PEACE *through*
COMMERCE

THE JOHN W. HOUCK
Notre Dame Series in Business Ethics

PEACE *through* COMMERCE

Responsible Corporate Citizenship and the
Ideals of the United Nations Global Compact

edited by

OLIVER F. WILLIAMS, C.S.C.

University of Notre Dame Press

Notre Dame, Indiana

Library of Congress Cataloging-in-Publication Data

Peace through commerce : responsible corporate citizenship and the ideals of
the United Nations global compact / edited by Oliver F. Williams.
        p.   cm. — (John W. Houck Notre Dame series in business ethics)
Includes index.
ISBN-13: 978-0-268-04414-5 (pbk. : alk. paper)
ISBN-10: 0-268-04414-7 (pbk. : alk. paper)
1. Social responsibility of business. 2. International business enterprises—
Social aspects. 3. Corporate power. I. Williams, Oliver F.
HD60.P35   2008
658.4'08—dc22

                                                                    2008026864

Contents

Part VI
SOME CONCLUSIONS AND A VISION FOR THE FUTURE

APPENDICES

Foreword

Sir Mark Moody-Stuart

It is an honor to introduce this volume containing the reflections of distinguished international scholars and renowned business leaders on the theme of corporate citizenship in a global economy. Some thoughts from my long career in business may serve to put some of these ideas in context.

The terms *corporate responsibility* and *corporate social responsibility* (CSR) are relatively new, but the concept is not. There were two schools of thought in the nineteenth and early twentieth centuries concerning this concept. One tradition is represented by Rockefeller and Carnegie and perhaps continued by Bill Gates and Warren Buffet: it is essentially philanthropy and not related to the source of the money being spent. The other tradition is that personified in England by the Quaker industrialists Cadbury and Rowntree. This was a concern for the effects of business and is integral to business, dealing, for example, with the improvement of living and working conditions. This was followed in the United States by Henry Ford paying his workers five dollars a day.

I will explore here the second approach—that is, activities integral to the business and not philanthropy alone, however important and beneficial philanthropy may be. If we are dealing with responsibilities that are integral to business, the first question has to be, What is the object of a business?

THE OBJECT OF A BUSINESS

Some time ago I heard a representative of Levi Jeans being interviewed on corporate responsibility. He spoke of the work the company was doing on responsible employment and monitoring in the supply chain and so on, but when pushed by the interviewer he said that, of course, businesses must make money. We agreed that, in fact, the object of Levi's business is to make the best jeans in the world. If they do that, people will flock to their door and they will certainly make money. To succeed and be sustainable, the company has to make money. But profit making should be an enabler, not an end in itself.

I recently spoke about climate change at a conference in Singapore. Someone from Procter and Gamble (P&G) was speaking before me on a different subject. The conference was (unusually for Singapore) running seriously behind schedule, so I was listening somewhat impatiently. But I was delighted to here him speak with enthusiasm of the three billion times a day that P&G products touch people on this planet, presumably some of them several times, and the benefits of these products. He was clearly passionate about what the products could do for consumers. He then added, "as a result of this, but please note that it *is* as a result, we make money." I recognized a kindred spirit.

In a recent book on the corporation, Joel Bakan puts overwhelming emphasis on his view that a corporation's legal fiduciary duty is to maximize profit and that if directors and management do not do this they can be sued.[1] I believe that this is a distortion of the duties of directors. During my years at Shell I was familiar with the Shell Business Principles, promulgated in the 1970s, which list obligations to what would now be called stakeholders—customers, employees, governments, etc. The responsibility to shareholders, according to these principles, is to provide an acceptable return and to protect the value of their investment. No one has sued us yet, although I suppose in this litigious world it may yet come to that.

One can perhaps draw an analogy with a car or automobile. The objective of a car is personal transportation from point A to point B. To do this you need to put gasoline into it. The gasoline is like the shareholders' funds or borrowings of a company, but it is not an end in itself. Of course, that fuel, that enabler, needs to be converted efficiently into forward motion. If the wheels spin and the vehicle does not move, or the engine does not convert the fuel properly, the vehicle is useless—like a business that does not make money. The nonprofitable business is utterly useless—and it will not survive. The fuel, the engine, and the wheels are essential to the vehicle, but they are not the object. The object is to move someone from A to B. Incidentally, that process is not very efficient. Only about

15 percent of energy expended actually moves the vehicle and its passengers—the rest is wasted. Only about 1 percent actually does the job of moving the person, and the remaining 14 percent moves the vehicle, which is not the real object of the exercise. The same lack of concentration on the real objective is true of many corporations.

I might add that of course for some people transport from A to B is not what they use the vehicle for—it is for show, cruising round town, making a lot of noise, beating the next person at the start at traffic signals, sometimes just the sheer pleasure of driving or the thrill of speed. That is similarly true of some people running businesses—they do it for kicks, or for fun, or for show, or to beat the guy next door. But the real objective of a business is to supply goods or services that its customers need or want, and to do so at affordable and probably decreasing prices while continuously improving on the product. Some of the other business motivators may be essential, and some of them are certainly fun, but they are not the real objective.

When I was a teenager my father asked me what I wanted to do as an adult. We lived on an island in the Caribbean and he was a sugar planter. I used to go with him to see ploughing or cutting of the cane. It was a great job and you could really see the results of the human effort working with nature, essentially producing sugar that was loaded onto ships. However, the industry came with many challenges. I said I wanted to do that. He said that that era had come to an end. I should go and do something else useful. So I taught myself geology at school, then studied it at university, and eventually joined Shell as an exploration geologist.

It is very important for people to enjoy and feel committed to their work. The ethics of the business or the utility of the product—whether you are a carpenter, an artist, an exploration geologist, or a financial wizard—are not the only important elements to a career. It is important for a person to enjoy the work and have the opportunity to apply his or her talents.

SUSTAINABLE DEVELOPMENT

I have never had a moment's doubt that the provision of energy to people is useful to society as a whole, and the same is true of the metals produced by the mining company at which I now work. The modern world depends on energy for everything from food to lighting to comfort to transportation. The metals are equally essential in that process. Energy and metals certainly meet the needs of modern society. In 1987 the UN Brundlandt Commission issued the report "Our Common Future," which defined *sustainable development* as development that meets the needs of the present without compromising the ability of future generations to meet their own needs.[2]

This is a brilliant definition. It is not static and means that if this generation is using up a finite resource, or a part of our natural capital, it will only be sustainable if we are converting it into other forms of capital— human capacity and education, infrastructure, etc. Our forebears radically changed the planet, just as we are changing it now. In the case of our forebears they made many mistakes, but they left us with legacies of education, art, science, commerce, religion, political systems, and infrastructure. I do not think that they have compromised our abilities to meet our needs. Far from it. You have but to look around the campus of the University of Notre Dame to see it. The words on the monument to architect Christopher Wren, in St Paul's Cathedral are just as appropriate here: *Si monumentum requris, circumspice,* "If you seek a monument, look around you!" But I am not at all sure that we can still claim the same. If we look at the proportion of people in the world who are not adequately fed, lack education, do not benefit from modern medicine, and do not currently have the means to earn an adequate livelihood, we are plainly not meeting the needs of the present generation. I do not take an apocalyptic view of the environment. Some countries demonstrate the means to ensure that the national environment is reasonably protected, although many countries do not. But in at least one urgent sense, it would appear that we are compromising the ability of future generations to meet their needs. It is plain that while we in the developed world can use energy much more efficiently, if the needs of the developing part of the world are to be met, large amounts of additional energy will be needed. And yet we know that our main sources of energy—the fossil fuels on which our own economies are built—are having an impact on our climate.

I have had the privilege of living in ten countries and visiting natural resource operations in another thirty or so. I have been able to see the impact on development over time. When I first worked in Oman in the 1960s as a field geologist, it was a medieval-like country. There were only a couple of doctors for a million people, the disabling eye disease trachoma was rife, female genital mutilation was common, and education was basic or nonexistent. In the intervening years, with a change of ruler and wise government, Oman has become a modern country, with a reasonable distribution of its oil income, an excellent education system, medical care to be proud of, and an elected Majlis, or parliament, with women represented. In the same period Malaysia has been transformed from an economy dependent on primary resources—oil and gas, tin, palm oil, and rubber—where race determined both perceptions generally and the actualities of occupations to a modern economy with a strong light manufacturing base, a sound educational system, and a society where one can no longer guess a person's occupation based on his race. In Nigeria, on the other hand, the outcome and application of income from oil and gas development has been less positive. Oil revenues have often been misapplied and in some cases stolen through corruption, and there are divisions in society due to arguments over the allocation of revenue expenditure to different parts of the country.

THE CAUSES OF DIFFERENT OUTCOMES
TO DEVELOPMENT

What causes these different outcomes? In each case, the main company operated with similar people and according to similar principles. The actions of the companies, both positive and negative, undoubtedly had some impact. If we take some pleasure and credit for the positive outcomes, we must also share the pain and the blame for the negative ones. But the real difference has come from the characters and motivations of the government leaders involved. Oman and Malaysia have been blessed with leaders with very clear visions and commitment to development and who have provided frameworks within which business and civil society can operate. One might not agree with the nature of the political system in either case, but there is no denying the results. In contrast, Nigeria has suffered from frequent changes of leadership, normally by military coup, and with leaders whose agendas have often been more personal than national. The present democratic government is making progress in the battle to establish sound and uncorrupted governance systems. President Obasanjo certainly established his national leadership credentials when he returned the country to civilian democratic government by stepping down as president in 1979 to make way for a civilian government.

But government alone is not enough—different parts of society need to cooperate. In Malaysia, perhaps as a result of staring into the abyss of racial slaughter in 1969, different ethnic groups have developed working compromises. In Oman it has been possible to build on strong social and religious structures. In Nigeria the creativity and energy of civil society is evident in that in response to a severe deterioration of the education system, people have organized and started their own schools. Religious institutions are strong, and family cohesion and support systems are something that would be beneficial in my own country, the United Kingdom. Without a government framework providing basic structure services in Nigeria, much creativity has gone into less socially constructive directions. Society's dependence on government only becomes clear through a lack of it. Commerce is essential to development and poverty eradication, but so is government. I believe this is the point often made by Father Theodore M. Hesburgh, C.S.C., former president of the University of Notre Dame, when he quotes the noted medieval theologian Thomas Aquinas: *Opus justitae pax,* "the work of justice is peace." In other words, if you want peace, you must work for justice.

LIMITS TO THE ROLE OF BUSINESS

If effective government and a functioning civil society are essential components of development, what can be said about corporations? What are the limits of their role? When I joined Shell in the 1960s, the involvement of ITT in the politics of a developing country was an issue, and the activities of United Fruit had given rise to the epithet "banana republic." Corporations sought to avoid involvement in political activity in any form. In the 1970s I and many of my colleagues believed that if a company ran an efficient operation with sound staff development, employment, safety and environmental policies; did not bribe anyone; paid our taxes honestly and in the country where income was earned; and engaged in a reasonable amount of community development, our responsibilities stopped there. The *Economist* still holds this line, expressing in a recent cover story the concern that companies might misguidedly take on responsibilities of host governments and vice versa. The article stated that "it is the job of elected politicians to set goals for regulators, to deal with externalities, to mediate among different interests, to attend to the de-both are then independently audited. It may be possible to extend this transparency to the vitally important ultimate use of the government revenue.

Similarly the Kimberley Process, which grew out of concerns over the use of diamonds as a source of funding for conflict, now covers 99 percent of diamond production and prevents the fueling of conflict through diamond revenues. In another example, the Voluntary Principles on Security and Human Rights were developed through cooperation between the UK Foreign Office and the U.S. State Department, with involvement of major companies and human rights NGOs. The Voluntary Principles provide guidelines for the use of armed security, the evaluation of risk, and the steps to be taken if government forces are used. Proper application of these principles helps protect companies from accusations of complicity in human rights abuses. There are similar efforts in Sustainable Fisheries and in the Forest Stewardship Council.

SUPRANATIONAL OR NATIONAL LEGISLATION?

There is a third and somewhat more contentious area where the building of mutual trust between companies and NGOs is needed. Many NGOs believe that international, legally binding regulation is needed to govern the behavior of multinational corporations (MNCs). NGOs view the strong opposition from companies to this proposal with deep suspicion. On the other hand, MNCs fear an extension of—mainly U.S.—judicial activity. They believe that it would result in a plethora of frivolous cases being brought in New York courts by ambulance-chasing lawyers, forcing companies to face an unattractive choice of making large out-of-court settlements—much of which goes to the said lawyers—or proceeding with lengthy and expensive litigation that ends before an unpredictable jury who is relatively unaware of the background and conditions against which the actions took place.

There is no doubt that there are many offenses against human rights and the environment carried out by companies, but the vast majority of these occur not in major transnational businesses but in poorly regulated national businesses, in manufacturing as well as artisanal mining, and underground coal mining in many countries. But despite clear and universally acknowledged agreements such as the Universal Declaration of

---

mands of social justice, to provide public goods and collect the taxes to pay for them, to establish collective priorities where that is necessary and appropriate and to organise resources accordingly."[3] This is fine as an aspiration, but what about the large areas of the world where governments are either incapable or unwilling to carry out this role, or worse still, steal the means by which they are supposed to carry out these tasks? Where the proceeds of industry, particularly extractive industry, are misspent or misapplied over long periods by governments, people turn to the company and say, "You made money, but there is little in the country to show for it." To protest that we paid our taxes is of no avail. It may not be our responsibility, but it becomes our problem. If we want the sort of functioning society in which we can do business, we need to work with others to create the capacities and conditions that sound governance requires. To say "once we have paid our taxes, responsibility stops," is like a passenger who has paid for his ticket refusing to help man the pumps on a foundering ship because it was the captain's incompetence that caused the ship to sink. This attitude is short-sighted at best and certainly not in the interests of shareholders.

Drawing the line of responsibility is difficult. Some time ago I had a discussion in London with a minister of a country in which the company I worked for played a major role. He asked me to intervene and attempt to stop the irregular activities of certain people in his country. We had, as a matter of deliberate policy and principle, avoided any connection with their activities and the minister knew it. When I pointed out that this was no concern of mine, that it was not my country or my government, he replied that when it all went wrong I could guess who would be blamed. At first this seemed to me to be unfair. But was it so unfair? We were friends of the country. Had the issue been a natural disaster, or even a social issue for the nation, we would have immediately offered to play our part. Is it the act of a friend to avert one's eyes and walk down the other side of the street when a crime is being committed, just because it is not our business?

At a meeting recently I was asked, slightly aggressively, if I could give just one example of a corporate contribution to the delivery of the Millennium Development Goals (MDGs). I was able to say that taking my own company, Anglo American, as a typical business example, we directly employ about 80,000 people in Africa and about the same indirectly through contractors. Assuming there to be about five members in each employee's family, that is almost a million people directly dependent on our operations. In Africa our direct payroll is some $3 billion a year. We spend some $8 billion a year on suppliers in developing countries, including some $1.6 billion a year to Black Economic Empowerment companies in South Africa, of whom almost half are small- and medium-sized businesses. We pay some $1.6 billion in taxes in developing countries. A large amount of employees' salaries then goes into housing, education, and local businesses and service employment. So simply in the normal line of business, without any consideration of corporate responsibility spending, this represents a significant injection of funds toward the MDGs. This is replicated by many other businesses in the developing world. In addition, we fund some 5,000 people through bursaries, scholarships, apprentices, and graduate training, and some 3,000 people on antiretroviral treatment for HIV/AIDS. By its very activity business makes a serious contribution to the eradication of poverty and the building of capacity.

We have a strong interest in sound governance but no mandate to impose it. We have to work with others—we need a collective approach. And for this we need to build trust.

THE GLOBAL COMPACT: BRINGING BUSINESS, LABOR, AND CIVIL SOCIETY TOGETHER

One of the biggest challenges for business in developing countries with weak governance is that it has a strong interest in the development of sound governance but no mandate to deliver it outside of the business itself. We have to work with others in a collective approach so that the influence of business is applied in conjunction with others, moderated by their views, and not applied in an unconstrained way.

At the World Economic Forum in Davos in 1999, Kofi Annan called for businesses to commit themselves to a Global Compact based on nine principles reflecting the major UN conventions on human rights, the environment, and labor standards. A tenth principle on corruption was added later. Some 3,000 companies in over 115 countries have committed themselves publicly to these principles. Part of Kofi Annan's genius was that he involved civil society and labor organizations in the process.

The Compact provides a forum where businesses, civil society, and labor organizations can develop practical approaches to the delivery of

the high-level principles. A second contribution is the develo
local and regional networks where different sectors of society
together on issues critical to that country. I recently attended
Compact Local Networks Forum in Barcelona, which included
participation from representatives from around the world.

Initially the Compact was criticized by some as being ju
"blue wash." Indeed, for some it may be so, but I was struck
regional Global Compact Summit in Shanghai how sessions w
ment representatives addressed practical and specific issues
corruption and working conditions in local manufacturing
mines. International labor organizations and human rights N
presence was facilitated by the Global Compact, actively
discussion and could see tangible benefits from their involv

If business is to work with others in societies around the
dress issues critical to those societies—be they issues of er
governance, of corruption, of the environment, or someth
essential to build trust, for trust in business, particularly b
generally low. How can trust be built between companies,
public at large? One way is through open reporting on sta
cators, such as those developed by the Global Reporting I
These indicators are developed by a transparent public pr
representatives from NGOs, UN agencies, labor organiza
panies. Reporting should cover the whole scope of a comp
Inevitable shortfalls in performance can be put in the c
performance. Clearly it is best if these indicators are inc
fied. The GRI also develops guidelines for specific
NGOs, national governments, and local governments
some local governments, and some NGOs are beginn
compatible reports on their own activities, joining co
around the world in building a global standard. The
the guidelines were launched in October 2006 in Ams

A second method for building trust is for groups of
nies to work together on particular issues. There are
amples of this. Arising from the "Publish what you
Global Witness and the Soros Open Society Foundatic
dustries Transparency Initiative was launched by th
involves oil, gas, and mining companies publishing
governments and the host government declaring wh

Human Rights, the International Labour Organization (ILO) Fundamental Principles and Rights at Work, the Rio Declaration on Environment and Development, and the UN Convention Against Corruption, offenses are daily committed in these areas in many countries. At the heart of the problem is an understandable lack of trust in national governance in many states, but superimposing international legislation applicable only to international companies does not address this issue. Business is prepared to work with governments and other sections of society to ensure that in each and every country national legislation is enacted, and then enforced, to ensure that the principles of these major UN declarations and conventions on which the Global Compact is based are honored. This is a major job, and it could not progress in every country simultaneously or evenly. But this long-term undertaking, not grandstanding in New York or Geneva, is what is needed if we are to make real progress across the world. Having said that there are clearly areas such as climate and trade where supranational regulation is required, I argue that these areas are limited to truly international issues.

In this process the practical learning and dialogue activities of the UN Global Compact are very important. Companies need the experience and expertise that civil society organizations and others can bring to bear. Groups of companies and NGOs, both national and international, need to continue to come together to make practical progress in the complexities of real world situations in various countries, and to support that progress with well thought out and properly enforced national laws and regulations.

APPLICATION ACROSS ALL SECTORS OF BUSINESS

It may appear that because I have discussed mainly the extractive industries these issues are only applicable to them. In my experience this is not so. Whether one speaks of a bank, a beverage company, a media company, a communications company, transportation, manufacturing, health care, or construction, the business has as its key role the provision of goods or services to its customers, who form a larger or smaller segment of society at large. That is the real aim of a business. Different people have different skills and enjoy working in different industries, but unless they focus on the essential objective of the business they will almost certainly fail. Of course it is necessary to make profits, but I would argue that profit is an essential enabler, not a pure end in itself. Profit is also a very useful indicator of the efficiency with which the business is using resources and capital. This may seem to be just a question of semantics, but I believe it to be fundamental to the way in which we set about doing business.

Some years ago I was talking to Barbara Hayes, who was on the Ecumenical Council for Corporate Responsibility at the time. I was drawing a diagram with the corporation in the center and its different stakeholders surrounding it. Barbara said that the diagram was typical of the corporate view of the world—I should redraw the diagram with Society in the center and others around it as stakeholders in Society. In this diagram, business is just one stakeholder in Society. I have never forgotten this conversation, and it goes very well with something that Bjorn Stigson of the World Business Council for Sustainable Development often says: business cannot flourish in a society that is not flourishing. All of us, including everyone in business, have a strong stake in the sound working of society.

NOTES

1. Joel Bakan, *The Corporation: The Pathological Pursuit of Profits and Power* (New York: Simon and Schuster, 2005).

2. UN Brundlandt Commission, *Our Common Future* (1987), http://www.un-documents.net/wced-ocf.htm.

3. "The Good Company," *Economist,* January 22, 2005, 22.

Introduction

Oliver F. Williams, C.S.C.

At the founding of the United Nations in 1945, political and business leaders as well as scholars shared the conviction that commerce could play an important role in fostering peace. Half a century later, with the emergence of the interlocking global economy and the enormous new reach of business, the business community faces new challenges in its engagement with societies emerging from conflict.

While business still retains its core responsibilities of creating jobs and wealth and thus contributing to poverty alleviation, under the rubric of global corporate citizenship business is increasingly developing new policies and practices aimed at promoting human rights, preventing violent conflict, and contributing to more peaceful societies. A prominent forum for such efforts is the United Nations Global Compact, a new initiative (started in 2000) intended to increase and diffuse the benefits of global economic development through voluntary corporate policies and actions. Over three thousand businesses throughout the world have already signed on as participants.

The ten principles of the Global Compact focus on human rights, labor rights, concern for the environment, and corruption and are taken directly from commitments made by governments through the UN: the Universal Declaration of Human Rights (1948); the Rio Declaration on Environment and Development (1992); the International Labour Organization's Fundamental Principles and Rights at Work (1998); and the UN Convention Against Corruption (2003). The principles are as follows:

Human Rights
Principle 1
> Businesses should support and respect the protection of internationally proclaimed human rights within their sphere of influence; and

Principle 2
> Make sure that they are not complicit in human rights abuses.

Labor
Principle 3
> Businesses should uphold the freedom of association and the effective recognition of the right to collective bargaining;

Principle 4
> The elimination of all forms of forced and compulsory labor;

Principle 5
> The effective abolition of child labor; and

Principle 6
> Elimination of discrimination in respect of employment and occupation.

Environment
Principle 7
> Businesses should support a precautionary approach to environmental challenges;

Principle 8
> Undertake initiatives to promote greater environmental responsibility; and

Principle 9
> Encourage the development and diffusion of environmentally friendly technologies.

Corruption
Principle 10
> Business should work against corruption in all its forms, including corruption and bribery.

The Global Compact was designed as a voluntary initiative. A company subscribing to the Principles is invited to make a clear statement of support and must include some reference in its annual report or other public documents on the progress it is making on internalizing the Principles within its operations. The company must also submit a brief description of this report to the Global Compact Website. Failure to submit such a description within two years of becoming a signatory to the Compact (and subsequently every two years) will result in being removed from the list of participants. The intention is that, through leading by the power of good example, member companies will set a high moral tone throughout the world. The overall thrust of the Global Compact is to emphasize the moral purpose of business, as summarized well by Ban Ki-Moon, the Secretary-General of the United Nations: "Business practices rooted in universal values can bring social and economic gains."[1]

The ten Principles of the Global Compact have been given added force by the Millennium Development Goals (MDGs), a blueprint for action agreed to by all the countries of the world as well as leading development institutions. With the target date of 2015 for completion, the eight MDGs are (1) eradicate extreme poverty and hunger; (2) achieve universal primary education; (3) promote gender equality and empower women; (4) reduce child mortality; (5) improve maternal health; (6) combat HIV/AIDS, malaria, and other diseases; (7) ensure environmental sustainability; and (8) develop a global partnership for development. Commitment to these ideals has brought businesses into new collaborative relationships with an unlikely partner: nongovernmental organizations (NGOs). In places such as Darfur, South Africa, Nigeria, and Afghanistan, NGOs and private firms are combining their unique capacities and strengths to provide an important new avenue for achieving social development.

To be sure, this new paradigm is not without its problems. This may appear to be a marriage of convenience or perhaps even an attempt to mix oil and water. Some of these issues have surfaced in debates over NGO participation in the Global Compact; several NGOs have actively participated as members of the Compact to promote change, even as others vigorously denounce it. Yet there is evidence that, at their best, such partnerships can yield positive results for developing countries while at the same time fulfilling the goals of the participating partners.

This volume will discuss what leading businesses are doing with NGOs in developing countries and explore the characteristics of successful partnerships. It seeks to advance the understanding of the conceptual foundations of the role of business in society and to encourage new and more effective partnerships. The book also hopes to lay the foundation for new courses in business schools on *Peace through Commerce.* This follows the recommendation of the Association to Advance Collegiate Schools of Business International (AACSB), through its Task Force on Peace through Commerce. The task force, chaired by Carolyn Woo, dean of the Mendoza College of Business at the University of Notre Dame, issued a report that is summarized in appendix 3.

The book opens with a foreword by Sir Mark Moody-Stuart, former chairman of the Royal Dutch/Shell Group of Companies, and now chairman of the Board of Directors of the UN Global Compact Foundation. The overarching theme of this volume is captured in Moody-Stuart's reflection that "All of us, including everyone in business, have a strong stake in the sound working of society." Moody-Stuart gets to the heart of the matter when he asks, *What is the object of business?* His answer, which opens the way to much discussion in future chapters, is that the object of business is to bring goods and services to the consumer, not to make a profit. Profit is the enabler of business, but it is not the end.

Part one of the volume has two chapters designed to direct our attention to the purpose of business. Marilise Smurthwaite, in chapter 1, offers a comprehensive survey of the literature and explains her own perspective based on Catholic Social Thought: "In fact, the purpose of a business firm is not simply to make a profit, but is to be found in its very existence as a *community of persons,* who in various ways are endeavoring to satisfy their basic needs and who form a particular group at the service of the whole society."[2] Her overview of the literature forms the context for much that follows in later chapters.

Tim Fort, one of the acknowledged pioneers in the scholarship on Peace through Commerce, and his colleague Michelle Westermann-Bahaylo argue that it is only a business with a "fairly sophisticated level of moral maturity" that can actually implement programs that consciously strive to build communities. "The higher good is pursued not for instrumental ends, but regardless of them, because it is intrinsic in the identity and culture of the corporation to help and to build community." Chapter 2 outlines how this might be possible using a "good trust" model of a partnership with NGOs.

Part two presents some conceptual issues from related disciplines that may be helpful in understanding the Peace through Commerce concept. Douglass Cassel and Sean O'Brien offer a legal perspective on the role of human rights in corporate action in chapter 3. John Paul Lederach, a scholar of peace studies, presents helpful concepts from that field in chapter 4. Chapter 5, authored by Willie Esterhuyse, a philosopher and advisor to the South African government, outlines how partnerships can vary depending on the context. In South Africa, because of the legacy of apartheid and the enormous socioeconomic inequalities that still exist today, the government has mandated a role for business designed to shape a more just society. One such initiative, the Broad-Based Black Economic Empowerment Act of 2003, is highlighted.

One NGO leader and one business leader offer their perspectives in part three. Mary Anderson, a respected spokesperson for the NGO community, draws on a large body of experience and points the way for corporations to ensure that they do not do more harm than good. She is convinced that business can play a constructive role in achieving peaceful societies, but there is a need for circumspection. She addresses these issues in chapter 6. In chapter 7 David Lowry, a former vice president of Freeport-McMoRan, a leader in the extractive industry, reflects on his experience and offers some suggestions on how business can make economic and social development as peaceful and beneficial as possible.

Part four presents the reflections of two experienced business leaders on this new role of business in society. Donal O'Neill, in chapter 8, argues that the only way to ensure that business has a positive effect in a host country is to anticipate problems and devise solutions in advance of the investment. He outlines an "impact assessment" process that strives to foresee social, economic, and environmental problems that could arise with an investment. Forging partnerships with NGOs and other institutions often is the key to finding solutions to socioeconomic problems and, therefore, to shaping a more peaceful society.

Chapter 9 is authored by Klaus Leisinger, who is both a business leader and a scholar. Leisinger asks how we can enhance and increase the efforts of business to reduce poverty and accelerate human development. He suggests that while some corporations may work for human development because it is the right thing to do, it may be advisable to employ a more market-driven approach for other firms. "Reputation capital"—the respect and admiration consumers might show for a socially responsible company—is a powerful incentive for many businesses to get involved in development programs. Education of the consumer about these issues is crucial. Another key issue identified by Leisinger is that today society's expectations for corporate involvement in the problems of society are quite high. When has a business done enough? What does it mean to be a good corporate citizen? The answers to these questions are clearly a work in progress.

Part five of the book contains ten case stories detailing what some companies are doing with regard to aiding development. While not all the companies profiled here are signatories to the Global Compact, they certainly do subscribe to its ideals. The first case, profiled in chapter 10, is authored by Ofelia Eugenio and describes a public-private partnership formed with the United Nations Development Program (UNDP), Chevron-Texaco, and the government of Angola. Called the Angola Enterprise Program (AEP), the goal of the project is to reduce poverty thru private sector development by supporting micro, small, and medium entrepreneurs. Eugenio offers some lessons learned for future projects.

Chapter 11, by Brigitte Hélène Scherrer, discusses how the NGO the Business Humanitarian Forum joined in a multistakeholder partnership with the European Generic Medicines Association, a local Afghan investor, and the UNDP to establish a generic medicine factory in Kabul, Afghanistan. The chapter also has a very helpful discussion of the phases of the partnership process. Emphasizing the crucial task of rebuilding trust in war-torn countries like Afghanistan, the chapter concludes with some lessons learned.

Authored by David Wheeler and four colleagues, chapter 12 focuses on grassroots enterprise development in post-conflict Southern Sudan and Darfur. This report shows how micro enterprises could assist in healing and peace building by restoring the social fabric of the community and preparing the way for private sector development and partnerships. The role of enterprises led by women is stressed in the study.

Chapter 13, authored by Gerald Cavanagh, S.J., along with another scholar and two senior managers of the Ford Motor Company, argues that Ford's reputation capital is a significant factor in selling vehicles. Thus Ford has social and environmental policies in place that are designed to meet society's expectations. The chapter outlines three areas of such policy: human rights and working conditions, greenhouse gas emissions, and material use and recycling. An interesting observation in the essay is that while the traditional role of the nation-state is to pursue the common good—by working for stability, peace, and prosperity—there is now a reversal of roles in a global economy. For example, with stakeholders in two hundred countries, Ford cannot afford to view its concerns in narrow, national terms but must pursue its quest for peaceful societies globally.

Chapter 14 focuses on Nestlé and is coauthored by the academic Lisa Newton and Nestlé executive John Bee. Eschewing the notion of charity, the authors argue that partnership necessarily entails some self-interest: "in a true partnership, all the parties benefit, and each is committed to the success of the others at least in part out of self-interest." Drawing on the notion of sustainability, the case is made that all activity should pass not only an economic test but also ethical and environmental ones as well. Examples of Nestlé partnership projects exemplifying sustainability in Pakistan, Colombia, South America, and Nigeria are discussed.

Chapter 15 is by the IBM executive Stanley Litow. For IBM the core concept in this discussion is corporate citizenship, which "describes a company's total dealings with the community, —local, regional, national, or global—encompassing traditional corporate philanthropy but also going far beyond." The author discusses many partnerships and sees their value as a way to tap into community interests. Social investments and policies flow from IBM's core values and business strategy and most often involve sharing technology innovations with communities in developing countries. IBM contributes about $150 million a year to such projects. Why does IBM do this? Litow notes that the *Financial Times* estimates that the reputation capital of IBM is worth about $55 billion; reputation capital, in part, tries to capture the payoff of corporate citizenship projects in such things as brand value, employee morale, and so on. While Litow is clearly an advocate of corporate citizenship, he is not unmindful of the problem raised earlier by Leisinger: When has a company done enough? IBM helped organize a group of companies to study the issue of how high to set the bar for citizenship. Called the Global Leadership Network, the coalition of companies continues to reflect on the corporate citizenship issue.

Chapter 16 is authored by Marshall Greenhut and Bob Corcoran and discusses General Electric's approach to corporate citizenship, focusing on its program to improve health care and infrastructure in hospitals in Africa. The chapter offers an excellent overview of poverty in Africa and the work of the Millennium Development Goals. It concludes with some insightful reflections on why a business like GE becomes involved in this sort of project.

Chapter 17, authored by Daniel Malan, an official of KPMG, discusses Barloworld, a diversified industrial company. The chapter offers an example of a partnership formed during the 1980s in the struggle against apartheid in South Africa. This partnership may provide a model for the resolution of many current problems in developing countries. In chapter 18 Alexandra Guáqueta discusses the implementation of a human rights, conflict-sensitive corporate code of conduct involving major multinational companies in the extractive business—Occidental Petroleum and Cerrejón—in partnership with global and local NGOs. The chapter offers much insight for others in similar situations. Based on the company's mission statement, "to extend and enhance human life," Bristol-Myers Squibb embarked on a program in nine African countries to help with the HIV/AIDS pandemic. Chapter 19 by Tom Costa, an official with Bristol-Myers Squibb, describes how the company dedicated over $150 million to this project through private-public partnerships.

Part six, the final section of the book, offers some concluding reflections and a vision for the future. Chapter 20 is authored by the well-known scholar in finance and ethics Lee Tavis. Drawing upon many of the insights and lessons learned from the partnerships discussed in the book, Tavis argues that partnerships are the new form of social responsibility in this era of Peace through Commerce.

In chapter 21 I argue that while corporate social responsibility is certainly not a new idea, what is emerging in some of these company accounts is a new role for the firm within society. Some companies have a view of corporate citizenship that implicitly envisions a state-like role for the corporation, which becomes a quasi-public institution that goes far beyond the traditional division of labor between corporations and governments. While affirming and applauding this view of corporate citizenship, Williams suggests some additional measures that will strengthen the democratic nature of society while the firm implements this new role.

Finally, appendix 1 lists the Principles for Responsible Management Education, a new initiative to expand corporate citizenship education; it was developed by a number of business schools in cooperation with the United Nations Global Compact. Appendix 2 lists the Principles for Responsible Investment, a program launched in April 2006 and coordinated by the UN Global Compact and the UN Environment Programme Finance Initiative (UNEP FI). By 2006 institutions representing more than

$2 trillion in assets owned had signed the Principles for Responsible Investment. Appendix 3 is a summary of the report from the Task Force on Peace through Commerce of AACSB International.

I am most grateful for our many benefactors who help support the work of the Center for Ethics and Religious Values in Business at the University of Notre Dame, and, in particular, William Lehr Jr. Also, a thank you is in order to Deb Coch, administrative assistant at the center, whose work enabled this project to move from an idea to a finished product. I am also grateful to Marshall Greenhut and Julie Ratliff, recent graduates of the Notre Dame M.B.A. Program, who provided outstanding assistance. Most of the essays in this volume were first presented at a conference in November 2006 at the University of Notre Dame; the conference was organized by the center with the cooperation of the United Nations Global Compact Office, the Joan B. Kroc Institute for International Peace at the University of Notre Dame, and AACSB International. To our partners, we owe a great debt of gratitude, in particular to Georg Kell, executive director of the Global Compact; Hal Culbertson, associate director of the Kroc Institute; Michael Wiemer, assistant vice president of AACSB International; and Lee Tavis, professor in the Mendoza College of Business at Notre Dame. To be sure, I want to thank all those who contributed to this volume and added to our understanding of responsible corporate citizenship.

Finally, I want to express my gratitude to Eon Smit and Frank Horwitz, directors of the Graduate Schools of Business of Stellenbosch University and the University of Cape Town, respectively. I served in a joint appointment at these universities during the 2007–2008 academic year and also as the Donald Gordon Visiting International Scholar at the University of Cape Town. This year in South Africa enabled me to focus on preparing this volume for publication, and I owe a great debt of gratitude to my many South African colleagues.

NOTES

1. See http://www.globalcompactfoundation.org.

2. Pope John Paul II, *Centesimus Annus* (Washington, DC: U.S. Catholic Conference, 1991), para. 35.

PART I

The Emerging Purpose of the Corporation

CHAPTER 1

The Purpose of the Corporation

Marilise Smurthwaite

The purpose of the corporation has been much discussed both in the academic literature and in business circles. This chapter will examine the notion of corporate purpose as presented in the academic literature, as well as that suggested by Catholic Social Thought. To fully comprehend this purpose and its implications, it is necessary to understand the debate surrounding other notions about the corporation, most notably its nature, its moral agency, and its role *in,* relationship *with,* and responsibilities *to* society. The way we conceive of the corporation's nature and moral agency has a direct bearing on the way we will view its purpose. The latter, in turn, is fulfilled by means of its relationship with society and its role and responsibilities in society. Mindful of the oversimplification that can result from such an endeavor, it might be helpful to summarize the focal issues in the debates concerning the above-mentioned aspects of the corporation:

The nature of the "corporation": the debate on the nature of the corporation turns on whether the corporation is merely a *legal entity* or *legal fiction;* or whether it is viewed as a *community* of some sort, as a *citizen,* or as a *group* loosely bound or contracted together to further its own interests; or whether it is the equivalent of an *individual person* or some combination of these.

Corporate moral agency: this debate turns on whether a corporation can be seen as a *moral agent,* and, therefore, whether it can be seen to have any moral responsibility. If the latter is true, the issue then becomes the *nature* of the moral responsibility and the accountability that the corporation can be said to bear—that is, *who* bears this moral responsibility and to *what extent?* Is the corporation to be treated as a *person* with respect of moral issues, as a *group,* or as a *legal entity?*

The purpose of the corporation: this debate revolves around whether the purpose of the corporation is *only* to make a profit (for owners or shareholders) or whether, in addition to making a profit, its purpose is a broader one—for example, to contribute to society in some way (for example, socially and ecologically), to contribute to the common good, or to develop human virtue. If it does indeed have a broader purpose, the question revolves around what *form* this purpose should take or by what *criteria* it should be determined or measured.

The role of the corporation, its relationship with society, and its responsibilities: the corporation's role and its relationship with society usually correlate to the way its nature, moral agency, and purpose are explained. Debate largely centers on conceptualizing the *nature* of the role and relationship of the corporation with society and on *defining* what *responsibilities,* moral or otherwise, the corporation has toward society. Various theoretical models explain *what* this role and relationship are or suggest *how* they should be conceived. Within the various approaches differing priorities are given to the responsibilities/obligations/duties that are said to derive from the corporation's role in and relationship with society. In its simplest form, the debate could be summarized as being between those who view the corporation's purpose as "profit only" versus those who view it as "profit-plus-extras." Given the latter dichotomy, the issue seems to be what the corporation's responsibilities are, and, flowing from this, the *model* that best reflects or represents the corporation's responsibilities and relationship with society.[1] At issue in all of these debates are questions about *what* responsibilities corporations have, *to whom* they owe these responsibilities, and *by whom* they are owed (that is, directors, all members of the corporation, etc.).

We will examine each of these issues by means of a brief literature survey[2] and in so doing will clarify the perspective of this chapter—that is, that of Catholic Social Thought—while acknowledging that the chosen paradigm is not the only available option.

THE NATURE OF THE CORPORATION: THE MEANING OF THE TERM *CORPORATION*

The first step in understanding the purpose of the corporation is to define *corporation* itself. The academic literature contains a few purely descriptive definitions. More frequently, the corporation is prescriptively defined, and the definition or explanation of what the corporation *is* actually indicates what the corporation *ought to be or do*. In addition, each discipline tends to have its own version of what the corporation is, but such versions do not provide a holistic view: "For ethicists the corporation is (or perhaps is not) a moral agent; for economists it is a set of relationships designed to optimize efficiency; for social scientists it is a social arrangement with its own culture, both like and unlike families and civil societies."[3] Even the law fails to provide a holistic perspective because its definition of the corporation is based on the problems it wishes to solve and varies according to particular problems.[4]

Broadly speaking, descriptions of the nature of the corporation seem to fall into one of two categories: (1) the corporation as legal entity only; and (2) the corporation as legal entity (stated or assumed) as well as something else, for example, citizen, community, etc. Phillips goes some way toward outlining the main conceptions of corporations in twentieth-century *legal theory*[5] as follows:

> *concession theory,* which views the corporation as an *artificial person* created by the state; it has no real existence other than according to the view of the law
> *aggregate theory,* which views the corporation as a *collection of smaller basic units*[6]
> *real entity theory,* which views the corporation as a *real entity* in the sense that it really exists, rather than being just an artificial creation of the law; such entities have qualities over and above those of the individual constituents.

Like the legal concession theorists, Samuelson and Nordhaus define a corporation as a legal entity owned by shareholders who have limited liability. It is an entity that can be sued and can function as a "good" means for raising capital or a "convenient" way to do "good" and "efficient" business without which the market economy would be less efficient.[7] This view, typical of the neoclassical/neoliberal economic paradigm, is clearly normative rather than descriptive and emphasizes the corporation as a legal entity rather than as a human enterprise or human endeavor. A similar explanation of the term *corporation* is given by Robbins: "Technically a corporation is a social invention of the state; the corporate charter granted by the state ideally permits private financial resources to be used for a public purpose." However, he adds that "at another level, it allows one or more individuals to apply massive economic and political power to accumulate private wealth while protected from legal liability for the public consequences."[8] Interestingly, Lutz notes that even though there could be "overpowering reasons to believe that the modern investor-owned corporation *ought not to exist*," economics, in line with its approach toward all "existing social institutions," accepts the corporation as an "unquestionable given."[9]

A very different view is taken by those who see the corporation as a community and/or as *part* of a community. This view is taken by adherents to Catholic Social Thought, among others:[10] "The challenge of Catholic social thought to our understanding of the role and place of business in modern capitalism goes to the heart of how we explain, legitimate and understand the economy, because it goes to the underlying values upon which both our economy and our understanding of the economy are based."[11] Catholic Social Thought differs from the neoclassical idea of the "firm," company, or corporation. The latter is based on a view of human nature and society rooted in "the marginal utility theory of value . . . which leads to the ultimate conclusion that the ultimate good in society is the consumption of utility achieved through market exchange."[12] On the other hand, in Catholic Social Thought, the *firm* is defined as a "community of persons."[13] It was Pope Pius XII who first expressed the idea that business was comprised of "persons who are partners . . . who together seek a common purpose" rather than being constituted by a group of shareholders only.[14] Furthermore, it was also Pius XII who stressed that those who work in such enterprises were "subjects" not "factors"—the latter being a "neutral" term used in economics.[15] It is significant that

> John Paul II's idea of business as a community of work does not suppose a disembodied community disconnected from the economic pressures of profit, risk, competition, and productivity. Rather, he sees that only through a community of work can these economic values be properly ordered within a business so that they serve to develop people and society. Because of the nature of business, profit and productivity are necessary and critical dimensions; but unless a

community develops within a business to provide a proper ordering of these economic dimensions, the possibility of the business becoming a place where people can develop evaporates.[16]

Thus, Melé and Fontradana state that businesses ought to be seen as *authentic communities:* they have goals and a mission, and they perform a task together that has an effect on society.[17]

Examples of "secular" writers inclining toward this view of business as a *community* include Solomon, an advocate of the virtue ethics approach to business ethics; Bowie, writing from a Kantian perspective; and Kelly. Solomon refers to business as a "human and social enterprise"; he believes the corporation is the "unit" of commerce in our time and that businesses are defined in terms of their roles and responsibilities in the community *outside* of their own internal setting.[18] They are both part of the community and comprised of individuals who in turn make up a community. For Solomon, "corporations are neither legal fictions nor financial juggernauts but communities, people working together for common goals."[19] Bowie argues that "A Kantian views an organization as a moral community,"[20] and Kelly also argues that the corporation is a community (not merely a group of stockholders) and cannot be seen as an individual or person as it is both larger than a person and is "immortal."[21]

On the other hand, a number of views cluster around the notion of the corporation somehow being a *part of the community*. Goodpaster and Matthews argue that business is part of the community, and, like the individual person, is a "juristic person" and therefore can be seen as a citizen with both "functional" and other roles.[22] Waddock holds a similar view.[23] King also seems to see the corporation as a citizen, while at the same time recognizing that it is created by statute and is *part* of the community.[24] Koehn argues that corporations *belong to* communities "in which they are bound to one another by ties of justice and trust,"[25] while Verstraeten argues that businesses are *social institutions,* not private organizations, and form part of the wider society. They incur their legitimacy by contributing to the community *of which they are part.*[26]

Those who believe the corporation is not a community, but rather a group of individuals united "by chance" or for particular purposes, include Keeley,[27] who sees the corporation as merely a group of individuals who have found certain relations between themselves to be of mutual benefit, and Van Gerwen, who, writing about business ethics from a social contract perspective, defines the corporation as a *group* that unites members *by chance* in their following of their individual interests.[28] Van Gerwen argues that few corporations will become communities because the latter offer "an all-embracing context for the socialization and interaction of their members. Social restraints of functional differentiation and of respect for the private life projects of the participants will preclude the occurrence of this type of process in most companies."[29]

In addition, a community does not merely unite its members by chance, as does a corporation. At the same time, those who view the corporation as the private property of individuals to be bought or sold at a profitable time have an incomplete picture of the corporation because it combines human capital (expertise) and contracts, is both a profit-making and a social group with history and expertise, and has a purpose as well as operating and decision-making structures.[30] Yet Donaldson, a leading advocate of the social contract perspective, differs from others advocating social contract theory and conceives of the corporation in terms of a contract between society and business, in which society sees the corporation as a single legal agent and grants it permission to use land and resources and hire labor.[31] However, what the corporation recognizes as "society" is more complicated because it includes consumers' and employees' interests in the contract agreement.

Velasquez, also a business ethicist, defines the corporation by citing its development from a "joint stock company" in the sixteenth century to its modern form, where the law "treats [them] as immortal fictitious 'persons' who have the right to sue and be sued, own and sell property, and enter into contracts, all in their own name." However, the corporation is also made up of shareholders, directors and officers, and employees who are coordinated and controlled by "bureaucratic systems of rules."[32] While he recognizes both legal and human aspects of the corporation, Velasquez does not go so far as to recognize that the corporation could be a *community*. Were he a legal theorist, we might say he combines the perspectives of concession theory and aggregate theory. Perhaps, from a business ethics perspective, he is best placed alongside the contract theorists. Finally, Korten, while agreeing that the corporation "is not a person"—though such an "illusion" is created by its legal standing and by public relations efforts, does not believe that it is a community. Rather, he sees it as "a lifeless bundle of legally protected financial rights and relationships brilliantly designed to serve money and its imperatives."[33]

Each of these above views has different implications for how we conceive of the "purpose" of the corporation. In summary, the corporation has been variously conceptualized as the following

a legal entity
a community
a part of a community
a citizen/juristic person/individual person
a chance group

What is interesting is that while these perspectives come from diverse fields—business ethics, legal theory, and economics—there are certain commonalities. One is that the corporation exists in law; a second is that it has to do with the human; a third is that it does not exist in a vacuum but in the context of the wider community in which it operates. This chapter argues that the corporation has been constituted in law but is more than a legal entity. It is a community of persons situated in a wider community, of which it is part and which it cannot ignore on the grounds of being merely a "legal entity."

CORPORATE MORAL AGENCY

The "nature" of the corporation is closely linked to the issue of corporate moral agency. Whether or not the corporation can be viewed as a "moral agent" has important implications for the corporation's purpose, its relationship with society, its responsibilities, its liability, and its accountability.[34] However, as Solomon notes, this is "one of the most prominent confusions and controversies in business ethics."[35] There seem to be three main approaches to the debate on corporate moral agency. First, the corporation is not a moral agent, does not have moral responsibilities or obligations, and carries only legal responsibility and accountability. In legal theory concession theorists take this view, as do some, but not all, of those classified as espousing "real entity theory."[36] They claim that the corporation is not the sort of entity that can qualify as a moral agent despite being a real entity.[37] In economics this view would be supported by the likes of Friedman and Galbraith, in philosophy by John Ladd,[38] and in business ethics in work like that of Sternberg.[39] If, as this first approach suggests, the corporation is not a moral agent, then it follows that it is not capable of acting morally and has no moral responsibilities. Therefore, it cannot be held accountable for its practices or behaviors (even if these are not ethical or moral), other than those actions that are defined by law, moral or not.[40]

The second approach argues that moral agency does not reside in the entity of the "corporation" per se but rather in the individuals who comprise it or in the individuals personally and as a community. In legal theory this view is espoused by aggregate theory, which claims moral responsibility rests with individual officers, employees, etc., and is determined under the normal standards applied to the natural person. Likewise, Catholic Social Thought does not place moral agency on the corporation per se but argues that *persons* carry the moral responsibility as individuals and as a human community. Melé and Fontradana explain that only the human person can be held as responsible, because only persons have morally free will and reason. Responsibility is the result of freedom and of "the capacity to discover the moral good."[41]

Within Church teaching, however, reference is also made to "certain collective or community responsibilities." This collective responsibility is based on the decisions and actions of individuals. Hence, merit or culpability is always that of the individual person, even when acting together with others. Even when referring to "social sin"—that is, where *collective* behavior is morally wrong—such sin is seen as the result of many personal sins on the part of many persons, and it is the individual persons who are responsible, not merely the group.[42]

Given that responsibility rests with the person, Melé and Fontradana question the use of the terms *corporate moral agency* and *corporate responsibility,* preferring to speak of *community responsibility.* Community responsibility is an integral part of being a member of the human community and encompasses more than one's job or contract responsibilities: "Community responsibility, far from eliminating individual responsibility, expands it by making the individual aware that there is something which affects each and every person by virtue of their being united among themselves and forming part of society."[43] To attribute all responsibility to the corporation would be to deny the autonomy of the person who is acting within the corporation.[44] Thus, the term *community responsibility* indicates "a responsibility to achieve something that must be accomplished among many people united by certain nexuses, not to eliminate personal responsibility for the sake of the responsibility of a 'moral agency.'"[45] Responsibility, therefore, is personal, but it also includes responsibility for actions carried out with others. The corporation per se cannot be said to be a moral agent, nor can it be claimed to be the equivalent of a human person for moral purposes—that is, an entity onto which we can project individual responsibility.

In the business ethics literature we find a similar view in Solomon, who states that "people in business are ultimately responsible as individuals, but they are responsible as individuals in a corporate setting, where their responsibilities are at least in part defined by their role and duties in the company and, of course, by 'the bottom line.'"[46] Bowie, too, contends that the "business firm" is a "moral community" where "each member of the organization stands in a moral relationship to all others."[47] A variation of this approach may be seen in Velasquez, who disagrees both with those who claim the corporation is like an individual moral agent and those who claim it is like a "machine" and can bear no moral responsibility.[48] In his view, the corporation is made up of individuals whom we agree by convention to treat as a unit. Corporations and their acts depend on individuals; because those acts originate in individuals, those individuals are morally responsible. To this extent Velasquez's view seems very like that of Catholic Social Thought. He continues, however, that "organizations have moral duties and are morally responsible in a secondary sense: A corporation has a moral duty to do something only if some of its members have a moral duty to make sure it is done, and a corporation is morally responsible for something only if some of its members are morally responsible for what happened."[49] According to this definition, then, a situation could arise for which no one is responsible, making this view problematic in the context of our society today.

Werhane, like Velasquez, contends that the corporation is not an autonomous moral agent itself but, given that the acts of the corporation derive from the acts of persons, these persons must be evaluated morally.[50] Furthermore, the rights of the corporation are not primary equivalent to those of persons but are secondary *to* those of persons. The implications of this view are that the individual members of the corporation are the moral agents, and for the purposes of accountability, they are liable for the moral or immoral actions of the corporation. This position becomes complicated when the corporation is large, as it is self-evident that individuals would bear differing degrees of moral responsibility as well as culpability for the corporation's policies and practices. It would seem reasonable to think that the leaders of the corporation are the responsible moral agents for policies and practices rather than the lower-level employees. Kaptein and Wempe criticize this view, which they term the "functional model," because it does not recognize the relevance of the culture and structure of the corporation and merely sees moral problems as the responsibility of individuals.[51] What happens if these individuals are replaced by others? Does responsibility for behavior (for example, pollution) cease when these individuals leave the corporation? Who then is responsible? Corporations are often enormous and complex in structure. Can management really be held responsible for all that the corporation does?[52]

The final approach to corporation moral agency argues that the corporation is indeed a moral agent. In legal theory some of the "real entity" supporters adhere to this view. Phillips notes that Peter A. French contends that the corporation is a moral person and that it has both intentionality and corporate moral agency because there is a decision-making structure whose operations can be described in terms of intentions and actions.[53] Van Gerwen believes that corporate moral agency is an issue that both exists and should be examined.[54] While many deny it and claim that only individuals can be moral agents—a claim based on methodological individualism and Kantian ethics that stresses human reason and personal autonomy—an alternative to this dominant paradigm of liberal philosophy is offered by the likes of MacIntyre.[55] This alternative has a communitarian view of social action, which leads to a development of an ethics of virtue including corporate virtues and vices.[56] It differs from the liberal model, which combines utilitarian and deontological arguments.[57] Some arguments of others who hold the view that the corporation is a moral agent include the following:

- Elfstrom notes that "Corporations, therefore, have the qualities required for moral agency, though in less elegant and more complex fashion than single human individuals."[58] Additionally, he states that "the contention that corporations are moral agents is supported by the fact that corporations clearly are held accountable in many ways . . . corporations themselves commonly acknowledge a distinct sense of *moral* responsibility when dealing with their employees and in their external business transactions."[59]

- Bowman-Larsen contends that "the issue of corporate personhood and agency is not to be settled once and for all. But insofar as a company (or its board of directors) deliberates and decides upon company policy and company strategy and acts in the name of the company, and insofar as a corporation is a legal entity that can be held liable as such, there is absolutely no reason that it cannot be responsible for its 'actions' as well . . . I do not think we need to establish metaphysical personhood in order to speak of corporations as moral actors."[60]

- Goodpaster believes the corporation, like the individual, is a citizen, and like the individual it has moral responsibilities.[61] He provides a carefully nuanced examination of corporate moral agency and notes that "our frame of reference does not imply that corporations are persons in a literal sense. It simply means that in certain respects concepts and functions normally attributed to persons can also be attributed to organizations made up of persons."[62]

- Donaldson believes that corporations, like individuals, are moral agents and that they can have moral responsibilities and rights, albeit not identical to those of persons.[63] Also representing this social contract approach to business ethics are Kaptein and Wempe, who contend that it is justifiable to view a corporation as a moral subject: "the corporate social contract theory portrays the corporation as the focal point within a network of contracts on the basis of which moral responsibilities can be ascribed to the corporation as an independent entity."[64]

- Brown notes that "because corporations have their own decision making structures, have choices and justify them with corporate reasons, it made sense to treat corporations as moral agents."[65]

- Morse views business as a "moral entity" and as a "moral member of the community" and contends business must view itself as such and acknowledge that it has considerable influence on the lives of people.[66] Hence, it has an "added moral responsibility of reinforcing the ends and desires which help people flourish."[67]

- Corlett, discussing the issue of corporate responsibility for environmental damage, contends that whether or not we conclude that the corporation is a moral person, corporations as collectives are responsible for certain actions (for example, environmental damage) and should be held liable and punished as collectives. In other words, she advocates "moral responsibility collectivism."[68]

This third perspective is an interesting theoretical position but poses difficulties in the practical sense. Those who advocate it do not define clearly who exactly would be accountable or how to decide who bears the moral responsibility. Communication is only possible, in practical terms, between individuals, not entities. Even in law, persons represent the organization, though they may not be held personally liable. Perhaps this is the advantage of this approach: individuals do not have to "foot the bill" for recompense in the event that they *should* have made more *moral* decisions.

This brief overview illustrates that there is considerable difference of opinion concerning the issue of corporate moral agency. Consequently, there will be differences in opinion as to whether the corporation can have any *moral* purpose or be held *morally responsible* for its actions at all. This chapter does not support the position of those who claim that because the corporation is not a moral agent, it has no moral responsibility and bears only legal accountability. Given the ethical framework presented in this chapter we would argue that moral agency rests with individuals in the first instance but rests with the individuals *as community* as well. Likewise, moral responsibility and moral accountability for policies and practices of the corporation rest with the individuals (as individuals and as community) who comprise the corporation. It is these human persons who devise the policies and who perform the actions, although the extent of each individual's moral responsibility and culpability will differ.[69]

THE PURPOSE OF THE CORPORATION

Having examined the notions of the *nature* and *moral agency* of the corporation, we now consider the *purpose* of the corporation. It was Berle and

Means, in *The Modern Corporation and Private Property,* who first posed the question of the purpose of the business corporation and concluded that it had to serve all of society.[70] However, this is by no means an accepted or unanimous view. The issue at stake, in its simplest form, seems to be whether the purpose or objective of the corporation is *only* to make a profit or whether it has some other *broader* purpose, for example, social, ecological, etc.

Those who adhere to the classical liberal economic paradigm, and what is called "the financial theory of business,"[71] such as Friedman, Soros, Sternberg, and others, believe that the *only* purpose of business is to make a profit. Thus, "the neoclassical theory of the firm contends that the firm works best when it fulfils the task of maximizing the shareholder value only."[72] Friedman argues that the purpose of business is "to use its resources and engage in activities designed to increase its profits . . . in open and free competition without deception or fraud."[73] Soros contends that the *single* purpose of the publicly owned corporation is to make money—other purposes merely distract from this.[74] In other words, business does not have communal goals. Sternberg states that "The defining purpose of business is maximizing owner value over the long term by selling goods and services."[75] She is critical of the plethora of additional objectives that have been given to business and states categorically that the purpose of business is neither to promote the common good, nor to improve employee well-being, nor to create jobs. While such things may be *side products* of business, they are not its key purpose.[76] This neoclassical economic perspective, "together with its applied 'arm' finance, has dominated contemporary discussion of the theory of the firm, propagating Friedman's view."[77] Clark, who examines three efforts of this neoclassical theoretical paradigm to delineate the purpose of the firm—namely, that the firm is a market, is a mental fiction, and exists due to transaction costs—argues that all three are "based on neoclassical theory's individualistic and mechanical conception of society, its hedonistic conception of human nature, and its assumption of a tendency toward general equilibrium."[78] He contends that these assumptions are unrealistic and are the weakness of this theory. Only in an economy that does not actually exist can maximization of shareholder value promote equity and efficiency; likewise, the assumptions about human beings and society "are unsupportable either in theory or in fact."[79]

In contrast to the neoclassical/neoliberal view, there are a number of other conceptions that advocate a *broader approach* to the purpose of business and the corporation. Among these broader conceptions, the "profit-plus-extras" contingent is that of Catholic Social Thought. John Paul II links "purpose" and "nature," acknowledging profit as having a legitimate role in business but emphasizing that, "in fact, the purpose of a business firm is not simply to make a profit, but is to be found in its very existence as a *community of persons* who in various ways are endeavoring to satisfy their basic needs, and who form a particular group at the service of the whole society."[80] Community and the individual are interconnected.[81] Thus, business has a *social* function and "is considered as a means to facilitate a wider sense of community. It is a community of persons who through the goods and services it produces stands at the service of the wider society and the common good."[82]

These views are echoed by others in this tradition. Riordan suggests that the purpose of the corporation is to contribute to the ultimate human good and is strongly critical of Sternberg's neoliberal/neoclassical view.[83] Zadek argues against the notion that profit is the *only* or even the *primary* purpose of all businesses and argues for including "human and moral factors."[84] Kennedy also believes the purpose of the firm is to "bring some human good into being" and to meet both economic criteria and those of becoming a true community contributing to the development of those who are involved in its activities.[85] Alford and Naughton note that while it is tempting to describe the corporation and its purpose only from a financial point of view because this is quantifiable, "the description is inevitably abstract and disconnected from the real world of business, compared to one which recognizes the fact that the members of a business build their own common good and may contribute to the wider common good."[86] They argue that acceptance of the principle of the common good enables people to move out of the dominant liberal paradigm. While business is not responsible *for* the common good, it is responsible *to* the common good and has its own common good.[87] The basis of the "common good model" is a distinction between foundational/instrumental goods like profit and excellent/inherent goods like human development and community. The former are not supreme but are necessary only as a means to obtain the latter, not as an end in their own right. This is where the shareholder model errs—in elevating such goods to being the sole goods.[88]

In other words, business must create profit but only as the first step to enabling human development.

Contributing to the common good, however, does *not* mean that business should be a social welfare agency; rather, as part of the community, it ought to share with other social institutions and agencies in the responsibility for that common good.[89] Catholic Social Thought, then, promotes "an understanding of the firm based on how firms actually behave and second on how they can best promote the goals of human dignity and the common good."[90] In contrast, "Friedman's teleology remains truncated until profit making is seen—as the principle of subsidiary demands—in terms of its overall role in achieving the common good."[91]

In this respect, Koslowski makes an interesting observation: Catholic Social Thought is based on the belief that human beings *can* do good and can, in the context of the firm, for example, choose to foster the common good. He argues that the Protestant understanding of the purpose of the "firm" would differ from this, however, because Protestants, especially Lutherans, believe that human beings cannot *intend good*. Thus, a contribution to the common good can only be made "as the invisible hand directs individuals' inevitably selfish intentions and needs to ends beyond them."[92] Therefore, shareholder maximization would be *the* primary purpose for the firm and *the* optimal way of contributing to the common good.

Let us examine other views on the purpose of the corporation. First, Goodpaster, an advocate of corporate citizenship, agrees with the approach of Catholic Social Thought but combines it with his view that the corporation should be a good citizen.[93] Its purpose, therefore, is to fulfill not only its "functional" role—that is, specialized tasks like the production of goods—but also to share responsibility for the common good, "for the community or the nation as a whole."[94] King, coming from the same perspective, believes that, because the corporation is part of the global and local communities, its purpose is to be a good citizen.[95] In addition, because it is the "medium" by means of which the gap between the rich and poor is widening, "if the corporation does not begin to act as a good citizen, it will be destroyed and capitalism will be destroyed with it."[96]

Second, Morse and Solomon reflect a virtue ethics approach to the corporation. Morse believes that business is not an end in itself but a means to promoting the good life of the citizens in the community in which it is situated. Therefore, it must, like society, produce good human beings. Merely focusing on profit alone would result in encouraging "vicious" persons.[97] Solomon states, "We can no longer accept the amoral idea that 'business is business' and that its purpose is merely "to make money."[98] Rather, its purpose is "to serve society's demands and the public good and be rewarded for doing so."[99] For Solomon, Friedman's "infamous" view is one that "betrays a willful misunderstanding of the very nature of both social responsibility and business."[100]

Third, there are a number of scholars who view the purpose of the corporation from a "corporate social responsibility" perspective. Samuelson and Nordhaus, despite their very neoclassical definition of the corporation, imply that the purpose of the corporation is to be financially successful and economically efficient and blend social responsibilities (like job creation, patronage of the arts, being a good corporate citizen) with profit making.[101] Post believes the corporation has *multiple* purposes that challenge its viability.[102] Nevertheless, its purpose must include profit making as well as contributions to its stakeholders. Krueger argues that generating wealth is the primary, but not only, purpose of the corporation.[103] In addition, corporations must serve the common good by contributing to an ecologically sustainable society and serving as "engines of growth" to relieve poverty, which is their key "moral challenge."[104] This view is echoed by Thompson, who points out that "multinational corporations [MNCs] can make valuable contributions to the alleviation of poverty, but their single-minded drive for profits often blinds them to the common good and the needs of the poor. Worse, the power that accompanies their size and wealth enables MNCs to manipulate the system in their favor so that the rules of the game oppress the poor."[105]

Finally, we consider two contrary voices: Keeley, who contends that organizations per se have *no purpose* and have no goals at all—it is the individuals who have the goals for the organization;[106] and Drucker, who argues that profit is not an absolute goal for business because profit shifts according to social and environmental factors.[107] Instead, the purpose of the business is "to create a customer," from which all other purposes flow.

In summary, approaches to the purpose of the corporation suggest that it should do the following" make a profit for shareholders/owners

make a profit as well as develop individuals and serve the common
good

be a good citizen

produce good human beings and contribute to the community as a
whole

be socially responsible in addition to making a profit (for example,
relieve poverty)

Or, alternatively, some argue that the corporation has not purpose at all.

It would seem that current writing on the purpose of business tends toward the "profit-plus-extras" view rather than "profit only" view. Exactly
how those "extras" are defined varies considerably, as does the ways in
which such purpose is fulfilled. This chapter takes the view that business
is part of the community and is made up of human persons, who themselves are part of this wider community as well as of the corporation *as
community.* Therefore, the corporation's purpose includes serving the common good and developing the human beings who work within the corporation in addition to generating a profit/wealth.

THE ROLE OF THE CORPORATION, ITS RELATIONSHIP
WITH SOCIETY, AND ITS RESPONSIBILITIES

The purpose of the corporation is not merely a matter of understanding
goals and aims in a generalized manner. In addition to being conceptualized and defined, a purpose must be realized and fulfilled. This process
depends on how the corporation's relationship (that is, connection) with
society is understood, its consequent responsibilities (that is, what it is
required to do as part of its role, moral or otherwise) and its role (that is,
function) in that society.[108]

At the outset, it is worth noting that this area in the literature is one of
the most complex and contentious and is difficult to clarify. There are a
number of reasons for this. First, the literature is prolific, yielding almost
as many explanations of these issues as individual authors. Not even
within the same theoretical paradigm is there agreement on what exactly
are the roles and responsibilities of the corporation. While this indicates

that the field is evolving and contains lively and interesting debate,[109] it also means that it is difficult to be definitive and to evaluate corporations in these areas because there is no agreement on constituent elements. Second, terminology is used imprecisely and variously. Thus, the terms *role, purpose, responsibilities,* and *relationship* are differentiated here, but elsewhere they may be used interchangeably. The corporation's *relationship* with society may be explained in terms of *responsibilities,* or the *role* of the corporation may be illustrated by discussing *specific duties.* It is also extremely difficult to pin down the meaning of either *corporate responsibility* or of *corporate social responsibility,* a difficulty acknowledged in the literature. What the actual responsibilities of the corporation *are* varies depending on the individual author's preference and/or approach. Third, the notion of *moral responsibility* is slippery. Some theorists do not acknowledge that business *has* such a responsibility. Others use the term to apply to certain *duties* of business, yet those same duties may not be seen as *moral* responsibilities/duties in another author's work. For these reasons, it is important to note that while the discussion below attempts to give some idea of the diversity of views on the role of the corporation, its relationship with society, and its responsibilities (moral or otherwise), and to acknowledge different ways of construing these concepts, it cannot cover all possibilities. We note further that the "ethical narrative" of the present chapter is that of Catholic Social Thought.

Danley provides a useful overview of the role and responsibilities of the modern corporation. He contends there are two main positions—the Classical and the Managerial business ideologies—and that most writers use the assumptions of one or the other.[110] Both frameworks are grounded in the liberal tradition, the key values of which are liberty and equality. At base the ethical value lies in determining the sort of person we should try to become and the sort of communities we should try to shape and challenging corporations to do more than make profits.

The Classical perspective holds that the main responsibility of the "company" is economic competition in the context of a limited government in order to make a profit for stockholders. Profit making is either the primary or the only responsibility.[111] Some call this approach the neoclassical stockholder/shareholder theory, which, as observed by Cortright and Pierucci, "refuses to die"; however, many versions of stakeholder theory appear to run counter to it.[112] Those who adhere to this "profit only" paradigm—the "amoral" position, or what McCann calls "the financial theory of business"[113]—opt for the "shareholder model" and claim that the role of the corporation centers on making a profit, while its chief or *only* relationship and responsibility is to shareholders and/or owners. This view is based on an economic paradigm that "has its roots both in the individualistic philosophies of the past few centuries and in the heavily quantified economic theories of the twentieth century."[114] As Phillips notes, it endorses only the profit-making responsibilities of business (as represented in legal theory by concession theory), argues that corporations are held responsible only for *legal purposes* (for example, for failing to avoid foreseeable harm), and contends that they do not have moral responsibility.[115]

Kaptein and Wempe provide some clarification on the ambivalence toward the moral responsibility of the corporation,[116] noting that this can be traced to classical and neoclassical economics, where ethical questions are seen as inappropriate. The view that business is amoral seems to have its origins in the differentiation between fact and value in the seventeenth and eighteenth centuries, as well as in the emphasis on efficiency, functionality, the concept of equilibrium, and the "scientific" approach to business. Morality came to be seen as irrelevant or counterproductive to prosperity and as a force that disrupts the economic order. Business was to run independent of morality—economics was based on the natural sciences and was seen as "neutral" or value-free. Elfstrom, explaining this resistance to moral responsibility on the part of the corporation, outlines four arguments used to claim that "corporations cannot be expected to shoulder more than minimal moral responsibility."[117] Rossouw, making a similar point, refers to business "myths," which are used to discount the importance of ethical behavior and moral responsibility on the part of business.[118] Sethi states "there is considerable resistance to the injection of moral and ethical values in the capitalistic system which depends on individual choices and is supposedly value neutral."[119] However, as Kaptein and Wempe point out, values have an important social role and influence on the corporation and cannot be discarded. No amount of efficiency will alter the fact that the manager is faced with moral demands.[120]

However, adherents of the neoclassical approach, such as Friedman, ask:

What does it mean to say that "business" has responsibilities? Only people can have responsibilities. A corporation is an artificial person and in this sense may have artificial responsibilities but "business" as a whole cannot be said to have responsibilities even in this vague sense. . . . I share Adam Smith's skepticism about the benefits that can be expected from "those who affected to trade for the public good"[;] . . . the use of the cloak of social responsibility . . . does clearly harm the foundations of a free society . . . In an ideal free market . . . there are no values, no "social responsibilities" in any sense other than the shared values and responsibilities of individuals. . . . [social responsibility is a] "fundamentally subversive doctrine" in a free society.[121]

Sternberg believes Friedman's views on corporate social responsibility are too mild and argues that the value maximized must be financial not moral, that the use of business resources for corporate social responsibility is "theft," and that stakeholder theory is a "mischaracterization of business,"[122] confusing its role with that of government and the nature of accountability. While business may be *affected* by many things or groups, it is nonsensical to say that business is *accountable* to all these things or groups. Furthermore, stakeholder theory has no criteria for *balancing* all of the stakeholders' interests.[123]

Yet while Friedman and Sternberg claim that profit making is the *only* responsibility of the corporation, they also suggest it should be done according to fair competition, without fraud or deception and according to the rules of human decency. This means business should be honest and fair and not employ lying, cheating, killing, stealing, coercion, and so on in seeking profit.[124] Sternberg also endorses the principles of distributive justice, which he believes "incorporates the purpose of business into its very definition."[125] This seems to indicate that in carrying out its primary responsibility, the corporation must indeed adhere to certain moral standards. This in turn suggests that corporations *do* have some limited *moral* responsibility and, dare we say it, moral accountability. Perhaps, therefore, the role of business is less amoral than it appears on the surface of this approach. Kaptein and Wempe, while criticizing this approach, also note that "the fact that the corporation is not the appropriate institution for pursuing social ideals (as Hayek and Friedman propose) does not mean that no norms at all should apply to the business context. There is a difference between the social responsibility and the moral responsibility of a corporation."[126] They also argue, however, that this "amoral model" fails to take into account the corporate context and the moral issues that arise in the course of a person's job in the corporation, and, because morality is viewed as a private and personal issue, real ethical problems in business are not acknowledged.

This neoclassical/neoliberal view[127] is in strong contrast to broader approaches to corporate responsibility and the role business could play in society—for example, Danley's Managerial perspective.[128] The Managerial perspective includes stakeholder theory and argues that the stockholder/shareholder theory of the Classical approach is both dated and morally wrong. Most business ethics researchers and social issues in management researchers believe the company is responsible to a wide range of stakeholders and must weigh their various interests before making a decision.[129] The role of the corporation in a free society is to be a good citizen and to act in a socially responsible way. As far as Danley is concerned, the discourse of this perspective is conceptually amorphous, with a high moral tone and little moral argument, and the definitions of corporate social responsibility are vague, "vacuous," and irrelevant because of a failure to consider the system within which the modern corporation functions.[130] In addition, both frameworks are inadequate for answering the question of the *role* of the corporation, particularly given the changes of the global world and the powerful role of the multinational corporation.[131] The role of the corporation in the new globalized world is *normative,* but exactly what this means needs to be worked out in conjunction with "the development of a coherent and defensible theory of political economy."[132] Danley's analysis is useful because it confirms, at the broadest level, that we are dealing with the "profit only" or "profit-plus-extras" dichotomy once again. It also confirms the diversity and confusion in this area.

Let us examine, then, some of the diverse approaches to the relationship, role, and responsibilities of the corporation that cluster in this broader "profit-plus-extras" perspective on how the corporation fulfills its purpose. We will examine here the notions of corporate *social* responsibility, the stakeholder model and approach, the corporate citizenship approach, the corporate governance approach, the social contract approach, and the approach of Catholic Social Thought concerning this vexed question of how the corporation fulfills its purpose through its relationship with, responsibility to, and role in society.

The notion of corporate social responsibility per se originated at the beginning of the twentieth century when social protest at the extreme size, power, and overcompetitive nature of corporations resulted in their being asked to consider using "their power and influence voluntarily for broad social purposes rather than for profits alone."[133] It was as a result of this new role for business that the principles of charity[134] and stewardship[135] emerged as the foundation for the modern notion of corporate social responsibility. It was the principle of stewardship that lay at the basis of the modern theory of stakeholder management.[136] Buchholz and Rosenthal contend that the issue of social responsibility grew particularly between 1960 and 1975 as a consequence of and in response to great social change and changing social values.[137] This "ethical" concept of social responsibility points to business corporations being both economic institutions and institutions that must play a role in assisting society to solve its many social problems,[138] some of which have been *caused* by business[139]:

> Corporate social responsibility challenges business to be accountable for the consequences of their actions affecting the firm's stakeholders while they pursue traditional economic goals. The general public expects business to be socially responsible, and many companies have responded by making social goals a part of their overall business operations. Guidelines for acting in socially responsible ways are not always clear, thus producing controversy about what constitutes such behavior, how extensive it should be, and what it costs to be socially responsible.[140]

This statement on corporate social responsibility bears out the criticisms of authors like Danley, Riordan, and De George. De George criticizes corporate social responsibility as a modern myth.[141] No one can adequately define what it means to be socially responsible, and so no one can apply standards to determine whether a corporation is or is not socially responsible. Therefore, corporate social responsibility ends up being little more than obeying the law, acts as a whitewash for amoral business practice, and hides the real ethical and moral responsibilities of business. De George states:

> economic responsibilities are not basic, if this means that a company must make profits and then ask what its ethical responsibilities

are. Its ethical responsibilities parallel its profit-making and should inform and be used to evaluate the means the company employs to make profits, the company's ends and the profit itself. Similarly, the firm's ethical responsibilities parallel the legal and discretionary ones and should inform them.[142]

The latter include operating according to consistent moral norms rather than changing these according to the country in which the corporation is situated and acknowledging that moral responsibilities (for example, not exploiting workers) are obligatory. De George's views are corroborated by Brown, who states: "corporate social responsibility has become a popular notion in business circles, with a variety of meanings. As Richard De George has pointed out the notion can refer to either moral or non-moral obligations. It can also refer to obligations or to voluntary actions."[143] Brown therefore chooses to use the term *corporate responsibility* rather than *corporate social responsibility* and suggests five theoretical approaches: the classic theory (which includes Friedman, socially responsible investment adherents, and the corporate governance movement in financial institutions); the contractual theory (which includes Donaldson and Dunfee); the stakeholder view (Freeman); the corporate agent theory; and the corporate citizen theory.[144]

Robert Samuelson, writing in *Newsweek* (July 5, 1993), even went so far as to state that the corporation that could blend profit and social responsibility, like IBM had done at its peak, would no longer exist in our globalized world.[145] Boatright argues that corporate social responsibility needs to be understood in the context of "the new world of investor capitalism" rather than in terms of "a managerial philosophy that guides business executives and board directors."[146] Sethi also refers to the "divergent nature of our expectations of a socially responsible corporation."[147] As mentioned, this lack of agreement on the meaning and form of corporate social responsibility is one of the most prominent difficulties with this approach.

Because of these difficulties, Buchholz and Rosenthal contend that there was a shift toward *social responsiveness* in the late 1970s,[148] while Post, Lawrence, and Weber date this shift to the 1960s.[149] Carroll and Buchholz explain *social responsiveness* as a corporate citizenship concept along with corporate social responsibility and corporate social performance.[150] Despite these confusions, social responsiveness seems to have emphasized business' response to social pressure rather than its *moral* responsibilities, as well as action and activity rather than obligation and accountability. However, *how* such a response is to be carried out also was debated.[151]

The stakeholder model approach, which could be viewed as one attempt to clarify precisely what corporate social responsibility envisages, originated in the 1960s in the work of Management theorists like Rhenman, Ansoff, and Ackhoff and is linked to a very old tradition that sees business as an integral part of society rather than as a separate economic institution.[152] The original idea of identifying all the constituents in a corporation was expanded to include interaction with stakeholders; this emerged in the 1980s as a method for taking into account in a systematic way the views of those who affect or are affected by corporate actions.[153] Freeman, a key figure in the development of stakeholder theory, believes that while this does not mean that business can solve all problems, it does mean that business can become a "truly human institution."[154] Stakeholder theory has been used to describe and analyze the corporation's relationship with society and advocates that business take into account the interests of both primary and secondary stakeholders.[155] Business is seen to have responsibilities other than financial and legal ones, but the exact nature of these responsibilities and how they are understood varies according to the theorist. Therefore, as in the case of the term *corporate social responsibility,* we see once again that there are difficulties in clarification.[156] However, some authors suggest that stakeholder theory has the advantage of embodying a relational view of the firm, and its power lies in focusing management decision making on the multiplicity and diversity of the relationships with which the corporation has its being and of the multipurpose nature of the corporation as a vehicle for enriching those relationships in their various dimensions.[157]

These advantages may outweigh the problems with the clarification of who is or is not a stakeholder. There are also other criticisms of this model, however, such as that it goes *too far* in the responsibilities set out for companies, fails to distinguish sufficiently between fiduciary and non-fiduciary relationships, needs to have a hierarchy of stakeholder duties, and needs to acknowledge that not all stakeholders are equal. Gordley points to these and states: "the trouble with it . . . is that it does not indicate how to weigh the conflicting claims of . . . groups. It does not explain why a management's responsibility to make a profit for shareholders seems basically different from its other responsibilities. Moreover, . . . the ethical foundation of the stakeholder model is not clear, particularly if we imagine each of these groups to be out for itself!"[158] Similarly, Fort contends that "if a corporation must take into equal account *all* of the various constituents who are affected by its actions (which is the charge laid on it by R. Edward Freeman), it serves too many masters." This could result in "gridlock or overreaching."[159]

In addition to stakeholder theory itself, there are other efforts to specify exactly what is involved in the *relationship* of business with stakeholders and what exactly its *responsibilities* are in this regard, including the corporate citizenship approach, the social contract approach, and the virtue ethics approach. The corporate citizenship approach originated in the 1990s and is based on building collaborative partnerships with stakeholder groups with a focus on mutual business opportunities and management of social and financial performance. Those who advocate that the corporation be viewed as a citizen for purposes of outlining and monitoring its conduct in the context of society include Goodpaster and King. Goodpaster argues that such conduct must fulfill both functional responsibilities and those for contributing to the common good.[160] Post, Lawrence, and Weber, discussing corporate citizenship, contend it is characterized by ethical business behavior, an attempt to balance stakeholder interests, and environmental protection.[161] Ethical behavior includes fair and honest business practice, good corporate governance, and high ethical standards for employee conduct. The corporation's relationship with society resembles the ordinary citizen's and includes similar responsibilities. King believes the corporation must act responsibly toward all stakeholders while being accountable to the company itself.[162] It must also act fairly, transparently, and with intellectual honesty. King, who also advocates good corporate governance, states "the inclusive approach [to corporate governance] recognizes stakeholders other than shareowners. The relationship between the company and some of these stakeholders is contractual—as with the customer and supplier—while some are non-contractual, such as the community in which it operates."[163] Thus, the corporation is a citizen, and in order for it to be a good citizen, it must conform to good corporate governance standards as well as perform well—a difficult balancing act.

Another way of conceptualizing this relationship between stakeholders and business is in terms of a social contract, that is, an agreement as to what obligations and responsibilities business owes society and what is owed by society to business. The social contract perspective originated in the 1980s, and according to Dunfee and Donaldson it is the only approach other than stakeholder theory and Friedman's market-based morality to establish itself as a core paradigm in the field of business ethics.[164] It emphasizes those fundamental or basic commitments necessary for two parties to co-exist as social agents. Its roots lie in Hobbes, Locke, Rousseau, and Kant. The assumption underlying the approach is that we can best understand the obligations of social institutions like business and government by trying to comprehend what a fair contract between these institutions and society, or among different communities within these entities, entails.[165]

While the old contract between business and society was based on the notion that economic growth was the basis for both social and economic progress and that business drove this growth by fulfilling its purpose to produce goods and services at a profit—thereby also fulfilling its responsibilities to society—the new, emerging social contract is somewhat different. It suggests that pursuing growth in this way imposes detrimental social costs and does not automatically result in progress. In some cases, for example, it causes damage to the environment. The new contract between business and society aims to oblige business to work for social *and* economic goals and redress these detrimental effects. Buchholz and Rosenthal contend that the contract between business and society that incorporates the social responsibilities of business is changing to reflect the altered social expectations of business by society. In addition, there are now laws and regulations to ensure business obeys the new rules.[166] Thus, this approach emphasizes social obligations to consumers and employees. Post also contends that a "new social contract" is "emerging" between business and *employees* that affects and has implications for business' relationship with society.[167] Business must indeed contribute economically to society, but in taking action it must take into account the benefits both to the society and to the corporation. He believes that while corporations are certainly responsible to stockholders, they also must discharge social responsibilities and be held accountable for actions that affect people, their communities, and their environment. This does not mean that the company must abandon its economic and legal responsibilities but rather that corporations have great responsibilities because they affect many lives. Therefore, they must balance these responsibilities and weigh the costs and benefits.[168] Kaptein and Wempe, who also favor social contract theory, say it "portrays the corporation as the focal point within a network of contracts on the basis of which moral responsibilities can be ascribed to the corporation as an independent moral entity."[169]

Koehn points out, however, that Donaldson "insists on the corporation's peculiar moral status: the corporation cannot be expected to accomplish social purposes such as the just redistribution of wealth within the community because it has not been designed as a political unit. Instead, Donaldson argues, the corporation's social responsibilities must be interpreted as those which can reasonably be imputed to a primarily economic entity."[170] Consequently, from a social contract perspective, corporate responsibility would be seen in terms of rights and duties of an *economic* entity and would not include "social purposes" like economic justice. Yet, having said this, we note that Dunfee and Hess, also adherents of the social contract approach, contend that business *cannot* turn a blind eye to the enormous human misery on our planet.[171] They therefore advocate "Direct Corporate Humanitarian Investment," which "involves a firm using its resources and know-how to alleviate a particular instance of human misery."[172] This is not just a matter of a cash donation but includes involvement in specific projects, such as the well-known example of Merck's efforts to combat river blindness. For Dunfee and Hess, such involvement is compatible with the social contract approach because it is voluntary and does not contend that such responsibility is the primary responsibility of the corporation, nor does it demand resources that the company does not have. Again, we are faced with various views on the nature of corporate (social) responsibility within the same paradigm.

An argument along the same lines, albeit from a utilitarian rather than a social contract approach, is given by Elfstrom.[173] He believes that a corporation, like an individual, must provide for the *basic* wants of others but does not have as much obligation, if any, to provide for *secondary* wants.[174] In his view, the corporation should make a contribution to society by creating jobs, providing goods and services, and managing resources. Its contribution should come from its commercial efforts, and it should avoid involvement in other areas such as social problems that government is better suited to handle. Business should not deal with social problems unless government has set priorities. This, of course, begs the question that if government never sets priorities or sets unjust priorities, should business merely note that social issues are not part of its purpose and not part of its responsibility?

A further variation on the social contract approach, and one that has been given much emphasis in South Africa during the postapartheid period, is that of corporate governance. Van Gerwen contends that the corporate governance approach is based on the social contract approach and Kantian deontology. In his view, it emerged in the Anglo-Saxon context and aimed to define a moral framework for corporate conduct.[175] It differed from previous models in that it did not want managers to have a central role in corporate conduct but rather advocated greater stockholder control and a focus on balanced control of power and ownership between stockholders and management. Therefore, property becomes the center of ethical reflection. Considerations include corporate structure and statutory rules and corporate law, as well as the debate on the link between ownership and the responsibility for the consequences and effects of corporate action. In South Africa the so-called King Code of corporate governance has been formulated to guide business conduct, but it is neither statutory nor mandatory. Calls for better corporate governance are often couched in terms of the so-called triple bottom line, that is, reporting on financial, social, and environmental issues, contributions, and/or behaviors. What is interesting about the *King Report on Corporate Governance for South Africa* is that it advocates good corporate citizenship.[176] This seems to contradict Van Gerwen's notion that corporate governance is based on the social contract approach.

Some theorists seem to suggest a virtue ethics approach to the role, relationship, and responsibility of the corporation. Thus Morse, like Post, contends that business has a great influence on the lives of people and on "all aspects of human existence."[177] As such it has an "added moral responsibility of reinforcing the ends and desires which help people flourish"[178] and thus is responsible for developing virtue and virtuous conduct. This will lead to the happiness of all persons in society. Solomon likewise points to the great power of corporations—power that is so great that the future of the world lies in their hands. Therefore, their conduct is not purely a *business* matter. Solomon's concern for the future arises because policies, decisions, and behavior in business continue to be based on profit making and stockholder return *alone*. Yet, those in business know well "that business is a human and social enterprise,"[179] that there is no law of nature that *insists* profit must be made no matter what, that corporations do have responsibilities to stakeholders and the community who have played a part in their success, and that returns for stockholders cannot eclipse other obligations. The corporation must, in the global context, care about the less fortunate. It must look to long-term rather than short-term goals within the context of a global future that will be shared by corporations, stakeholders, and the wider community alike. However, there are also those like MacIntyre and Dobson who contend that the current market system, with its emphasis on individualism and acquisitiveness, excludes the development or even the possibility of "virtuous" behavior. As Dobson contends, a *truly* virtuous corporation would not be suited to economic activity at all.[180]

Given this variety and somewhat contradictory plethora of views, what then is the approach of Catholic Social Thought to the corporation's role, responsibilities, and relationship with society? Melé contends that "the Catholic Social tradition considers the common good as the basic reference point for any human society, and for business as well. In this regard, John Paul II does not hesitate to affirm that the Church 'recognizes the positive values of the market and of the enterprise but at the same time points out that these need to be oriented towards the common good.'"[181] Therefore, the corporation has responsibilities that go beyond itself. It enables the human person to express his/her freedom and talents; gives each person an opportunity to work, which is part of the dignity of the human person; and advances the spirit of solidarity enabling the individual to make a contribution to others. The "role of business in the modern economy demands the person's best qualities: the capacity to investigate and to know, the capacity for solidarity in the organization, and the capacity to work toward the satisfaction of the needs of fellow employees. Unfortunately, however, not enough businesses reach their full potential for developing people and instead they alienate them."[182]

Kennedy notes that for business to make a contribution to others as advocated by Catholic Social Thought does not require that it use its resources to solve whatever problems exist in the community, as appears to be the argument of the corporate social responsibility approach. Rather, businesses have a duty to conduct their operations by choosing courses of action that deliberately support not only the common good of the business itself but the common good of the society as well.[183] This may mean, for example, making a bit less profit or not producing goods that can harm people. In other words, decisions are to be taken in solidarity with others.[184] Melé says there are three "essential elements" in the common good: respect for humans and their rights, "social well-being and group development," and "stability and security within a just order."[185] Serving the common good can be achieved through the products or services offered; through the work done by the company; through the organizational culture and leadership; by providing investment channels; by "creating and distributing economic value added"; and by "providing continuity to the company itself."[186] To evaluate the responsibility of the corporation means to weigh actions taken or omitted in terms of the principles of justice and solidarity and their consequences.[187]

Goulet, too, makes a number of important observations concerning the corporation and its role and responsibilities in society. First, he notes that corporations, like other large, powerful institutions in society, "have an inherent tendency to impose their own dynamics and rules upon society at large,"[188] and that this is especially the case with transnational corporations. Second, he observes that one of the challenges faced by the Church is how to get these corporations to behave ethically—the implications being both that ethical behavior is desirable and that it is absent from corporate conduct. However, because the corporation and the Church have different goals and criteria for success, conflict over values is inevitable. Third, he notes that the Gospel does not show approval or condemnation for corporations but that Christians should critically view these and other powerful, wealthy organizations as human creations that do not automatically deserve legitimacy in society. Such legitimacy cannot be taken for granted but must be negotiated with society in general.

Finally, Novak contends that business, just by being what it is, serves the common good and has seven corporate responsibilities that emerge from its very nature: satisfying customers with really valuable goods and services; making reasonable profits for shareholders; creating new wealth; creating new jobs; enabling upward mobility and demonstrating that hard work is rewarded and so dissipating envy; promoting invention, ingenuity and progress in arts and sciences; and diversifying the interests of all in the country.[189] Whether this list could be seen as representative in terms of Catholic Social Thought is doubtful: Novak's perspective is one that doubtless would be countered by those of a more radical persuasion, particularly those from the third, rather than the first, world environment.

CONCLUSION

As the above discussion demonstrates, the issue of the role, relationship, and responsibilities of the corporation vis-à-vis society is both complex and contentious. Even within the same approach, we find a variety of corporate responsibilities. For our purposes, we argue that the corporation is a part of society and that, while its profit-making role is clearly important, this role may not eclipse its relationship or role with regard to human beings, be they employees or others affected by the policies and practices of the corporation. Responsibilities to the common good include responsibilities for the environment in which the corporation operates and for environmental damage that these operations may have caused. From our perspective the corporation bears both legal responsibilities and *moral* responsibilities and cannot merely be held accountable to legal obligations.

NOTES

1. For example, where the only purpose of the corporation is to maximize profits for the owners/shareholders, it is seen as having only legal obligations to society and the obligations of fair competition within the market: the "shareholder model." However, where the purpose of the corporation is conceptualized as including social, financial, and ecological contributions, the corporation must take into account the interests of all its stakeholders, balancing these and delivering on the basis of the so-called triple bottom line. This approach is represented by the "stakeholder model." Related to the latter model is the social contract model and the corporate citizenship view. A further possibility found in the literature is that of "virtue ethics" and the "virtuous corporation."

2. Throughout the discussion below, only selected examples from the literature will be given in support of our analysis of each issue.

3. R. G. Kennedy, "Does a Business Corporation Have a Responsibility to Society?" *Religion and Liberty* 13, no. 6 (November–December 2003): 2, http://www.acton.org/publications/randl/nl_article_479.php?view=print.

4. Ibid., 4.

5. M. Phillips, "Corporate Moral Personhood and Three Conceptions of the Corporation," *Business Ethics Quarterly* 2, no. 4 (1992): 439.

6. What exactly these units are varies according to the theorist: for example, Robert Hessen believes that human beings are the most vital constituents. See R. Hessen, *In Defense of the Corporation* (Stanford: Hoover Institution Press, 1979). However, other nonhuman constituents may be chosen—for example, contracts. See Phillips "Corporate Moral Personhood," 439.

7. P. A. Samuelson and W. D. Nordhaus, *Economics,* 12th ed. (New York: McGraw-Hill, 1985).

8. R. H. Robbins, ed., *Global Problems and the Culture of Capitalism,* 3rd ed. (Boston: Pearson, 2005), 35.

9. M. A. Lutz, *Economics for the Common Good: Two Centuries of Social Economic Thought in the Humanistic Tradition* (London: Routledge, 1999), 181.

10. Abrahams notes: "It is generally accepted that all ethical reflection takes place within a particular tradition, or what some scholars call 'an ethical narrative.'" Catholic Social Thought is, then, the "ethical narrative" of the present chapter. See M. Abrahams, "Responsibility in Business," *Grace and Truth* 20, no. 3 (2003): 38–49.

11. M. A. Clark, "Competing Visions: Equity and Efficiency in the Firm," in *Rethinking the Purpose of Business: Interdisciplinary Essays from the Catholic Social Tradition,* ed. S. A. Cortright and M. J. Naughton (Notre Dame, IN: University of Notre Dame Press, 2002), 83.

12. Ibid., 86. This in turn means that the neoclassical theory of the "firm" merely extends the values and value judgments of neoclassical economic theory—namely, individualism, a hedonistic concept of human nature, and market competition—as *the* way of resolving the conflicting desires of human beings.

13. Pope John Paul II, *Centesimus Annus* (Washington, DC: U.S. Catholic Conference, 1991), para. 35. This idea is also found in Pope John XXIII, *Mater et Magistra* (1961), para. 92, and Second Vatican Ecumenical Council, *The Church in the Modern World* (1965), para. 68.

14. Abrahams, "Responsibility in Business," 40.

15. J. Calvez, "The Catholic Social Tradition and the Purpose of the Corporate Enterprise" (paper presented at the Second International Symposium on Catholic Social Thought and Management Education, University of Antwerp, Belgium, 1997), 2.

16. J. Calvez and M. J. Naughton, "Catholic Social Teaching and the Purpose of the Business Organization: A Developing Tradition," in *Rethinking the Purpose of Business: Interdisciplinary Essays from the Catholic Social Tradition,* ed.

S. A. Cortright and M. J. Naughton (Notre Dame, IN: University of Notre Dame Press, 2002), 12.

17. D. Melé and J. Fontradana, "Individual and Corporate Responsibilities in the Social Teaching of the Church" (paper presented at the Second International Symposium on Catholic Social Thought and Management Education, University of Antwerp, Belgium, 1997), 7.

18. R. C. Solomon, "Business with Virtues: Maybe Next Year?" *Business Ethics Quarterly* 10, no. 1 (2000): 340.

19. R. C. Solomon, *Ethics and Excellence: Cooperation and Integrity in Business* (New York: Oxford University Press, 1992), 109.

20. N. E. Bowie, "A Kantian Approach to Business Ethics," in *Ethical Issues in Business: A Philosophical Approach,* 7th ed., ed. T. Donaldson and P. H. Werhane (Upper Saddle River, NJ: Prentice Hall, 2002), 68.

21. M. Kelly, *The Divine Right of Capital: Dethroning the Corporate Aristocracy* (San Francisco: Berret-Koehler, 2001), 87.

22. K. E. Goodpaster and J. B. Matthews Jr., "Can a Corporation Have a Conscience?" in *Harvard Business Review on Corporate Social Responsibility* (Boston: Harvard Business School, 2003), 131–55.

23. S. Waddock, *Leading Corporate Citizens: Vision, Values, Value Added* (Boston: McGraw-Hill, 2002), 50–52.

24. M. King, "Good Corporate Governance: A Fundamental Value for New Citizenship in South Africa," in *Defining a New Citizenship for South Africa and the Fundamental Values That Will Shape It* (Johannesburg, South Africa: Konrad Adenauer Stiftung, 2001), 21–27.

25. D. Koehn, "Rethinking the Responsibility of International Corporations: A Response to Donaldson," *Business Quarterly* 3, no. 2 (1993): 180.

26. J. Verstraeten, ed., *Business Ethics: Broadening the Perspectives* (Leuven: Peeters, 2000).

27. M. Keeley, *A Social Contract Theory of Organizations* (Notre Dame, IN: University of Notre Dame Press, 1988).

28. J. Van Gerwen, "Corporate Culture and Ethics," in *Business Ethics: Broadening the Perspectives,* ed. J. Verstraeten (Leuven: Peeters, 2000), 42–78.

29. Ibid., 48.

30. Ibid.

31. T. Donaldson, *The Ethics of International Business* (Oxford: Oxford University Press, 1989).

32. M. G. Velasquez, *Business Ethics: Concepts and Cases,* 6th ed. (Upper Saddle River, NJ: Prentice Hall, 2006), 13.

33. D. C. Korten, *The Post-Corporate World: Life after Capitalism* (San Francisco: Berret-Koehler, 1999), 75.

34. Note that the term *moral agent* as used in philosophy implies that the individual can be responsible and held accountable.

35. Solomon, *Ethics and Excellence,* 132.

36. See, for example, J. Ladd, "Morality and the Ideal of Rationality in Formal Organizations," *The Monist* 54, no. 4 (1970): 488–516; and M. Keeley, "Organizations as Non-Persons," *Journal of Value Inquiry* 15 (1981): 149–55.

37. See Phillips, "Corporate Moral Personhood."

38. Solomon, *Ethics and Excellence,* 132. See also J. K. Galbraith, *American Capitalism: The Concept of Countervailing Power,* rev. ed. (Cambridge, MA: Riverside Press, 1956); M. Friedman, *Capitalism and Freedom* (Chicago: University of Chicago Press, 1962); and J. Ladd, "Bhopal: An Essay on Moral Responsibility and Civic Virtue," *Journal of Social Philosophy* 32, no. 1 (1991): 15–25.

39. E. Sternberg, *Just Business: Business Ethics in Action* (Oxford: Oxford University Press, 2000).

40. So, for example, in the case of economic justice in South Africa, this would mean that the corporation has no moral responsibility to contribute to remedying economic injustices and cannot be held accountable for not doing so. Any contribution in this sphere would be entirely voluntary.

41. Melé and Fontradana, "Individual and Corporate Responsibilities," 4.

42. Pope John Paul II, *Reconciliation and Penance* (1984), http://www.cin.org/ipZeney/reconcil.html.

43. Melé and Fontradana, "Individual and Corporate Responsibilities," 6.

44. L. Kaufman, "Mining the Sources of Moral Values," *Grace and Truth* 20, no. 3 (2003): 5–15.

45. Melé and Fontradana, "Individual and Corporate Responsibilities," 6.

46. Solomon, *Ethics and Excellence,* 209.

47. Bowie, "A Kantian Approach," 67–68.

48. Velasquez, *Business Ethics,* 17–18.

49. Ibid., 18.

50. See Melé and Fontradana, "Individual and Corporate Responsibilities," 3.

51. M. Kaptein and J. Wempe, *The Balanced Company: A Theory of Corporate Integrity* (Oxford: Oxford University Press, 2002), 121.

52. Kaptein and Wempe give a very comprehensive treatment of this complicated area of corporate moral agency in *The Balanced Company.*

53. Phillips, "Corporate Moral Personhood"; see also L. Bowman-Larsen, "Reconstructing the Principle of Double Effect: Towards Fixing the Goalposts of Corporate Responsibility," in *World Business: Managing Harmful Side-Effects of Corporate Activity,* ed. L. Bowman-Larsen and O. Wiggen (Tokyo: United Nations University Press, 2004), 82–98.

54. Van Gerwen, "Corporate Culture," 65–66.

55. A. MacIntyre, *After Virtue,* 2nd ed. (London: Duckworth, 1985).

56. Van Gerwen, "Corporate Culture," 44.

57. J. M. Lonzano, "Companies and Society, Ethical Responsibilities," in *Business Ethics: Broadening the Perspectives,* ed. J. Verstraeten (Leuven: Peeters, 2000), 11–40, also deals with the communitarian model of ethics.

58. G. Elfstrom, *Moral Issues and Multinational Corporations* (New York: St. Martin's Press, 1991), 14.

59. Ibid., 15 (emphasis in the original).

60. Bowman-Larsen, "Reconstructing the Principle," 86.

61. See K. E. Goodpaster, "Can a Corporation Be a Citizen?" *Praxis* 2, no. 3 (2001): 2–7.

62. Goodpaster and Matthews, "Can a Corporation Have a Conscience?" 147.

63. Donaldson, *Ethics of International Business,* xvii.

64. Kaptein and Wempe, *The Balanced Company,* 208.

65. M. T. Brown, *Corporate Integrity: Rethinking Organizational Ethics and Leadership* (Cambridge: Cambridge University Press, 2005), 128.

66. J. Morse, "The Missing Link between Virtue Theory and Business Ethics," *Journal of Applied Philosophy* 16, no. 1 (1999): 48.

67. Ibid., 56.

68. J. A. Corlett, "Corporate Responsibility for Environmental Damage," *Environmental Ethics* 18 (Summer 1996): 197.

69. See Velasquez, *Business Ethics,* 46–54, for details on this issue.

70. A. Berle Jr. and G. Means, *The Modern Corporation and Private Property* (Chicago: Commerce Clearing House, 1932).

71. See D. P. McCann, "Business Corporations and the Principle of Subsidiarity," in *Rethinking the Purpose of Business: Interdisciplinary Essays from the Catholic Social Tradition,* ed. S. A. Cortright and M. J. Naughton (Notre Dame, IN: University of Notre Dame Press, 2002), 169–89.

72. P. Koslowski, "The Shareholder Value Principle and the Purpose of the Firm: Limits to Shareholder Value," in *Rethinking the Purpose of Business: Interdisciplinary Essays from the Catholic Social Tradition,* ed. S. A. Cortright and M. J. Naughton (Notre Dame, IN: University of Notre Dame Press, 2002), 102.

73. M. Friedman, "The Social Responsibility of Business Is to Increase Its Profits," *New York Times Magazine,* September 13, 1970.

74. G. Soros, *Open Society: Reforming Global Capitalism* (London: Little, Brown and Company, 2000), 161.

75. Sternberg, *Just Business,* 32. She points out that owners may not be synonymous with shareholders.

76. Ibid., 35–36. However, that it is not the purpose of business to foster moral good is not the same as saying that business is immoral.

77. Cortright and Naughton, *Rethinking the Purpose of Business,* 24. For a thorough discussion of the normative presuppositions underlying this view see H. J. Alford and M. J. Naughton, "Beyond the Shareholder Model of the Firm: Working Toward the Common Good of a Business," in *Rethinking the Purpose of Business: Interdisciplinary Essays from the Catholic Social Tradition,* ed. S. A. Cortright and M. J. Naughton (Notre Dame, IN : University of Notre Dame Press, 2002), 29–35.

78. Clark, "Competing Visions," 87.

79. Ibid., 92.

80. Pope John Paul II, *Centesimus Annus,* para. 35.

81. Clark, "Competing Visions," 94.

82. Abrahams, "Responsibility in Business," 41. Melé and Fontradana make the same point: "The firm, like every human community, has not only certain goals selected by its senior executives, but also a mission to fulfill in society in the service of the common good" ("Individual and Corporate Responsibilities," 7). The common good is *the promotion of all the goods necessary for integral human development in the organization, in such a way as to respect the proper ordering of these goods* (Alford and Naughton, "Beyond the Shareholder Model," 38; emphasis in the original).

83. P. Riordan, "The Purpose of Business and the Human Good" (paper presented at the Second International Symposium on Catholic Social Thought and Management Education, University of Antwerp, Belgium, 1997).

84. S. Zadek, *The Civil Corporation: The New Economy of Corporate Citizenship* (London: Earthscan, 2004), 138–40.

85. R. G. Kennedy, "The Virtue of Solidarity and the Purpose of the Firm," in *Rethinking the Purpose of Business: Interdisciplinary Essays from the Catholic Social Tradition,* ed. S. A. Cortright and M. J. Naughton (Notre Dame, IN: University of Notre Dame Press, 2002), 57.

86. Alford and Naughton, "Beyond the Shareholder Model," 28.

87. Ibid., 28–29.

88. Ibid., 35–36. See also Clark, "Competing Visions," 94, 97.

89. Abrahams, "Responsibility in Business," 43.

90. Clark, "Competing Visions," 97.

91. McCann, "Business Corporations," 183.

92. Koslowski, "Shareholder Value," 123.

93. Goodpaster, "Can a Corporation Be a Citizen?"

94. Ibid., 57.

95. King, "Good Corporate Governance," 23.

96. Ibid.

97. Morse, "The Missing Link."

98. Solomon, *Ethics and Excellence*, 102, 110.

99. Ibid., 110.

100. Ibid., 149.

101. Samuelson and Nordhaus, *Economics.*

102. J. E. Post, A. T. Lawrence, and J. Weber, *Business and Society: Corporate Strategy, Public Policy, Ethics,* 10th ed. (Boston: McGraw-Hill Irwin, 2002), 50.

103. D. A. Krueger, *The Business Corporation and Productive Justice* (Nashville, TN: Abingdon Press, 1997), 38.

104. Ibid., 54, 43.

105. J. M. Thompson, *Justice and Peace: A Christian Primer,* 2nd ed. (New York: Orbis Books, 2003), 43.

106. Cited in Melé and Fontradana, "Individual and Corporate Responsibilities," 2.

107. Cited in McCann, "Business Corporations," 183. See also P. Drucker, "The Age of Social Transformation," *Atlantic Monthly* (November 1994): 80.

108. The way these elements of purpose are viewed depends in turn on the view adopted toward the nature of the corporation and corporate moral agency notions discussed previously. While it may seem that the choice is between "shareholder" and "stakeholder" versions of this relationship, a number of scholars point out that this choice is a false one, especially given our global economy. In fact, business must both be profitable and take into account other responsibilities.

109. For example, the revival of the "shareholder-stakeholder conversation," initiated by Freeman, remains "inconclusive" even while being "compelling." See S. A. Cortright and E. S. Pierucci, "Clearing Ground: Toward a Social Ethic of Corporate Management," in *Rethinking the Purpose of Business: Interdisciplinary Essays from the Catholic Social Tradition,* ed. S. A. Cortright and M. J. Naughton (Notre Dame, IN: University of Notre Dame Press, 2002), 136.

110. J. R. Danley, *The Role of the Modern Corporation in a Free Society* (Notre Dame, IN: University of Notre Dame Press, 1994). While claiming there are only two approaches may seem to be an oversimplification, Danley believes they deal with the main issues.

111. Ibid. Writers in this tradition include Adam Smith, David Ricardo, Jeremy Bentham, and the Social Darwinists. However, over time much of the richness and nuance of these writers was lost, and so classical liberalism today advocates a free market capitalist economy and a laissez-faire government policy concerning the economy.

112. Cortright and Pierucci, "Clearing Ground," 138.

113. McCann, "Business Corporations," 188.

114. Kennedy, "Virtue of Solidarity," 49.

115. Phillips, "Corporate Moral Personhood."

116. Kaptein and Wempe, *The Balanced Company*. Their view is that on the one hand, the corporation is held morally responsible, but on the other, this responsibility is not seen as that of a person.

117. Elfstrom, *Moral Issues*, 12. The arguments he outlines are (1) the corporation cannot be a moral agent; (2) the pressurized, competitive nature of the business environment precludes time or energy for moral considerations; (3) profit making is the only responsibility, moral or otherwise, of business; and (4) corporations are not individuals and so persons in the corporation cannot accept moral responsibility on behalf of the organization, other than that pertaining to their particular corporate role.

118. D. Rossouw, *Business Ethics in Africa*, 2nd ed. (Oxford: Oxford University Press, 2002), 11–21.

119. S. P. Sethi, "Moving from a Socially Responsible to a Socially Accountable Corporation," in *Is the Good Corporation Dead? Social Responsibility in a Global Economy*, ed. J. W. Houck and O. F. Williams (Lanham, MD: Rowman and Littlefield, 1996), 90.

120. Kaptein and Wempe, *The Balanced Company*, 109–10. They note three positions on corporate moral responsibility: (1) the amoral, where it is believed that there is no such responsibility for the corporation or for individuals who perform certain functions there (for example, as argued by Friedman, *Capitalism and Freedom;* and F. A. Hayek, *The Road to Serfdom* [Chicago: University of Chicago Press, 1944]); (2) the functional, where it is believed that the individual company representatives are morally responsible; and (3) the autonomous, where the corporation is seen as a "social entity" and corporate social responsibility is seen as being separate from those individuals who represent the company.

121. Friedman, "Social Responsibility," 1–5.

122. Sternberg, *Just Business*, 41, 49.

123. Ibid., 54.

124. Ibid., 79.

125. Ibid., 80.

126. Kaptein and Wempe, *The Balanced Company*, 117.

127. That is, that corporations are only responsible to the shareholders for whom one is bound to make a profit, that the relationship with them is paramount, and that it is to them that business is accountable (other than being accountable to the law of the land).

128. Danley, *Role of the Modern Corporation*.

129. Writing within this framework includes John Dewey's pragmatism, Frederick Taylor's scientific management, Elton Mayo's social responsibility, and Jon M. Keynes's "new economy."

130. Danley, *Role of the Modern Corporation,* 144.

131. Ibid.

132. Ibid., 288.

133. Post, Lawrence, and Weber, *Business and Society,* 60.

134. That is, voluntary actions to promote social good (ibid., 61–64).

135. That is, acknowledging the interdependence of business and society and balancing the interests and needs of many diverse stakeholders. It incorporates the duty to ensure that resources are used for the good of society and not only for profits (ibid., 63).

136. Ibid.

137. R. A. Buchholz and S. B. Rosenthal, "Social Responsibility and Business Ethics," in *A Companion to Business Ethics,* ed. R. E. Frederick (Oxford: Blackwell, 2002), 303.

138. Ibid., 304.

139. According to Buchholz and Rosenthal, while social responsibility has numerous ethical facets, proponents argued seven points:

> business should adapt to social change if it was to survive
> business should view self-interest from a long-term perspective and contribute to solving social problems and so create a better environment for itself
> being socially responsible would improve business' social image
> government regulation could be avoided if business voluntarily met social expectations
> business has huge resources that could assist in solving social problems
> social problems could be profitable business opportunities
> business is morally obliged to assist in solving social problems that it has caused/perpetuated

From this account, corporate social responsibility seems to be a variation on the theme of self-interest and represents the views that Riordan so roundly condemns. However, not all authors treat social responsibility in this way.

140. Post, Lawrence, and Weber, *Business and Society,* 56.

141. R. T. De George, "The Myth of Corporate Social Responsibility," in *Is the Good Corporation Dead? Social Responsibility in a Global Economy,* ed. J. W. Houck and F. O. Williams (Lanham, MD: Rowman and Littlefield, 1996), 17.

142. Ibid., 24.

143. Brown, *Corporate Integrity,* 13.

144. Ibid., 14–22.

145. Cited in Houck and Williams, *Is the Good Corporation Dead?* vii.

146. J. R. Boatright, "The Future of Corporate Social Responsibility," *Business and Professional Ethics Journal* 20, nos. 3–4 (2001): 12.

147. Sethi, "Moving from a Socially Responsible," 83.

148. Buchholz and Rosenthal, "Social Responsibility," 303.

149. Post, Lawrence, and Weber, *Business and Society,* 83.

150. A. B. Carroll and A. K. Buchholz, *Business and Society: Ethics and Stakeholder Management* (Cincinnati: Thomson South-Western, 2002), 31.

151. See Buchholz and Rosenthal, "Social Responsibility," 307; Carroll and Buchholz, *Business and Society,* 31; and Post, Lawrence, and Weber, *Business and Society,* 83.

152. R. E. Freeman, "The Possibility of Stakeholder Capitalism," in *Ethics and the Future of Capitalism: Praxiology: The International Annual of Practical Philosophy and Methodology Volume,* ed. L. Zsolnai (New Brunswick, NJ: Transaction, 2002), 111. See also E. Rhenman, *Industrial Democracy and Industrial Management* (London: Tavistock, 1968); I. Ansoff, *The New Corporate Strategy* (New York: Wiley and Sons, 1988); and R. Ackhoff, *The Democratic Corporation* (Oxford: Oxford University Press, 1994).

153. Ibid., 112.

154. Ibid., 116.

155. Primary stakeholders include, for example, customers, suppliers, employees, stockholders, etc. Secondary stakeholders include local communities, the general public, media, business support groups, government, social activist groups, etc. Stakeholders are the people and groups affected by or that affect an organization's decisions, politics, and operations.

156. See Buchholz and Rosenthal, "Social Responsibility," 315–16.

157. Ibid., 316.

158. J. Gordley, "Virtue and the Ethics of Profit Seeking," in *Rethinking the Purpose of Business: Interdisciplinary Essays from the Catholic Social Tradition,* ed. S. A. Cortright and M. J. Naughton (Notre Dame, IN: University of Notre Dame Press, 2002), 65–66.

159. T. Fort, "Business as a Mediating Institution," in *Rethinking the Purpose of Business: Interdisciplinary Essays from the Catholic Social Tradition,* ed. S. A. Cortright and M. J. Naughton (Notre Dame, IN: University of Notre Dame Press, 2002), 248; emphasis added by the author.

160. Goodpaster and Matthews, "Can a Corporation Have a Conscience?" 57.

161. Post, Lawrence, and Weber, *Business and Society,* 81–83.

162. M. King, "Good Corporate Governance: A Fundamental Value for New Citizenship in South Africa," in *Defining a New Citizenship for South Africa and the Fundamental Values That Will Shape It* (Johannesburg, South Africa: Konrad Adenauer Stiftung, 2001), 21–27.

163. Ibid., 24.

164. T. W. Dunfee and T. Donaldson, "Social Contract Approaches to Business Ethics: Bridging the "is-ought" Gap," in *A Companion to Business Ethics,* ed. R. E. Frederick (London: Blackwell, 2002), 38, 41.

165. Ibid., 38.

166. Buchholz and Rosenthal, "Social Responsibility," 317.

167. Post, Lawrence, and Weber, *Business and Society,* 51.

168. Ibid., 71–72.

169. Kaptein and Wempe, *The Balanced Company,* 208.

170. Koehn, "Rethinking the Responsibility," 177.

171. T. W. Dunfee and D. Hess, "The Legitimacy of Direct Corporate Humanitarian Investment," *Business Ethics Quarterly* 10, no. 1 (2000): 95–109.

172. Ibid., 95.

173. Elfstrom, *Moral Issues.*

174. By *basic* wants he refers to sustaining life; having a basic diet, shelter, clothing; and basic medical care. These items are, in his view, not so costly that the industrial nations could not afford to support the whole world. *Secondary* wants (for example, a satisfactory career, a rich cultural life) vary and change and derive from basic wants—they cannot exist if the basic wants are not fulfilled.

175. Van Gerwen, "Corporate Culture," 57–62.

176. Institute of Directors in Southern Africa, *King Report on Corporate Governance for South Africa–2002* (Parklands, South Africa: Institute of Directors in Southern Africa, 2002).

177. Morse, "The Missing Link," 55.

178. Ibid., 56.

179. Solomon, "Business with Virtues," 340.

180. See A. MacIntyre, "A Partial Response to My Critics," in *After MacIntyre,* ed. J. Horton and S. Mendus (Notre Dame, IN: University of Notre Dame Press, 1994), 283–304; J. Dobson, "MacIntyre's Position on Business: A Response to Wicks," *Business Ethics Quarterly* 7, no. 4 (1997): 127–32; and A. Wicks, "On MacIntyre, Modernity and the Virtues: A Response to Dobson," *Business Ethics Quarterly* 7, no. 4 (1997): 133–35.

181. D. Melé, "Not Only Stakeholder Interests: The Firm Oriented Toward the Common Good," in *Rethinking the Purpose of Business: Interdisciplinary Essays from the Catholic Social Tradition,* ed. S. A. Cortright and M. J. Naughton (Notre Dame, IN: University of Notre Dame Press, 2002), 194.

182. Calvez and Naughton, "Catholic Social Teaching," 12.

183. Kennedy, "Virtue of Solidarity," 61.

184. Ibid., 62.

185. Melé, "Not Only Stakeholder Interests," 194–95.

186. Ibid., 197–98.

187. Ibid., 202.

188. D. Goulet, "Economic Systems, Middle Way Theories, and Third World Realities," in *Co-Creation and Capitalism: John Paul II's "Laborem Exercen,"* ed. J. W. Houck and O. F. Williams (Washington, DC: University Press of America, 1983), 142.

189. M. Novak, "Seven Corporate Responsibilities," in *Is the Good Corporation Dead? Social Responsibility in a Global Economy,* ed. J. W. Houck and O. F. Williams (Lanham, MD: Rowman and Littlefield, 1996), 192–95.

CHAPTER 2

Moral Maturity, Peace through Commerce, and the Partnership Dimension

Timothy L. Fort and Michelle Westermann-Behaylo

INTRODUCTION

In the space of a few short years, the idea that businesses might be able to make positive contributions to sustainable peace has come a long way. In 2006 at least four U.S.-based academic institutions—George Washington University, Case Western Reserve University, the University of Maryland, and the University of Notre Dame—held conferences on the topic of Peace through Commerce. The accrediting body for business schools in seventy-two countries, the Association to Advance Collegiate Schools of Business (AACSB), issued its Task Force's report on the topic, and at least two special journal issues—*American Business Law Journal* and *Journal of Corporate Citizenship*—solicited papers for publication. In addition, several books have been completed or are being developed on the topic. Looking back only to 2001, when Jane Nelson published her book *The Business of Peace*[1] and the William Davidson Institute's first of three Corporate Governance, Stakeholder Accountability, and Sustainable Peace conferences commenced, the level of activity on this topic has flourished. Special sessions now are being held at the annual international meetings of academic organizations such as the Academy of Management and the Society for Business Ethics.

In important ways, of course, the concept is nothing new. Montesquieu, Kant, and Hayek all believed that economic trade lessened the likelihood of war. Too much can be made of this concept, of course. All the parties involved in World War I traded with each other prior to hostilities, as did Germany and the Soviet Union just prior to the Nazi invasion. Nevertheless, the economic ties of countries that resort to war to settle disputes are disrupted—to put it mildly. In the United States both Democrat Bill Clinton and Republican George Bush believed that economic trade could promote foreign policy stability. Indeed, it seems something of an article of faith that trade dampens the fires of war.

It is important to be careful about this linkage, however. Just what kind of economic activity promotes peace? Any kind? Do we want to claim that exploitative colonialism will create sustainable peace? Aren't businesses often perceived as being culturally and religiously insensitive and exploitative? Will an extractive industries model of commerce cause peace? These issues are important because it seems that not just any kind of commerce will foster peace. In fact, it is important to delineate what we mean by *Peace through Commerce* in two important ways.

First, we focus on the actions of *businesses* rather than on macro-level economic policy. We must remember that when we talk about trade between countries, the agents of that trade are businesses. How do *those businesses* promote (or not promote) Peace through Commerce? Focusing on business activity brings the issue to a meso or micro level of analysis rather than the macro level of analysis of economic policy. Second, if we are talking about actions of businesses, then what kinds of business actions promote Peace through Commerce? We know policies of exploitation and cultural domination do not promote piece; instead, we look to actions that foster multifaceted economic development, attention to rule of law institutions and practices, and the development of businesses as communities, both in an external corporate citizenship sense as well as in the sense of corporations developing a sense of their own organizations as communities. This focus raises issues of ethical corporate behavior. In other words, it is not *any* kind of business that promotes Peace through Commerce but a *particular kind* of business that does so: that is, an ethical corporation.

Many political scientists thought they had completely discredited the notion that trade would result in peace. If it did, they argue, World War I would not have occurred because all of the warring countries previously had traded with each other. However, by specifying that a certain kind of business—ethical business—might make such a contribution, we differentiate the actions sufficiently to provide a new way of looking at the

Peace through Commerce equation. As we see enthusiasm for the idea of Peace through Commerce growing, we need to be very careful to avoid blithely assuming that any old kind of business activity will do the trick—it won't. Unethical business activity may make things worse because it sows the seeds for resentment and animosity.

Putting the notion of Peace through Commerce in terms of business ethics, however, raises as many questions as it answers. To paraphrase Alasdair MacIntyre, whose ethics, which economics?[2] Those questions can be answered, at least in broad terms. What is more difficult is the level of cognitive awareness that is necessary to put whatever answer one comes up with into practice. The preceding two sentences provide the organizational framework for this chapter. The first section argues that a corporation seeking to actualize a contribution toward peace through its activities has to have a fairly sophisticated level of moral maturity. Corporations that operate on a profit-only basis will not take into consideration a sufficient number of financially ambivalent factors necessary to contribute to peace. Yet some companies do have this moral maturity, and we can learn from them as well as studies in various fields that indicate the specific ways in which corporations can contribute to sustainable peace.

Section two recognizes, however, that corporations frequently do not possess the moral maturity to make such contributions. In many cases a partnership with a nongovernmental organization (NGO) can not only promote contributions to sustainable peace but, indirectly, can inspire improvements in the moral development of the firm. This section reviews the types of partnership models that can develop. The Hard Trust model of corporate-NGO relationships is not partnering in a traditional sense; it is more of an adversarial approach used by NGOs to push for social justice through regulation, litigation, or public shaming. The Real Trust model is employed when corporations take an instrumental view of their efforts to contribute to peace; action is taken when it is perceived to improve the corporation's marketing efforts, reputational capital, and, essentially, its bottom line. The Good Trust model of partnering is for those corporations that have a sophisticated level of moral maturity and seek proactively to partner with and tap the expertise of NGOs in order to maximize the impact of their efforts to do good.

In the final section of this chapter, these three models are defined in further detail and tied to recent related academic research; case studies are examined in order to further demonstrate the nature of these partnerships. Future research topics derived from these models are discussed in the conclusion.

CORPORATE MATURITY

Although the comparison may be a bit unfair, corporations have much in common with a toddler. For all the positive satisfaction one may get in dealing with them, a corporation and a toddler are generally selfish. They are interested in claiming what is "mine" to the exclusion of others. When it comes to moral virtues, whether positively inclined ones such as sharing or those with a negative association such as do no harm to others (a vulnerable customer for a corporation, the family dog for the toddler), following through on a moral course of action can be quite difficult. Frequently, the level of moral maturity for both corporations and toddlers involves doing whatever one can get away with as long as one does not get caught. As a result, some overarching authority (Mom or Dad, the Securities and Exchange Commission or Internal Revenue Service) has to remain vigilant in order to correct misbehavior. In his model of moral development, Lawrence Kohlberg would describe this level as the first preconventional stage: one is moral in order to avoid punishment from others.[3]

Kohlberg has theorized that in the preconventional level of the process of moral development, individuals pass from the first stage, punishment avoidance, to a second stage where moral behavior is engaged in because it is in the child's self-interest—good behavior is rewarded. Thereafter, most people reach what Kohlberg calls the "conventional level" of moral development, where social conformity or law and order motivate moral behavior. Few people reach Kohlberg's postconventional level of moral development: where the individual sees herself as a member of a wider society with an obligation to contribute, to uphold ethical principles, and to be consistent with a commitment to justice—that is, social justice.[4]

Continuing our comparison of corporations to toddlers, one can see how corporate actions, and the maturity demonstrated in corporate cultures, could arguably follow a similar course. While some corporations engage in ethical business practices only when pressed into compliance by the threat of sanctions, others may progress to the self-interest level—

the point where ethical business practices are seen as instrumentally beneficial for purposes of economic gain. In other words, good behavior may generate better marketing opportunities. Some firms may develop to what could be called a conventional level of corporate moral responsibility; for example, pursuing social conformity in the form of maintaining a good corporate reputation in the eyes of peers and investors.[5] A limited number of firms may reach the stage analogous to a corporate postconventional level, where they recognize their role in the wider society and embrace their obligations to contribute to the interests of a wide range of stakeholders.[6]

The good news about toddlers is that they can and do mature. They enjoy doing good things, and they internalize both punishments and rewards. They learn to balance many conflicting demands to become adults. Indeed, to be an adult is to live with conflicts of interest. Corporations, on the other hand, have a more difficult time growing up for three reasons.

First, corporations have no soul or conscience. Corporations are things that are created by human beings to achieve desired purposes. Although corporations can be legally punished and can hold legal rights, their conscience cannot be shocked, nor can they fear divine justice (whether bad karma or hell), nor can they have their spirits uplifted with an ideal of achieving peace through their activities.

Second, our current market structure strongly encourages corporations to maintain their toddler maturity. That is, the market frequently demands that corporations maximize short-term profitability or else be punished. Falling stock prices and fired executives can result in companies practicing short-term grasping rather than long-term citizenship. Developing complex notions of long-term values that would integrate peace-seeking activities is very difficult to do under the pressures of quarterly financial reports.

Third, pursuing any nonfinancial objective becomes more difficult the bigger the company. The larger the number of shareholders, the more likely it is that there is no other binding objective to invest in a stock other than to make money. In a smaller, family-owned company, the investors could have a wider set of interests, such as supporting the local community in which they are residents. But common denominators for thousands, even millions, of investors are hard to come by. Money may very well be the only guiding maxim, which only reinforces the market-driven issues.

The good news, however, is that corporations can still internalize a sense of moral maturity and indeed may have to do so, also for three reasons. The first reason is more of a possibility than a need: while the market may insist on short-term financial performance, the law has always been and remains open to managers taking into account nonfinancial objectives in running a company. There have been a multitude of cases where courts have upheld a director's actions in favor of other stakeholders to the detriment of shareholder wealth maximization. For instance, courts in most states have upheld charitable giving by corporations; in fact, most states have a statute permitting unprofitable philanthropic donations.[7]

In cases where shareholders complained that corporate decisions favored community or family interests over profits, courts have upheld family-friendly policies. For example, shareholders once sued Wrigley, the chewing gum company that owned the Chicago Cubs, and asserted that all games should be scheduled at night because they would be more profitable. However, the court agreed with Wrigley's arguments that daytime games are better for families and the surrounding community. Therefore, Wrigley was not required to pursue profits to the exclusion of other interests.[8]

In hostile acquisition circumstances, which usually benefit shareholders, courts have upheld actions to deter hostile takeovers for purposes of protecting the interests of employees.[9] Furthermore, the Supreme Court of Delaware allowed directors to reject a premium offer for shares in favor of a merger that would preserve a firm culture of journalistic integrity in *Paramount Communications v. Time, Inc.* (1989), stating: "a board of directors is not under any per se duty to maximize shareholder value in the short-term, even in the context of a takeover."[10] Thus, corporations have the legal freedom to engage in non-profit-maximizing activities—including activities involving the surrounding community and an organizational culture that can promote sustainable peace.

Second, numerous studies have examined the links between corporate social performance and social financial performance. While many scholars have come down on either side of the debate over whether socially responsible corporate activity contributes or is detrimental to corporate financial performance, the general conclusion is that it generally does not negatively impact the corporation's finances, and, indeed, it may have indirect benefits.[11] For example, Godfrey suggests that corporate social responsibility can contribute to financial performance in terms of providing insurance-like protection for intangible assets.[12] Furthermore, studies have shown that large companies frequently are capable of devoting the dollars necessary to differentiate products to high-end consumers who will purchase a product because of its social benefits.[13] Thus, where companies are open to taking a long-term view, activities that can promote sustainable peace may have a positive economic impact.

Third, while corporations may not have souls and consciences, they do have cultures and traditions. Legally, there are increasing demands, such as through the Federal Sentencing Guidelines, for corporations to develop cultures that lead to ethical behavior. In order to qualify for reduced penalties under the guidelines, an effective corporate ethics program must promote "an organizational culture that encourages ethical conduct" and focuses on being a "good corporate citizen."[14] Thus, the goal is not simply to prevent employees from engaging in illegal activities. Through their ethics and compliance programs, corporations are increasingly charged with implementing a fundamental change for the good in the nature of the organizational culture.[15]

In fact, some companies do seem to have these kinds of cultures. The U.S. Secretary of State has given the Award for Corporate Excellence to companies whose ethical practices have resulted in positive diplomatic efforts between the United States and a host country.[16] International Alert, in its report *Local Business, Local Peace,* has documented dozens of case studies in which businesses engage in attempts to alleviate interethnic clashes, foster gender equity, and provide support for dialogue among warring factions.[17] There is an economic argument for why companies may want to engage in these activities, but they are not likely to be arguments that can be quantified in a quarterly income statement. If there is an economic argument, it will be projected into the long term. The more likely drivers for such engagement will be those of a sincere desire to make a noneconomic contribution for the betterment of the society in which the company is doing business, resulting in a balancing of economic and noneconomic factors that is the hallmark of moral maturity. The fact that there are companies that *already* do these things demonstrates the possibilities. Perhaps these companies are exceptions; indeed, we are not sure what else to call them but exceptions. But exist they do, and they provide examples of (1) how companies can act with moral maturity through their cultures, decisions, leadership, and decision-making processes; and (2) how companies can apply that maturity directly to issues of peace.

MATURITY AND PARTNERSHIPS (WHETHER ONE WANTS THEM OR NOT)

A toddler does not develop moral maturity simply by growing older. She becomes more mature because others around her—parents, siblings, friends, teachers—object to some actions and reward others. Whether the toddler likes it or not, she has partners in her moral development, and those partners teach lessons. At some point, the toddler matures and internalizes those lessons in developing her own moral character, typically by digesting the various lessons she has learned from various partners over the years and then choosing which ones define her as a person.

Companies that have embraced the notion of peace have, in some way, internalized similar kinds of partner teachings as the toddler being corrected or rewarded by parents, the child seeking the acceptance of social conformity, and finally the adult committing to the principles underlying a pursuit of social justice. Who are the relevant partners for business? Often, NGOs act as the partner to business by objecting to certain behaviors, working out solutions to others, rewarding positive behaviors with recognition and incentives, and inspiring an interest in issues of social justice that can contribute to sustainable peace. Together, some companies and NGOs have been able to generate norms and values that allow business to integrate the many different pressures and opportunities companies face and to work through the difficult tradeoffs that justify taking the time and effort to work toward peace.

There can be many different types of NGO partnerships, which we categorize according to three levels of corporate maturity. For those firms that do not care about such issues at all absent some kind of punishment, the kind of partnerships they have with NGOs may be more confrontational, even coercive. For those that do care but require some kind of incentive, a more constructive, yet transactional, approach may be possible. Finally, for corporations that "get it," a true partnership built on inspiration and common commitments may emerge.

In his book *Business, Integrity, and Peace,* Timothy Fort identifies three types of trust that must be integrated for corporations to contribute to sustainable peace: Hard Trust, Real Trust, and Good Trust.[18] Hard Trust relates to coercive actions, such as government regulation, that act as the parent reining in the toddler and result in corporate compliance with the law. There is evidence of compliance practices that are associated with peace. Rule of law practices like avoidance of corruption, creation of rational property rights systems and contractual protection as well as development of fair dispute resolution processes are all associated with less violence.[19] Laws that enforce these kinds of peace-producing practices can coercively move corporations to practice them simply by obeying the law and staying out of trouble.

Real Trust relates to business efficacy, where the business case for engaging in socially responsible behavior is made, including concepts such as strategic philanthropy, instrumental stakeholder engagement, and the relationship between corporate reputation and financial performance. Corporate values such as integrity are aligned with rewards and incentives. Elements of Real Trust also relate to peace. Studies have shown correlations between poverty and violence; therefore, business involvement in economic development can decrease poverty and break that link.[20] Where businesses promote value-added economic development, they can also transfer knowledge and managerial skills that facilitate contributions in other parts of society. Where businesses can achieve a profit while improving the economic and social circumstances of the surrounding communities, there is a win–win–win situation: the corporation profits, the stakeholders benefit, and the conditions for sustainable peace are improved.

The final piece is the concept of Good Trust, which is the aesthetic quest for a higher good through ethical business behavior. Businesses adhering to this model of trust care intrinsically about ethics, and the positive impact of ethical behavior becomes the aspirational aim of corporate action. The higher good is pursued not for instrumental ends but regardless of them because it is intrinsic in the identity and culture of the corporation to help and to build community. Good Trust actions, such as those that support employees and engage with the surrounding community, can contribute to peace. These three dimensions of trust link to three contributions to peace: rule of law aspects (Hard Trust), economic development (Real Trust), and building empathic communities (Good Trust).

The partnerships that develop between NGOs and business also reflect these three dimensions, and NGOs can have a role in encouraging corporations to engage in each of these three levels of trust.

For those companies that may care very little about contributing to a stable society, a kind of "partnership whether you like it or not" can force corporations to consider Peace through Commerce notions. The Hard Trust model of corporate-NGO relationships is not really partnering but more of an adversarial approach used by NGOs to push for social justice through regulation, litigation, or public shaming. In terms of Hard Trust, NGOs can motivate reluctant corporations to comply with standards or regulatory requirements by organizing consumer activism, negotiating tougher industry standards, invoking the legal coercive power of government through initiating lawsuits, and using technology to monitor and report on compliance.

Some companies may require an economic rationale for engaging in such activities. For those looking for the "business case," an NGO may help them make it. The Real Trust model is employed when corporations take an instrumental view of their efforts to contribute to peace; action is taken when it is perceived to improve the corporation's marketing efforts, reputational capital, and, essentially, its bottom line. In the Real Trust model relationships between business and NGOs are initiated by either party with these instrumental goals in view. Real Trust can involve mutually beneficial partnerships where NGOs and businesses recognize and emphasize both the contribution that business can make to building peaceful societies as well as the reputational and branding benefits that make such actions desirable to corporations.

For those companies that think contributing to peace is a good idea but have no idea how to go about it, partnerships can make all the difference in the world. Certain businesses have the moral maturity to look beyond an instrumental rationale for acting; NGO partners can provide the inspiration for acting toward the greater good and can also facilitate the most effective use of corporate capabilities to maximize the positive impact. The Good Trust model of partnering is for those corporations that have a sophisticated level of moral maturity and proactively seek to partner with and tap the expertise of NGOs in order to maximize the impact of their efforts to do good.

TRUST AND PEACE PARTNERING: THE POSSIBILITIES FOR
CORPORATE-NGO PARTNERSHIPS

The Hard Trust, Real Trust, and Good Trust models of corporate-NGO
partnerships are rooted in recent literature from the larger domains of
nonprofit and business and society research, as well as in current social
activism. These dimensions of peace partnering will be discussed individually, including a review of relevant academic publications and case
studies. The Good Trust model is the least discussed of the three within
management literature; therefore, we will emphasize this model in the
following discussion.

Hard Trust

NGO engagement with corporations originated with a hard trust model.
In the last twenty to thirty years, the perception of corporate power in the
global economy increasingly has overshadowed the power of governments. In this time period NGOs changed their focus accordingly from
influencing governments to engaging in corporate activism.[21] Activist
NGOs initially took the role of moral compass and ethical watchdog
against corporations and capitalism.[22] From a position of skepticism,
NGOs would attack corporations with the intent of changing their behavior under threat of financial harm. Along with social justice issues, Hard
Trust also includes concerns such as avoiding corruption and bribery and
compliance with laws such as environmental regulation and child labor.
These are the very issues that NGOs found could be more effectively advocated for through corporate, rather than government, activism.

NGO Hard Trust tools range from arranging consumer pickets, protests, and boycotts with the intent of disrupting business to using the
media, the Internet, and letter-writing campaigns to widely distribute a
critical message and inflict reputational harm.[23] Another way NGOs ensure corporate Hard Trust is by using technology to monitor corporate adherence to these standards and "trying" corporate misbehavior in "the
court of public opinion." An example of this sort of behavior is the use of
video cameras to record environmental damage (for example, Amazon
Watch, the Earth Films Toronto Video Activist Collective) or breaches of

labor laws or human rights (for example, Witness, Globalvision.org, Labor Beat) and releasing the tapes to the media in order to incite change.

It is a misnomer to call the interaction between the NGO and corporation a "partnership" under the Hard Trust model. While partnerships can evolve once corporate consciousness is raised, initially corporate action primarily consists of denial, reactive damage limitation, and avoidance of reputational harm. Simon Zadek suggests that corporations move from a defensive stage to a compliance stage early in the path to corporate responsibility.[24] Spar and LaMure have characterized corporate reaction to NGO activism in terms of three strategies: preemption, capitulation, or resistance.[25] All of these strategies are more or less adversarial between corporations and NGOs and do not necessarily leave room for the possibility of a meeting of the minds and development of a common purpose between the NGO and firm. Indeed, corporations are seen as a vehicle for the NGOs' pursuit of social justice, and it is suggested that NGOs would lose credibility among their public and peers if they were seen as working too closely with businesses.[26]

Well-known examples of the Hard Trust model are Greenpeace's activities against Shell regarding the Brent Spar oil rig and Global Exchange's campaign against Nike with regard to sweatshop labor.[27] Both of these activist campaigns seemed to surprise Shell and Nike. These events are cited by the corporations as a turning point—the companies learned of the importance of evaluating and complying not just with the law but with standards of social acceptability in business decision making as well.[28] In the years since these activist campaigns, both Shell and Nike have come to be leaders in their industries in terms of environmental and supply chain impact, respectively. This goes to show that Hard Trust activism can affect a company's moral maturity.

In terms of the development of moral maturity of corporations, using Hard Trust engagement NGOs can act as an overarching moral authority that keeps tabs on and corrects misbehavior of the corporation as toddler. While this form of engagement continues to be the primary nature of contact between a great number of NGOs and corporations, in some cases new models of corporate-NGO engagement have arisen.[29] When corporations develop beyond the toddler stage—the obedience and punishment orientation of moral development according to Kohlberg—they realize they can make money by being good, that is, they reach the second level in human terms: the self-interest level of moral reasoning. At this stage, a less adversarial and more partnership-based relationship can develop. We call this the Real Trust model of corporate-NGO engagement.

Real Trust

Much of the recent management research studying corporate-NGO partnerships has focused on the instrumental Real Trust level. The concept that a business case must be made for socially responsible activity that benefits society and contributes to peace goes back to a Friedmanesque view of corporations: the business of business is business, and any activities that do not contribute to the bottom line are inappropriate.[30] Thus, a great deal of ink has been spent on establishing why engaging in activities that benefit society are good for business and how NGOs can further this connection. Zadek suggests that as businesses go from a managerial stage to a strategic stage along the path to corporate responsibility, they understand how benefiting society can lead to competitive advantage and long-term success.[31] It has even been suggested that NGOs themselves benefit from collaborating with business through improved efficiency and economic sustainability.[32]

The most frequently mentioned business rationales for partnering with NGOs for social benefit relate to improving the reputation of the company, differentiating their brands among consumers, developing new markets or marketing techniques, and improving organizational commitment among employees by demonstrating organizational values. Thus, Real Trust is the economization of goodwill. NGOs can help companies strategize as to how to engage stakeholders in the dialogues that can create peace. NGOs lend credibility to companies and provide them with access to otherwise unavailable groups. NGOs can also explain nonfinancial concerns to corporations.[33] In terms of reputation, while Hard Trust relates to a company's reactive defense of a reputation under attack by NGOs, in Real Trust partnerships NGOs can help businesses to proactively pursue reputational benefits.

Business and NGOs can partner to create new markets and develop new marketing techniques. Many such partnerships recently have begun to, on the one hand, promote fair trade products to sell in developed markets[34] and, on the other, bring capitalist efficiency and products to Bottom of the Pyramid (BOP) consumers.[35] NGOs promoting fair trade seek to break cycles of poverty by ensuring ethical treatment of small producers and opening wider markets for their products. Obtaining direct access to Western markets can reduce resource dependency issues that contribute to poverty by cutting out the middle man and thereby gaining more sustainable sources of income. Global corporations can benefit from the market differentiation that fair trade branding can provide as well as an improved reputation. Some issues corporations face, however, are (1) educating consumers to ensure market demand for more ethically produced goods, and (2) ensuring that high-quality fair trade goods are produced in quantities necessary in highly competitive global markets.[36] This is where corporate-NGO partnerships can be very beneficial because business's credibility among consumers and the success of the marketing message may be improved by association with the NGO. Additionally, NGOs may be able to intermediate among providers by training small producers and certifying quality production. Likewise, where NGOs work with businesses to seek a BOP commercial solution to poverty issues, they can provide deep local knowledge needed to develop and access markets and cope with infrastructure and distribution issues.[37]

An instrumental partnership between NGOs and business is very important because it brings that many more actors into the picture. When more companies engage in Real Trust partnerships that build peaceful communities while benefiting at the bottom line, the more it becomes necessary to remain engaged in order to keep up with the competition. Thus, the more we can encourage Peace through Commerce activities from a Real Trust perspective, the more likely it is to become a necessary business strategy. This can be seen from a few analogies: Quality management was not viewed as important until Japanese automakers used it in the 1970s to gain a competitive advantage over U.S. automakers, at which time U.S. businesses suddenly saw the efficacy of quality. Environmental concerns were not central to businesses two decades ago, but now green marketing has become an important part of many companies' identities. Likewise, concerns regarding fair trade and ethical supply chains are changing the way companies source materials and products to ensure that workers are paid fair wages and work amidst reasonable health and safety standards. The same can hold true of Peace through Commerce activities: even if a company does not care, Hard Trust public pressure from NGOs can make it care. Moreover, where consumers and socially responsible investors increasingly discriminate in favor of companies engaging in Real

Trust measures that do well while doing good, market forces can reward companies that work with NGOs to promote peace.

Good Trust

Companies can change. There are more and more examples of companies that have moments of epiphanies, whereby NGOs or others hold up the standards of what is possible and the company chooses to embrace it. One analogy, from David Bollier, is the story of viatical insurance settlements for AIDS patients after a Prudential Insurance adjuster was confronted with the death of AIDS patients in a nonprofit hospice. The experience made the adjuster search for a creative solution, and he developed a way for Prudential to pay out insurance proceeds prior to death for a terminally ill patient.[38] These settlements did not provide any economic benefit to Prudential—quite the opposite. Nevertheless, it was the right thing to do and Prudential's agent was inspired by an NGO, hospice, to do it. Companies change.

Until recently, there have been a number of case studies but a dearth of theoretical academic contributions concerning the phenomenon of NGOs inspiring and partnering with businesses to engage in what we call Good Trust activities. NGOs have helped businesses to start caring intrinsically about ethics such that the positive impact of ethical behavior has become the aspirational aim of corporate action. An important impact of the Peace through Commerce movement in academic research is the understanding that by recognizing the dignity of their employees and stakeholders, practicing cultural sensitivity in different parts of the world, respecting the environment through ecological stewardship, maintaining transparency, protecting human rights and gender equity and encouraging voice in the workplace, and philanthropically supporting the development of a civil society, corporations with an ethical culture can demonstrate citizenship, mitigate tensions, and help build communities where there was once divisiveness. NGOs must be given credit where credit is due for inspiring the epiphanies that lead corporations to pursue these activities and for partnering with corporations to give these activities more impact.

Our conception of Good Trust in corporate-NGO relationships goes beyond most of the existing management literature. Even Zadek's final civil stage on the path to corporate responsibility does not go far enough. Zadek suggests that in the civil stage corporations go beyond their own competitive interests to promote collective industry action to address society's concerns. This is done largely in order to ensure consistency so that the industry as a whole is perceived in a good light and, also, to preempt restrictive legislation.[39] Thus, from a moral development perspective, Zadek suggests that corporations take a conformity, or law and order, stance toward responsible behavior—this is comparable to the conventional level of Kohlberg's moral reasoning. Our contemplation of Good Trust is more like Kohlberg's highest level of moral development: the corporation sees itself as a member of a wider society with an obligation to contribute to its stakeholders, uphold ethical principles, and make a commitment to justice—that is, social justice.

There are a limited number of corporations that are founded upon the principle of taking on this kind of responsibility and acting in this manner because it is right, and not because of self-interest, as part of the corporate identity. One example is Seventh Generation in terms of its environmental and social commitments. Another is Johnson and Johnson, as exemplified by its corporate credo. Corporations in Good Trust partnerships proactively initiate relationships with NGOs in order to utilize their expertise and maximize the positive effect of the corporation's efforts.

From a normative perspective, we argue that companies and NGOs adopting a Good Trust partnership benefit not simply in terms of the more quantifiable Real Trust financial advantages but, more importantly, from an unquantifiable and intrinsic telos of peace within their relationship. This higher purpose will spill over into the culture of both the firm and the NGO, bringing intangible benefits that will make work and life more meaningful for all participants. By contributing to combating poverty, sustaining the environment, establishing more equality between the sexes as well as socioeconomic classes, and building communities in the external environment where firms pursue business opportunities, firms and NGOs will lay the groundwork for more peaceful societies while building stronger communities within their own work environments.

We close this discussion with one more example. In a 2006 *Foreign Affairs* article, anthropologist Robert Sapolsky related the story of "the Forest Troop."[40] The Forest Troop was a group of baboons who lived on the edge of a recreational park. They ate the leftovers from campers and other users of the park. The baboons' social structure was very hierarchical, with alpha male baboons violently competing for the food and not sharing much of it with others in the troop. Then, according to Sapolsky, tuberculosis swept through the Forest Troop, killing most of the violent males. The results were intriguing. The remaining population, comprised of less aggressive males and the remaining females, practiced a much more egalitarian, sharing approach to resources. That in itself may not be particularly surprising. What is surprising is that these practices continued. In what may be a hardwired understanding of the need to avoid incest, baboon males move from troop to troop. Males from typically aggressive baboon troops joined the Forest Troop, as would be expected; however, the now more pacific culture of the Forest Troop did not change. Even the newly arriving, aggressive males adopted the cultural practices of the Troop rather than re-instituting the competitive, violent, and hierarchical style to which they were accustomed. As Sapolsky argues, the cultures and traditions of the Forest Troop changed and continued to remain pacific even when aggressive individuals joined the group. And so, we might ask, if baboons can change, why can't corporations?

Indeed, the point of Sapolsky's piece is that countries change, too. Germany and Japan look much different than they did seventy-five years ago. So, too, do countries like Sweden and Switzerland, which are bastions of peace now but could hardly be described that way two centuries ago. Baboons change. Countries change. Corporations can change, too. They can change by paying attention to the coercive, Hard Trust demands of society, or, even better, by integrating Real Trust strategies that connect financial success with long-term reputational effects and social capital resources. And they can unleash the desires human beings have to do good—to seek peace—in their work.

CONCLUSION

This chapter discusses a framework for considering the nature and benefits of relationships between business and NGOs. NGOs have provided incentives, expertise, and inspiration that have been important factors in the development of moral maturity within many corporations. The role of NGOs in a Hard Trust, adversarial relationship has been extensively discussed in the general media as well as academic literature. Likewise, much management research has focused on the instrumental relationships that corporations can develop with NGOs to seek mutual benefit through positive social actions. This chapter seeks to broaden the discussion within academic circles as well as the wider public to reach an understanding of the inspiration and intrinsic value that a Good Trust relationship between business and NGOs can generate. Further case studies and research are necessary to identify, characterize, and seek to understand the intangible benefits these relationships can generate in building peaceful communities wherever business is done.

NOTES

1. Jane Nelson, *The Business of Peace: The Private Sector as a Partner in Conflict and Resolution* (London: Prince of Wales Business Leaders Forum, 2000).

2. Alasdair MacIntyre, *Whose Justice? Which Rationality?* (Notre Dame, IN: University of Notre Dame Press, 1998).

3. L. Kohlberg, *The Philosophy of Moral Development* (San Francisco: Harper and Row, 1981).

4. Ibid.

5. C. J. Fombrun and M. Shanley, "What's in a Name? Reputation Building and Corporate Strategy," *Academy of Management Journal* 33 (1990): 233–58.

6. T. Fort, "The Corporation as Mediating Institution: An Efficacious Synthesis of Stakeholder Theory and Corporate Constituency Statutes," *Notre Dame Law Review* 73 (1997): 173–203.

7. See, for example, *Theodora Holding Corp. v. Henderson,* Court of Chancery of Delaware, 257 A.2d 398 (1969); *Kahn v. Sullivan,* Supreme Court of Delaware, 549 A.2d 48 (1991); and E. Elhauge, "Sacrificing Corporate Profits in the Public Interest," *New York University Law Review* 80 (2005): 733.

8. *Shlensky v. Wrigley,* Appellate Court of Illinois, 237 N.E.2d 776 (1968).

9. *Cheff v. Mathes,* Supreme Court of Delaware, 199 A.2d 548 (1964).

10. *Paramount Communications v. Time, Inc.,* Supreme Court of Delaware, 571 A.2d 1140 (1989).

11. J. P. Walsh and J. Margolis, "Misery Loves Companies: Rethinking Social Initiatives by Business," *Administrative Science Quarterly* 48, no. 2 (2003): 268–305.

12. P. C. Godfrey, "The Relationship between Corporate Philanthropy and Shareholder Wealth: A Risk Management Perspective," *Academy of Management Review* 30, no. 4 (2005): 777–98.

13. A. McWilliams and D. Siegel, "Corporate Social Responsibility: A Theory of the Firm Perspective," *Academy of Management Review* 26, no. 1 (2001): 117–27.

14. U.S. Sentencing Commission Guidelines, Section 8B2.1(a)(2) (2004).

15. T. L. Fort, D. Hess, and R. S. McWhorter, "The 2004 Amendments to the Federal Sentencing Guidelines and Their Implicit Call for a Symbiotic Integration of Business Ethics," *Fordham Journal of Corporate and Financial Law* 11 (2006): 725–64.

16. See http://www.state.gov/e/eeb/ace/2007/.

17. See http://www.international-alert.org/our_work/themes/LBLP.php.

18. T. Fort, *Business, Integrity, and Peace* (Cambridge: Cambridge University Press, 2007).

19. T. Fort and C. A. Schipani, *The Role of Business in Fostering Peaceful Societies* (Cambridge: Cambridge University Press, 2004).

20. Ibid., 26–29, 46, 143.

21. D. L. Spar and L. T. LaMure, "The Power of Activism: Assessing the Impact of NGOs on Global Business," *California Management Review* 45, no. 3 (2003): 78–101.

22. P. A. Argenti, "Collaborating with Activists: How Starbucks Works with NGOs," *California Management Review* 47, no. 1 (2004): 91–116.

23. Spar and LaMure, "Power of Activism," 81.

24. S. Zadek, "The Path to Corporate Responsibility," *Harvard Business Review* 82, no. 12 (2004): 125–32.

25. Spar and LaMure, "Power of Activism," 79.

26. Ibid.

27. Zadek, "Path to Corporate Responsibility."

28. K. Starkey and A. Crane, "Toward a Green Narrative: Management and the Evolutionary Epic," *Academy of Management Review* 28, no. 2 (2003): 220–37.

29. Michael Yaziji, "Turning Gadflys into Allies," *Harvard Business Review* 82, no. 2 (2004): 110–15.

30. M. Friedman, "The Social Responsibility of Business Is to Increase Its Profits," *New York Times Magazine,* September 13, 1970.

31. Zadek, "Path to Corporate Responsibility."

32. D. Rondinelli and T. London, "How Corporations and Environmental Groups Cooperate: Assessing Cross-Sector Alliances and Collaborations," *Academy of Management Executive* 17, no. 1 (2003): 61–76.

33. Ibid.

34. D. Lewis, "Nongovernmental Organizations, Business and the Management of Ambiguity," *Nonprofit Management and Leadership* 9, no. 2 (1998): 135–51.

35. C. K. Prahalad, *The Fortune at the Bottom of the Pyramid* (Upper Saddle River, NJ: Wharton School Publishing, 2005).

36. Lewis, "Nongovernmental Organizations."

37. Prahalad, *Fortune at the Bottom.*

38. D. Bollier, *Aiming Higher* (New York: American Management Association, 1996).

39. Zadek, "Path to Corporate Responsibility."

40. R. Sapolsky, "A Natural History of Peace," *Foreign Affairs* 85, no. 1 (2006): 104–20.

P A R T II

Influences from the Disciplines of Law
and Peace Studies

CHAPTER 3

Transnational Corporate Accountability and the Rule of Law

Douglass Cassel and Sean O'Brien

INTRODUCTION

In June 2006 Professor John Ruggie, the United Nations Secretary-General's Special Representative on Business and Human Rights (hereafter the SGSR) reflected on his mandate and the status of the draft of *Norms on the Responsibilities of Transnational Corporations and Other Business Enterprises with Respect to Human Rights,*[1] which was adopted in 2003 by the United Nations Sub-Commission on the Protection and Promotion of Human Rights. Describing the Norms as a "train wreck" that could lead to "utterly perverse consequences" if enacted as law, Ruggie pronounced that, under his mandate, "[T]he Norms are dead."[2]

As Ruggie went on to note, the death of the Norms does not put to rest the "challenges they sought to address," which remain the "essence of [his] mandate."[3] Nor does it put to rest the legal principles on which the ill-fated Norms were based. If the SGSR is to bury the Norms, he should take care not to dig the grave too deep, as there remain existing sources and legitimate roles for international human rights law to play in sanctioning the misdeeds of transnational corporations (TNCs).

If indeed some level of international legal regulation of corporate conduct is both beneficial and inevitable, the question arises, By what means and through which laws should TNCs be regulated? Following a critique of both the Norms and the wholesale rejection of any legal norms, this chapter will identify sources of existing and emerging international law that might be used to hold TNCs accountable for human rights violations.

THE ROLE OF LAW AND TNCS

Both national and international law have legitimate roles to play in regulating the conduct of transnational corporations. National law creates corporations and makes them economically viable by generally shielding corporate investors from legal liability for corporate conduct. International law creates a framework for trade and investment that enables TNCs to engage in international business transactions.

Despite the importance of the regulatory role of law in shaping corporate behavior, perhaps the paramount guarantor of legal and "human rights–friendly" corporate behavior is the "culture" of a corporation. Regulation and culture can either be at odds with or can complement each other, although neither by itself is sufficient. Law without a culture of responsible corporate conduct is hollow, somewhat like the constitution of the former Soviet Union—beautiful in print but ineffective in practice.[4] Culture without law may work well in some circumstances but lacks consistency and uniformity. Healthy corporate cultures that encourage respect for human rights may also place good corporate citizens at a competitive disadvantage versus cutthroat operators. Therefore, the best conditions for good corporate conduct combine elements of culture and law. This assumes, of course, that the laws are well designed and well targeted and are neither too lenient nor unnecessarily intrusive. Law in this context may serve at least three beneficial roles:

1. To serve as a catalyst, an incentive for good or better corporate behavior
2. To standardize good practices and to generalize a "floor" of good conduct
3. To catch corporate laggards and thereby level the playing field among all corporate participants in a given industry or market

As TNCs have grown in both power and reach, a commensurate increase in public scrutiny has led to a proliferation of voluntary codes that define, assess, and remedy their conduct. Individual corporations have developed codes of conduct that govern their relationships with other companies in their supply chain.[5] Industry associations have self-policed, and partnerships between governments, TNCs, and nongovernmental organizations (NGOs) have resulted in voluntary principles in the high-risk extractive and energy sectors.[6] Intergovernmental organizations are involved as well; the Organization for Economic Co-operation and Development (OECD) has its *Guidelines for Multinational Enterprises*,[7] and the International Labor Organization (ILO) has adopted a *Tripartite Declaration of Principles Concerning Multinational Enterprises and Social Policy*.[8]

The United Nations Global Compact is one of the most well-known of these voluntary regimes.[9] Established in 2000 at the behest of then Secretary-General Kofi Annan, the Global Compact describes itself as a "social learning network . . . intended to identify, disseminate and promote good practices based on universal principles."[10] These principles are contained in "ten short sentences" recommending what TNCs "should" do in the areas of human rights, labor standards, protection of the environment, and preventing corruption.[11] A business can participate in the Global Compact upon submitting a letter of support for the Compact and promising to incorporate the principles into its corporate culture and publish an annual report describing the ways in which it is supporting the ten principles.[12]

Aiming for universality through flexibility, the pithy principles suffer from a lack of specificity.[13] This lack of specificity can lead to absurd results, as exemplified by Global Compact member BHP Billiton's interpretation of its obligations under Principle 3: "businesses should uphold . . . the effective recognition of the right to collective bargaining."[14] Despite the plain meaning of the text, BHP interprets the obligation as permitting them to force new employees to sign individual contracts.[15] BHP suffers no consequences for its aggressive posture; the Global Compact continues to embrace BHP as a member and BHP touts its membership in the Global Compact as evidence of its commitment to human rights. In fact, the Executive Head of the Global Compact seemingly ratified BHP's anti–collective bargaining policy in a letter to the company, stating "It is true that the Global Compact principles have the potential to be interpreted in different ways by different stakeholders. This is inherent in the nature of the principles and is not necessarily a negative thing."[16] BHP is not the only company that has been accused of "wrapping itself in UN blue"[17] as a way to insulate its controversial human rights behavior.[18]

As of April 2007, approximately 3,139 businesses were participating in the Global Compact, of which a significant number—618—were labeled as "non-communicating participants."[19] With more than 60,000 TNCs making decisions that affect human rights today, TNCs actively participating in the Compact represent only a small fraction of possible participants.[20] While varied in their scope, many of these voluntary regimes share common deficiencies:[21] (1) they are entirely voluntary and do not address the behavior of laggards; (2) their multiplicity has led to definitional problems; (3) their lack of universality has led to jurisdictional problems; and (4) they have weak, if any, accountability mechanisms.

THE DRAFT NORMS

In response to these perceived weaknesses, the United Nations Sub-Commission on the Promotion and Protection of Human Rights (a subset of the former UN Commission on Human Rights, now the Human Rights Council) established a working group in 1998 "to examine the working methods and activities of transnational corporations."[22] By August 2001, the mandate of the working group specifically included the authority to "[c]ontribute to the drafting of relevant norms concerning human rights and transnational corporations and other economic units whose activities have an impact on human rights."[23]

After a series of seminars and consultations with stakeholders—including representatives of NGOs, states, and TNCs—the Sub-Commission approved the draft Norms on August 26, 2003. The Norms consist of two parts—the Norms themselves and an accompanying Commentary that serves as a "useful interpretation and elaboration of the standards contained in the Norms."[24]

Context and Foundation

While much of the draft Norms is a comprehensive listing of substantive human rights provisions, most of the significant contributions of the Norms to the discussion regarding TNCs and human rights are contained in four background sections that provide context and a foundation for the substantive provisions. These sections include a lengthy Preamble as well as General Obligations (para. 1), General Provisions of Implementation (para. 15), and Definitions (paras. 20–23).[25]

Preamble

The Preamble is critical to understanding the breadth and scope of the regime that the draft Norms purport to create. The Preamble proclaims—using the term "reaffirming"—"that transnational corporations and other business enterprises, their officers . . . and persons working for them have, inter alia, human rights obligations and responsibilities and that these human rights norms will contribute to the making and development of international law as to those responsibilities and obligations."[26] Beyond the self-reference to the Norms themselves as a source, the Preamble cites the Universal Declaration of Human Rights and an open-ended list of more than forty specific human rights instruments of varying legal character as the source of these "obligations and responsibilities."[27] Despite the fact that these instruments—both "hard" and "soft" law—are nearly all directed at states, the Preamble announces the intent of the Norms to "provide a basis for imposing, at an international level, a public law oriented constituency model on corporate organization."[28]

General Obligations

The General Obligations section of the Norms confirms the Preamble's view of TNCs as the objects of international human rights law. With a nod to the "primary responsibility" of states with respect to human rights law, the Norms announce that TNCs have a parallel "obligation to promote, secure the fulfilment [*sic*] of, respect, ensure respect of and protect human rights recognized in international as well as national law."[29] The Commentary notes that this paragraph "reflects the primary approach of the Norms and the remainder of the Norms shall be read in the light of this paragraph."[30] In addition, the Commentary creates an additional "responsibility [for TNCs] to use due diligence in ensuring that their activities do not contribute directly or indirectly to human abuses, and that they do not directly or indirectly benefit from abuses of which they were aware or ought to have been aware."[31]

Definitions

The Definitions section extends the duties and substantive provisions of the Norms to a wide range of actors, including "transnational corporations" and "other business enterprise[s]."[32] The category of *TNCs* "refers to an economic entity operating in more than one country or a cluster of economic entities operating in two or more countries," while *other business enterprise* broadly refers to any business entity that has any relation with a transnational corporation."[33] As one commentator has observed, "It is not clear whether there are any economic enterprises, except perhaps the most isolated, that do not constitute a 'transnational corporation or other business enterprise' to which most of the substantive provisions of the Norms apply."[34]

The term *stakeholder* is defined by the Norms to include "stockholders, other owners, workers and their representatives, as well as any other individual or group that is affected"—either directly or indirectly—"by the activities of transnational corporations or other business enterprises." This expansive definition creates substantive rights for a large and seemingly all-inclusive category of rights holders under the Norms.

General Provisions of Implementation

The Norms include a number of creative forms of implementation, some of which are novel in the field of public international law. As a starting point, TNCs are required to adopt the Norms internally and to incorporate the Norms in "their contracts or other arrangements and dealings with contractors, subcontractors, suppliers, licensees, distributors, or natural or other legal persons that enter into any agreement with the transnational corporation or business enterprise."[35] This use of private law to enforce human rights obligations allows the Norms to be efficiently and flexibly implemented without the intervention of state actors.[36]

Accountability under the Norms is ensured through an interconnecting web of nonjudicial and quasi-judicial mechanisms. First, TNCs are required to conduct a public and transparent "human rights impact" assessment prior to launching any "major initiative or project."[37] It is hard to underestimate the sea change that this requirement would signify: to date, not a single human rights impact assessment has been made public, save for the summary of BP's liquefied national gas project in Indonesia.[38] Second, TNCs "shall be subject to periodic monitoring and verification by United Nations, other international and national mechanisms already in existence or yet to be created, regarding application of the Norms."[39] The Norms envision a supervisory role to be played by the treaty bodies, the special procedures (including thematic and country mandate holders), the Sub-Commission, and the nascent Human Rights Council. Third, each TNC must engage in a dynamic and periodic review of its compliance with the Norms, "taking into account comments from stakehold-ers."[40] The inclusive nature of the "stakeholder" category means that governments, unions, indigenous communities, individuals, and others would have a say in this review process.

Substantive Provisions

The Preamble, Definitions, General Obligations, and General Provisions sections reveal the intended breadth of the Norms and provide the con-text within which the Norms' substantive provisions should be read. Clearly, the Norms were meant to be a departure from all previous at-tempts at creating a blueprint for achieving corporate accountability.

With respect to human rights, the Norms require TNCs to respect and ensure, prevent violations of, and promote the following human rights (Norm 1):

equality of opportunity and nondiscrimination (para. 2)

security of persons, including not engaging in or benefiting from inter-national crimes against the human person (para. 3),[41] and ensuring that corporate security arrangements observe norms of interna-tional humanitarian law (para. 4)

rights of workers, including no forced or compulsory labor (para. 5), no exploitation of child labor (para. 6), a safe and healthy working en-vironment (para. 7), compensation that ensures an adequate stan-dard of living for workers and their families (para. 8), and freedom of association and collective bargaining (para. 9)

respect for national sovereignty and human rights, which covers a broad range of obligations:

- recognition and respect for applicable norms of international law; the rule of law; national development objectives; eco-nomic and social policies including transparency, account-ability, and a prohibition of corruption (para. 10)
- refraining from bribery and from any activity that supports, solicits, or encourages human rights abuses and seeking to en-sure that a corporation's goods and services are not used to abuse human rights (para. 11)

- respect for civil, political, economic, social, and cultural rights and seeking to contribute to their realization and to refrain from obstructing them (para. 12)

consumer protection, including fair marketing standards applicable to human rights performance (para. 13)
respect for all laws and policies relating to respect for the environment (para. 14)
prompt, effective, and adequate reparations for violations of the Norms, to be enforced by national courts (para. 18)

The Norms also make clear that states retain primary responsibility for protection of human rights (para. 1) and that nothing in them diminishes either the responsibility of states or any more protective human rights norms (para. 18).

CRITIQUE OF THE DRAFT NORMS

While intended as a response to the weaknesses of the voluntary regimes that dominated the corporate social responsibility (CSR) landscape before their promulgation, the draft Norms suffer from their own weaknesses. Viewed as hortatory guidelines, the Norms are expansive, ambitious, and generally laudatory. Viewed as law, however, they are open to serious question, for at least four reasons.

First, the draft Norms characterize as "nonvoluntary"[42] a host of substantive provisions whose status as legally binding on private corporations is less than evident. Most generally, Norm 1 refers to the "obligations" of TNCs to respect human rights, to ensure human rights, to prevent human rights violations, and to promote human rights. While international law imposes such an array of obligations on states, it is by no means clear that international law, to the extent it imposes human rights obligations on TNCs, requires them to do anything more than simply refrain from committing or being complicit in a narrowly defined range of gross violations of human rights, as discussed below.

This overstatement of the current international legal obligations of TNCs[43] contradicts the claim of the Norms' authors that "[t]he legal authority of the Norms derives principally from their sources in treaties and customary law, as a restatement of international legal principles applicable to companies."[44] In support of this claim, the Norms' primary author, David Weissbrodt, cites two draft documents of the International Law Commission.[45] These documents, however, highlight the various ways in which states can be said to be responsible for an "internationally wrongful act."[46] A state commits an international wrong through an act or omission that "[i]s attributable to the State under international law" and that "[c]onstitutes a breach of an international obligation of the State."[47] The fact that the conduct of third parties (for examples, individuals or TNCs) may be attributable to the state does not necessarily mean that the third party conduct in question violates international law.[48] Furthermore, even if these draft documents could be construed as supporting the proposition that international law places the extensive obligations on TNCs claimed by the Norms, the documents have never been approved by any authoritative body.[49] To be sure, it is within the prerogative of states to create an international legal regime to hold TNCs accountable for their misdeeds. There are no legal impediments to states adopting a regime like the Norms.[50] To suggest that they have already done so, however, is premature.

Second, there are also particular Norms that arguably go beyond current international law, even for states. For example, paragraph 2 prohibits discrimination based on "other status . . . unrelated to the . . . job," which the Commentary defines to include discrimination based on "sexual orientation." While discrimination based on sexual orientation is barred in certain contexts by the European Convention on Human Rights,[51] and the Human Rights Committee has condemned criminal sodomy laws as discriminatory,[52] a broad ban on sexual discrimination goes well beyond current international human rights law. It would also create difficulties for corporations operating in Muslim communities and other cultural contexts.

Third, despite their attempt at specificity and comprehensiveness, the draft Norms raise serious issues of vagueness for TNCs that might attempt to comply with them. Under paragraph 10, for example, what does it mean for a corporation to respect "applicable" norms of international law? The "rule of law"? "Development objectives"? "Social, economic and cultural policies"? How does a TNC know whether it is or is not in compliance with such broad and vague norms? Under paragraph 12 TNCs must "contribute" to the realization of rights. How? How much? Again, how does a TNC know whether it is in compliance with paragraph 12? Vagueness is also found in the Commentaries to the Norms, such as Commentaries 3(j), TNCs must refrain from trade "known" to lead to human rights violations; 10(a), TNCs must "encourage social progress"; and 14(b), TNCs are responsible for the health impacts of all their activities.

The very concept of "human rights" within the Norms lacks precision. As defined in the final paragraph of the Norms, "human rights" includes rights enumerated in unspecified "other human rights treaties" and "other relevant instruments adopted within the United Nations system."[53] The concept is also treated in the Preamble, which roots the human rights obligations of TNCs in dozens of treaties incorporated into the Norms by mere reference, including the unspecified category of "other instruments."[54] These imprecise definitions and sweeping references would be understandable in a document that merely identifies the aspirations of the political community but not for a "binding" treaty upon which liabilities will be determined.

Fourth, the broad sweep and vague definition of the substantive Norms are aggravated by Norm 18, on reparations, which requires "prompt, adequate and effective" reparation to persons adversely affected by a TNC's failure to comply with the Norms.[55] Reparations would include, among other measures, "restitution, compensation and rehabilitation," with precise amounts to be determined by national courts and/or unnamed "international tribunals."[56] Thus, a TNC is not only at risk of an unknowing breach of the Norms but may face the risk of having to pay substantial money damages for its unknowing breach.

Given these weaknesses, it is not surprising that many in the business community have rejected the draft Norms outright. Two of the major participants in the UN Global Compact—the International Organisation of Employers (IOE) and the International Chamber of Commerce (ICC)—called the Norms "counterproductive," arguing that "many IOE and ICC member companies have moved beyond such a legalistic approach to human rights."[57] In contrast to the Norms, the IOE and ICC stated that "business principles and responsibilities should be developed and implemented by the companies themselves" so as not to limit the "innovation and creativity" shown by TNCs in addressing human rights concerns.[58]

In contrast to the laissez-faire attitude of the IOE and ICC, a significant business-led initiative undertook to engage constructively with the draft Norms. In 2003 a group comprised of seven corporate members formed the Business Leaders Initiative on Human Rights (BLIHR) with the principle purpose of finding "practical ways of applying the aspirations of the Universal Declaration of Human Rights within a business context and to inspire other businesses to do likewise."[59] With the Norms being adopted by the Sub-Commission at nearly the same time, the BLIHR took on the task of "road-testing" the Norms over a three-year period through a series of projects, dialogues, and collaborations. The conclusions of the road-testing were published at the end of 2006.[60] As tactfully summarized by Honorary BLIHR Chair Mary Robinson, former UN High Commissioner for Human Rights,

> [T]he BLIHR companies found much in the draft Norms that was helpful within their respective companies as a benchmark to check and develop their own policies and practices. At the same time, as the conclusions of their road-testing point out, a number of important questions still require answers not provided by the draft Norms and there is a recognition that the debate must now move on.[61]

Significantly, the draft Norms were not adopted by the Sub-Commission's parent body or by any other body within the UN. The Commission on Human Rights declared that they had never requested the Sub-Commission to draft any such Norms "and that, as a draft proposal, [they have] no legal standing, and that the Sub-Commission should not perform any monitoring function in this regard."[62] Furthermore, the draft Norms were met with dismay by officials of the UN Global Compact, which promotes a cooperative, voluntary partnership to promote corporate responsibility.

The Special Representative

In response to the stalemate between the Sub-Commission and its detractors among state bodies, UN officials, and TNCs, the UN Commission on Human Rights requested that Secretary-General Kofi Annan "appoint a special representative on the issue of human rights and transnational corporations and other business enterprises"[63] with the following mandate:

(a)   To identify and clarify standards of corporate responsibility and accountability for transnational corporations and other business enterprises with regard to human rights;

(b)   To elaborate on the role of States in effectively regulating and adjudicating the role of transnational corporations and other business enterprises with regard to human rights, including through international cooperation;

(c)   To research and clarify the implications for transnational corporations and other business enterprises of concepts such as "complicity" and "sphere of influence";

(d)   To develop materials and methodologies for undertaking human rights impact assessments of the activities of transnational corporations and other business enterprises;

(e)   To compile a compendium of best practices of States and transnational corporations and other business enterprises.[64]

Annan responded by appointing his former close aide, John Ruggie, to the post. Ruggie's first report, published in January 2006, criticizes the Sub-Commission Norms and promises an approach of "principled pragmatism."[65] What this means is not entirely clear, but at minimum it includes an effort to identify best practices with an emphasis on what works. Ruggie continued to explore with experts the question of what international legal norms are applicable to TNCs and reported his findings in a second report in February 2007.[66] In that report he also requested an extension of his mandate in order to complete his study and to prepare recommendations.[67] In the event his mandate is extended, however, Ruggie is not likely to recommend measures that will not command support in the UN Human Rights Council. Therefore, his recommendations are likely to be quite modest.

Moving Beyond the Special Representative

Modest proposals, however, need not represent a step back from the current state of international law with respect to TNCs. Ruggie's measures should reflect the fact that at least five categories of international law currently, or by a slight conceptual extension, could be applied to TNCs.

First, the Nuremberg Trials established that individuals have definable duties under international law and that those duties may be violated without the intermediary "state action" requirement.[68] Challenged, refined, and applied in the decades since Nuremberg, individual responsibility for crimes such as genocide, war crimes, and crimes against humanity are firmly included in the Rome Statute establishing the International Criminal Court.[69] Private individuals, including corporate executives, may commit genocide and war crimes, and also crimes against humanity, provided they act pursuant to an "organizational policy."[70] To be sure, legal persons are not generally prosecutable before international tribunals.[71] However, there is a nascent, but growing, body of jurisprudence from those domestic fora that allow for jurisdiction over corporations that indicates that international law places obligations on nonstate actors, including corporations.[72]

Second, corporate activity that aids and abets, or is otherwise complicit in, state violations of human rights can lead to corporate liability. In *Doe v. UNOCAL* a panel of a federal appeals court held that a corporation could be held civilly liable for aiding and abetting alleged forced labor in Myanmar if it provided "knowing practical assistance or encouragement that has a substantial effect on the perpetration of the crime."[73] Third, corporations that undertake privatized government functions may be liable in some jurisdictions as state actors.[74] Fourth, some international law obligations are nominally directed at states but in reality mainly seek to govern private conduct. For example, treaties prohibiting racial or gender discrimination in private employment obligate states to prohibit such practices. Is it not a short step simply to "leave out the middle man" and to argue that international law, in substance if not in form, already requires TNCs to meet basic labor standards? Fifth, under regional and UN human rights treaties, states have affirmative duties to ensure the enjoyment of human rights by all persons within their jurisdictions. To the extent this entails a duty to prevent private actors from engaging in, say, disruption of free association and assembly, it might again be but a short step to say that international law imposes the duty to respect such human rights directly on private actors, including private corporations and their executives.

CONCLUSION

In the end we need just enough law but not too much. If the Sub-Commission has overreached, then to date it appears that Ruggie may be en route to underreaching. Unlike the Sub-Commission's draft Norms, effective legal norms concerning TNCs and human rights should not only protect basic rights but should also be, and be perceived as, clearly defined, fair, and reasonable in what they demand of TNCs and feasible to implement in practice. They should also be developed by a transparent and inclusive process and adopted by an authoritative body.[75]

Perhaps the most significant impact of the draft Norms and the reactions to them—both positive and negative—is the rejection of the view that "there is one and only one social responsibility of business—to use its resources and engage in activities designed to increase its profits so long as it stays within the rules of the game, which is to say, engages in open and free competition, without deception or fraud."[76] The claim that corporations have such starkly limited "social responsibility" is no longer credible as either a legal or business matter: corporations are being held responsible for human rights violations, especially at the domestic level, and want to be seen by their peers, the public, and investors as protective of human rights.

The future course of international legal regulation of TNCs and human rights is uncertain. One can imagine a more robust international regulatory framework in at least two scenarios. One may arise if major TNCs fail to get ahead and stay ahead of the curve on human rights. If they fail, there will be pressure on states to enact national and international laws. The other scenario is the opposite: "responsible" TNCs do adopt reasonable norms, but laggard corporations fail to do so and then undercut the responsible corporations in cost competition. In that event the major TNCs themselves may support legal regulation of minimum human rights standards for TNCs in order to outlaw what would amount to unfair competition.

The narrative of human rights throughout the twentieth century is that of a normative framework expanding in its embrace of human dignity. From humble beginnings as the right of a state to claim violation of its sovereign rights for the mistreatment of its citizens in another state, human rights now establish rights of all persons against all governments. Human rights have also fueled the expansion of individual criminal responsibility for serious violations of international law. It may be only a matter of time before corporations become subject to explicit international human rights obligations. Meanwhile, there remains time for all stakeholders—including TNCs—to advocate responsible approaches to legal accountability.

NOTES

1. *Norms on the Responsibilities of Transnational Corporations and Other Business Enterprises with Regard to Human Rights,* UN Doc. E/CN.4/Sub.2/2003/12/Rev.2 (2003), hereafter referred to as "the Norms"; see also *Commentary on the Norms on the Responsibilities of Transnational Corporations and Other Business Enterprises with Regard to Human Rights,* UN Doc. E/CN.4/Sub.2/2003/38/Rev.2 (2003), http://daccessdds.un.org/doc/UNDOC/GEN/G03/160/08/PDF/G0316008. pdf?OpenElement.

2. Remarks by John G. Ruggie at a Forum on Corporate Social Responsibility, June 14, 2006, Bamberg, Germany, http://www.reports-and-materials. org/Ruggie-remarks-to-Fair-Labor-Association-and-German-Network-of-Business-Ethics-14-June-2006.pdf.

3. Ibid.

4. Constitution of the Union of Soviet Socialist Republics (October 7, 1977), http://www.departments.bucknell.edu/russian/const/1977toc.html.

5. See *Report of the Special Representative of the Secretary-General on the Issue of Human Rights and Transnational Corporations and Other Business Enterprises,* UN Doc. A/HRC/4/35, Advance Edited Version, February 19, 2007, paras. 63–81, http://www.ohchr.org/english/issues/globalization/business/reports.htm.

6. *Voluntary Principles on Security and Human Rights in the Extractive Industries and Kimberley Process Certification Scheme (KPCS),* http://www.kimberleyprocess. com; and *Extractive Industries Transparency Initiative (EITI),* http://www. eitransparency.org/.

7. *The OECD Guidelines for Multinational Enterprises* (Revision 2000), www. oecd.org/daf/investment/guidelines.

8. ILO, *Official Bulletin* 61, no. 1, series A (1978), as amended, ILO, *Official Bulletin* 83, no. 3, series A (2000), http://www.ilo.org/public/english/ employment/multi/download/english.pdf.

9. See *United National Global Compact* (2000), http://www.unglobalcompact.org/.

10. John G. Ruggie, "Symposium: 'Trade, Sustainability and Global Governance': Keynote Address," *Columbia Journal of Environmental Law* 27 (2002): 301.

11. David Weissbrodt, "Eighteenth Annual Corporate Law Symposium: Corporate Social Responsibility in the International Context: Business and Human Rights," *University of Cincinnati Law Review* 74 (2005): 66.

12. See http://www.unglobalcompact.org/HowToParticipate/Business_ Participation/How_To_Join_the_Global_Compact.html.

13. See Lee A. Tavis "Novartis and the UN Global Compact Initiative," *Vanderbilt Journal of Transnational Law* 36 (2003). "The Global Compact is not specific

in its seventh principle, asking firms to 'support a precautionary approach to environmental challenges'" (743).

14. *United Nations Global Compact,* Principle 3, http://www.unglobalcompact. org/.

15. See Surya Deva, "Global Compact: A Critique of the UN's 'Public-Private' Partnership for Promoting Corporate Citizenship," *Syracuse Journal of International Law and Commerce* 34 (2006): 131.

16. Letter from George Kell to Ian Wood, December 1, 2003, http://www. bhpbilliton.com/bbContentRepository/docs/SustainableDevelopment/policiesAndKeyDocuments/UNLetter.PDF.

17. Ruggie, "Symposium," 305.

18. According to Surya Deva, BHP "shares the dais with other well known MNCs such as Bayer, Nike, Shell, Rio Tinto, and Nestle" ("Global Compact," 148).

19. See *United National Global Compact.*

20. United Nations Conference on Trade and Development, *Development and Globalisation: Facts and Figures,* UN Sales No. E.04.II.D.16 (2004), http://www. unctad.org/en/docs/gdscsir2004i_en.pdf.

21. For a general discussion, see *Interim Report of the Special Representative of the Secretary-General on the Issue of Human Rights and Transnational Corporations and other Business Enterprises,* UN Doc. E/CN.4/2006/97 (February 22, 2006) 13, 14, http://daccessdds.un.org/doc/UNDOC/GEN/G06/110/27/PDF/G0611027. pdf?OpenElement.

22. Sub-Commission on the Promotion and Protection of Human Rights, res. 1998/8, UN Doc. E/CN.4/Sub.2/RES/1998/8 (1998) para. 4, http://ap.ohchr. org/documents/E/SUBCOM/resolutions/E-CN_4-SUB_2-RES-1998-8.doc.

23. UN Sub-Commission on the Promotion and Protection of Human Rights, res. 2001/3, UN Doc. E/CN.4/SUB.2/RES/2001/3 (2001) para. 4(c), http:// www1.umn.edu/humanrts/links/subcommissionres2001.html.

24. *Norms on the Responsibilities,* Preamble, http://www1.umn.edu/humanrts/links/CommentApril2003.html.

25. Ibid.

26. Ibid.

27. Ibid.

28. Larry Catá Backer, "Multinational Corporations, Transnational Law: The United Nations' Norms on the Responsibilities of Transnational Corporations as a Harbinger of Corporate Social Responsibility in International Law," *Columbia Human Rights Law Review* 37 (2002): 334.

29. *Norms on the Responsibilities,* para. 1.

30. Ibid., para. 1, Commentary (a).

31. Ibid., para. 1, Commentary (b).

32. Ibid., paras. 20 and 21.

33. Ibid.

34. Backer, "Multinational Corporations, Transnational Law," 339.

35. *Norms on the Responsibilities,* para. 15.

36. Backer, "Multinational Corporations, Transnational Law," 335.

37. *Norms on the Responsibilities,* para. 16, Commentary (i).

38. *Report of the Special Representative of the Secretary-General on the Issue of Human Rights and Transnational Corporations and Other Business Enterprises: Human Rights Impact Assessments—Resolving Key Methodological Questions,* UN Doc. A/HRC/4/74 (February 5, 2007) para. 9, http://daccessdds.un.org/doc/UNDOC/GEN/G07/106/14/PDF/G0710614.pdf?OpenElement.

39. *Norms on the Responsibilities,* para. 16.

40. Ibid., Commentary (g).

41. These are defined by the Norms to include "war crimes, crimes against humanity, genocide, torture, forced disappearance, forced or compulsory labor, hostage-taking, extrajudicial, summary or arbitrary executions, other violations of international humanitarian law and other international crimes against the human person as defined by international law, in particular human rights and humanitarian law" (para. 3).

42. David Weissbrodt and Muria Kruger, "Norms on the Responsibilities of Transnational Corporations and Other Business Enterprises with Regard to Human Rights," *American Journal of International Law* 97 (2003): 903. The article was written by the main drafter of the Norms and published six months after the Norms were approved by the Sub-Commission; he describes the Norms as "the first nonvoluntary initiative accepted at the international level."

43. Backer, "Multinational Corporations, Transnational Law," 374.

44. Weissbrodt and Kruger, "Norms on the Responsibilities," 913.

45. International Law Commission, "Draft Code of Offences Against the Peace and Security of Mankind, Report of the International Law Commission on Its Sixth Session," *Yearbook of United Nations International Law Commission* (1954). "Draft Articles on Responsibility of States for Internationally Wrongful Acts," in *Report of the International Law Commission on the Work of Its Fifty-third Session,* UN GAOR, 56th Sess., Supp. No. 10, at 43, UN Doc. A/56/10 (2001), http://untreaty.un.org/ilc/texts/instruments/english/draft%20articles/9_6_2001.pdf.

46. Draft Articles on Responsibility of States," Article 1.

47. Ibid., Article 2(a) and (b).

48. Carlos M. Vazques, "Direct vs. Indirect Obligations of Corporations Under International Law," *Columbia Journal of Transnational Law* 43 (2005): 947.

49. UN Commission on Human Rights, E/CN.4/2004/L.11/Add.7 (2004) para. 81, http://www.unhchr.ch/huridocda/huridoca.nsf/e06a5300f90fa02380 25668700518ca4/169143c3c1009015c1256e830058c441/$FILE/G0413976.pdf.

50. Vazques, "Direct vs. Indirect Obligations," 947.

51. See, for example, *Karner v. Austria,* (Eur. Ct. H.R. 395, July 24, 2003); *S.L. v. Austria* (Eur. Ct. H.R. January 9, 2003).

52. *Toonen v. Australia,* CCPR/C/50/D/488/1992 (1992).

53. *Norms on the Responsibilities,* para. 23.

54. *Norms on the Responsibilities,* Preamble.

55. *Norms on the Responsibilities,* para. 18.

56. Ibid.

57. *Joint Written Statement to the UN Sub-Commission on the Promotion and Protection of Human Rights Submitted by the International Chamber of Commerce and the International Organization of Employers,* E/CN.4/Sub.2/2003/NGO/44 (July 29, 2003), http://www.unhchr.ch/Huridocda/Huridoca.nsf/3d1134784d618e28c125 6991004b7950/918bbd410b5a8d2cc1256d78002a535a?OpenDocument.

58. Ibid.

59. See *http://www.blihr.org/*.

60. Business Leaders Initiative on Human Rights, *Report 3: Towards a 'Common Framework' on Business and Human Rights: Identifying Components* (2006), http://www.blihr.org.

61. Ibid., Foreword, 2.

62. UN Commission on Human Rights E/CN.4/2004/L.11/Add.7 (2004), para. 81.

63. UN Commission on Human Rights, Res. 2005/69, *http://ap.ohchr.org/documents/E/CHR/resolutions/E-CN_4-RES-2005-69.doc.*

64. Ibid.

65. *Interim Report of the Special Representative of the Secretary-General on the Issue of Human Rights and Transnational Corporations and Other Business Enterprises,* UN Doc. E/CN.4/2006/97 (February 22, 2006), part II.B, http://www.ohchr.org/english/issues/globalization/business/reports.htm.

66. See *Report of the Special Representative of the Secretary-General on the Issue of Human Rights and Transnational Corporations and Other Business Enterprises,* UN Doc. A/HRC/4/35, Advance Edited Version (February 19, 2007), http://www.ohchr.org/english/issues/globalization/business/reports.htm.

67. Ibid., para. 10.

68. Vazques, "Direct vs. Indirect Obligations," 939.

69. *Rome Statute of the International Criminal Court,* July 17, 1998, art. 6-8, UN Doc. A/CONF.183/9, 37 I.L.M. 999, http://www.un.org/law/icc/statute/romefra.htm.

70. Ibid., art. 7.2 (a).

71. Ibid., art. 25.1. See also *Statute of the International Criminal Tribunal for Rwanda,* art. 5., S.C. Res. 955, UN Doc. S/RES/955 (1994), http://www.ictr.org/ENGLISH/basicdocs/statute.html.

72. A. Clapham, *Human Rights Obligations of Non-State Actors* (Oxford: Oxford University Press, 2006), 251.

73. *Doe v. UNOCAL,* 395 F. 3d 392 (9th Cir. 2002), vacated for rehearing en banc, 395 F. 3d 978 (2003). The full Court never heard the case, however, as it was settled. While the panel opinion is thus not formal legal precedent, its reasoning could be resurrected by other courts addressing the issue.

74. See generally Clapham, *Human Rights Obligations,* 460–99; and, for example, *Burton v. Wilmington Parking Authority,* 382 U.S. 296 (1961).

75. Development by such a process would likely enhance the "compliance pull" of the resulting norms (see T. Franck, "Legitimacy in the International System," *American Journal of International Law* 82 [1988]: 712) and ease the way for corporations to internalize them in their culture and behavior, much as states internalize international norms through an iterative process of interactions (see H. Koh, "Why Do Nations Obey International Law?," *Yale Law Journal* 106 [1997]: 2599.

76. Milton Friedman, "The Social Responsibility of Business Is to Increase Its Profits," *New York Times Magazine,* September 13, 1970.

CHAPTER 4

The Role of Corporate Actors in Peace-Building Processes

Opportunities and Challenges

John Paul Lederach

INTRODUCTION

Within the field of peace building I work in the tradition of a practitioner-scholar. I have spent more time in the field than the classroom, working with peace initiatives and people in settings of deep-rooted conflict. Three recent experiences from my work in the field speak to the challenges of commerce and peace building at both the macro and micro levels.

Several years ago I remember sitting with a number of grassroots leaders in Myanmar. While our wider focus was the question of how to approach the challenges of peace in this ultra-controlled setting, the immediate discussions swirled around recent sanctions and boycotts placed on the import of fabrics produced in Myanmar by a number of countries in the international community. Many in our group had extended family members affected by the resulting layoffs. Within weeks of the international community's actions, producer factories moved from Myanmar to China and neighboring countries; at the same time, China made several transfers of money to the military Junta. The net result, as expressed by some in the group, was a sharp rise in unemployment in the fabric sector and no noticeable effect on the government. As noted by Seagrave in *Lords of the Rim,* Chinese and diaspora-based Chinese capital moves with extraordinary ease and fluidity throughout Southeast Asia.[1] Practical capacities to mobilize the connections between peace and commerce rarely move with the same ease.

In Nepal, where civil war has been raging for nearly a decade and is now on the cusp of a major positive transformation, intriguing examples exist of innovation in the commerce sector in the midst of war. As a notable example, there is the Three Sisters Trekking Agency—a trekking company for women operated by women—formed in the years just prior to the war. They made a serious organizational commitment to employ women and to do so across caste groups, including the most marginal and excluded groups in rural areas. Thirty staff were hired and trained. The women worked and ate together. Developing their primary excursions from Pokhara, a major tourist area in Nepal that experienced a significant decline in tourism during the war, this company, unlike others, prospered. Interestingly, they undercut the Maoist revolutionary taxes, though they have no ideological or direct connection with them. Their strong sense of social justice and equality, focus on marginalized women, and inclusion of low castes served as a kind of vaccination against the demands of the Maoists, with whom they stood fast on principle, refusing to pay revolutionary taxes. Three Sisters Trekking was the only trekking agency not forced to comply with the revolutionary tax, and it was one of the few companies that has grown in size and extended its area of operations throughout the past eight years.[2]

At a training program on peace building for Catholic bishops held in San Diego in 2005, a case study emerged in our discussion about the difficulties of local conflict, the extractive industries, and globalization. In Peru a mining company based in the United States had contracts with the Peruvian government to pursue extraction of minerals. The effects of this arrangement were twofold: an increased level of employment and a sharp rise in environmental degradation and pollution. The Catholic bishop in the area began to pursue the issue of environmental impact and corporate responsibility. He found significant resistance and opposition from influential locals and those employed by the corporation because they feared losing their jobs. His strategy, as he described it, took him to Detroit and Boston, where he formed alliances with scientists who helped provide environmental assessments. Yet he increasingly experienced tension and pressure from people within his own diocese associated with the company and the government. Ironically, his efforts were received more favorably in Boston than locally.

These examples point toward the complexity of the issues faced when commerce and peace building are linked from the standpoint of on-the-ground challenges and impacts. I believe they set the stage for identifying important opportunities for and difficulties of this very necessary but much underdeveloped aspect of peace building. For the purposes of this chapter, and for those who may have had less exposure to peace building from the perspective of commerce, it will be useful to revisit several basic lenses, tools, and definitions that have emerged in the peace-building field and seem particularly relevant to this discussion.

THE LENS OF PEACE BUILDING

At the Kroc Institute for International Peace Studies at the University of Notre Dame, we have been working on our understanding of a concept we refer to as *strategic peace building*. While still under a process of definitional development, we are converging on a more concise understanding of the need for peace building to sharpen its capacity for significant impact on situations of protracted conflict. Generally speaking, protracted conflicts are those that have displayed a long history of open violence coupled with patterns of structural injustice and, therefore, have been especially difficult to transform constructively. In my own trajectory of the past twenty-five years in the field, I started using the term *strategic peace building* in the mid-1990s, mostly driven by my work with local nongovernmental organizations (NGOs) and their peace-building initiatives in these settings of deep-rooted division and open war. My concern was precisely what the research of Mary Anderson[3] bore out some years later in the field of peace building, we have too much good work that is less than strategic. The formative question is this: How exactly does constructive change happen in settings beset with cycles of violence?

Sorting through definitions of peace building can, in reality, be mind-numbing. Most definitions attempt to include such a wide range of concerns and issues that just the core concepts are enumerated in one or more paragraphs. At the Kroc Institute's recent twentieth anniversary (November 2006), I offered what I referred to as a haiku approach to the definition, or what the scientific community might refer to as the challenge of parsimony: "Peace building represents the intentional confluence—the flowing together—of improbable processes and people to sustain constructive change that reduces violence and increases the potential and practice of justice in human relationships." Each of these elements can be highlighted in more detail.

"Improbable processes and people" suggests that people and activities that would not likely come together under their own volition and connection are encouraged to do so with intentionality. This means that people who are not like minded and not like situated within the conflict context find themselves in relationship—flowing together—with a purpose of finding greater understanding and constructive engagement. In a word, this kind of confluence points toward the idea of creating space for meaningful though very unusual interaction.

Constructive change provides a goal and a direction for this flowing. In more specific terms it suggests that transformation is needed that reduces violence and increases justice in human relationships. These are not easy goals to attain in settings of violence, inequity, and structural injustice, but they clearly articulate a horizon: violence must be stopped and human dignity, equality, fairness, and human flourishing must be pursued and increased.

As we turn toward concepts that underpin this approach to strategic peace building, we find a number of challenges. At the turn of the millennium I identified three gaps in peace-building initiatives based on the rapid increase of peace processes during the 1990s: the vertical gap, the justice gap, and the interdependence gap.[4] These seem relevant to our discussion of commerce and peace building, and each illustrates both a conceptual component of peace building and a particular platform for thinking about the nexus between commerce and constructive change in settings of protracted conflict.

The vertical gap is based on a descriptive or mapping tool for looking at conflict known most commonly as "the pyramid" (see figure 1).[5] This descriptive tool suggests that conflict settings rarely have *a* "peace process." Rather, they experience multiple levels of simultaneous processes of peace building. The higher up the pyramid the more visible the process and actors, though often the key actors involved can be counted on two hands. Known as the official, or sometimes the national, peace process, and based extensively on a model of direct negotiations between leaders of warring factions and governments, this process functions as a top-down approach to peace. At the base of the pyramid we find the wide variety of local communities affected by the conflict, and within local villages, districts, and regions exist an extraordinary range of grassroots initiatives and efforts to work on peace. Being far more numerous and far less visible, these efforts propose a bottom-up approach to change. In the middle we have the range of unique spaces and efforts that link up the grassroots with the higher official process while attending to the existing divisions within the society, or what I have come to call the "web" approach to change. The web approach in particular requires the development and integration of "vertical" and "horizontal" capacities. Vertical capacity focuses on locating and encouraging relational spaces that link the higher-level people and processes with those that are engaging the grassroots. Horizontal capacity focuses on finding and sustaining relationships that cut across the existing boundaries and divisions created in and through the years of polarized conflict.

The "vertical gap" suggests that the most difficult aspect of peace building is how higher-level leaders and official initiatives connect with those myriad of people and processes located in the heart of everyday peoples' lives on the ground. We typically find that peace builders function more easily at the horizontal level—that is, they are more likely to meet with their counterpart across the divide at the level where they are located in society—but they rarely are in relationship vertically—that is, up and down within social structures. To deal with conflicts diplomats meet

Figure 4.1   Actors and Approaches to Peace Building

TYPES OF ACTORS:

Level 1: Top Leadership: Military/political/ religious leaders with high visibility

Level 2: Middle-Range Leaders: Leaders respected in sectors, ethnic/religious leaders, academics/intellectuals, and humanitarian leaders

Level 3: Grassroots Leaders: Local leaders, leaders of indigenous NGO's, community developers, health officials, refugee camp leaders

APPROACHES TO PEACE BUILDING

Level 1: Focus on high-level negotiations, emphasis on ceasefire, led by highly visible, single personality

Level 2: Problem-solving workshops, training in conflict resolution, peace commissions, insider-partial teams

Level 3: Local peace commissions, grassroots training, prejudice reduction, psychosocial work in postwar trauma

Source: John Paul Lederach, *Building Peace* (Washington, DC: U.S. Institute of Peace, 1997).

with diplomats, NGOs meet with NGOs, opinion leaders meet with opinion leaders. The vertical gap rises with how high-level officials and processes find meaningful spaces of interaction, strategic planning and participation with middle- and local-level leadership, and processes of change.

The justice gap identified a different challenge. Early peace studies pioneers suggested the useful differentiation between positive and negative peace, which included the idea of direct and structural violence.[6] Negative peace is the absence of open conflict and violence but justice is not yet present—that is, inequalities and inequities still exist though no open fighting is raging. The concepts of positive and negative peace correspond to Galtung's proposal of structural as opposed to direct violence. Structural violence arises from the impact of systems, institutions, and wider social or cultural patterns that inhibit or diminish the realization of basic human flourishing. In other words, some people benefit from the systems and social, political, and economic structures as they exist while others suffer under inequity, racism, inequality, or the inability to access basic needs, though there exists no direct, personal intent of direct, open violence.

With this differentiation as a backdrop, the field of peace building has found it easier to envision and practice a range of mechanisms and processes focused on ways to end open violence. This comes primarily through conflict resolution approaches that have evolved an increasingly sophisticated capacity, particularly through mediation, facilitation, and negotiation, to address and bring conflicting groups to agreements. Approaches of this natures are often referred to as *national peace processes* in settings of macro conflict, of which there have been more than eighty in the past twenty years.[7] The capacity to address the underlying roots of the open violence in ways that more systematically redress fundamental patterns of injustice, particularly in the arena of poverty and economic disparity, has proved more difficult for the field of peace building to achieve.

However, everyday people affected by violence have a more robust expectation of peace than the attainment of a ceasefire alone. While peace may first translate into an image of safety and security, it also has very powerful connotations about the quality of life, livelihood, and social well-being. These latter qualities are specific, including decent employment or a piece of land, a house, access to education, and food on the table. Or as they say in Spanish, *trabajo, techo, tortilla.* The justice gap happens when open violence diminishes through national accords but people's expectations for some level of incremental improvement of their basic needs are not met in practical and palpable ways. A deep sense of betrayal and of a cheap, political peace is often experienced.

A final significant gap in peace building rises from what I called the interdependence gap. A comprehensive view of peace requires that a wide range of people and processes contribute pieces to a very complex puzzle of change as whole societies move from deep division, structural injustice, and open violence toward a new way of relating. In such complex processes of change no one process, person, or level of activity can initiate, build, deliver, and sustain peace on its own. Peace as a dynamic and complex phenomenon requires a myriad of contributions and wide participation. In turn, this requires that people understand that in order to achieve some level of sustainability in the change they seek, they and their particular piece of the wider puzzle must be in relationship with other actors, levels, processes, and activities.

The interdependence gap rises from an inability to see oneself and preferred activities as needing and relying on others, including those that on the surface appear distant, different, and perhaps even threatening. Constructive change cannot be achieved in isolation from the complexity of a very diverse multilayered and multileveled world of actors and activities. In a word, peace requires a rather strong dose of humility. Peace is not possible to control from or by a single actor or activity. People and processes, no matter at what level of society, must envision their interests and goals as not only related but ultimately dependent on a wide range of factors that includes others, even those they may most dislike, fear, or wish to ignore.

OPPORTUNITIES

Given this basic range of lenses we can address more directly the opportunities for commerce and the business sector to contribute to peace building. First, commerce links two key elements necessary to peace building: livelihood and relational interdependence. Business fundamentally operates according to the capacity to bring together diverse sets of people within and beyond a given context, from employment and production to locating and providing resources and linking those resources with outlets where they are needed and useful. In all instances this requires relationship building with a wide range of people. In addition, commerce functions on the basis of meeting human needs, many of which are related to very basic needs.

In recent years we have seen a sharp increase in the cooperation between the fields of sustainable development and conflict transformation. The conflict transformation field focuses on how to get polarized, conflicting groups to cooperate on common initiatives, while the development field is concerned with increasing the capacity of local communities and groups to sustain and improve their lives. The nexus of the two creates energy, particularly around processes that link livelihood needs and cooperation across lines of conflict. With imagination and innovation, business and commerce can serve as an extraordinary center of that nexus.

Second, inherent to the activities and needs of commerce and the wider business community are unnoticed and unique relational spaces and relationships in reference to conflict settings. These often cut both vertically and horizontally across the divisions within societies. In other words, good business practice requires an ability to develop relationships across lines of conflict and from local to national and global levels. This is pursued, in my mind, not so much due to visionary insight about peace building but rather due to the inherent goal of commerce: achieve a profit. Nonetheless, this practice suggests two important things. On the one hand, good business practices often have developed an unusual knack to understand and build on relational spaces where very diverse sets of people must interact, understand each other, and move in common directions. Second, business entrepreneurs, generally, are less concerned with the polarizing demands of conflict than with what they need to do good business. By virtue of this adventurous spirit they frequently find themselves as forerunners moving across lines of polarization, sometimes to the chagrin of their corresponding politicians.

Finally, commerce has what the conflict and peace-building fields refer to as "the power of the convener." In settings of polarization a rather consistent strategy for overcoming its paralyzing effect on a society and groups is to ask who people on various sides of a conflict might accept as a leader in convening a common process, meeting, or encounter. Typically, this is seen as the role of quasi-mediator. More broadly, however, it often involves finding unique points of commonality around which enemies can agree to sit and talk. Commerce and business, with its potential for livelihood, resources, and benefits, can often serve in very unique ways to create this kind of a "magnet."

CHALLENGES

These opportunities are accompanied by a series of important challenges that cannot be minimized for the commerce and business community working in settings of conflict. First and foremost, the fact that opportunity may exist and that a general ability to work with people of different persuasions and interests does not automatically translate into a capacity to understand and creatively deal with the level of intensity that accompanies settings of deep-rooted and violent conflict. The commerce sector would be well advised to develop both a greater capacity to analyze the dynamics and process of conflict and its constructive transformation and to know when specialized expertise in outside facilitation process design is needed. Perhaps the worst case scenarios are ones where overconfidence prevails concerning the ability of commerce entrepreneurs to do this on its own. The simple antidote is basic good business practice: make sure the best expertise for the situation—in this case, commerce working in settings of deep social conflict—is found and engaged. For the business sector this places an equal emphasis on conflict analysis and process facilitation as may be placed on security. It certainly affirms and suggests a partnership that more closely links the fields of peace building and commerce.

Second, commerce often operates on too narrow a view of self-interest and too short of a time frame for gauging success when working in areas of social strife. Settings of conflict require that commerce think about success in terms of broad and diverse constituencies rather than one driven by self, company, or profits. When that happens the business sector loses sight of the uniqueness of its wider interdependence. Conflict settings, particularly those that have a longer protracted history, cannot be redressed through quick solutions. While the profit lines are driven by the literal and metaphoric image of quarterly reports, success in places where conflict is highly polarized requires a long-term commitment to relationship building and needs to be held in a wider metaphor of strategic investment rather than quick turn around. If the exclusive goal of commerce, given the nature of a particular company or business, is a quick turn of profit based on an in and out action, I believe ethical questions must be raised about how this affects, and likely adds to rather than alleviates, the volatility of the conflict and those affected by it locally.

As a final observation, partnership with peace building expands the frame of reference for accountability that commerce may typically employ. Many companies use shareholders and investors as their point of reference for accountability. Peace building suggests that when commerce engages parties in settings of protracted conflict, a shift from shareholders to stakeholders gains importance. Beyond shareholders, stakeholders suggests a wider accountability is needed that recognizes and engages those affected by commerce-related decisions and processes in the setting of conflict. Framing accountability as including stakeholders requires that commerce act creatively in seeking out spaces of participation and benefit that include those who bring hard capital, social capital, and moral capital. While those with social capital would inquire how people affected by the commerce are included and taken into consideration, stakeholders with moral capital would ask how the wider social good and flourishing of local communities in conflict are affected by the presence and activity of the particular businesses involved.

CONCLUSION

The gaps identified in peace building potentially may be redressed through a greater connect between actors in the peace process and the business and commerce sector. Two immediate points of summary come to mind from our discussion. First, commerce may be among the most well-positioned and experienced sectors that constantly create and nurture vertical capacity. The basic necessity of business to hone a wider interdependence among people who are not like minded or like situated— because commerce, to be successful, must find ways to relate to and move seamlessly between higher-level leadership and the grassroots—creates unique potential for the intersection with peace building. Second, commerce also finds itself in a unique position to mobilize and bring livelihood and basic justice issues to the fore in concrete ways. Given that commerce has the potential to create mechanisms that can potentially increase employment, provide services and goods, and generate wealth, commerce is inherently attractive to people struggling to meet their basic needs across the divisions of protracted conflict.

In sum, interestingly, commerce has the potential to help address the vertical, the interdependence, and the justice gaps found in peace building. Conversely, peace building may have many tools and processes that could enhance the ability of commerce to be present in new and more effective ways in settings of conflict. The fundamental question may be one of mutual recognition and partnership between these two broad fields. For peace building this suggests the need to recognize in commerce its unique potential, which for too long has been ignored. For commerce in settings of social conflict, the challenge is how to develop a perspective that includes and addresses the well-being of local communities caught in cycles of strife as part and parcel of investment, accountability, and outcome of their activities.

NOTES

1. Sterling Seagrave, *Lords of the Rim* (New York: Putnam Books, 1995).

2. Ameet Dhakal, "Supporting National, Provincial and Grassroots Private Sector Actors in Peace-Building" (draft paper presented to International Alert, 2005).

3. Mary Anderson, *Do No Harm: Supporting Local Capacities for Peace Through Aid* (Boulder, CO: Lynne Reiner, 1999).

4. John Paul Lederach, "Justpeace: The Challenge of the 21st Century," in *People Building Peace* (Utrecht: European Centre for Conflict Prevention, 1999).

5. Ibid., fig. 1.

6. Adam Curle, *Making Peace* (London: Tavistock Press, 1971); Johan Galtung, *Essays in Peace Research* (Oslo, Norway: PRIO Institute, 1975); and Kenneth Boulding, *The Image* (Ann Arbor: University of Michigan Press, 1984).

7. John Darby and Roger MacGinty, *Contemporary Peacemaking* (New York: Palgrave, 2003).

CHAPTER 5

Broad-Based Black Economic Empowerment and the Deracialization of the South African Economy

Willie Esterhuyse

INTRODUCTION

Globally the debate on the changing role of business in society recently has gained momentum in both scope and intensity. The Millennium Developmental Goals (MDGs), the UN Global Compact, the World Summit on Sustainable Development, the increasing importance and role of civil society and globally connected NGOs, the influence of global leaders such as Kofi Annan, and international conferences on the issue of Peace through Commerce provided much-needed energy and focus to an idea and new trend "whose time has come."

This energy and focus have not bypassed South Africa, a relatively young democracy and a country still in the throes of a complex transition. In fact, the transition from authoritarian rule to democracy gave additional leverage to the private sector to play a more decisive social role than it was allowed to play under authoritarian conditions. The private sector, including international companies, admittedly played an important role in preparing the ground for South Africa's transition, with many companies practicing forms of brinkmanship. Most of them, for either moral or strategic reasons—or both—did not ascribe to the traditionalist view of corporations as "islands of managerial coordination in a sea of market relationships."[1] In fact, given the nature of the apartheid system and its impact on social, political, economic, educational, and environmental issues, business leaders could not allow themselves the luxury to ascribe to the view that their responsibilities "stopped at the boundaries of their firms." They were obliged to accept the idea of the "boundaryless corporation."[2]

Concerning the idea of Peace through Commerce, South Africa provides a special case. The translation of this idea into applicable policy terms, however, requires careful consideration of the context. The idea will be ineffective if the context is not well-understood. This chapter will, first of all, consider some of the characteristics of the new worldwide support for the idea of Peace through Commerce. A "national context" is inevitably interconnected and interrelated with the global context. In fact, part and parcel of South Africa's emerging democracy is acceptance of the principle of multilaterism and the reality of interconnectivity and interdependence. From this broader perspective the focus will shift to the South African context. South Africa's transition will be discussed, including some of the policy requirements and policy positions taken.

THE GLOBAL CONTEXT

As discussed in the introduction to this volume, the post–World War II interest in commerce's ability to foster peace has recently gained momentum through the emergence of the global economy. The increasing willingness of the business community to form partnerships with NGOs has opened important new avenues for achieving social development. From these and other signals it should be clear that "partnerships as the new paradigm" has emerged as a new trend in the world's search for answers to developmental and other global problems. The emphasis on business, and their relationship with NGOs, has taken on a new and very promising dimension, as borne out by a wealth of literature on the connections and interactions between business, government, and society.

To give perspective to this dimension, it is necessary to refer to the Millennium Development Goals (see chapter 16). The target date of 2015 for achieving these goals is rather ambitious and is coincidentally close to the target dates set by the South African government for goals such as land reform and Broad-Based Black Economic Empowerment (BBEE). At the World Summit on Sustainable Development, a set of very similar goals was accepted, although the emphasis here was on natural resource and energy issues. Discussion papers on the reform of the governance structures of international financial institutions are emerging. Panel discussions on the UN in the twenty-first century, and how to deal with new threats, challenges, and change, have raised the level of consciousness regarding global cooperation and rule making. An insightful contribution in this regard, and one that reflects the new consciousness, is Susan Rice's "The Social and Economic Foundations of Peace and Security: Implications for Developed Countries."[3]

Another dimension in the discussion is the focus on the increasing importance and role of civil society and, in particular, NGOs. This discussion highlights ways in which civil society organizations could be strengthened and enhanced in order to promote a peaceful and secure future. In fact, it is conceded that globally connected civil society organizations, whether in an institutionalized form or specifically organized around pressing issues, have played a decisive role in the trend toward greater transparency in both the UN and global economic institutions. In the case of South Africa, the strong trend toward workable partnerships between business and NGOs is one of many reforms inspired by the government's acceptance of the importance of civil society and its network of NGOs. The MDGs and the World Summit on Sustainability are important driving forces in these developments.

Sweden, incidentally, is regarded as a front runner in realizing the idea of Peace through Commerce in everyday life; the idea was incorporated into a policy position by the Swedish government and enacted in the 2003 bill Shared Responsibility—Sweden's Policy for Global Development. Development aid remains a priority and is envisaged to increase to 1 percent of GDP. Most important, however, was the decision to align all government policies around a guiding principle of equitable and sustainable global development.[4] The paradigmatic thinking behind this new consciousness and its policy articulation is represented by what has become known as "Society as the Macroenvironment." The importance of this phrase has been enhanced by globalization and the new security threats that accompany this process.

SOCIETY AS THE MACROENVIRONMENT

The idea of the macroenvironment was thoroughly developed by Fahey and Narayanam.[5] Theyidentified four interlocking and interacting components in the macroeconomic environment: social, economic, political, and technological. One of their main arguments was that shifts in the core factors of the *social environment* (demographics, lifestyles, and social values) have an impact on all organizations, including business organizations, and their functioning. The *economic environmental* component focuses on the nature, direction, and impact of value creation, with civil society increasingly becoming a referee regarding who should obtain "the license to operate." The *political component,* affecting such things as the process of policy making, regulation, taxation, long-term planning, and the quality of governance, has a decisive impact on society and business, both negative and positive. The *technological component,* in particular technological change, directs and facilitates development and processes in all of the other components of the macroenvironment. As a result of this view of the macroenvironment, the idea of the corporation as an island in a sea of market relationships has become something of the past, with "pluralism" now the name of the game; wide decentralization and diversity of power concentration has become the norm. Power has become dispersed as a result of continuing democratization and globalization, and civil society organizations in developed countries are benefiting from this with regard to the issue of power.

The MDGs, the emphasis on sustainable development, and conference themes such as Peace through Commerce display the fundamentally changed views on the interactive relationships between business, government, and society. Such views require a rethinking of the way in which these relationships should be developed and managed. They also underline something very significant, that is, an acknowledgment of the decisive importance of business in the developmental process given the expertise of business in the macroenvironment. In important instances, and among significant stakeholders, the view of business as capitalist villain has changed for the better; business is now viewed as a partner, and in some instances even as a savior.

The idea of Peace through Commerce is given practical effect in a number of ways. For example, the joint statement of a task force of the World

Economic Forum, "Global Corporate Citizenship: The Leadership Challenge for CEO's and Boards," contains a framework for action.[6] The explanation for the statement mentions the need for business leaders and managers "to develop a strategy for managing their company's impact on society and its relationship with stakeholders." It makes the point that issues such as corporate responsibility, sustainable development, and the triple bottom line are "not an 'add-on' but are fundamental to core business operations"; hence the objective "to identify some key leadership actions that can be adapted by most business leaders to their own circumstances."

The declaration, focusing on the challenge to leadership posed by the forces of globalization, political transition, and technical innovation, sounded a positive note in that these challenges have created new opportunities for the improvement of the living standards of millions of people. The declaration admitted the existence of widespread concerns that the potential could be destroyed. It noted the fact that many people are still facing high levels of inequality, insecurity, and uncertainty. New sources of conflict, environmental decline, and lack of opportunity are also presenting serious risks to many. The declaration stated that "leaders from all countries, sectors and levels of society need to work together to address these challenges by supporting sustainable human development and ensuring that the benefits of globalization are shared more widely. It is in the interests of business that these benefits continue both for companies and for others in society."[7] How are these challenges being met in the South African context?

THE SOUTH AFRICAN CONTEXT

It is important to note that South Africa is a country in transition. Transitions from authoritarian rule to democracy are structural in nature; they are managed revolutions over time, not adaptations. In the case of South Africa, given the nature and legacy of the apartheid system, the transition is playing itself out on, broadly speaking, three interrelated levels: the political level, the economic level, and the social level.

In an early 1990s scenario exercise[8] sponsored by two major South African companies, (Old Mutual and Nedcor), the team—of which I was a member—argued that a successful transition should meet at least the following requirements: (1) a stable democracy; (2) rising incomes (earned rather than borrowed); (3) a reasonable distribution of incomes; and (4) a stable social fabric. An important assumption—albeit not the only assumption—was that a very close relationship exists between democracy and income levels. Democracies are more sustainable in higher-income countries. Generally speaking, South Africa has done quite well with regard to the first two requirements. The country has been less successful on requirement 3 and is, in the case of requirement 4 (social capital and social cohesion), still in a very problematic state.

Incidentally, this particular requirement is multifaceted—requiring policy interventions by the state and committed, consistent, and concerted actions by the leaders and organizations of civil society. The state and its institutions alone cannot create a stable social fabric—at least not if the state is of a democratic nature. Failure in this respect is in the main a failure of civil society, and civil society, of course, is not a creation or extension of the state (in a democracy). The state, admittedly, has to create the material, regulatory, security, and other conditions under which civil society can flourish. In transitional societies, with high levels of social instability and violence, a partnership between the state, business, and organizations of civil society designed to effectively deal with the issue of social disintegration—or, positively stated, the creation of social capital—is of paramount importance.

The Nedcor/Old Mutual scenario team concluded that South Africa needed three miracles: a peaceful political transition; a resuscitation of the economy; and social development. The team described the last miracle as the most difficult and warned that it would take a few generations to be realized. The first phase, political transition, took less than five years (from February 1990 to April 1994). The second phase, economic resuscitation, took ten years (from 1996 to 2006) and is of course ongoing work. The third phase, social development, is where we are now. And it must be stated quite bluntly: Violence inhibits successful transitions because it impacts negatively on the creation and broadening of social capital in historically divided societies.

South Africa ascribes to the MDGs, the objectives of the World Summit on Sustainable Development, and other global initiatives on the issue of development. One can safely say that South Africa's economic transition—that is, the restructuring of the South African economy and the integration of the restructured economy into a globalizing economy (a very complex process)—was a remarkable success. Making a profound impact on poverty, joblessness, and social stability, however, has been less successful and visible. The country's "pyramid of socio-economic migration" is not as solid and progressive as it should be.[9]

At the bottom of the pyramid we find the underclass, subsistors, and survivors, constituting roughly 30 percent of the total population. They are followed by the informal entrepreneurs, who are active in the informal economy, and those making a living from nonpermanent work. They constitute roughly 20 percent of the population. The "entrants," "participators," "movers and shakers," "big guns," and "rich and retired" make up the other 50 percent of the population. Thus, South Africa is still a society in which socioeconomic inequality is depressingly high, constituting an extremely complex situation. Although the very close relationship between race and class has improved for the better, the conflict inherent in the existing overlap of race and class, together with the continuing violence in the country, pose serious challenges to government and business. The democratized social macroeconomic environment, as well as the acceptance of the MDGs and the objectives of the World Summit on Sustainable Development, have inevitably created very high expectations among the poor, of which the vast majority is black and young.

BROAD-BASED BLACK ECONOMIC EMPOWERMENT

How to deracialize the South African economy, creating opportunities and a better life for all as well as establishing a nonracial middle class, is—within the South African context—the primary issue if one talks about Peace through Commerce. It has to be kept in mind that the old apartheid state has been transformed into a market-friendly developmental state—a social democracy rather than a typical liberal democracy. Whether South African businesses fully understand this transformation is doubtful. BBEE fits into the present government's dream of a nonracial, market-friendly social democracy. It is a structured policy intervention by the state aimed at redressing the inequalities of the past, as well as creating opportunities and access for people deliberately disadvantaged because of ideological and racist reasons. Or, stated somewhat controversially: Is a deracialized middle class, with shared values and interests, possible in an ethnically divided society in which the wealth of the country is still in the hands of the previously privileged ethnic minority? Will such a middle class impact constructively on the pressing issues of poverty, skills shortage, social disintegration, and joblessness?

One must take serious cognisance of the fact that those with a socialist ideological inclination, like, for instance, the unions united in Cosatu, are well-informed about South Africa's inequalities. Based on an analysis of data from the year 2000, the World Bank reported that South Africa ranks twelfth in terms of socioeconomic inequalities among 126 countries, such as Bolivia, Colombia, Brazil, and Paraguay.[10] BBEE is a deliberate state intervention to impact constructively on the situation. It is, in the first place, a developmental project aimed at creating access and opportunities for the historically disadvantaged. As such it makes political, strategic, and moral sense because it creates space for viable partnerships and the sharing of wealth and opportunities across a very broad spectrum. In fact, it is a new way of doing business in South Africa.

The Broad-Based Black Economic Empowerment Act (2003) provided the legal framework for government to achieve its empowerment objectives. On the basis of this act, Empowerment Codes of Good Practice were developed, which provide practical guidelines for the implementation of Broad-Based Black Economic Empowerment. This means "that business in South Africa will in future have to comply with BBEE legislation (such as the Employment Equity Act and Preferential Procurement Policy Framework Act) as well as meet other non-legal requirements (such as black shareholding) in order to retain their competitive position."[11]

The BBEE Code includes a "scorecard," or a set of quantifiable guidelines, in terms of which a company's compliance with the BBEE policy should be measured; a company's compliance determines its access to state-funded projects or other forms of financial assistance. These guidelines include access to equity (shareholding), including board representation; management control; skills training; corporate social responsibility (corporate citizenship); employment equity; the development of new enterprises; and preferential procurement. The outcome of this policy initiative is something quite significant: mandatory black economic empowerment charters that outline targets for specific industries, such as building and construction, communications and technology, etc.

Admittedly—and as a negative of "political credibility"—some (black) newcomers on the economic scene became very rich over a short period of time. There was corruption, such as "fronting"—that is, putting "black faces" up front but without decision-making powers or responsibility. Despite these negatives, however, major strides were taken in deracializing South Africa's economy. Initially, "equity" (shareholding) dominated. A new, very positive, trend is toward capacity building and skills training. Another positive trend is the setting up of multiracial partnerships, contributing to the creation of much-needed social capital as well as competitive advantage through diversity.

CONCLUSION

South Africa's emerging developmental state has taken an active role in molding the interactive relationships between business, society, and government. It accepts the decisive importance of business in the developmental process and is actively trying through policy interventions to provide leadership and direction in this regard. It is accepted, as a policy position, that sustainable development within the global and South African context requires viable public-private sector partnerships. This view, however, is premised on the assumption that, given the legacy of apartheid and the nature of South Africa's socioeconomic inequalities, the state has a political and moral obligation to intervene in the structure of the economy. BBEE is an example of such an intervention.

A very promising facet of what has been achieved is a growing consensus between business, political, and societal leaders on the requirements for successful partnerships across the divide of race and culture. These requirement include sharing of risk and reward; long-term relationships; capacity and capability building; shared values; and trust and confidence among partners. We have reason to believe that "a better life for all" is within our reach.

NOTES

1. G. B. Richardson, "The Organization of Industry," *Economic Journal* (October 1972): 883.

2. Joseph L. Badaracco, *Business Ethics: Roles and Responsibilities* (Boston: Irwin, 1995), 395.

3. Susan Rice, "The Social and Economic Foundations of Peace and Security: Implications for Developed Countries" (Report for the UN and Global Security Project, 2004), http://www.un-globalsecurity.org/pdf/Rice_paper2.pdf.

4. H. French, G. Gardner, and E. Assadourian "Laying the Foundations for Peace," in *State of the World 2005,* ed. L. Starke (New York: W.W. Norton, 2005), 171.

5. Liam Fahey and V. K. Narayanam, *Macroenvironmental Analysis for Strategic Management* (St. Paul, MN: West Publishing, 1986), 28–30.

6. World Economic Forum, "Global Corporate Citizenship: The Leadership Challenge for CEO's and Boards" (January 2002), http://www.weforum.org/pdf/GCCI/GCC_CEOstatement.pdf.

7. Ibid.

8. Bob Tucker and Bruce R. Scott, *South Africa–Prospects for a Successful Transition* (Kenwyn: Jura, 1992).

9. Unpublished paper by W. P. Esterhuyse (2000).

10. United Nations Development Programme, *Human Development Report 2005: International Cooperation at a Crossroads: Aid, Trade, and Security in an Unequal World* (New York: UNDP, 2005).

11. Frans van Wyle, personal discussion with the author, October 2006. Van Wyle is an expert on empowerment issues at PriceWaterhouseCoopers.

PART III

Some Lessons from the Experience
of Seasoned Professionals

CHAPTER 6

False Promises and Premises?

The Challenge of Peace Building
for Corporations

Mary Anderson

Peace cannot be mined, manufactured, outsourced, hired, contracted, bought, or sold. Peace is essentially a political process, not an economic one. How, then, is peace the business of business? Do corporations really have any business engaging in peace building? In the following pages I will argue both that they do not—and that they do. Building on the collected experience of many peace agencies and on the experience of multiple corporations that have operations in areas of conflict, this chapter will delineate the aspects of peace building that fall outside the purview of corporations and, then, describe the very real and direct ways in which corporate activities can have profound influence on the likelihood that peace is, or is not, achievable.

The chapter is organized into four sections. The first section describes two projects run by CDA Collaborative Learning Projects, of which I am the executive director. These projects provide the evidence on which this chapter is based. In the second section we turn to an examination of peace building, outlining the factors that, experience shows, are central to effective peace work. We then report on findings with regard to the interactions of corporations with conflict and with peace, showing how, through their daily operations, companies can have potentially significant impacts on peace and conflict. Finally, we bring the learning about peace building and corporate interactions with peace and conflict together to draw conclusions regarding the practical ways in which, indeed, corporations can and should assume limited but meaningful responsibility for the pursuit of peace.

BACKGROUND AND EVIDENCE

Two "collaborative learning projects" provide the information and evidence for the arguments put forth in this chapter. As developed by CDA,[1] a collaborative learning project is a process through which a large group of agencies involved in some type of activity join together to pool their experiences. By analyzing their experiences comparatively across many contexts, they can derive useful lessons for how to achieve their intended results more effectively. The two projects that provide data for this chapter are the Reflecting on Peace Practice (RPP) project, which includes a broad range of agencies involved in conflict prevention and peace building worldwide, and the Corporate Engagement Project (CEP), which involves a range of international corporations that work in societies where there is conflict and instability.

Over six years ago, acknowledging the increasing number of nongovernmental peace initiatives that have been undertaken since the 1990s, CDA organized a collaborative effort in which individuals and agencies involved in such work could assemble and analyze their collective experience. Since its beginning, the Reflecting on Peace Practice project has engaged well over two hundred agencies involved in peace work around the world. Of the agencies involved, about one-third are international, meaning that they cross borders to work on conflicts in other nations, The remaining two-thirds are local; they are based in an area of conflict and work directly on solving that conflict. The purpose of the effort was to systematically compare and analyze the broad range of existing experiences in order to learn what does and does not work, and why, in conflict prevention and peace building.

Experience was gathered through a series of field-based case studies. Each case followed a particular peace effort and asked the following questions: What did the peace effort intend to do? What actually happened? How do people judge the impacts of the effort? What evidence do they cite to support their judgments? As the case studies were written, CDA brought together groups of active peace practitioners in three-day workshops to read and analyze the findings. As cases were written and multiple workshops were held, the analysis continually deepened. Over time, through this iterative process, it has been possible to identify which issues and factors appear again and again, across varying contexts, and which are specific to local circumstances. Through sorting the general from the contextual, the group involved in the RPP has been able to derive specific lessons about how to improve the effectiveness of their future peace work.

Similarly, over five years ago, CDA began a collaborative learning project involving a number of international corporations that have operations in conflict areas. This Corporate Engagement Project employed the same process of collecting the experiences of individual corporations in over twenty locations around the world and comparing and analyzing these experiences in consultations involving corporate managers and others.[2] Similarly, this project has identified a number of lessons about how corporations influence the circumstances of peace and conflict.

Both of these projects are ongoing; we continue to gather experience and to derive lessons for improving impacts. Therefore, the evidence provided in the following sections does not constitute a "final word." However, much has been learned that is helpful for identifying the processes that are likely to contribute to peace and for examining how corporations relate to these processes.

Before turning to these findings, it is important to clarify one definition and offer one caveat. First, as we use the word *conflict* in the pages that follow, we will always be referring to destructive, often violent, intergroup conflict. There are other useful ways to use this word, including to refer to the dynamics of disagreement and struggle that often underlie social and political progress. For our purposes, however, our meaning is always focused on conflict that is destructive and dangerous in its effect on relations among societal groups and that often ends in open warfare.

Second, the evidence we offer below is always focused on international peace agencies and/or international corporations. Through the RPP and CEP projects we have found that the lessons for international agencies differ in some significant respects from the experiences of local NGOs and local businesses. It is important, therefore, that the following be read as applicable only to agencies that work in countries other than their own.

WHAT HAS BEEN LEARNED ABOUT EFFECTIVE PEACE WORK

From the many lessons gathered through the Reflecting on Peace Practice Project, five findings seem of particular relevance for our purposes of examining how corporations can and cannot be effectively involved in peace.

There is no clear knowledge about how to do effective peace work. The evidence shows that much (and perhaps most) peace practice is not as effective as those who undertake it intend and hope it will be. That is, although many people work on peace, the record of success is mixed and, largely, disappointing. This is not a judgment made by CDA. Rather, this is the judgment of many who are, themselves, engaged in peace work. We learned this because, in the consultations of peace practitioners organized by the RPP, we often asked people to assess their own effectiveness. To do this, we asked that they give themselves a "grade" (from A for excellent to F for failure) for some peace activity in which they had been involved. With remarkable consistency, these highly motivated, intelligent, and dedicated people self-reported that, although they gave themselves an A for effort, their *results* only deserved anywhere from a C (passable) to an F (failure). Consistently, people felt that they worked hard but that they had less than desired effectiveness. Although many people work on peace, the field of peace building is not yet a well-defined field with clear guidelines for how to achieve desired results.

There are reasons why peace practitioners do not concern themselves with effectiveness. Given the evidence of weak effectiveness, we next asked why this was the case. Many peace practitioners act out of a deep concern for the suffering they see around them. Many assert that it is better to do anything for peace than to do nothing. They feel that any good effort—that is, anything undertaken to improve any aspect of people's lives—will ultimately contribute to a larger "peace." In addition, many peace efforts are small and funding is modest. As a result, many people feel that they cannot expect too much from any given peace effort; many say that, because peace takes a long time to achieve, they cannot know whether or not they are effective until many years later. All of these attitudes and beliefs can work together to weaken strategic analysis and planning. If one thinks all good works will, in some way and over time, "add up" to peace, and this belief is combined with the notion that we cannot really know our effectiveness until some years hence, then the motivation—even urgency—to assess the effectiveness of every small peace effort is undermined.

To be effective, peace programming must be focused specifically on a conflict analysis. The RPP found that to be effective, a peace activity must be based on an up-to-date and accurate analysis of the conflict. A *conflict analysis* differs in important ways from a *context analysis.* Whereas a context analysis includes a comprehensive review of all social, economic, political, environmental, demographic, and historical (etc.) issues, a conflict analysis should be focused explicitly on identifying the key driving factors for and actors in the specific conflict at a specific time. Many factors in a context may be important for the quality of people's lives, but not all will be central to whether or not a conflict emerges or continues.

Many activities are undertaken by concerned people who want to promote peace based more on a context analysis than on a conflict analysis. As a result, we often see projects and programs that are helpful to the people who are involved in them but that, in the context of an intergroup conflict, are either irrelevant to the conflict or, in some cases, actually worsen intergroup relations. For example, after the end of the civil war in Afghanistan, some agencies promoted postwar development through microfinance projects for women. Often such projects are organized so that women receive their loans in a group and, as a group, are responsible for repayment. This model has been successful in a number of locations where women are poor and have little access to credit. The Afghan planners knew that these two conditions—poverty and little access to credit—existed in the context of post-conflict Afghanistan.

With additional conflict analysis (as opposed to context analysis), however, these planners realized that groups that would include women who had remained in the villages during the war as well as women who had just returned from refugee camps in Pakistan could face important intergroup challenges. Whether people remained in Afghanistan or fled to Pakistan often reflected divided political and clan alliances. If, in the microcredit program, a woman from one group failed to repay her loan on time, rather than all women readily helping her due to a sense of common identity, there was a high probability that the existing, deep political and experiential differences between the two groups of women (those who stayed and those who left) would be exacerbated. The Afghan planners of one such microcredit program, realizing the circumstances that divided the women they intended to include in the program, reconsidered the usefulness of their approach. By analyzing how the conflict affected the relations of the two groups, they redesigned their program in order to address directly these continuing divisions and ways of overcoming them. The redesigned program was, therefore, a much more effective peace program; it dealt directly with the realities of conflict rather than simply "doing something good."

A conflict analysis is the basis of strategic peace programming. Experience shows that a conflict analysis must include, at a minimum, two things. First, it must identify and clarify the key driving factors of and the key constituencies involved in the conflict. That is, a conflict analysis must determine which, of all the many issues at play in a context, are the issues that underlie and are central to the divisions that drive the conflict. It must identify the specific people, individuals, and groups who gain through the conflict and those who can be most instrumental in ending or reversing conflict. Without an understanding of and focus on the issues and individuals who drive the conflict, many well-intended peace activities "miss the mark." They may do "good work," but this work may be disconnected from the driving factors, or constituencies, of the conflict. Although it seems self-evident, it is (we have found) worth stating that it is critical to identify with precision what the war is about if one intends to work on ending it.

Second, the Reflecting on Peace Practice project also found that it is important for a conflict analysis to ask "What is the war *not* about?" This question, again, highlights the fact that all issues that are of importance in a society are not, essentially, also of importance to that society's conflictive status. This is a lesson that surprised me personally when I learned it. As an economist I had believed that by working on economic development—by working to enlarge the "pie" so that all could enjoy more goods—I was also, *ipso facto,* working on peace. If scarcity were a factor in conflict, I reasoned, then by reducing scarcity my work would also be reducing the likelihood of conflict. Through several CDA collaborative learning projects, I found that I was sadly and completely mistaken.

The evidence shows instead that the introduction of new resources into a resource-scarce society that is also in conflict rarely (if ever) leads to people sharing these resources and living happily together. Rather, resources brought into a conflict environment always become a part of the conflict. The warring sides see the resources both as the spoils of war ("If we are the stronger side, we can gain access to these things") and as the means of war ("If we control these things, we can use them to fight better against the other side").

Further, the evidence shows that greed, not poverty, is often a key driving factor of warfare. All war leaders claim that the battles they fight are undertaken to achieve "justice" for the poor. In addition, it is true that poor people fight in wars and, as warriors, sometimes have access to a livelihood that they would not otherwise. However, few wars are actually started by poor people as a means for gaining economic justice, and war is not ever an effective instrument for achieving economic justice and equality. Rather, war enriches some people and impoverishes many more. Some people gain a great deal economically, but the majority, and especially the poor, suffer losses of livelihoods, infrastructure, health, education, and more as wars are fought. For corporate managers, this finding should not be surprising. We often have seen how the entry of a corporation into a poor area sets into motion a series of demands and intergroup competition and struggle among local people for access to corporate resources that can have significant and lasting negative impacts on that area.

Peace essentially is not achievable through economic processes. Peace is not essentially about economics; it is about politics. Peace seems to rest on political arrangements in which people have confidence. Such political arrangements are seen as providing predictable and acceptable processes for redressing injustice and unfairness when it occurs. Economic processes may buttress, or undermine, such political arrangements, but, by themselves, they cannot ensure peace.

"Peace is not an area for amateurs." Finally, this "lesson" was strongly stated by one of the experienced peace practitioners involved in the RPP. This woman has been involved in many peace initiatives in her own region, which has been embroiled in conflict for many years. She has seen many international peace activists come to her region to "do peace work." And, she has seen many of these efforts fail and even worsen the situation. Her plea was that those who intend to become involved in peace take on the discipline and learning required to be effective.

The evidence of our research supports this comment. International actors who intend to engage effectively in peace processes must possess certain key skills. They must be able to do accurate and up-to-date conflict analysis. They must be able to establish comfortable, trusting, and transparent relationships with a wide range of people and types of people, often including those who do not share their own values. They must have mediation skills, including highly specialized listening and responding skills, through which effective peace practitioners are able to identify common concerns that can unite antagonists while also respecting fundamental differences and opposing positions. Finally, peace practitioners must have the ability to be calm and comfortable in situations of danger, threat, and emotional and physical stress.

These are the lessons learned about peace practice that are relevant for our discussion of the role of corporations and businesses in peace. Peace practice is not easy. The skills that are central are not common, everyday skills found among corporate managers. The centrality of accurate conflict analysis, and the importance of politics over economics in the achievement of peace, provide a cautionary background for any corporate efforts to connect with, and promote, peace.

THE EXPERIENCE OF INTERNATIONAL CORPORATIONS IN CONFLICT AREAS

What has been observed about the role of international corporations in conflict areas? What lessons can be derived from this experience? CDA's Corporate Engagement Project has found several general patterns across varying contexts that are helpful as we consider these questions. The first finding of note is that when a corporation has operations in a context of conflict, the corporation becomes a part of that context and, hence, has direct influence on the conflict (or potential conflict). Even when a company has a policy of noninterference in political issues and claims to maintain a neutral stance in relation to the issues driving a conflict, by its very presence it is seen by people in the country to be involved. The impacts of corporate operations in areas of conflict are, the evidence shows, never neutral.

The second finding relates to the resources that a company's presence introduces into the context. As noted above, these are, inevitably, viewed by people in the context as relevant, instrumental, and useful in relation to any power struggles that are underway. Furthermore, the evidence shows that these resources do have direct, and often negative, impacts on conflict by exacerbating, prolonging, and worsening the divisions in societies. The CEP found that a company's most significant impacts on conflict occur as a result of its daily, core operations and not, as many expect, through its explicit community relations programs. There are four ways in which daily operations may have negative impacts on local conflicts.

Distributional Impacts

When a company enters a poor area where there are tensions, every decision about how to transfer funds into that society has distributional implications.³ Some people benefit and some people do not. When the benefits all go to one particular group of people and not to another group, and these two groups are engaged in potential or actual conflict, the resources are seen to strengthen one group vis-à-vis the other. This feeds conflict. For example, many companies hire "on merit," with the intention of avoiding bias or any appearance of bias in employment opportunities. However, in areas where there are historical patterns of privilege and exclusion that have favored some groups and marginalized others, especially where such patterns have had implications for educational access and completion, the decision to hire on merit in fact reinforces the historical advantage/disadvantage divide. In some instances, even where a company hires many young men and feels it is, thereby, helping to develop an economy in a way that is "bound to support peace," the actual result is heightened intergroup tension and, possibly, violence.

Equally damaging, compensation policies that are directed toward mitigating a company's impact on the "most affected" can, inadvertently, favor groups and disfavor groups that have existing tensions among them. Land compensation that pays "owners" may exacerbate tensions between them and the "tenants" who actually use and rely on the land. When owners are compensated but tenants are not, the latter not only receive no compensation but, also, lose their means of livelihood. Where this occurs, tensions between groups inevitably rise. When such tensions exist between groups that already are divided by class and historical marginalization (as are land owners and tenants), the results can be dangerous.

Many company managers talk about the economic "contributions" they make to a region through hiring, compensation, subcontracting, etc., and many see these efforts as contributing positively to peace. One often hears company people assert that by offering jobs to unemployed groups, they are helping address the causes of conflict. This analysis fails to take into account the distributional effects of these same economic "contributions." Important to any assessment of a company's impact on peace or conflict is recognition of the fact that when company benefits go to one group and not to others, and when these groups are historically or currently divided over other issues, the effect is to exacerbate preexisting divisions, often leading to increased violence.

Legitimization Effects

Experience also shows that companies very often legitimate troublemakers more than people who work quietly for community progress. In many places CEP has heard local people report that hotheaded troublemakers dominate the meetings with the company so that the rest of the community does not receive any attention. They note that the people who threaten the company get extra meetings with company managers and often end up being employed or receiving some other compensation. People point out that corporate managers who are busy and overstretched tend to respond to crises. When things proceed quietly within a community its members are ignored, but when tension arises, the people who create the tension receive immediate attention and, often, financial rewards.

At its worst, this tendency results in a company inadvertently rewarding, and thus encouraging, violence. In many communities that surround corporate operations, people describe how they attempt to raise a matter of concern with a company. Sometimes they have small problems, sometimes much deeper ones. However, when they write to the manager or try to arrange a meeting in a calm and nonthreatening way, communities report that they get no answer or find that their concerns are "put off" to a later date. However, these communities see that other groups block roads or close down a pipeline or sabotage a production site and receive immediate attention. Sometimes, such groups even end up with a contract to "protect" the site they just damaged. This undermines the communities who have tried to approach the company cooperatively, sometimes leading them to resort to violence against the company as well because they see this as the only way to get the company's attention.

On the other side, companies very often interpret their interactions with troublesome groups, especially groups of young men, as "managing" the environment in which they work. They fail to see that many of the approaches they use to respond to such groups actually set into motion and reward continuing violence both from the community toward the company and, often, among different groups within a community. These approaches further reinforce violence as "the most effective means" by which to interact with others and gain rewards.

Substitution Effects

Because peace is essentially political—depending on systems of governance that manage competition among groups in ways that everyone sees as legitimate and fair—any activities that a company undertakes that undermine the capacity of government may also undermine the potential for peace. When a company builds roads, schools, and clinics or provides electricity and water—all aspects of corporate work intended to better the lives of local communities—they are performing the functions that should be done by a government. They are substituting for the government. Very often, corporate managers complain about the necessity of taking such roles. They decry the inadequacies and incompetence of government that force them to do so. In community meetings they agree with the dissatisfactions of communities as they complain about "government incompetence and corruption." Furthermore, when a company builds a school or opens a newly furnished clinic, very often it puts a plaque on the door that tells the world that this structure was given by the company, reinforcing the widespread recognition that government is failing in its duties.

These actions—substituting for government and highlighting the failures of government—reinforce and deepen government weakness and awareness of it. In the long run, this inevitably weakens any potential for government to become more competent and responsible. Companies do not invent or create the failures of governments. However, by paying taxes to governments (which is necessary) and also taking on governmental functions that these taxes should have funded, companies add to and perpetuate the cycle by which corruption and inattention to public responsibility for the quality of civilian life continue.

Companies cannot change or reform governments, but they can support community efforts to hold government accountable for the use of tax monies. They can work with those committed and struggling civil servants who do, in fact, want to do a good job in education, health, and other fields with inadequate resources and training. And they can develop relationships with government by which they contribute to the strengthening of the capacities of civil servants. Companies too often take the relatively "easy" route of doing a job themselves rather than working to support—or force—processes by which indigenous systems function better.

Cash Effects

Finally, the introduction of sizable amounts of cash into cash-scarce areas, which is one result of the arrival of a company, sets into motion a number of factors that threaten peace and exacerbate conflict. Communities describe two specific changes that cash brings to their societies and affects the likelihood of conflict. First, cash often displaces age and experience as the dominant criteria by which people assume community leadership positions. A company's arrival and the sudden influx of cash very often causes younger, entrepreneurial types of people to challenge traditional, usually elder (and possibly calmer and wiser) leadership. Communities describe these new leaders as "brash" and driven by self-interest. They report that they become "leaders" by gaining access to company cash (through threats and other unethical dealings). Such shifts in leadership often bring about change in intergroup relationships as well. Decisions made by the new leaders may alter or undermine past agreements or arrangements that facilitated intergroup cooperation; forms of rapprochement that have been in existence may be ignored as the new leadership pursues economic wealth over community welfare. Second, many communities report that the influx of cash allows people to purchase guns. The presence of small arms in volatile areas, where other changes are also occurring in traditional forms of leadership, can make eruptions of violence more likely.

All of the above examples of distributional, legitimization, substitution, and cash effects are found in many locations. The very fact that these represent common and general patterns found across varying contexts allows us to anticipate and predict such effects, however. When problems are predictable, it is possible to plan for them and to avoid or mitigate them.

PEACE, CONFLICT, AND CORPORATIONS

We have seen that peace is a specialized field, requiring specific skills and approaches. We have seen that individuals' and companies' naiveté while working in areas of conflict can, and too often does, result in worsening relations. The relationship of economic progress to peace is more subtle than usually imagined by economic actors—that is, there are ways in which economic forces interact with existing patterns of intergroup relations that can, if not analyzed and addressed, contribute to and exacerbate conflict among groups. In addition, these same forces often feed into and worsen negative relations between corporations, who want to be helpful to progress in communities, and the communities they mean to help.

A fundamental reality shapes any efforts by corporations—or peace agencies—to support peace in conflicting societies: namely, no one ever makes another society's peace. People and societies themselves must create and sustain the conditions by which they live together without intergroup violence. If someone "brings peace" to another society, this peace is not integrated into the structures of that place and is not "owned" and supported by local people. Thus, it cannot be said to be durable or deep. The best outsiders can do in relation to peace, therefore, is to tie into the forces that locally support peace, connect to the processes that enable people to solve problems without violence, and reinforce the systems and structures that make intergroup relations positive. Our evidence makes clear that corporations do affect these local forces, processes, systems, and structures. Sometimes these effects are sizable and profound. They occur primarily through the core and daily operations of companies and, secondarily, through explicit community relations programs initiated by companies. If the core operations of a corporation consistently feed into and worsen suspicious and competitive relations among groups, the best corporate social responsibility programs in the world cannot counterbalance and correct these negative impacts. The single most important lesson for corporations concerned about their impacts on peace and conflict, therefore, is that they must attend to the impacts of their core operations—hiring, compensation, contracting, etc.—on the lives and relationships of local people.

The economic benefits that can be derived from the arrival and operations of a company in a poor and unstable society can be positive, both for the relatively more affluent individuals and families and for the larger pursuit of peace. However, the connection is not automatic. The connection requires thoughtful analysis, sophisticated understanding of intergroup relations, and a conscious programmatic design that ensures that existing peace forces and connections among groups are reinforced and existing divisions are lessened. Every corporation that claims to support and promote peace can (and should) take on these lessons in each overseas operation. Corporations *can* promote peace in this way. Therefore, they should do so.

NOTES

1. CDA Collaborative Learning Projects is a nonprofit organization based in Cambridge, Massachusetts, that works with humanitarian and development agencies, peace groups, and international corporations to gather and analyze their field experiences in order to improve their future work with local communities in the countries where they work.

2. CDA's Corporate Engagement Project is directed by Luc Zandvliet.

3. Distributional effects, as well as the legitimization and substitution effects discussed below, also have been traced as they arise from humanitarian and development assistance provided by NGOs, UN agencies, etc. These have been documented and discussed in Mary B. Anderson, *Do No Harm: How Aid Supports Peace—or War* (Boulder, CO: Lynne Rienner, 1999), which analyzes a CDA Local Capacities for Peace project.

CHAPTER 7

International Concord
and Intranational Discord

A Study of Freeport-McMoRan

Reverend David B. Lowry

It is difficult to come to grips with the complexities of commerce and the role it plays in both peace and conflict. It seems to me, based on fifteen years of experience in developing countries, that international peace is much enhanced by international trading—that is, by active commerce. For many developing countries, however, the only way to have goods to trade internationally is to exploit local labor (through sweatshops) and natural resources in ways that often fail to take into account land rights, cultural values, and environmental protection. This is the irony of post–World War II international prosperity and tranquility: the developing world remains mired in poverty, corruption, and environmental degradation—that is, intranational chaos and conflict. At the center of this irony are governments in developing countries that are corrupt and rapacious; international lenders (multilateral and private) that are insensitive to cultures; and multinational corporations that too often are driven by the need to return value to shareholders without broader considerations of the long-term good of the countries where they work and the people who are most impacted by their operations.

Although the evidence of developing-world manufacturers exploiting workers (directly or through subcontractors) is great, the extractive industries most directly affect peace and stability in the developing world. With their massive size and social and environmental impacts, as well as their presence in the least developed areas of the world, the extractives have the potential to positively "jump-start" the economic and social development of people in remote and underdeveloped areas. Equally, they have the potential to disrupt fragile societies and cause conflict and even civil war.

The following is a study of extractives that work in developing countries and in more developed countries with regions that are substantially undeveloped. I have patterned it on Mary Anderson's pioneering work concerning multilateral development projects.[1] Although I have based this study on Freeport-McMoRan's mine in Irian Jaya (West Papua), it is not my intent to either praise or condemn Freeport. I have used Freeport only because I know its operations best, having worked for the organization for fourteen years, mostly in connection with mines in Irian Jaya. I believe Freeport has done some very creative and forward-looking things that have helped the local population and the company. I also believe Freeport has taken actions that have hurt the company and the local population. I have tried to be objective and fair in these matters. It is my hope that in analyzing the nearly forty years Freeport has worked in Irian Jaya, themes will emerge that will help companies, local communities, and NGOs better understand the dynamics of development and discord in communities.

I also wish to inform readers that most of my observations come from personal, in the field observations rather than through reading other people's work on related topics. For that reason I have included limited references, such as works on the topic that I have found helpful and studies about Freeport that have been done by the company and NGOs. There is much in these studies with which I disagree, but I urge interested readers to refer to them for other opinions concerning topics about which I have written.

ESTABLISHING A THEORETICAL FRAMEWORK FOR THE ISSUE

Commerce, at least in theory, thrives when and where there is peace. It may also be said that peace thrives where there is vital commerce. Money and goods flow where there are open borders and tranquility. Since the end of the Second World War there has been unprecedented global economic growth—and no major wars. To be sure, the Cold War limited global economic growth during the early part of that period, but since the end of the Cold War in 1990, the expansion of global economic activity has quickened greatly. During this time of economic growth, relative international peace, and global interconnectedness, however, there has been a troubling trend toward intranational discord in the form of civil wars, suppression of indigenous and minority groups, and, in extreme cases, genocide.

These trends toward expansive, international peace and local discord can be seen most distinctively in the regions in which global extractive industries operate. Critics of the extractives blame mining and oil and gas industries for the discord and violence in the areas in which they operate. The industries must shoulder some, but not all, of the blame. By their very nature, extractive industries operate on the edge of development. As one can see in the histories of countries such as the United States, Canada, Australia, and Chile, the discovery and development of natural resources have "jump-started" broader economic and social development. At the same time, the history of these countries and their economic and social development are a testimony to the violence and discord that often follows extractive-driven economic development.

Many of the areas in which development is taking place are in former European colonies south of the equator and in parts of the former Soviet Union. They are new to "free-market" economic development, and the success of their economic and social development process remains to be determined. However, it is clear that in many places the process of current development is difficult and troubled. The questions that must be raised are what can be done to make the process of economic and social development as peaceful and beneficial for the majority of people in the areas where development is taking place, and what role extractives, where they are a major driver in that development, should play in making the development process as positive as possible.

Some theoretical background may be of help. In 1795 Immanuel Kant wrote an essay entitled "Eternal Peace."[2] In it he set out the three principles he considered necessary for international peace: (1) republican/democratic governance, (2) international law and conflict resolution mechanisms, and (3) enhanced economic activity, especially in the form of international commerce. History has, by and large, proved that Kant's insights were correct. Nations with democratic governance are less apt to enter into wars; international law and international conflict resolution mechanisms, although they falter from time to time, help preserve peace; and trade between nations has made the world both more prosperous and more peaceful.[3]

A rather different view may be of some help as well. In 1942 Joseph Schumpeter wrote an extended study of economics entitled *Capitalism, Socialism and Democracy.*[4] He raised important questions about the long-term efficacy of capitalism. Part of his critique of capitalism was to introduce the concept of "creative destruction," in which old social and economic structures are destroyed by new processes and new economic and production possibilities. Schumpeter's concept of constant creative destruction is as appropriate for developing economies where extractives are present as it is for advanced capitalist economies where there is a high level of manufacturing and technological activity. The difference is that the societies in the newly developing areas are less equipped to deal with changes that extractives bring than societies that have broader experience with economic development and change. The implication is that corporations and development organizations must bring special sensitivity to those communities that are least accustomed to rapid societal and economic change.

In this chapter I wish to assume the reality of Kant's vision of commerce as a component of international peace and focus upon the "other side of the coin," which is the unfortunate reality of persistent intranational conflict in developing areas in which large extractive operations dominate the economic and social life of the area. In order to tease out the important issues and to make what follows more than just a general and theoretical exercise, I will focus on Freeport-McMoRan's giant mining operation in southern Irian Jaya (West Papua), Indonesia.

Among the challenges that extractives face are the following:

1. Most extractives operate in partnership or by contract with nation-states whose legal and/or moral control over the area in which they are located is in question. Further, many of the nation-states in developing areas that are of interest to the extractives are corrupt and inept, which fosters distrust and discord in the local communities. Finally, the security forces in many developing countries are ill-trained, poorly paid, and therefore prone to human rights violations.

2. Land ownership and land rights in areas inhabited by indigenous people are often confused and poorly regulated. Contracts of work and revenue-sharing contracts often assume the right of the government to all surface and subsurface resources. However, the "land interface" is often in the hands of local communities and multinational corporations rather than the government.

3. The operational and economic development changes caused by the activities of extractives have profound effects upon the structure and day-to-day living in areas around extractive operations. Although many of these societal changes are (or will be) advantageous to local communities, the immediate effect of those changes can be very disruptive and can cause conflict.

4. Extractive industries change landscapes and can cause serious environmental problems. For communities rooted to the land such changes can cause serious and long-term societal problems.

All of the above "extractive issues" are evident in the history of Freeport in Irian Jaya. Of course, the "problems" and "challenges" that extractives and local communities face do not reflect the whole picture. While extractive industries may have a very mixed effect upon the communities in which they operate, they are often the economic engine for countries in which they operate, provided that these countries use the revenues from the extractives in a responsible and far-sighted way and avoid the so-called Dutch Disease. Instances of this "good use" of revenues generated by extractives in developing areas have not been numerous in recent history, however.

During the period from 1968, when the Freeport Minerals Company signed the first Contract of Work for mining activities in West Papua, to the present day, Freeport's mining activities have been an economic boon for Indonesia. According to Freeport, since 1992 the company has paid the government of the Republic of Indonesia $5 billion in taxes, royalties, and dividends. In 2006 alone, Freeport paid $1.6 billion to the Indonesian government. In addition, Freeport has produced many secondary economic benefits for Indonesia as a whole and especially for the substantially undeveloped area of southern Irian Jaya where the mine is located. All of this has been greatly beneficial for Indonesia and, in some ways, for the local Papuan population. On the other hand, Freeport's mining operation has been one of the focuses of rebel activity, social discontent, and internal conflict between and among indigenous peoples throughout Irian Jaya.[5]

This situation is not unique to either Irian Jaya or Freeport's operation. It has been played out in numerous undeveloped and developing areas throughout the world. Large extractive operations disturb the natural social order of local communities, thereby exacerbating internal tensions, fanning the flames of long-standing internal conflicts, and creating new areas of strife, some of which can be directly attributed to enhanced local economic activity. The irony is that what is very positive for the larger nation-state and in many cases for international peace and tranquility is at best a difficult mixed blessing for local communities, which often host extractive industries without having granted permission or full understanding of the consequences of such industry. Yet before condemning Freeport or extractive industries in general, it is important to take a careful and nuanced look at this phenomenon. We must consider whether it is better, in order to keep peace within local communities, to rob those communities and peoples of their right to develop. If one looks at the history of local and national development in the countries we now consider to be substantially economically established, we cannot help but recognize that a real price was paid in the past for development.

For an example of the internal conflicts that rapid social change and economic development can cause, one needs only look at Europe in the late eighteenth and nineteenth centuries. During that time England, France, and the German territories were convulsed time and time again by social and political conflicts sparked by the social dislocations of the Industrial Revolution. Some of these conflicts were caused by the exploitation of workers in the newly developed factories; others, however, were caused by the more general issues of urbanization and the transformation of a society moving away from an agrarian lifestyle.

Since extractive industries, in many cases, operate on the periphery of socially and economically developed areas, they are always dealing with cultures and societies that are least ready to face the difficult issues raised by a large and relatively technologically advanced industrial operation. Traditional ways of life, traditional leadership structures, and traditional power relationships collapse in the face of the new paradigms of development and industrialization.

It would be easy to condemn the extractive industries for the conflict and chaos they create in these undeveloped communities and to demand their closure and limit their access to such areas where one might reasonably expect there to be social and cultural dislocation. However, such a one-sided action would be virtually impossible and probably unwise. The difficulties caused by the presence of major extractive operations in developing areas of the world can, if managed correctly, bring potential long-term benefits to the local areas in which extractives operate, as well as the larger nation-state. This can happen, however, only when there is a concerted effort by the extractive industries, national governments, and the international community to create structures for managing social change in order to minimize local conflict and social dislocations while maximizing long-term benefits for the local community and the nation.

In the remainder of this chapter I will consider Freeport's mining operation from the singular perspective of conflict within the local communities that are most deeply impacted (positively and negatively) by Freeport's presence. First, I will describe briefly Freeport's history in Irian Jaya, Indonesia. Then I will spotlight a series of events and situations that have caused conflict, whether between the community and Freeport, between the community and the government, and/or between different groups within the local community. Finally, I will try to look at ways in which the various parties could have avoided conflict and how conflict can be minimized in the future.

PAPUA AND FREEPORT IN IRIAN JAYA: A SHORT HISTORY

The Freeport Minerals Company began exploration in West Papua (Irian Jaya) in 1968.[6] At that time West Papua was a United Nations Protectorate under the administration of the government of the Republic of Indonesia. The people of West Papua awaited a definitive decision about their future because a vote of the tribal leaders of the West Papuan community was required to determine the ultimate status of the area. This complex and in some ways convoluted process was arranged by the United Nations after the 1961 invasion of the Dutch territory of West Papua by the military forces of the government of the Republic of Indonesia. In spite of the uncertainty about the ultimate political status of West Papua, Freeport concluded a Contract of Work with the government of Indonesia in 1968 to begin exploration of whether a mining facility in West Papua was feasible.[7]

In 1969 chosen leaders of the Papuan communities in Irian Jaya voted unanimously to join Indonesia. From the time of the vote until the present time, many Papuans believe that the so-called Act of Free Choice was in reality an act of no choice, manipulated by Indonesia and the United Nations in order to assure peace and stability in the Pacific region. Therefore, from the beginning of Freeport's exploration activities up to the present time, there has been a perception among the Papuans that the determination of their future was unfairly, and quite possibly illegally, determined. The election process, the role the United States played in that process, and the signing of a Contract of Work with the Indonesian government prior to the Act of Free Choice has caused great tension in Papua for the past thirty-five years and has colored Freeport's relationship with the leadership of the Papuan community. When Indonesia formally took over West Papua, it changed the name of the province to Irian Jaya.

In spite of these questions, Freeport and the government of Indonesia proceeded with the Freeport Minerals Mining Project. In 1972, after three years of arduous and difficult development, Freeport produced the first copper concentrate through its mill in Irian Jaya. Even before the opening of mining and milling operations, however, there were protests, especially in the Waa-Banti community (the indigenous community located closest to the mine and to Freeport's administrative and residential town), against Freeport's activities. There were numerous incidents of hex poles being placed at strategic points where Freeport was building infrastructure for the mine and the mill. The local community, however, felt quite powerless in the face of the technological prowess and machinery that Freeport possessed. The construction of the mine continued unabated.

At the time that Freeport began operations, it is estimated that 1,000 indigenous Papuans (500 in the highlands and 500 in the lowlands) lived in the 320-square-mile area stretching from the Arafuara Sea, where Freeport built a small port to receive necessary goods for its operation and to export copper concentrate, up to the Ertsberg deposit, which was being mined in the mountains at an elevation of nearly 13,000 feet. The highland Papuans were from the Amungme tribe, and the lowland Papuans were from the Komoro tribe.

It was not until January 1974, nearly two years after mining commenced, that an agreement was made between the highland Amungme and the government of Indonesia and the Freeport Minerals Company to provide economic and social benefits for the Amungme people on whose traditional land Freeport was operating. The so-called January 1974 agreement required Freeport to build houses and places of worship and provide free medical care for the Amungme who lived in the vicinity of Freeport's operation. In 1977, however, during government military activities against rebel forces active throughout southern Irian Jaya, the infrastructure constructed by Freeport as part of this agreement was destroyed.[8] In some cases the destruction was undertaken by the Papuans themselves and in others by the military. For nearly a decade after the infrastructure was destroyed, little was done by Freeport or the government to rebuild the community infrastructure of the Amungme Papuans.

In the early years of Freeport's operation there was very little migration of Papuans into Freeport's Contract of Work area. Part of the reason for this was the lack of development of general infrastructure in Irian Jaya, which made gaining knowledge about Freeport's industrial operation difficult. Freeport employed only a small number of local Papuans, so there was little pressure from outsiders to gain employment with Freeport. Freeport's mine remained very small because the price of copper was depressed through much of the late 1970s and into the 1980s. In fact, several times between 1975 and the mid-1980s plans were set forward either to sell or to close the operation outright.

In the late 1980s all of that changed. James Robert Moffitt became Freeport's chairman, and he brought new vision and aggressiveness to Freeport's mining operations. As a geologist Moffitt took personal interest in exploration for larger and richer deposits near the Ertsberg mining site.

Success came in 1988 when Freeport geologists discovered that a grassy area above the Ertsberg deposit covered a vast deposit of copper, gold, and silver. In time this grassy area came to be known as Grasberg, and it has proved to be the largest single, integrated deposit of copper and gold in the world. The development of the Grasberg mine created a complex new social situation for Freeport and the Papuan people. As construction moved forward, not only of the mine and mill but also of the support infrastructure for the largest mining complex in the world, the allure of the Freeport site for Papuans from many parts of Irian Jaya grew. Migration to the outskirts of Freeport's core town of Tembagapura in the highlands and the expansion of Freeport's support operations in the lowlands caused about 15 percent population growth per annum.[8]

As Papuans arrived seeking work, education, medical care, and in some cases just the excitement of something new, they also brought with them disease, unresolved conflicts from times past, and a society that had been built on close internal relations within family units and a deep distrust of outsiders, including fellow Papuans. For many centuries Papuans had tended to separate themselves from all but their closest intimates. The difficult terrain on the Island of New Guinea made much of that separation natural. In the mountains deep valleys and rushing rivers made travel and interconnection between peoples difficult. This natural separation can be seen in the numerous languages found in New Guinea; over time the separation of peoples allowed them to develop completely different words for similar things and events. It is reported that when a person wandering far from his native village encountered an outsider, he would ask questions and ascertain whether they shared common family ties and language. If no commonality was discovered, the outsider was either shunned or killed.

The movement of people into Freeport's area of operation increased the Papuan population in the area from a mere 1,000 in the early 1970s to nearly 60,000 today, creating troublesome tensions within the community. These tensions were exacerbated by an ongoing, unresolved conflict between Papuans who believed that Irian Jaya had been granted independence by the Netherlands prior to the intervention of the United Nations and that Freeport supported the Republic of Indonesia in blocking the Papuans' quest to be separated from the Republic of Indonesia.

Although Freeport continuously has stated its neutrality in the conflict between the Papuans who are seeking independence and the government of Indonesia, Freeport's actions have been confusing to all parties. On the one side, Freeport set up an innovative and generous program of support for the Papuans in and around its area of operation. This program, known as the Freeport Partnership Fund, has received 1 percent of Freeport's net revenues for a period of more than ten years. This has provided nearly a quarter of a billion dollars in support for education, health care, and economic development for the so-called seven local tribes (*tuju suku*). In a sense this has been an unexpected and unintended support for Papuan independence, even though Freeport has worked assiduously to prevent any of the funds from the Freeport Partnership Fund from supporting political and independence activities. On the other side, Freeport has provided substantial support for Indonesian security forces through the Octagon

Project, which built housing and other infrastructure for the police and the armed forces in the area. In addition, Freeport has provided annual operating grants to Indonesian security forces. This has led the Papuans to feel that the police and the army work for Freeport and that Freeport supports what the Papuans perceive to be a long history of human rights violations against their communities by Indonesia and the Indonesian security forces. Freeport insists that its support for the police and the army has been given only for the most necessary purposes and in order to prevent the security forces, which have been notoriously underfunded, from devolving into unacceptable behaviors such as owning businesses and outright extortion to cover their costs.

CONFLICT IN FREEPORT'S CONTRACT OF WORK AREA: DESCRIPTION AND ANALYSIS

Conflict in Freeport's Contract of Work area can be attributed to three issues: (1) disputes about land ownership and land usage; (2) security and human rights violations; and (3) changes in Papuan traditional society caused by migration, demographic transition, and economic development. Clearly these three issue cannot be easily separated—they are intimately interrelated. Although I will try to highlight each of these areas of conflict in the following narrative, I will proceed chronologically because events flow from one another even though they can be categorized in different ways.

As the description of Freeport's more than thirty years in Papua indicates, the presence of a giant industrial operation in the middle of one of the least developed areas of the world has been a mixed blessing. Freeport has brought education, health care, employment, and, in many cases, wealth to a good number of Papuans. Regrettably, it has also brought internal strife, intertribal conflict, and pollution. While large corporations like Freeport tend to trumpet the benefits they have brought to the national economies and the local people in the areas in which they operate, many local, national, and international NGOs attack companies like Freeport for the environmental and social damage they cause. Neither position is accurate or helpful. In reality, the type of economic and social change that large industrial operations create in undeveloped and newly developing societies causes substantial instability by changing virtually all social and economic relations within the local communities affected by such sudden and radical development. This sounds very bad, but as was noted in the introductory section of this chapter, history is filled with examples of short-term chaos, including conflict within and between communities that became long-term, beneficial development leading to prosperity and stability. If poorly managed, however, the same chaos can become endemic.

A number of specific issues that have arisen during Freeport's tenure in Irian Jaya illustrate the ways, many of which are totally unintentional, that discord and violence can occur in places where extractives operate. As noted above, Freeport's first Contract of Work was signed with the government of the Republic of Indonesia in 1968, a year prior to the Act of Free Choice and the formal assumption of territorial control of West Papua by Indonesia. From a psychological perspective, at least, the date of the signing of Freeport's Contract of Work has loomed important in the minds of some Papuans; they claim that any contract between Freeport and the government of Indonesia is illegal because it predated the Act of Free Choice. Freeport's contract has become a potent symbol of American and Indonesian imperialism and a source of continuing anxiety for Freeport, the government of Indonesia, and the local communities.

Beyond the legality of the contract between Freeport and the government, the local community was perplexed by the very act of giving land to Freeport to operate a mine on their traditional land. Papuan indigenous communities do not "own" land, but they have a clear sense of who can use land and under what circumstances. The government of the Republic of Indonesia has laws and regulations about land ownership that are very different from the land-use traditions of the Papuans. Of even greater importance in the case of Freeport, the Indonesian government claims all surface and subsurface minerals for the "benefit of all the people of Indonesia." The communities with traditional land claims gain virtually nothing from mining on traditional land. The only exceptions to this are that owners of "improved land"—that is, land that has structures built on it or that has been cultivated—must be compensated according to government guidelines and buildings for public use are to be constructed on land that is taken by eminent domain as negotiated by the government. The issue of indigenous land rights and land title is complex. Indigenous groups throughout the world have no title to land and therefore seldom benefit financially from their traditional land. The Amungme in Irian Jaya are a prime example of this situation. The Amungme could not sell land to Freeport because, in the eyes of the Indonesian government. they did not own the land. Fernando de Soto has made the case that the inability of the poorest people in the world to "leverage" their land puts them at a great disadvantage in a global, capitalist world.[9]

As has been described above, Freeport and the local Amungme community near the mine negotiated a land rights agreement six years after the development of the mine began and two years after the first ore was produced. The January 1974 agreement provided for a few buildings in the highland village of Waa and several other buildings in the government relocation village for highland Papuans in the lowlands. By 1977 all those buildings had decayed or were destroyed during rebel activities or by government security forces searching for rebels.

In the late 1990s and early 2000s new land rights agreements were negotiated with lowland residents, most of which are from the Komoro tribe, when Freeport began to use large areas in the lowlands to impound mill tailings. These land rights agreements were much more favorable to the local people. However, the government would not permit renegotiation of earlier land rights agreements with the highland Amungme.

In 2001 Freeport took the bold step of privately negotiating "informal, addition land rights compensation"[10] with the Amungme and Komoro. Ironically, this agreement became the foundation for better relations between Freeport and the Amungme and Komoro tribes and the cause of widespread unrest among the other tribes that had moved into the area. The issue was complex; since there is no clear land title in traditional Papuan communities, there are real and imagined disputes concerning on whose land one lives. Such issues are played out individually, by family units within tribes, and between tribes. When the opportunity presented itself for compensation for land use by Freeport for its mine and support facilities, every tribal group in the area vied for a piece of the pie. The Papuans not only beat down a path to Freeport's door; they beat on each other to get to the door. Although in time the conflicts moderated, they have not entirely dissipated. The lure of quick money is too great.

The second major issue is security and human rights. Freeport's presence in Irian Jaya has always been seen by the Papuans as a reason for the presence of the Indonesian military in Irian Jaya. Although this may not be accurate, it has become an enduring perception. Even before the Act of Free Choice, the Indonesian army was accused by local church leaders and members of the international community of violating the human rights of the Papuan people. Following the Act of Free Choice, accusations of human rights violations increased, and they continue to the present day. Because Freeport utilizes the Indonesian army and police to protect its operations and property, there have been accusations that Freeport has colluded with the Indonesian security forces to take actions against Papuans "beyond what is necessary to protect Freeport's operations and property."[11] Freeport denies such accusations and has stated that it has taken positive actions to make certain no further violations occur.

Freeport's relationship with Indonesian security forces is very complex. Initially Freeport needed little regular protection for its operations since the mine was small and the local population was sparse. The few times the army came into Freeport's area of operations were because of army operations against rebels rather than at the behest of Freeport to protect its assets and operations. The case could be made that Freeport was happy to have the security forces stay away. However, after the expansion of the mine and its operations in the 1990s, the rapid increase in the general population at the mine, and the influx of large numbers of Papuans and non-Papuans to the area around Freeport's operations, it became increasingly necessary for Freeport to have governmental security to protect employees, their dependents, Freeport's assets, and its operations. Since the government was hard-pressed to provide the resources necessary to house and feed the additional security forces required to protect Freeport and the growing population around Freeport's operations, Freeport agreed to build the infrastructure in which the additional security would be housed and fed.[12]

The local population—and especially the Papuans within that population—distrust the Indonesian security forces. Freeport's very visible support for the Indonesian security forces made clear to many Papuans that Freeport and the government of Indonesia were "one" and that both Freeport and the government were aligned against the Papuan people. Freeport would certainly argue that such perceptions are untrue and that its support for the Indonesian security forces in the region is an attempt to help those forces be more professional and protective of the overall welfare of the people in the area around its operations, including, of course, the company and its employees. However, the local community did (and does) not see Freeport's support for Indonesian security forces in that way, and in this case perceptions are very important.

To further complicate the issue and the perceptions, over the past decade Freeport has provided operating expenses for the army and the police in the form of food and cost-of-living subsidies. In the past few years, it has been shown that Freeport also paid substantial sums directly to high-ranking police and military officers. Freeport claims these payments were intended for distribution to subordinates, but NGOs claim they were payoffs to gain preferential treatment.

Freeport counters that the security forces are poorly paid and, until Freeport constructed facilities for them, were terribly housed. Freeport notes that under such conditions security forces are virtually forced into behaviors that threaten rather than enhance peace and tranquility. This was certainly the case up to the time that Freeport constructed facilities for the army and police. From 1972 until Freeport's rapid period of expansion in the early 1990s, a minimal regular cohort of government security forces was assigned to Freeport and the area around Freeport. From time-to-time enhanced security forces entered the area when there was rebel (*Organisasi Papua Merdeka*) activity in the vicinity. Two periods of such activity were 1977 and 1984. In 1984 Freeport's pipeline that carries slurry to the port for export was cut by rebels. The local community, church leaders, and international NGOs accused the military of using excessive and indiscriminate force and of violating human rights during those campaigns.

However, the period of greatest interest for the local community and NGOs came between 1994 and 1996. In April 1994 a rebel band led by Kelly Kwalik (an Amungme and native of Freeport's Contract of Work area) occupied the Amungme village of Tsinga, located several miles to the east of Freeport's Grasberg mine. Several months later the army sent troops into Tsinga to hunt down Kwalik and his men. They found the village abandoned. Many Amungme who fled from Tsinga came to the areas around Freeport's operations. There was high anxiety among the Amungme people and at Freeport about possible rebel and military action in the vicinity of Freeport's operations and the Amungme villages of Waa and Banti. On November 18, 1994, one Freeport employee was shot and killed and another seven were wounded by a sniper along the Freeport road. Freeport shut down its road (which is necessary for the mining operations to continue) and asked the government of Indonesia to supply sufficient security personnel to allow operations to continue. Within a short period of time, an additional 600 army and police personnel arrived, bringing the total number of security forces in the area around Freeport's operations to more than 800. Over the coming two years the number of police and army personnel in the area increased to nearly 1,500. In part the increase was a result of the security problems in the area and in part because the area had been granted the designation of a *kabupaten* (county), which required an increase in governmental services, including security.

After the shooting incidents, the army sought to capture Kelly Kwalik and his followers once again. Part of the strategy for their capture was to detain and interrogate relatives of Kwalik. By all accounts, the interrogations were brutal and clearly crossed the line into the area of human rights violations. One of those interrogated (Yosepha Alomang) was locked in a shipping container for days in high heat and with little food or water; five others disappeared and have never been found. It is suspected they were killed by the army before, during, or after interrogation. Finally, on Christmas morning 1994, the army shot dead a man who raised a Papuan independence flag in Freeport's residential and administrative town (Tembagapura). Reports differ as to what happened thereafter, but the final result was that local Papuans were arrested, Freeport vehicles were commandeered, and at least two other Papuans died at the hands of the army. The outcry of the local community, Papuan human rights activists, and the Papuan churches was heard far beyond Irian Jaya. In Australia the Australian Council for Foreign Aid (ACFOA), a little-known human rights organization, used the report produced by the office of the Catholic Church in Jayapura to attack Freeport and the security forces of Indonesia—the security forces for gross human rights violations and Freeport for complicity in those violations. Freeport defended its actions vociferously if in the end ineffectively. Freeport and Papua were on the international human rights map and the global Web.[13]

Tensions throughout the area rose dramatically. Indonesian NGOs, led by WALHI (Friends of the Earth, Indonesia), organized the community and planned lawsuits against Freeport to be filed in the United States using the Alien Tort Claims Act. The expectation of a major lawsuit against the largest foreign corporation operating in Irian Jaya fanned hopes for a financial bonanza and, possibly, independence. Over a two-year period the lawsuits were dismissed on procedural grounds.

Tensions increased again in January 2006 when Kelly Kwalik and his followers kidnapped expatriate and Indonesian biological researchers working for the Worldwide Fund for Nature (WWF) in the area of Gila, some one hundred miles east of Freeport's operations. Although the kidnappings were not related to Freeport or its operations (although Freeport had contributed funds to WWF), the kidnappers publicly stated that they would release the captives if Freeport ceased operations.

Because of the nature of the kidnappings and because nine of those kidnapped were expatriates (mostly Dutch and English), the actions of the government to effect a release were closely watched worldwide. The International Red Cross came in to negotiate with the captors, the Indonesian government assigned President Soeharto's son-in-law to lead the military's action, and England engaged foreign mercenaries to assist the Indonesian army (although it appears they only observed operations). Timika, the fast-growing city in the lowlands of Freeport's Contract of Work area, became the staging area for the Red Cross and the Indonesian military.

On Sunday, March 13, 1996, in the latter stages of the kidnapping saga, rioting broke out in Freeport's town of Tembagapura. Although most of the rioters were Papuan, videotapes of the riots revealed that the leaders of the riot (who had and used walkie-talkies) were non-Papuan Indonesians. The riots caused over $3 million in damage in Tembagapura but no injuries. It was clear that the riots were carefully and well orchestrated. Freeport shut down operations for two days to make certain the situation was stabilized. On Tuesday, March 15, the rioting moved to Timika. Unlike the riot in Tembagapura, the rioting in Timika was spontaneous, violent, and totally uncontrolled, resulting in three deaths.

The two days of rioting were the most violent and damaging in Freeport's history. Although the people of the two local tribes (the Amungme and Komoro) did not participate in the riots, other Papuans made many demands on Freeport for better treatment. Interestingly, there were few demands made to the government or the army. There also was little evidence in the field of who was behind the rioting. Soon after the riots the Indonesian army produced intercepted e-mails that suggested the riots were planned and carried out by a coalition of Indonesian (WALHI) and international (Rivers Network) NGOs. The NGOs denied their role in the riots, suggesting the Indonesian military had a role in the riots and their orchestration. Some years later the Indonesian Minister of Defense stated that the local military command in Irian Jaya had planned and carried out the riots. Whoever was behind the rioting, there is little doubt that the kidnappings had changed the dynamics of the Papuan community and its relationship to Freeport, as well as the relationship of Freeport to the local community.

This leads to the most complex issue that engenders conflict in Freeport's operations area: employment and the provision of social and economic benefits to the community. Everyone wants to receive these benefits. Unfortunately, these benefits create instability in two ways: they establish new leaders in the community, and they threaten old and cherished traditions within society. The aftermath of the 1996 riots provides an instance of these twin "destabilizers" at work. A month after the riots, Freeport and the Indonesian government announced a series of initiatives to improve Freeport's relationship with the local community. The initiative had three foci: (1) increased Papuan employment at Freeport's mine; (2) the establishment by Freeport of a fund to be used by the government to aid the social development of the local Papuan people (originally called the Freeport Fund for Irian Jaya Development—now known as the Freeport Partnership Fund); and (3) development of programs to end the human rights violations that had plagued the company and the government over the previous several years. Surprisingly, the initiatives did not make life more peaceful for the local community, the government, or Freeport. Following the announcement of the program, which was to be funded with one percent of Freeport's net revenue, further riots broke out in Papuan communities as local leaders vied to gain control over the "cargo" that was to be bestowed on their communities.

The failure of the programs to make the area around Freeport's mining operation more peaceful came as a surprise to the company. It should not have. In spite of the best intentions of the company, the initiatives created new inequalities within the Papuan communities around Freeport's operations area that would be difficult to resolve. These inequalities came in several forms. First, Freeport's commitment to Papuan employment was not culturally sensitive. Freeport believed that "a Papuan was a Papuan." Hence, Freeport looked to employ the best-educated and most-experienced Papuans. These Papuans came almost exclusively from the north coast of Papua (that is, from Biak and Jayapura). They were influenced the most by the Dutch and had the greatest opportunity for education and work experience. While Freeport proudly announced the success of the Papuan employment program, the local Papuan tribes, known as the seven *sukus,* fumed that they had been shut out of the new job offerings. Protests and strikes followed. It took several years for Freeport and the local Papuan community to establish programs to right the balance between the local Papuans and those from the north coast.

In spite of the litany of conflicts, large and small, that have surrounded Freeport and the local communities since the inception of exploration in 1968, the first mining and milling in 1972, and the expansion of mining activities in the 1990s, the period since 2000 has been relatively quiet. It appears that the disparate efforts of the company in the areas of human rights, Papuan employment, and sharing the economic benefits of Freeport's operations with the local population have begun to pay off. It is important to note a number of activities that appear to have helped the transition from constant conflict to relative calm.

First, in spite of the numerous questions that have been raised about Freeport's support for the Indonesian security forces around Freeport's mine, the behavior of the police and military in the area, while not exemplary, is far better than it has been in the past and far better than it has been elsewhere in Papua. It is a well-known fact that the police and military in Indonesia receive far less than half of the funds necessary to do their work from the government. Often, this means that security personnel have to raise additional funds for their food and lodging. Sometimes this is done through large-scale military- and police-directed businesses, such as owning and operating hotels and an airline. In other cases the money-making activities are less formal and less savory. For example, there are rumors of prostitution and illegal trade being part of the military and police's "second function." Although such activities in Freeport's Contract of Work are not unknown, they have become less prevalent since the building of dormitories, mess halls, and recreation facilities for the police and military. In the cases of officers, a good number now have their families residing with them in the Timika area, which allows the police and military to be part of the communities in which they work. While other areas of Papua have had escalating problems with human rights over the past five to seven years, reports of human rights violations in the Timika area have dropped substantially.

Second, Freeport has taken proactive steps to strengthen its relationships with the local community. The Freeport Partnership Fund is now administered by a board of local community leaders. Although these leaders are still learning their trade (administering programs worth more than

$25 million a year), there is an increasing belief that "community owner-ship" of education, health care, and community development belongs to the Papuan community, not to Freeport.

Third, Freeport established a board-approved Social, Employment, and Human Rights Policy to assure that the commitments made to the Papuan community in April 1996 were known within the company and beyond. This policy was first approved in 1999 and was updated in 2001. In addition, Freeport agreed to undertake a comprehensive audit of the company's compliance with the Social, Employment, and Human Rights Policy. This audit, which has taken more than two years, is being done by the International Center for Corporate Accountability (ICCA), a New York–based NGO specializing in monitoring multinational corporations' social performance. The first phase of the audit indicated that Freeport had made good efforts to implement its social policies but that there were areas in which improvement would be necessary; the second phase of the audit was released on December 3, 2007. It indicated that improvements have continued, especially in the area of human rights compliance.

CONCLUSION

We can conclude from this analysis of the rich and complex history of Freeport in Irian Jaya that the management of relations between corpora-tions and local populations is far more complex than anyone wishes to be-lieve. It is now clear, not only in the case of Freeport but with regard to extractive projects in general, that finding an effective way to manage se-curity is most problematic. Companies quite rightly do not want to be the protector of last resort for their personnel, operations, and property. How-ever, the record of security forces in remote areas of Indonesia (and in many other places in which extractives operate) is so mixed (if not down-right poor) that using government-provided security forces is apt to pro-duce a result as bad as not utilizing them at all. On the other hand, using company security forces can be just as uncertain, and, when matters re-ally go wrong, it is not at all clear that the governmental security forces will be willing to "bail out" the company. BP, which is developing a natural gas operation in Irian Jaya, has widely publicized its "community policing program," which uses local community leaders along with BP's security personnel to maintain peace and tranquility. It is an interesting idea, and many companies operating in developing regions are watching its evolution closely. The test, however, is not "in theory"; it will be in practice during a time of conflict and crisis, and how the Indonesian security forces respond (or do not respond) will be the real test.

If the security-related issues and the conflict they have engendered are no great surprise, the increase, rather than prevention, of conflict caused by Freeport's "positive" actions in the areas of employment and community development has come as a major and disappointing surprise. The lesson in this case is that even good things cause tension and stress, some of which can be played out violently. That Freeport's operations area has been more peaceful over the past seven or so years than it has been since the expansion of the mining activities began in the early 1990s is not only a testimony to the intensive work done by Freeport but also to the work done by the leadership of the local Papuan communities. Finally, the Freeport story is a cautionary tale for all extractives interested in working in communities during the early period of their development; there are numerous surprises to be confronted, and many will be troublesome. However, if all sides persevere, eventually there can be some positive outcomes.

NOTES

This chapter is dedicated to Mary Anderson

1. Mary B. Anderson, *Do No Harm: How Aid Can Support Peace—or War* (Boulder, CO: Lynne Reiner, 1999).

2. Immanuel Kant, "Eternal Peace," *Philosophical Works,* ed. Carl J. Friedrich (New York: Modern Library, 1942), 430–76.

3. Bruce Russett and John Oneal, *Triangulating Peace: Democracy, Interdependence, and International Organizations* (New York: W.W. Norton, 2001).

4. Joseph Schumpeter, *Capitalism, Socialism and Democracy* (New York: Harper and Brothers, 1942), esp. 81–86. See also Thomas K. McCraw, *Prophet of Innovation: Joseph Schumpeter and Creative Destruction* (Cambridge, MA: Belknap Press, 2007).

5. Freeport-McMoRan Copper and Gold, *Underlying Value: Annual Report* (2006), http://www.fcx.com/inrl/annlrpt/2006/fcx%20ar%202006.pdf.

6. Forbes Wilson, *Conquest of Copper Mountain* (New York: Atheneum, 1981).

7. John Saltford, *The United Nations and the Indonesian Takeover of West Papua, 1962-1969: The Anatomy of Betrayal* (New York: RoutledgeCurzon, 2003).

8. George Mealey, *Grasberg: Mining the Richest and Most Remote Deposit of Copper and Gold in the World* (Freeport-McMoRan Copper and Gold, 1996).

9. Fernando de Soto, *The Mystery of Capital: Why Capitalism Triumphs in the West and Fails Elsewhere* (New York: Basic Books, 2000).

10. D. Lowry, "Working toward Sustainability" (unpublished internal document, Freeport-McMoRan Copper and Gold, 2002).

11. "The Cost of Gold. The Hidden Payroll: Below a Mountain of Gold, a River of Waste," *New York Times,* December 27, 2005, 1. See also "Indonesian Military Admits Being Paid by U.S. Mining Firm," *Guardian,* December 30, 2005, 5.

12. "Paying for Protection," *Global Witness* (July 2005), http://www.globalwitness.org/media_library_detail.php/139/en/paying_for_protection.

13. Australian Council for Foreign Aid, "Trouble at Freeport," (1995); see also the report on which the Australian Council report was based by H. M. H. Munninghof, Bishop of Jasyapura, in Project Underground, "Report on Freeport" (undated), http://www.projectunderground.org.

PART IV

Ensuring the Success of
Peace through Commerce

CHAPTER 8

Impact Assessment, Transparency, and Accountability

Three Keys to Building Sustainable Partnerships
between Business and Its Stakeholders

Donal A. O'Neill

INTRODUCTION

Wealth matters. It pays for clean water, for vaccinations, for education, for the onslaught on infant and maternal mortality. It pays for the transportation and communication infrastructure that opens opportunities and for the energy that liberates humanity from millennia of soul-destroying, back-breaking toil. It kick-starts economic growth and generates employment, and in a self-reinforcing virtuous spiral it creates more employment and more growth, neutralizing in the process the discontents and frustrated ambitions that otherwise undermine personal and communal security.

Wealth ensures human dignity. Good intentions alone will not ensure social and economic progress. Of the UN's Millennium Goals, six are "cash sinks" in the short to intermediate term, aspirations that though noble in themselves will demand vast wealth for their realization. Only two of these goals—"Promote Gender Equality and Empower Women" and "Develop a Global Partnership for Development"—can be regarded as short-term enablers for wealth creation. Without wealth the Millennium Goals are impossible. Margaret Thatcher summarized the challenge when she remarked "No one would remember the Good Samaritan if he'd only had good intentions—he had money, too."[1]

Wealth—in the form of money—must come from somewhere: from exploitation of natural resources, from the application of human ingenuity, from recognition of opportunities hitherto overlooked. And history has shown us—in societies as diverse as ancient Phoenicia, the Venetian Republic, the great European mercantilist empires, Meiji Japan and its inheritors, the United States since its creation, and more recently Taiwan, Malaysia, and South Korea—that private business is the most effective mechanism known to humanity for sustained wealth creation. Business creates wealth through a combination of enterprise, ingenuity, creativity, skillful design, and use of capital markets and flexible organizational structures, not to mention an appeal to the basic human craving for a better life for one's family and descendents.

Business—which ultimately consists of millions of ordinary people who are investors through pension trusts and mutual funds—gains from the process. But so, too—and often more so—does government, not only through direct taxation on business (and, in the case of the extractive industries, through royalties) but through government's relentless pursuit of personal and value-added taxation of direct and indirect employees. This taxation pays for education, welfare, health care, and infrastructure—and for realization of the UN's Millennium Goals.

There is an implicit deal involved. Government takes its share, but business expects in return physical security, property rights, and rule of law to protect and regulate the arena in which it operates. But rule of law is a two-edged sword, imposing obligations on business as well as rights. The most significant obligations, and those least understood and least well-managed by both business and government, relate to the long-term socioeconomic impact of business on its host societies. It is with such socioeconomic impact that this chapter is concerned.

IMPACTS

Business changes the environment it operates in, not just in the immediate term but sometimes over decades. This statement applies as much to the convenience store on the street corner as to the huge manufacturing plant, but in no case is the impact as dramatic as in the extractive industries—mining, oil, and gas. It is on these industries that this chapter concentrates. Extractives probably have received more attention than other industries with regard to impact management, but the principles involved and the lessons learned—both about successes and failures— are applicable across a wide range of other business activities, in particular diffuse ones such as alcohol sales, gambling, and tourism, which governments are often keen to support without evaluating long-term consequences.

Extractive industry undertakings represent enormous investments— with budgets of billions of dollars—and over many decades generate vast revenues for host governments and large profits, as well as risks, for the investors. Challenges such as development of mines in difficult terrain, of oil or gas fields below thousands of feet of water, or of liquefaction of gas and its transport in refrigerated ships between continents demand sophisticated technical solutions, deployment of massive construction workforces, and availability of many specialist contractors to support operation and maintenance. But in addition, such undertakings impact massively on the host societies and economies, and some of the impacts carry the seeds of serious long-term difficulties if not properly managed. I discuss some of these difficulties below.

Revenues

If well managed revenues to government from taxation and royalties can fund improvements in education, health care, and infrastructure and support growth of local industries. Conversely, if the host government has neither the structures in place to manage increased revenues responsibly and transparently, nor has consensus as to equitable distribution between the national, provincial, and local levels, nor—worst of all—has the legitimacy and will to address these issues, then misappropriation, corruption, and waste are inevitable. The most notable example is perhaps Nigeria, a major oil and gas producer. Through the fiscal system and direct participation in joint ventures with international companies, the government takes over 90 percent of the value of every barrel of oil produced. Yet in 2005 the chairman of the Economic and Financial Crimes Commission, set up by the Nigerian government in 2002, stated that £220 billion (close to US$400 billion) had been "squandered" between independence from Britain in 1960 and the return of civilian rule in 1999. This figure corresponds almost exactly with the £220 billion of Western aid given to

Africa between 1960 and 1997 and represents six times the amount given by the United States to reconstruct postwar Europe under the Marshall Plan.

Employment and Economic Opportunities

Except during initial construction—when many of the workers will be migrant specialists—the extractive industries are not necessarily large direct employers. A "mom and pop convenience store" employs more people per thousand dollars invested than does a large oil production venture. Extractive industries do, however, generate significant secondary employment through specialist maintenance and other service contractors during their production phases and large demand for tertiary services such as hotels and transport, all providing a substantial "multiplier effect" in the economy. However, unless there is a conscious strategy to ensure that local interests receive early support to participate in such activities; to build on existing skills, which may not be adequate initially; and to assist if necessary with financing, then there is a serious risk that this sector will remain largely the province of established international companies. Countries such as Norway, the United States, and the United Kingdom have used development of a supply capability for goods and services for their domestic oil industry as a foundation for establishing themselves as major international suppliers in the sector, while Australia and Malaysia have built strong international presences in mining and oil and gas development on the basis of expertise gained initially in domestic production.

Distortion of Existing Economy

Massive investments imply the necessity to initiate production quickly and maintain production at high levels. This in turn justifies high salaries for qualified workers. In developing countries this may mean that established industries struggle to compete in the skilled-labor market—and in a worst case scenario, fail entirely. This phenomenon has led to Nigeria, once the world's largest palm oil producer, now importing the commodity from Malaysia and allowing its rubber plantations to revert to forest. An even worse phenomenon may be "Dutch Disease": the failure to plan for massive increases in government revenue from extractive industries with a consequent strengthening of exchange rates and rising noncompetitiveness of traditional exports. Even a nation as economically and politically sophisticated as the Netherlands plunged into this trap in the 1960s and 1970s, while Norway managed to avoid it by judicious planning, an example that Azerbaijan appears to be following today.

Boom Town Effects

Extractive industries' workers—well paid and often in remote locations—can afford to spend heavily. "Boom towns" grow around them, inducing high living and entertainment costs and major stresses on existing, possibly rudimentary, infrastructure. Goods and services, especially housing, are in short supply and local price inflation follows inevitably. The burden falls on those outside the extractive industries—especially government workers such as police, nurses, and school teachers. Large numbers of transient workers living away from home face boredom and isolation. Prostitution becomes an irresistible temptation—a deadly one since the arrival of HIV/AIDS—and drugs may make their first appearance. Ironically, industry employees who become HIV positive may be guaranteed antiretroviral treatment by their employers, while persons in the community whom they infect—typically young women—have no such fall back. The icon of the boom town phenomenon is the nurse or school teacher who earns more in a week as a night-club hostess than in a year in her original profession, though her new career may be a short one. The saddest stage of the boom town life cycle is perhaps the last: the ghost town that has lost its reason for existence once the resource that sustained it—minerals, oil, or gas—has run out.

Environmental Effects

Badly engineered and badly maintained mining or oil ventures can cause massive environmental damage. The 1996 Marcopper incident in the Philippines, in which vast quantities of tailings from a mining site found their way into a local river, causing massive devastation, is perhaps the most spectacular example of the consequences of poor environmental management. However, systematic, thorough engineering can prevent such incidents, as is shown by the fact that unprecedented large-scale offshore oil and gas developments in environments as hostile as the North Sea have been accomplished by responsible operators without pollution.

But though direct environmental impacts can be minimized or eliminated, indirect ones can be equally serious. Opening roads into hitherto remote areas creates vectors for uncontrolled immigration, unsustainable slash-and-burn farming, illegal logging and—in the worst cases— introduction of new diseases. These effects may not have been consciously intended by the extractive industry, but once the road is in place it may be impossible to control its use.

Conflict

A single major extractive project in a small, hitherto poor country, where no such industry existed before, may double government income almost overnight or increase it by an even larger factor. The revenue can become a target for the unscrupulous and the avaricious, the prize for which ruthless factions will struggle, plot, and stage coups or even civil wars. There will be conflict at the local, provincial, and national levels over division of the revenue, and ethnic and tribal divisions will be exacerbated to support the claims of individual interests. Nigeria's fragmentation from three federal states at independence in 1960 to thirty-seven today, with the murderous Biafran War of Secession a milestone on the way, is an example. At the local level the conflict may not even be ethnic but between villages, as they vie with each other to extract access fees or to sabotage pipelines and facilities to cause spillages so as to claim compensation from the companies operating in their midst. The more such groups are "paid off," the stronger the incentive to cause further disruption, and communities can descend into a self-reinforcing spiral of violence, distrust, and extortion.

The problems discussed above are only a sampling of what may arise; however, they are alike in that they have massive potential for damaging the host society. Some may have immediate consequences, but others may be "slow burn" issues that may smoulder for years before bursting into flame. Yet experience across a wide range of countries and differing societies has shown that if such social, economic, and environmental problems can be foreseen, then imaginative solutions can be devised and put in place as an integral part of any industrial development. The critical process in doing so is *impact assessment,* which identifies the likely consequences, both ecological and socioeconomic, of a specific proposed development on its host environment and society.

This impact assessment process is well-established, and large numbers of competent organizations are available to execute such studies. Thus, the question may well be asked, If these problems of business impact matter so much, why do companies and governments not do more to recognize and pre-empt them? The answer lies in a clash of cultures between the business and the public—in the widest sense—sectors, as discussed below.

THE CLASH OF CULTURES BETWEEN THE BUSINESS AND PUBLIC SECTORS

A major business project—a mine, an oilfield development, a processing or manufacturing plant—may well cost billions rather than millions of dollars, typically may take five years to recover the investment before a cent of profit is made (though in some sectors even longer times may be involved), and may have a productive lifetime of many decades. The decision to authorize the investment is a weighty one, taken only after extensive studies, and will normally reflect concerns related to managing risk and uncertainty in the following areas.

Technical: Is the proposed development technically feasible? Typical concerns might be whether a process that works on a laboratory test-rig will work satisfactorily on an industrial scale; the possible extent of mineral ores buried deeply in difficult to access terrain; whether an offshore oil-production platform can be designed to withstand extreme weather conditions in water depths well in excess of a thousand feet; or whether gas can be safely refrigerated, liquefied, shipped over thousands of miles, and regasified for use by consumers. The concerns refer not only to initial design and construction but to safety, reliability, and maintainability over decades. As many as twenty individual scientific and technological disciplines may need to be integrated in the design process, and a complex project management process will be required for the costing, scheduling, contracting, and supervision of the execution.

Commercial: Is the proposed development commercially viable? The issue is not just whether it will make a profit but whether it will provide a return on capital that will equal, or surpass, other investment opportunities available. Detailed knowledge of markets—and informed judgement—will be needed as to the likely range of prices that may be obtainable for the product well into the future. Prediction is impossible, so ranges of risk and uncertainty must be assessed and the robustness of the investment evaluated against them. Similar concerns apply to future costs, such as goods and services needed for operation and maintenance. The extent to which alternative products, or innovations by competitors, may undermine these assumptions must be taken into account. Recommendations also are needed as to whether the company should be the sole participant in the development or whether for risk spreading, necessary business relationships, technology access, or other reasons a joint venture should be created with another entity, or entities, that will then become joint investors in the project.

Environmental: Is the ecological footprint of the proposed development acceptable? Compliance with statutory regulations for minimization of air, water, and ground pollution by effluents is the most straightforward challenge. More difficult are indirect impacts such as the influence on breeding habits of local fauna and the long-term consequences, as mentioned earlier, of providing access by road to remote areas. Developments concentrated in a relatively small area—such as a process plant—represent lesser challenges than "transit" developments such as pipelines that traverse long distances and varying terrain. In some cases it may be appropriate in remote areas for ecological (and public health) reasons to decide against surface transportation and to rely instead purely on water or air transport for getting personnel and equipment to the site. Associated with this may be a decision to treat the site as an "island" on land, with clearly defined boundaries beyond which personnel are not allowed to venture. Opportunities for proactive ecological management—for example, by working with government and civil society for creation of wildlife reserves in the areas of operation—can also be sought. The most important consideration, however, is that the environmental impact not be regarded as a stand-alone issue, to be managed in isolation from technical and commercial concerns, but rather as integral with them. Environmental management is a discipline based on hard scientific principles, and there is every reason to treat it with the same rigor as, for example, geology, structural engineering, or process design.

Social: Will the host society be a better place to live if this proposed development proceeds? The term "host society" may cover several levels of community, from the villages in the immediate vicinity of the development, to the province or state in which the development is located, and, for major projects that are massive revenue producers, to the nation as a whole. The concerns may include "boom town effects," as discussed earlier, public health, migration of labor and changes of ethnic balances, creation of internal tensions and rivalries where they did not exist previously, challenges to existing social and behavioral norms, and massive strains on infrastructure, education, and health care provision. Positive effects may include widening of expectations and opportunities, including for women, and impetus for local business and industry to expand—or grow from scratch, if suitably supported—to support the development's needs. If "maximization of local content" is addressed as an integral part of the technical and project management, with hard targets set and realized, then the impact in terms of job creation can be massive. However, all these issues, positive and negative, need to be addressed in the context of total venture life—which may be decades—and not during the initial construction period only. The challenge involved in long-term commitment is obviously daunting.

Economic: Will the host society's economy be improved if this proposed development proceeds? At first glance it would appear that the answer must always be yes since royalties and taxes, direct and indirect, must contribute to the country's exchequer and a company's investment is always welcome. The "Dutch Disease" problem discussed earlier is one reason, however, why this may not be the case, and the distortions involved when a country becomes overdependent on the revenue yield of extractive industries, which by their nature have a finite life span, can be disastrous as natural resources run out. International trade agreements may have similar impacts. Some 50,000 jobs were created in the garment industry in Lesotho by East Asian investors in the 1990s as a means of getting imports into the vast U.S. market. The expiration in 2005 of the World Trade Organization's (WTO) thirty-year-old Multi-Fibre Agreement (MFA) opened this market to Chinese imports. Jobs in Lesotho evaporated as rapidly as they were created originally, and it has taken resolute action by the Lesotho government to establish the country as "a destination of ethical choice" for customers to counter the trend. Fiscal and taxation policy may be similarly important for long-term investments and uncertainty on this score, as well as the propensity of some governments to change the ground rules after costs have been sunk—or the suspicion that they might—may alter the perception of business of the desirability of investing in the country in the first place, as will concerns about currency volatility and inflation.

Political: Will the host nation's political stability improve if the proposed development proceeds? As discussed earlier, substantial increases in government revenues may become destabilizing factors. Unless there already is a strong tradition of the rule of law, an impartial judiciary, and a civil service of unimpeachable integrity, corruption and peculation may be serious threats. When ethnic or tribal tensions are added to the mix, the situation may become explosive, with civil war or secessionist movements real possibilities. Even where this is not the case, the business activity may become a "political football" to be struggled over by contending parties and to be subjected to the threats of whole or partial nationalization, changes of taxation, and nomination of political nominees to positions for which they are unfitted. In the worst case a country may descend to the level where only the most unscrupulous businesses are prepared to operate. Such operations may cut deals that are not to the benefit of the vast majority of the citizens and exploit resources in inefficient and irresponsible ways that provide short-term benefit, with the knowledge that the current situation cannot last but that substantial profits can be reaped before the inevitable crash occurs.

In dealing with the above concerns, influence is brought to bear by both the business entity promoting the development and by what business would see as *third parties*—a term that covers government, civil society, media, and communities, both represented and unrepresented. The power to influence these groups varies very significantly across the range of decision areas and is represented schematically in figure 1.

In the *technical* area specialist expertise built up by the company over many years allows a high degree of independent decision making with minimum input from third parties, who in general neither understand these aspects of the business nor have the expertise or inclination to learn about them. Government input may be restricted to no more than ensuring that specific regulations—for example, for integrity of pressure vessels, or for rates of extraction that will ensure maximum oil recovery—are observed. In crucial areas, such as the assurance that adequate technical and safety standards are being observed, government may have de facto transferred its responsibilities to recognized certification bodies such as Lloyds, Bureau Veritas, ABS, or Det Norske Veritas.

Commercial aspects are subject to a higher degree of third party influence, most notably from competitors and market forces. Government and civil society impact is low, however, again not least because the processes

Figure 8.1   Relative Powers of Business and Third Parties to Influence Areas of Concern

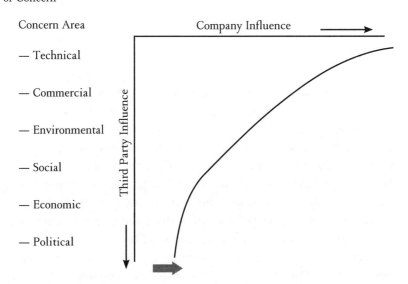

involved are alien to those who have been trained in the noncommercial sector and many affect contempt as well as ignorance for the wealth creation as opposed to the wealth distribution process. The financial media often represent a significant external influence in this area, but their focus is on the business aspect and shared value, and as such their commentaries are often ignored by civil society.

It is in the *environmental* area that government, civil society, and media begin to influence decision making in roughly equal measure to the company. The company is likely to have its own highly competent environmental specialists, even if the broader implications of their findings are not always welcome. Government, at least, is likely to have the specialist technical expertise available to address the issues involved in objective terms, even if civil society and media may well focus on emotive and sensational aspects, often as part of a wider agenda that has little to do with the specific development in question. Business often tends to argue its environmental case in terms of narrow compliance with regulations—and regulations, though they prevent bad practice, do not necessarily promote good practice. Through this narrow focus the wider, and indirect, environmental issues may be overlooked by the company, and yet it is about these that civil society and media are most likely to be concerned. Thus, the stage is set for confrontation based on mutual miscomprehension and distrust.

The *social* area sees the balance of influence swing decisively toward the third parties, even if they themselves are not fully aware of their own strength, are slow to recognize the potential long-term impacts of the business development on them, and are usually uncoordinated and reactive in their responses. Government, civil society, and media are likely to concentrate on the construction phase and on the immediate consequences of the business development—employment, local disruption, surges in revenue, etc.—rather than the longer-term impacts that are likely to change the host society, locally or nationally, over decades. Business, generally lacking the skills and, more importantly, the aptitude to address social issues comprehensively (this will be discussed in detail below), will also concentrate on achieving acceptability of its venture in the immediate term, often by "buying off" communities with "Social Development Projects" and "Corporate Social Responsibility" gestures that are just that—gestures. As a result, a fool's paradise situation is created in which serious long-term issues go unrecognized, thus becoming "sleepers" that smolder for years until they finally burst violently into flame.

In the *economic* sector government reigns supreme. It sets licensing policy for exploration and production, deciding what geographic areas will be opened for access by business, when they will be opened, and what bidding or award process will be used. It decides what companies—and what types of companies—will be welcome to bid and is in a position to play one business off against the other. It decides taxation and royalty levels and has the power to alter them arbitrarily in the future. It has the freedom to institute tax holidays or other incentives to stimulate investment. It is most likely to be able to control interest rates through the central bank and will have inside knowledge on macroeconomic trends in the country. Business—particularly international business, and especially if it is entering the country for the first time—is weak by comparison and to a great extent has to accept what government decrees. It may lobby against measures that it sees as counter to its interests, but it is always up against the ultimate sanction of government—its freedom to pick and choose between competing companies eager to gain access to what are perceived as attractive opportunities and ready to yield to any government demands.

The *political* area sees business at its least knowledgeable and its least influential. In many countries it is a given that a large part of the political spectrum is automatically and unthinkingly suspicious and hostile to business, and demands for policies such as nationalization or changes in taxation levels may be important campaign issues. It is easy, then, for business—like many politicians themselves—to become focused on the immediate political situation, with a time scale no longer than the next election, and to miss the longer-term sociopolitical trends that may totally transform a society in the intermediate term and render the business environment hostile. Resentment of business presence, and of the social, cultural, and economic changes it brings, can trigger new and unexpected political movements; major increases in revenue may trigger internal conflicts, changing the political environment irrevocably. However, business often shows itself to be singularly inept in either recognizing or coping with such trends.

For the oil industry in particular the economic and political powers of government often combine in a way that reduces yet further the power of the private company to influence outcomes. Participation by the private company may only be acceptable if it enters into a joint venture with the government's own national oil company, with a majority shareholding for the latter a nonnegotiable condition but with the private company acting as the operator. Depending on the terms of the production agreement negotiated—"imposed" may often be more appropriate—the company may be required to carry part or all of the national oil company's share of the investment until such time as it can be repaid by production revenues. The company then has the option of accepting participation on government terms or of losing the investment opportunity outright. Large numbers of other companies will be ready to take up the opportunity if the first company declines. In such circumstances it is not unusual for companies to avoid outright even the mildest potential confrontation with government on issues that are perceived as sensitive, with responsible revenue management topping the list.

The six areas of concern discussed above—which must be addressed in an integrated fashion if major investment decisions that are acceptable and beneficial to all parties are to be reached - fall into two categories, as seen in table 1.

There is a very human tendency to shrink back from areas in which one's power to influence decisions will always be weak, and to learn less

Table 8.1   Areas of Concern between the Business and Public Sectors

Technical and Commercial	• Business expertise, power, and influence dominant • Third party understanding and influence limited
Environment, Social, Economic, and Political	• Third party power and influence equal or dominant • Business undersatnding generally weak • Business impact may be very significant • Understanding by both business and third parties of long-term implications of investment decisions limited

about these areas than about those where it is stronger. This attitude ignores the fact that increased knowledge leads to increased insight, and this in turn to increased influence. Willingness by business to spend more time and effort learning about the underlying dynamics, relationships, and complexities of the social, economic, and political environment in which it wishes to operate, not only in the short term but over the longer term as well, can substantially improve its power to influence third party actors. With this increased knowledge, the business' sphere of influence vis-à-vis third parties will shift substantially, as illustrated in figure 2.

Though decision making should take all these areas of concern into account, it seldom does. It is notable, however, that the consequences of making serious errors in the two general categories described in table 1 are significantly different. A serious misjudgement with regard to technical or commercial aspects may have serious consequences in terms of human and material loss and decreased profit. For major companies, however, for which a single plant or project represents only one element in a much larger portfolio, the loss may well be survivable. For example, the 1984 Bhopal disaster in India, in which safety systems failed in a pesticide factory, resulted in the deaths of several thousand area residents. Yet the company responsible, Union Carbide, survives today, albeit as a subsidiary of another industrial group. Likewise, despite the explosion of the Piper Alpha oil and gas platform in 1988, which killed 167 people and is the worst in the history of the UK's North Sea development, Occidental Petroleum continues to thrive today.

Figure 8.2 Business Sector's Level of Influence with Increased Knowledge

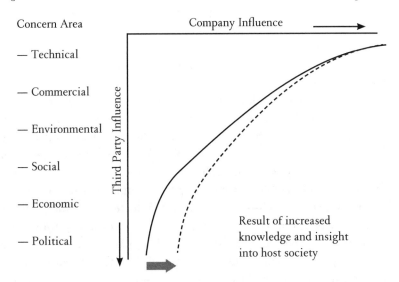

In contrast, decisions that take insufficient account of environmental, social, economic, and political factors tend to have more far-reaching consequences. The impacts triggered may take longer to manifest themselves, and the discontents and grievances may lie hidden as "sleeper issues" for long periods, but resentments ultimately boil over. And though business may suffer, the greatest loser may well be the general population. A notable example is the widespread discontent in Iran in the 1970s, which was fueled by the perceived misuse of oil revenues and challenges to cultural norms. The situation was exploited by the Islamic Fundamentalist movement and led to the 1979 Revolution, the ultimate consequences of which are unclear even today. Another example is the descent of the Niger Delta into near anarchy in recent years, largely as a result of ethnic tensions and rivalry over allocation of revenues and access to benefits distributed by oil companies that have increasingly taken over local government responsibilities in the face of government's retreat from the area. Finally, the use of oil revenues by one political grouping, and of diamond revenues by its rivals, funded the long cycle of civil wars that plagued Angola for some thirty years. The willingness of international business to exploit opportunities in Angola throughout this period was a major factor in prolonging the conflict.

In the light of the above discussion we must ask, Where does business expend most effort when planning a new venture or project? The answer, sadly, is predominantly in the technical and commercial areas, significantly in the environmental area, and hardly at all in the social, economic and political areas. The reason for these disparities is not surprising: business recruits its executives from graduates in the "hard disciplines"—engineering, accounting, law, the natural sciences, etc. Both by original aptitude and by virtue of their education, which is usually significantly meager in the "softer" human disciplines, these graduates often have little understanding—or perhaps more importantly, sympathy—for a worldview that assigns as much value to the interests of the wider society as to those of the employing company. The employee from this background will perform well—even superbly—in the technical and commercial areas, where the hard disciplines in which they are qualified and comfortable are needed; and they may well function effectively in the environmental area, since this also has a quantifiable scientific basis. However, the typical employee will distrust—even shrink back from—wholehearted engagement with the less quantifiable, certainly more anarchic, wider society in which intuition, emotional intelligence, and the ability to reach a compromise through long and frustrating dialogue count for more than technical expertise.

This discomfort with wider society often is reinforced through experience within the company. Dealings with regulators, government, or civil society who seek to influence or set limits on company plans will be seen as battles in a zero-sum game in which one side wholly wins or wholly loses. An often beleaguered "us and them" mind set will become entrenched, distinguishing "We, the Company" from the "Outside World" and ignoring the fact that the "We, the Company" represents a tiny fraction of the totality of humanity. The company's often reluctant concessions to demands for compliance with rising societal demands for transparency, accountability, and responsibility may reveal a high degree of cynicism among employees, often masked by ostentatious, even obsequious, public support of the "Company Line" on these issues. Despite attitudes of this sort, however, promotions and bonuses will be overwhelmingly determined by contributions to short-term profitability and the extent to which the "Outside World" is compelled to accept company solutions. The strength of company culture in reinforcing such behavior often is evident in the phenomenon of employees who in their private lives would be quick to sign petitions or join protests against the location of cellular phone masts, fast food outlets, or shopping malls close to their residences, but who during business hours feel genuinely aggrieved that anybody could object to their plans for open-cast mining, pipeline laying, or effluent discharge wherever this best suits company interests.

Poor qualification and aptitude for the "softer" disciplines translates into reluctance to engage wholeheartedly in the socially, economically, and politically dominated decision areas, precisely because company influence is—and indeed should be—weak in these sectors. It would be a mistake to believe, however, that weakness equates with impotence. Willingness to listen as well as dictate, to persuade and to explain; skills in alliance building and compromise; and readiness to accept that a solution that business might see as "partial" and "a concession to critics" might be more beneficial over the long term than an "absolute victory" in the short term are all qualities that will allow business to function more effectively and sustainably in these areas.

Business' reluctance to adapt its behavior in this way will result in failure to secure the informal "license to operate" and "license to grow" from the host society. These so-called licenses are not formal authorizations but rather represent the willing assent of the host society in its widest sense to accept business as a valid member of the community and to cooperate with, or at the very least not to hinder, its activities. Without these informal licenses no business is sustainable. This is especially the case for the extractive sector, which impinges so dramatically on adjacent communities and is so vulnerable to their ability to hinder access, while at the same time impacting so powerfully on the national economy through its generation of tax and royalty revenues.

THE ENVIRONMENTAL AND SOCIOECONOMIC IMPACT ASSESSMENT PROCESS

How can business better prepare itself to make decisions that are simultaneously and equally responsible to shareholders, employees, and the wider host community? The answer lies in strict execution of the environmental and socioeconomic impact assessment process and in implementation of its findings in venture planning, execution, and operation. The process predicts possible complex problems and identifies imaginative

Figure 8.3   The Impact Assessment Process

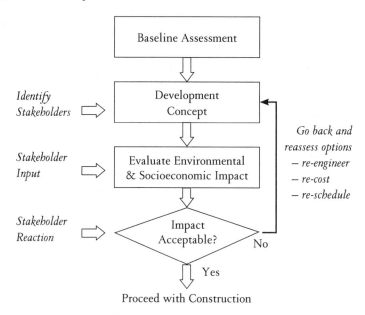

solutions that have the ownership of all the involved parties. The process itself is simple, as seen in figure 3.

The starting point of the process is a baseline assessment—a picture of the host environment and community before any development is initiated by business. Both quantitative data and qualitative description should be employed; the latter is especially important with regard to quality of life issues. The assessment must be undertaken by an independent entity—an established specialist contractor, a respected NGO, or a development agency—and though paid for by the company its integrity and objectivity must be above reproach. It may be appropriate at this stage to appoint a review committee consisting of impartial and respected representatives from academia and civil society as well as from the company itself. The ethics committees commonly used in the medical and pharmaceuticals field are good models for ensuring that the terms of reference for the assessment are sufficiently broad and that the methods used and results obtained are comprehensive.

The greatest challenge for the baseline assessment stage is identifying the host community and determining its boundaries. For a small undertaking, the host community may represent no more than those living in the immediate surroundings of the development. For a large industrial plant or extractive venture, however—which will have a life of several decades, will deliver substantial revenue flows to government, may be a major spur to other industrial and commercial growth, will employ large numbers indirectly as well as directly, and will have a significant ecological footprint—the term *host community* may embrace substantial aspects of the national economy and communities remote from the venture's actual physical location.

The company's development concept is now established. It does not have to be complete in all details, but the concept should be firm and the major parameters and dimensions should be specified. These will include the following:

> the physical location of the business and plans for land acquisition and clearance
> facilities to be constructed and infrastructure required to support them
> effluents and discharges
> numbers, qualification levels, and origin of those employed directly and indirectly during both construction and subsequent operation
> provisions for housing of temporary workers, if required
> likely values of payrolls during both construction and operation phases
> sources of goods and services required
> likely number and value of contracts to be available
> production volumes and consequent tax and royalty revenue streams
> company policies in place, or envisaged, with regard to environmental and human resource management, community relations, government relations, security management, etc.

The obvious next step is to evaluate what impact the proposed development concept could have on the host environment. For this assessment to be meaningful, however, it cannot be done by the company or its contractors in isolation, and it must involve the representatives of the host community—the stakeholders—who will be affected. Such stakeholders do not exist in isolation—issues create stakeholders, no less than stake-holders create issues—and the starting point for this evaluation is identi-fication of the likely issues that the development concept will create. With issues specified, stakeholders can be identified and a matrix com-pleted that identifies who is likely to be interested in specific issues (see figure 4).

This is only a starting point. The matrix will have to be updated con-tinuously; however, it does provide the basis for creative dialogue and fu-ture alliance building. The following points must be stressed concerning the matrix:

- Identifying the first stakeholders and the first issues on the matrix is easy, but extending the axes vertically and horizontally is more difficult.
- Some of the most important stakeholders may not have any formal representation at present—they may consist of dispossessed groups;

Figure 8.4   Identifying Issues and Stakeholders

Issues

		Issue 1	Issue 2	Issue 3	Issue 4	Issue 5	Issue 6	Issue 7	Issue 8	Issue 9
Stakeholders	S/H A	X		X					X	X
	S/H B		X				X	X		
	S/H C			X	X				X	
	S/H D	X					X			X
	S/H E			X		X		X		

or they may not even be in the country, but they still have strong interest in what is happening there.

- A sober assessment is needed of the legitimacy of each stakeholder. The most vocal groups, including NGOs, may be self-appointed spokespersons with little backing in the community, and the stances they take may be subordinate to some wider agenda.
- Some of the most important issues may not emerge until many years into the operational life of the venture, though their seeds may have been sown during initial construction. By the time these "sleepers" burst into life it may be too late to remedy them.
- Only continuous and open dialogue with stakeholders will enlarge the matrix and ensure that all valid viewpoints are recognized.

The evaluation of the venture's impact can now commence. It must be comprehensive in scope, addressing the full range of potential consequences discussed above not only in the short term but over the full lifetime of the venture. Environmental assessment is perhaps easiest because it deals with measurable physical quantities and generally hard scientific facts. Social and economic impacts are more difficult to predict, depending as they do on picturing how complex communities, with different dynamics, interests, and concerns, may react over years, even decades, to the stimulus of an industrial or commercial development. A degree of scenario creation and even storytelling may be needed to envisage how certain decisions may have certain consequences over a long period. Thus, a single apparently simple decision—such as work schedules and accommodation policy for a temporary workforce—can have major long-term implications.

For example, let us envisage a scenario in which a large industrial plant is to be built in a remote area in a developing country, adjacent to a small town that serves the needs of local subsistence farmers. It is estimated that to construct the plant some 1,000 specialist construction workers, supported by 2,000 laborers, will be required for a three-year period. Some 100 employees will be required to operate the plant thereafter. The 2,000 laborers are not available locally, but because there is a work shortage in the country, workers will undoubtedly turn up once they hear of work being available. Where the 1,000 specialist workers will come from will depend on what international contractor wins the construction tender, but they will come from overseas since the expertise is not available locally.

Several issues and questions must be considered in this situation:

- How will the temporary labor be housed? Will the company provide, or subsidize, housing? Does this represent an opportunity or a threat for the existing community?
- Will the arrival of the extra labor create ethnic or other tensions in the community and do the administrative and other provisions exist to cope with it if it does?
- The international workforce may move on when construction finishes, but what about the laborers native to the country? Will they stay on, hoping for further work, and thus change the community?
- Can the existing social and community infrastructure—roads, water and electricity supplies, education, health care, security—cope with the influx of workers? What responsibility does the company have to finance expansion of this infrastructure?
- Will the existing population be hit by local inflation caused by the presence of highly paid labor?
- Are the local authorities aware of what the long-term impact on their community may be? Do they have the necessary skills to identify the issues or address the challenges that will arise?
- Who speaks for the community concerning the question of whether the social changes that will come about are desirable? Who can be consulted? Who speaks for the unrepresented?
- What rotation and work cycles will be applicable to foreign specialist workers? The longer the cycle, the more likely that they will resort to prostitutes and drug use.
- If prostitution is identified as a potential problem, what alternative, high-income jobs can be made available for young women, and what is the company's responsibility to ensure their creation?
- What policy in relation to HIV/AIDS and STDs will the company adopt not only with regard to its own and its contractors' workers but also the local population?
- Are local health facilities capable of coping with increases in HIV/AIDS and STDs, if these are foreseen as potential problems? What is the company's responsibility for supporting expansion of such facilities?
- The presence of so many workers will create legitimate small-scale business opportunities for the local population, including catering,

lodging, and transport. The local residents, however, may not have the financial resources to take advantage of these opportunities. What "soft loan" provisions could be made to assist such enterprises?

The identification of impacts, much less their quantification, is a slow process, necessitating not just dialogue but exploratory discussion and speculation with a range of stakeholders and analysis of what has occurred elsewhere when similar ventures have been undertaken. Significant time may need to be invested in gaining stakeholders' trust and in explaining in simple, unambiguous terms exactly what is intended. Short "in and out" visits to village communities by specialists who deal only with government officials or perhaps self-appointed community leaders will not suffice. Time must be spent understanding the internal dynamics of the community—the respective roles, for example, of women and youths' groups, as well as of elders—and understanding how these impact on decision making. Particularly challenging for extractive industries will be assessment of the impact of tax and royalty revenues, including how these will be distributed by government to the national, provincial, and local levels, how transparently they will be employed and for what purposes, and whether these revenues in themselves may become the source of internal conflict. The "resource curse" that has plagued so many developing countries will need to be addressed honestly. Entities with expertise in this area, such as the World Bank, may need to be involved at this stage, either in the role of advisors or as intermediaries with government in assessing the likely impact.

The outcome of the evaluation stage will be a list of impacts, such as those outlined above. Before addressing the key question of whether these impacts are acceptable or not, however, the company must decide whether it will publish the full assessment, making it available not just to stakeholders dealt with earlier but to any party expressing interest. *This is perhaps the critical moment for establishing the company's credibility as a transparent and accountable corporate citizen in the eyes of the host community.*

The method of "publishing" is relevant. Holding a presentation in an urban hotel far from the community that will be most directly affected, and announcing that it is open to all interested parties, may in theory count as transparency but in practice will do nothing to alert the broadest range of citizens of that community—who may be semiliterate and live in remote swamp or bush locations—as to what is being considered for them. The assessment documentation may be thorough and fully supported by scientific data, but unless it is supplemented by a simplified version written in terms clear to the intelligent but not well-educated lay person, then it may not be appropriate. Attempts to withhold findings on impacts, unwillingness to discuss them openly or to discuss ways in which they can be minimized or eliminated, or presentations that have more "spin" than substance may not be seen through immediately, but in the longer term the lack of trust will inevitably reveal itself. Company credibility and trustworthiness will then be damaged, perhaps irreparably, and the trust of the community will be forfeited. From that moment the license to operate—and the license to grow in the future—will be seriously at risk.

At this point the company must decide whether the overall socioeconomic and environmental impacts of the venture are acceptable. If the answer is yes—or more likely, yes, with some adjustments to the development concept to ensure full acceptability—then the next step is obvious: proceed with construction. If the answer is no, however, then it is necessary to go back to the original development concept and re-engineer, recost, or reschedule the concept so as to eliminate the concerns identified. In an extreme case it may be necessary to alter the development concept fundamentally—to choose another location for a plant, to reroute a pipeline to avoid a specific community or terrain, to rely on air transport rather than cutting roads through rain forest, to isolate construction workers completely from surrounding communities to avoid the risk of introducing infections to which they had not previously been exposed. Where such an extreme overhaul of the development concept is required, the entire impact assessment cycle needs to be repeated, resulting in considerable delay in construction.

Deciding what constitutes acceptability is an action that cannot be taken—morally or ethically—by the company alone, though in practice it often is. The input of valid stakeholders, primarily those involved at earlier stages, is essential in order for the decision to be accepted, even owned, by the host community. Uniform assent is unlikely, but support should be forthcoming from what would be widely regarded as the majority of the valid stakeholders. If an independent review committee has been set up at the baseline assessment stage, then it would represent the ideal body for debating the acceptability of potential impacts.

Reworking a concept to address unacceptable impacts inherent in it will always be an unwelcome step for the company. It is inevitable that alternatives to doing so will be sought. A major temptation will be to leave the concept essentially unchanged but to gain the support of the stakeholders—or bribe them into acquiescence, depending on one's viewpoint—with a package of "community development initiatives" that have little or nothing to do with the impact per se. The likelihood is that these initiatives will be accepted with little thanks by the community. A degree of acceptance is purchased for a short period, but resentment at the unresolved impact issue will smolder and build, only to blaze up at a later stage. Such measures can be fairly compared with giving an aspirin to a patient complaining of a headache but who is in fact afflicted with a slowly growing brain tumor. Adherence to the impact assessment process can be viewed as the acid test for the sincerity of any company regarding its societal obligations. It does, however, have major implications for the company's way of doing business, as will be discussed in the next section.

IMPLICATIONS OF THE IMPACT ASSESSMENT PROCESS

The greatest single implication of the impact assessment process is that if it is taken seriously it can add significantly to the time required to realize a project, especially if it uncovers unacceptable impacts that demand significant re-engineering or re-scheduling of the original concept. Business generally bases investment decisions on discounted cash-flow economics, which are built on the concept of the "time value of money." Simply stated, the time value of money means that a dollar spent today is worth more than a dollar earned in five years time, and significantly more than a dollar earned in ten years time. The extent to which this is the case is determined by the rate of return an investor could obtain elsewhere for the same investment. The consequence for the economic attractiveness of a capital-intensive project is that up-front investment in construction is offset ever more weakly by future earnings from production the further into the future that production occurs. The incentive exists, therefore, to commence production—that is, move into earning mode—at the earliest possible moment, and anything that prevents production must be resisted as much as possible.

Given this pressure the impact assessment process will be seen by many within the company as an expensive luxury that is undertaken only to fend off external critics and as an activity not integral to the project as a whole. The entire consultation-based methodology and its orientation toward compromise between technical and commercial imperatives and wider societal needs may be regarded by many in the company as culturally alien; the tension between the "hard" and "soft" disciplines discussed above now comes to center stage. The requirement for impact assessment may be complied with, but it will not be perceived as adding long-term value to the venture. Rather, it is seen as an obligation to be complied with reluctantly, at the minimum level possible, and in such a way as to ensure that the plans and schedule already envisaged—perhaps even agreed upon—for the project will not be affected by the findings. Cases exist of baseline assessments being started after construction was already far advanced and of impact assessment contractors being told to produce a report only after the project in question was complete. These may be extreme instances, but they are symptomatic of an attitude not uncommon in industry.

Amelioration or elimination of some impacts may demand significant changes in cherished ways of working. In many industries the "Engineer, Procure, Construct" (EPC) model of contracting may be the preferred method for realizing large projects. In this model the overall concept and performance specification for an industrial plant is drawn up by the client—the company that will own and operate the plant—and a contractor, chosen by competitive tender, will then take over the detailed engineering, the procurement of all equipment, and the construction of the plant. Such contracts are often referred to as "turn key" because the client can enter into the contract, essentially sit back until construction is complete, and then "turn the key" to start up and begin operation of the plant. Unless the tender documentation specifies in considerable detail how the contractor will manage details such as sourcing and accommodation of labor, rotation schedules, community interactions, etc., the contractor will be wholly at liberty to make whatever arrangements it sees fit. Similar freedoms will exist in all other areas related to construction, including sourcing of goods and services—freedoms that will not necessarily provide the assistance needed so that local industry and commerce can benefit from the opportunity to expand or adapt their capabilities to support the new business in their midst.

The following discussion will show that it is extremely difficult to manage socioeconomic impacts during the construction phase under an EPC contract because it is in the contractor's best interest is get mobilized, get the job done as quickly as possible, and then get out. Good relations with the local community may be "purchased" by the contractor by spending large sums on activities that produce short-term goodwill but that are by their nature unsustainable since the contractor will disappear upon completion of the project. This mode of operating, however, will create an expectation in the community of continuing largesse at this same high level throughout the plant's operational life. Because the contractor's interest ceases with plant start-up, there is no reason for it to take the long-term interests of the host community into account. If the client company does not write such obligations into the EPC contract, the contractor's true legacy may be in terms of slums created on marginal land by casual laborers who have flocked to the worksite and stayed on after the end of construction; degradation of local society through prostitution and drug use; the introduction of new strains of STDs or HIV/AIDS; and the despair that results when the mushroom economy of a boom town collapses once construction is completed.

The tendency of contractors to believe they can buy themselves community cooperation during the construction period may be matched by a similar conviction from the company side. Where negative socioeconomic impacts on the community have been identified, it may seem easier to purchase community goodwill with development programs that have little to do with the company's activities per se but that may be seen as casting it in a beneficial philanthropic light. Major risks are inherent in this approach, however. Unless undertaken in partnership not only with the community but with government as well, many of the development projects may not achieve either community ownership or sustainability. Construction of a school or a clinic may sound admirable, but a school building is not education and a clinic building does not provide health care. Unless provision is made for staffing, for procurement of necessary supporting goods and services, and for ongoing maintenance, then projects of this sort are futile and may end up creating more resentment than goodwill. In the worst case the community may see the construction contract for the school or clinic as an end in itself and demand a string of similar projects, each to stand unused and with the only benefit the provision of temporary employment.

Likewise, investment by a company in activities that are the legitimate responsibility of government—especially a government that is in receipt of very significant royalty and tax revenue from an extractive industry— runs the risk of the responsibility being transferred over time from government to the company. The process may be a slow one, but once private business assumes responsibility for road and bridge construction, for electricity and water supply, for construction of clinics and schools—as oil companies have done in the Niger Delta, under pressure from local communities—government will inevitably retreat from its responsibilities and its credibility and authority will be impaired. The company, present and visible in the community in a way in which government is not, will be under constant pressure, often violent pressure, to provide ever more services. In the process the company engenders a dependency culture—akin to the World War II Cargo Cults in the Pacific region—in the communities they originally set out to assist.

Many of the "fixes" required for problems identified in the impact assessment will be organizational and social rather than technical. They will demand finding solutions in areas in which the company has little or no expertise—public health, for example—and getting solutions in place may necessitate long and patient alliance building with partners who initially may not see eye-to-eye with the company and may lack the necessary experience themselves. The process will be slow—and frustrating. There often will be a reluctance to call in external help, especially from an entity such as an NGO that has major cultural and value differences with the company and that is accustomed to different ways and tempos of working. The process will go more smoothly, however, if the entity in question has been recognized as a stakeholder during the assessment process and if it has been consulted, and involved, in the evaluation of impact acceptability. The next section discusses the challenges—and opportunities—of alliances and partnerships.

PARTNERSHIPS: THE WAY AHEAD

Rather than classifying the impacts of business activities as positive or negative, it is more rewarding to identify them as threats or opportunities. The more obvious threats include boom town effects, "Dutch Disease," and poor environmental management, while the opportunities include stimulation of industrial and commercial growth and increased employment opportunities. There is, however, a third grouping of impacts that, depending on how they are managed, could be transformed either into threats or opportunities. These include increased government revenues—whether they will be used well, or badly, or even misappropriated, and whether the provisions for their distribution and use could become a trigger for internal conflict; societal change, such as the transformation from a subsistence economy to an industrializing one; and changing personal expectations, including employment and personal development opportunities for women and other previously disadvantaged or marginalized groups in a society in which prospects previously were limited to subsistence farming or childbearing. Environmental impact also need not be wholly negative; careful management of industrial development and wise use of revenues may allow for protection of threatened species and habitats in a way previously unaffordable.

The challenge for business is to ensure that the threats are eliminated, or, at worst, managed so that their impact is minimized; that opportunities are exploited to the maximum; and that issues that hover on the threat/opportunity borderline are decisively converted into opportunities. Doing so will mean recognizing not only the necessity of involvement in areas and activities that may be outside the perceived core competence of the company but also that the ability to do so is indeed an integral part of that same core competence. This does not mean that a company needs to do everything in such areas itself, but it does need to know enough about them to work with specialists who do. There is nothing new in this scenario. Oil and mining companies do not regard support activities such as large-scale catering or air transport as core competences, but they know enough about these subjects to be able to specify their needs and employ competent contractors to provide the necessary services. The key to success in managing socioeconomic impacts, no less than support services, is to possess enough knowledge about the subject to recognize its importance to the success of the business and to be able to work with specialists and others who can provide pragmatic solutions.

The range of institutions that can be drawn upon for assistance is wide and includes the following:

academia and research institutes, both international and existing ones in the host country; the latter may be underfunded but can prove very effective if given financial backing

development agencies, both international (for example, the UN Development Program) and national (for example, the U.S. Agency for International Development, AusAID, the UK Department for International Development)

multilaterals, such as the World Bank, with significant experience in management of large-scale social issues such as community relocation and responsible revenue management

government agencies, including national ministries such as education, health, the interior, finance, justice, etc., as well as local government agencies

international NGOs, and their national affiliates, with proven and nonpartisan track records in areas such as community development, ecosystem conservation, women's and children's rights, HIV/AIDS, etc.

local NGOs, which although often very small, underfunded, and lacking resources, have deep roots in the community, possess high identification with its needs, and are energetic, enthusiastic, and potentially very effective if given the right backing

community groups, such as youth clubs and women's and church organizations already involved in development activities

chambers of commerce and trade associations; it is essential to establish early links with these groups in order to identify what goods and services are already being produced locally and provide assistance to increase their capacity to meet the company's needs if necessary

Many of these entities should already have been consulted or involved to some extent during the impact assessment process if it was undertaken comprehensively. Others will be approached for the first time, but in all cases it will be essential to convince the other party that the company is sincere in wishing to establish a mutually beneficial, long-term relationship. Who represents the company in these negotiations is critical. If relationship building is left entirely to some entity with a name such as "Public Affairs" or "Community Relationships," rather than involving operational and business development departments with clear profit-generating responsibilities and, for at least part of the time, top management, then the exercise will be widely perceived as no more than an insincere image-building exercise. Gaining early successes will be critical in establishing company credibility. Examples of activities that can assist in building trust and credibility include facilitation of loans for local businesses to provide catering and transport services; support of local fabrication yards and equipment suppliers; management of the accommodation and behavior of migrant workforces such that the dignity of the local community is respected; establishment of links with local educational establishments—artisan as well as academic—to train locals to take on responsible positions in the company; and launching programs to reduce the likelihood of introduction of HIV/AIDS and other infectious diseases to the host community.

The different paths open to companies in this regard are illustrated in the decisions made and activities developed by two international oil companies. The first company undertook field development for which a large offshore platform was required. The platform would require "topsides" weighing several thousand tons and involve complex processing, power generation, and control and pumping facilities. The oil industry had been moribund for some time in the country in question, and though a substantial fabrication industry existed, the companies and yards were small in size and had never undertaken a project of this scale. The largest items constructed by these companies were determined by the lifting capacity, some four hundred tons maximum, of the only large floating crane in the country. Thus, the oil company has two alternatives. It could construct the topsides in over forty separate modules, ranging from one hundred to four hundred tons, in several separate local yards—itself a nightmare in terms of interconnectivity and coordination. The modules would then be transported offshore, lifted into place individually, and joined with pipework and electric and control cables offshore, an operation demanding the presence of several hundred workers at any time and with very significant management challenges. Completing the project in this way, however, would raise the overall capacity of the local fabrication industry to handle major projects of this type in the future. In contrast, the company could go overseas to yards capable of constructing the topsides in as few as three separate modules, transport the completed modules to the country in question, float them over the platform, and lower them into place. Only yards with extensive experience of such construction would be invited to tender, and since a minimal number of interconnections would be required offshore, much of the commissioning work could be done at the fabrication yard. Minimal input would be required from local industry, and the risks of getting off schedule and increasing costs would thereby be minimized.

The estimated costs would most likely be similar for both options, but the first alterative had higher risks with regard to scheduling and implementation and considerably higher demands on supervision. The oil company chose the first alternative. The project proved even more complex and difficult than anticipated. The problems were overcome, however, and in the process a high degree of mutual respect and trust was created between the oil company and the local fabrication industry and its workers. The completed platform was of high standard and has operated successfully and profitably since commissioning. It is seen by all parties as a major success.

A year later another international oil company needed to construct a platform of similar dimensions in the same country. It chose the second construction method. The three massive modules arrived from overseas on sea-going barges and, while arrangements for mounting on the platform were completed, were moored opposite the main town in the area. This coincided with a period of down-turn of available work in the local fabrication yards, with consequent short-time working and large-scale layoffs. Unemployed workers looked out toward the three massive modules they themselves might have constructed and were resentful. It will take years of goodwill gestures before the second company's claims to be a good corporate citizen, interested in a mutually beneficial relationship with its host community, will be accepted locally. Both companies faced the same choice. One saw it purely in technical and commercial terms. The other recognized that its impact on the socioeconomic well-being of the host community was an equally valid consideration. Both companies ended up making money, but only one did it in a way that recognized the interests—and the dignity—of all stakeholders.

To be effective over an extended period, relationships need to be formalized—not in very rigid fashion but according to a framework that recognizes the interests of all parties, provides mechanisms for resolving differences and reaching consensus, specifies in general terms what each party will contribute to the relationship, and has the flexibility to develop and mutate over time to accommodate changes in circumstances. Once such frameworks are established, specific projects can be undertaken within their boundaries and renegotiation of the relationship will not be necessary. Instead, the relationship between the company and its stakeholders will strengthen over time as trust is built on shared achievement. In the process the relationship will become a partnership based on mutual interest.

The ideal partnership between business and community is rarely a bilateral one. The company does not have all the skills required to support the community in its development aspirations, and the community may well view the company in one of two equally undesirable ways: either as an organization so powerful and so incomprehensible that it cannot be engaged with on equal terms, or as an entity that is vulnerable by virtue of the susceptibility of its operations to disruption and, therefore, a cashcow that can be milked by threats. In either case, the stage is set for longterm dissatisfaction and confrontation. The involvement of third parties, however, can transform the relationship into one that is mutually beneficial. These third parties can play many roles—as mediators, as advisors, as specialists on confidence building, empowerment, and organization creation—and draw on experiences of what has worked elsewhere in comparable circumstances. In some cases the government itself, or its agencies, may be the third party that is involved, and its involvement may include ensuring that the government lives up to its own obligations with respect to provision of health care, education, and infrastructure. The resulting tripartite partnership model is illustrated in figure 5.

The key element in ensuring a sustainable, mutually beneficial, and mutually respectful relationship is that the input of each party should be recognized as being roughly equal. This cannot be an exact calculation but rather is a subjective feeling of "fairness" by all involved and a conviction that the others are "pulling their weight" and not getting disproportionate benefits. Reviewing and maintaining this equivalence is a key responsibility of the steering committee, which should be set up to oversee the workings of the partnership and include representation from all parties involved. The responsibilities of the company would be as follows:

Funding: Economic assistance required to support the activities agreed to be of mutual benefit should be provided by the company *but only where the responsibility for such expenditure does not already rest with*

Figure 8.5   Relationships among the Company, the Host Community, and Third Parties

Ideally the total input of each party is roughly equivalent and matched.

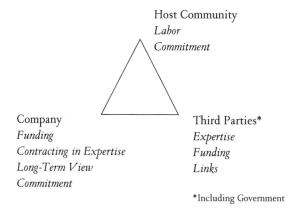

Host Community
Labor
Commitment

Company
Funding
Contracting in Expertise
Long-Term View
Commitment

Third Parties*
Expertise
Funding
Links

*Including Government

government, which should otherwise be persuaded to accept its responsibilities. This is essential if the company is to avoid becoming a government surrogate. In general the funding should cover materials (and expertise, as discussed below) but not labor.

Contracting in of Expertise: It may be necessary to bring in outside workers with specialist skills that may not be present in the community but that will be needed to realize the company's projects. An example would be electricians contracted to wire safely a clubhouse being built by a local youth group.

Long-Term View: This means creating and sharing an understanding of how the presence of the company will affect the community over the long term, including provision of jobs, possible requirements for further land acquisition, and the need to develop alternative sources of employment if the company's activities are likely to have a finite life, as is the case with extractive industries.

Commitment: Companies must share the conviction with the community and other partners that positive change is possible, that difficulties exist to be overcome, and that the company will stand by its obligations to its partners in times of economic hardship as well as in times of plenty.

The community's responsibilities include the following:

- Labor: This may be the only material resource the community can bring to the partnership, but by doing so it ensures that it has ownership of what it builds, even if the raw materials are funded by the company and much of the specialist advice and expertise comes from third parties. By volunteering labor, which ideally should not be remunerated by the company at full commercial rates or, at best, not at all, the community begins to shape its own future.

- Commitment: This is perhaps the most difficult element to achieve since it may require competing factions within the community to settle their differences and agree on common goals. The facilitation of a third party, ideally by a representative that lives in the community for a period of time, may be the best way to achieve this agreement. It may be necessary to foster the growth of entities such as women's or youth groups that will promote and foster community commitment over the long term. The primary objective must be to create a conviction in the community that it can deal on fair and equal terms with the other parties to the tripartite agreement and that there is nothing to be gained either by supine acquiescence or belligerent confrontation.

Third parties are responsible for the following:

- Expertise: NGOs and development agencies will have relevant skills and experience that are not available within the company. They also will be viewed as impartial and may be the ideal mediators and facilitators for setting up the tripartite agreement in the first place. Correct selection is essential, however; NGOs, no less than companies, should be prepared to listen rather than dictate preconceived solutions to communities without adequate consultation or as part of some wider agenda. Particular attention should be paid to the potential of small, local NGOs, which know the culture and community dynamics and which, with support, may prove most effective of all in addressing community issues. Expertise combined with funding, constituting influence that amounts to pressure, is the contribution that may be called on from entities such as the World Bank and the International Monetary Fund (IMF) when they become partners through underwriting government investments in joint ventures with private business. In this process they may be capable of applying a degree of pressure to government to conform with acceptable standards—for example, population relocation or revenue management. A private company would be incapable of applying such pressure without jeopardizing its relationship with the government. It is possible, however, that this power of multilaterals to influence may decline significantly as revenues start to increase and the country is no longer heavily dependent on loans. A situation such as this occurred recently in Chad when the government felt itself sufficiently liberated from previous commitments due to increased oil revenues as to amend substantially the previously agreed upon Petroleum Revenue Management Law.

- Funding: Both government and development agencies may feature as providers of funding in addition to, or in place of, the company. In the case of government it is a question of fulfilling its obligations, which may be highlighted through the partnership creation process, while development agencies may see an opportunity for inclusion of activities under the umbrella of some larger scheme.

- Links: A key contribution of NGOs and development agencies is their networking capability, which allows them to bring in expertise and insights other than they themselves can provide, should this be necessary. This is a capability that no other group possesses to the same extent, and it may well be an important element in ensuring that the partnership develops and adapts over time as new challenges arise.

There is nothing conceptually difficult about the partnership creation outlined above, any more than there is about the impact assessment process. The next section addresses the question of why neither is more widely employed in practice.

BLOCKERS TO PROGRESS

The impact assessment process sounds logical and straightforward, yet despite often lofty intentions, companies run into problems applying it in practice. Why? The first complication is that mentioned earlier: it represents an extra step in the development schedule, and if the findings indicate that significant rework is needed, then commencing production is delayed even further. There may be a strong temptation to argue that the results are not as serious as they seem, or to fudge the issue and implement solutions that are suboptimal. The chances of this happening are higher if the impact assessment process is seen as an add-on, undertaken reluctantly to keep potential external critics quiet, and executed by some entity that is separate from the project or venture-management structure of the company. The chances of delays being minimized are highest if the responsibility for the impact assessment rests squarely with the venture or project manager, and if the assessment is recognized as being as integral to the planning and success of the venture as strict engineering design and sound financial management. In this case the concept definition stage will be undertaken with as much attention paid to socioeconomic and environmental factors as to technical and commercial ones, and challenges in these areas will be addressed at this stage rather than left to be identified later during impact assessment.

A further complication is that impact assessment often involves reporting unwelcome truths: the likelihood that a delay or extra costs will be inevitable if certain impacts are to be minimized or eliminated; that work practices previously considered acceptable must be changed; or that the development concept envisaged may prove acceptable to all parties in the short term but is likely to raise significant socioeconomic problems over the longer term. In the worst case the assessment may recommend that the company not get involved in the country at all or abandon its activities there. This decision was made by several Western oil companies in relation to Myanmar and the Sudan over the last fifteen years. No chief executive, no board of directors, hears such news with pleasure, and it takes a high degree of moral courage for subordinates to report such findings and to spell out their implications—and for boards and chief executives to listen to them.

The "two cultures" challenge for business has been discussed at length above. Unless the challenge of "two cultures" in business is recognized and steps are taken to address it with regard to sensitization of executives and operators, it can be a major blocker to progress. The situation is worse in the case of international companies that deploy large numbers of expatriate specialists and managers to developing countries. Standards of living and security in the host country may be substantially lower than in the expatriate workers' countries of origin; therefore, workers may need to be enticed by creation of secure housing and recreational enclaves, which, though providing a refuge from the real conditions existing in the country, rapidly become claustrophobic and isolated cocoons. In general in situations such as this, briefings on local culture and potential challenges will have been perfunctory, seldom taking up more than a single day, if that. Knowledge of the host country is limited to the commute between home and office and to business relationships only, while social contacts are almost entirely within the circle of the wider expatriate community. This phenomenon is visible even in Western capitals where security is not an issue but where it is not uncommon to meet expatriates who have spent years in the country without learning a word of the local language.

In countries considered "hardship postings" it may be unusual for any expatriate personnel, including senior managers, to be assigned for longer than four to five years. This means that within two to three years of arrival, the individual's focus is on leaving and on the move to the next job. Thus, the incentive to know more about the country, its culture, and its politics is largely eliminated. Upon initial arrival in the country the expatriate manager may well suffer from a degree of "culture shock," possibly heightened by language difficulties, and may well find him or herself wholly dependent on the advice and interpretation of events and circumstances provided by local employees established in senior positions. That this advice and interpretation may represent only a single viewpoint, and one that consolidates the view of staff in positions that benefit them personally and their relationships with "elite" groups in the country, may never be realized. Such local senior staff in powerful positions may have few—or worse still, failing—links with other groups in the country, including the poor, the dispossessed, and ethnic groups other than their own. They may also have agendas that are more focused on their own benefit than the good of the wider community. To a great extent, senior staff represent the local public face of the international company. The local community's perception of the company as no more than a tool of senior executives' personal interests could be a major threat to maintenance of the company's license to operate and its license to grow. Company executives who fall unthinkingly into this trap—often as a result of being insufficiently and too narrowly briefed—may well deliver short-term results. They may, however, be unwittingly complicit in the destruction of the long-term interests of the company, not to mention of the host country.

The most subtle blocker of all to full utilization of the impact assessment process is also cultural: the necessity of admitting that the company is not in total control of its own business. Rather, stakeholders ranging from government to local communities may have not just the power—but a moral right—to comment on, to approve, or to disapprove of what the company wishes to do, and to back this up with action against it. It is not easy for business executives to accept that these stakeholders will demand ever greater transparency concerning not just what the company is doing today but what it plans to do in the future as well. They will demand that the company makes commitments with respect to its impacts on the stakeholders, and they will demand that the company holds itself accountable by reporting progress made toward these commitments. This issue—the company's unwillingness to accept the reality of reduced control—is perhaps the greatest single blocker to success of the impact assessment process.

ENABLERS OF PROGRESS

There are two possible reactions by business to the realization that stakeholders may have more control over its long-term viability than it has itself: anger or acceptance. Anger is natural, but if allowed to become the basis for policy making and behavior, it may result in an endless series of legal confrontations. Points may sometime be scored and small victories won, but the overall campaign to win a long-term license to operate from the host society will be lost before it even starts. Worse still, the anger may decline into grudging, resentful acquiescence, with external demands complied with to the lowest level possible so that relationships never advance beyond suspicion and tit-for-tat trade offs.

Acceptance may be reluctant initially, but once it is recognized that dialogue is essential, and that most valid stakeholders are interested in creating alliances that lead to mutual benefit, the process becomes easier. The first step may be the hardest: admitting that "business does not know best," that there are potential problems related to a venture for which solutions have not yet been identified by the company, and that the company would welcome other views and suggestions and be willing to sit with others and discuss solutions. In some cases it may be necessary to re-plan and reschedule a development completely or site it somewhere else. Stakeholder input concerning such decisions would be welcomed.

Cultural change within business must start from the top—from the board itself. Real change in this regard comes not merely by setting pious aspirations but by ensuring that these are translated into workable procedures, that their implementation is scrupulously monitored, and that subordinates are held accountable accordingly. Clausewitz's dictum that "What is not inspected is not done" is as true in the business world as in the military. In practice this means that the venture or project manager, and his or her staff, must be aware of the importance of "softer issues" (as discussed above) and that they are held accountable for delivering solutions that are valid over the entire life of the venture, not only in the period leading up to and including production start-up. By background and training most of such staff will be graduates in "hard disciplines" and will not have had the necessary sensitization to the "softer issues." Therefore, the challenge for the company is to ensure that the necessary change in mindset is effected. This may not sound easy, yet the success achieved in many companies over the last two decades in relation to management of safety indicates that such change is possible.

Until the 1980s most companies regarded "safety" as a matter for a "Safety Department"—a separate entity within the organization that issued exhortations, provided advice, investigated accidents, and kept statistics. Operational departments were responsible for profit-generating activities, and though they were obliged to pay at least lip service to the Safety Department and its recommendations, operations generally found safety issues onerous and risible and bypassed them when they could. The situation was not helped by the Safety Department sometimes being regarded as a convenient place to re-assign staff who had proved less than effective in operational activities.

Throughout this period a few companies—most notably Dupont—achieved safety performances that were not just better than others in comparable industries but better by factors of several times. The secret was that such well-performing companies did not assign responsibility for safety to a "Safety Department" but rather directly to the managers of the operational departments, who were held accountable for planning, managing, and reporting safety with exactly the same degree of rigor that was applied to their engineering, operational, and financial responsibilities. It was recognized that accidents did not just "happen"; they were the result of combinations of technical and procedural circumstances and of identifiable mind sets and behaviors. As such they could be prevented by redesigning systems, techniques, and processes; by systematic observation to identify vulnerabilities; by retraining personnel; and, above all, by holding chief executives and mangers accountable. *Accountable* in this context meant annual salary increments and bonuses being as much dependent on meeting safety targets as targets for production and financials. "Safety Departments" continued to exist under this model, but they had no direct responsibility for operational safety. Their role was purely advisory and monitoring, but often their authority for monitoring was strengthened by having them report directly to the chief executive.

From the mid-1980s what might be called the "Dupont Model" was accepted widely as the basis for safety management, to the extent that it is now the norm in most major industries. It demanded a significant cultural shift, and in most cases this took upwards of a decade. But the change happened—and because of it hundreds, perhaps even thousands, of lives have been saved worldwide and even larger numbers have been spared injury and permanent disfigurement. A similar challenge faces business today with respect to managing impact.

No less a challenge faces educational establishments. Too many, including some of the most eminent, seem to be rigid embodiments of C. P. Snow's "Two Cultures."[2] They churn out technically, scientifically, and commercially qualified graduates who know nothing of human skills—and feel even less for them—while simultaneously producing graduates in the softer disciplines who are their mirror images. The question for both business and education is whether they will face these challenges willingly, or whether it will take external pressure to force them to change.

NOTES

1. Interview with Margaret Thatcher, *BBC Weekend World,* January 6, 1980.
2. The British scientist and novelist C. P. Snow coined the term "the Two Cultures" when giving the 1959 Rede Lecture at the University of Cambridge.

Snow drew attention to the breakdown of communication between the "two cultures" of modern society—the sciences and the humanities—and cited it as a significant barrier to solution of the world's problems. With an established position in both cultures—as a physicist and as a successful novelist—Snow was well-qualified to raise the issue. Snow's lecture formed the basis for his book *The Two Cultures and the Scientific Revolution* (New York: Cambridge University Press, 1959) and triggered widespread debate in both Britain and the United States in the early 1960s.

CHAPTER 9

Stretching the Limits of Corporate Responsibility

Klaus M. Leisinger

Our experience with the Global Compact over the past four years has shown conclusively that voluntary initiatives can and do work. But we have also learned that they have to be made to work. Governments have to do the right thing: to govern well, in the interests of all their people. Business must restrain itself from taking away, by its lobbying activities, what it offers through corporate responsibility and philanthropy. And civil society actors need to accept that the business community is not a monolithic bloc; that it has leaders and laggards; and that leaders should be encouraged when they take positive steps, even though they may occasionally stumble, and not to be frightened off from trying in the first place.

—Kofi Annan, UN Secretary-General

GLOBAL CORPORATE RESPONSIBILITY IN CONTEXT

The State of Human Development

The UN Secretary-General rightly asks the business community to refrain from taking away, by its lobbying activities, what it offers through corporate responsibility and philanthropy.[1] This chapter will look into ways and means to encourage exemplary corporate conduct, including philanthropy, to enhance efforts to reduce poverty and accelerate human development. It will also deal with attitudes of civil society actors, whom Kofi Annan rightly challenges, to distinguish between leaders and laggards in the business community and to encourage leaders to take positive steps in this difficult area. In the first place, one has to understand that the state of human development is not a good one. Despite significant socioeconomic progress made over the past forty years, about 2.5 billion people must eke out their living on US$2 or less a day, infant and child mortality continues to waste 10 million lives per year, about 800 million people go hungry, more than 800 million women and men cannot write and read, more than a billion people do not have access to safe water and even more lack access to sanitation, and communicable diseases (tuberculosis, HIV/AIDS, diarrhea, measles, malaria, schistosomiasis, and infections of the lower respiratory tract) create a health burden of more than 57 million deaths and 610 million death and disability adjusted life years (DALYs).

Poverty is not only a cause, an associated factor, and a catalyst of ill health, it is also its result. Poverty keeps the poor in ill health and ill health keeps the poor in poverty—a vicious circle.[2] And there are challenging times ahead. The world population will grow from today's more than 6.5 billion to more than 9.2 billion by the year 2050. More than 98 percent of this population growth will occur in the less-developed countries.[3] Even under the best case scenario of achieving the Millennium Development Goals,[4] hundreds of millions of people in future generations will continue to live in misery.

Given the dimensions and complexity of the greatest social challenge of our time, all people and institutions—national governments, the international community, business, and civil society—are called to contribute their reasonable share of resources, skills, and know-how to solutions in the spirit of a fair division of labor.[5] The *primary responsibility* for making progress in human development rests, however, with national governments, and the extent of progress depends on government doing its job right.[6] Whatever opportunities the global economy offers, whatever resources are made available by the international community, good governance is the single most important factor for human development. The task to create the necessary preconditions—such as *transparency* in policy and social decision making, *accountability* for the policies and work performed by state employees, the *rule of law,* an independent and efficient judicial system, *institutional pluralism, participation* in all decisions impacting the lives of people, and *responsiveness* to the most pressing needs—cannot be delegated to any other societal institution.

The State of Corporate Reputation

State governance is unsatisfactory in many countries and scandalous in some. Corporate conduct, as well, is not always ideal.[7] The worst cases of corporate misconduct have a significant negative impact on the overall reputation of a whole industry; any corporate scandal is a burden for the image of business in general. A majority of citizens in forty-seven industrial and emerging countries does not perceive global corporations to work in the best public interest. These surveys also reveal that 65 percent of the interviewees think that NGOs—mainly the corporate "watchdogs" and whistle-blowers—work in the best interest of society.[8] The challenge for companies competing with integrity is to remove this generalized public distrust and receive credit for what they do at least by a differentiating judgment—at best through "reputation capital" granted. The most important precondition for achieving this is a flawless corporate responsibility performance. As Michael Keeley points out, people are very different in what they aim for in social life but very much alike in what they aim to avoid or find harmful. Therefore, corporations must prioritize minimization of harm over other organizational concerns.[9] This makes compliance management very important.

While effective legislation and enforced regulation at the national level are important pillars to enforce a minimum of responsible corporate conduct and prevent corporate ruthlessness, reference to law and regulation alone will only take care of part of the issue. Law is always the ethical minimum, and *legality* is in some cases not sufficient to lend *legitimacy* to corporate conduct. Reliance on law alone triggers legalistic, compliance-based attitudes and, where the quality of law is insufficient, opens vulnerabilities even for corporations acting legally.

CORPORATE RESPONSIBILITIES

The Concept

Ninety years ago, J. Maurice Clark concluded his article on "The Changing Basis of Economic Responsibility" as follows:

> The world is familiar enough with the conception of social responsibilities. These do not need to be rediscovered in the year of our

Lord 1916. But the fact that a large part of them are business responsibilities has not yet penetrated, and this fact does need to be brought home to a community in which business men and theoretical economics alike are still shadowed by the fading penumbra of laissez-faire. The issue is deeper and much more far-reaching than anyone can realize who has not tried earnestly to understand the sources of the deep sense of injustice that animates the discontented classes. The trouble is not that the unfortunate are not helped, but that they are helped in the name of charity, regardless of whether they are victims of their own weakness or of the misfit grindings of our non-too-perfectly-adjusted industrial machine. To many the very word "charity" is as a red flag to a bull, and this will never be otherwise as long as so much that passes for charity is merely repairing the damage or salvaging the wreckage for which industry is the chief responsible cause; the same industry which distributes the dividends out of which charity funds so freely come.[10]

Clark's insistence that corporate philanthropy should not be confused with corporate responsibility is still relevant. Today corporate philanthropy should be seen as an activity to be undertaking in addition to responsible business activities, and not as a way to repair the damage enacted due to a lack of corporate responsibility or compensate for harms done. For example, it would be cynical at best to use child labor in corporate core business and sponsor kindergartens as philanthropic highlights.

As far as conceptual clarity is concerned, we do not seem to have gained a lot of ground. One of the latest comments on this issue comes (this time "in the year of our Lord 2006") from Lisa Whitehouse, who states that "despite 70 years of vociferous academic debate regarding the concept of 'corporate social responsibility' (CSR), it is possible to say, with certainty, that there exists no one universally accepted definition of the term."[11] Yet corporate responsibility belongs to the top five global issues with increasing importance.[12]

A Religion with Too Many Priests

Prominent observers see corporate responsibility as "a religion with too many priests."[13] Mainstream business ethics and the larger part of the corporate responsibility literature suggest that acting in a responsible way means choosing a "legitimacy" rather than a "legality" approach, and judges the former as *the right thing to do*. But, then, what is "the right thing" according to the varied tastes of pluralistic societies?

According to a European Commission's Green Paper,[14] corporations qualify as socially responsible if they voluntarily take on commitments that go beyond common regulatory and conventional requirements, and if they endeavor to raise the standards of social development and environmental protection, respect fundamental rights, and embrace an open governance, reconciling interests of various stakeholders in an overall approach of quality and sustainability. Just like the UN Global Compact, the European Commission sees stakeholder relations as an integral part of corporate responsibility and specifies that "being socially responsible means not only fulfilling legal expectations, but also going beyond compliance."[15]

Today, corporations trying to achieve sustainable financial results are expected not only to avoid scandals but to consistently meet social, ecological, and political standards that will stand up to the judgment of a fair-minded, impartial third person.[16] In effect, this "impartial observer" seems to have rising expectations, while remaining skeptical. A recent Swiss poll shows that a clear majority of the public expects companies to go beyond fulfilling legal duties and to contribute to a better world. When companies actually do so, however, many people do not appreciate those efforts as a genuine motive to make the world a better place and accuse companies of simply polishing their image.[17]

Enlightened companies have long recognized that unfair labor conditions, destructive environmental standards, or "collateral damage" to human rights are unacceptable. For them, the fact that insufficient national legislation results in a low standard of "legality" is no excuse for deficits in corporate responsibility. Instead, they apply intelligent self-restraint by avoiding morally ambivalent business and are willing to pay the (investment, training, and compliance monitoring) costs necessary to avoid substandard corporate conduct. But the difficulties are not yet resolved by *doing no harm*. The far greater challenge is *to do good* or, even more ambitious, to do *the right thing even when difficult*—for example, under conditions of failing markets or failing states.

What It Takes to Do "The Right Thing"

Make the Right Value Choice

Controversies over what the *right thing to do* really is frequently suffer from the fact that the disputants base their norms on different values, personal experiences, or vested interests (often held implicitly). What one party holds to be an absolute value the other may see in a concrete situation as just a minor issue. For example, financial analysts—although becoming increasingly appreciative of a "triple bottom line" philosophy—still focus predominantly on the profitability data of businesses in relation to the benchmarks provided by the best in class. People who lose their employment due to corporate cost-cutting exercises intended to raise profitability to an international benchmark will understandably view the world differently than those who have to meet the expectations of financial markets. The same is true from a societal perspective: Where societies have to bear the social costs of high and rising unemployment (for example, disrupted families, violence, crime, alcohol and drug abuse), there will be no understanding for dismissals with the explanation that these were necessary in order to reduce the danger of "unfriendly takeovers" that could result in even more jobs being lost.

Study the Facts

We often fail to make a distinction between the *value judgment* and the *facts of a case,* although sound judgment ought to presuppose scrupulous clarification of the facts. This happens even if there is broad consensus over a particular value, for example, the quality of human life with good health as its precondition. The controversy over patents and the lack of access to medicines for poor people in developing countries is a case in point. The easily accessible facts do not support the argument that patents are the main obstacle to access to medicines for people living in poverty. Out of the 319 products on the World Health Organization's Model List of Essential Drugs, only 17 are patentable (5 percent) and most of them are not actually patented. Thus, the overall amount of patented drugs is 1.4 percent, and most of those are concentrated on larger markets.[18] Those who argue that patents are the problem tend to ignore other major access issues: lack of doctors, nurses, and laboratories for an appropriate diagnosis; lack of logistical essentials (for example, peripheral warehouses and refrigerators); lack of a general health infrastructure (for example, health centers located within reach of poor and isolated communities); and, last but not least, assurance of patient's compliance with complex and long-term therapy—especially in cases of stigmatized diseases (HIV/AIDS, tuberculosis, leprosy) where lack of compliance could result in resistances to available drugs.

Deduce the Right Norms

The essence of morality is that it points out the road to be taken to achieve results and poses demands on duty bearers. Norms function only to the extent that—and for as long as—they appear self-evident to the party who is expected to respond. And here we come to the central question: What can *reasonably* be demanded from a company, and "where does the buck stop?"[19] While it is obvious that it is morally wrong to accept or provoke human rights violations for the sake of increasing profits, the judgments on, for example, positive corporate obligations to fulfill the "right to health" of poor people are quite different for corporate management compared to right-to-health activists. It is relatively easy to pose demands on "Big Pharma" by pointing to the misery of those living in absolute poverty and criticizing the size of corporate profits. It is less easy for those who have to bear the costs in order to cover the needs of at least some of the patients who lack the purchasing power to buy medicines. The right-to-health debate is a good example to demonstrate how the neglect of complexity and a moralizing "simplification of the terrible" can distort a debate—and how this distortion impacts on what people perceive to be (or not to be) responsible corporate conduct.

Corporate Responsibility for the "Right to Health"

To discuss some of the corporate responsibility issues a bit more concretely, we will explore the complexities and diversities of an issue that involves more and more the pharmaceutical industry: the "right to health."

The Background

Article 25 of the Universal Declaration of Human Rights (UDHR) from 1948 mentions the "right to medical care." The understanding of this right evolved over the past fifty years under the influence of the constitution of the World Health Organization, the International Covenant on Economic, Social, and Cultural Rights from 1966 and other international human rights treaties, the "Health for All by the Year 2000" objective of the Alma-Ata Conference on Primary Health Care, and the UN Millennium Declaration adopted by the world's leaders. Today, there is a broad international and institutional consensus that every human being is entitled to *the highest attainable standard of health conducive to living a life in dignity.*[20]

The academic "right to health" debate took off following an article by Jonathan Mann in 1994, and since then it has gained in political impact.[21] In the context of the ravaging HIV/AIDS pandemic, Mann discussed the positive and negative impacts of different health policies, programs, and practices on human rights (he argued, for example, that a state's failure to recognize health problems that affect a marginalized or stigmatized group violates the right to nondiscrimination) and the health effects of human rights violations (such as torture, imprisonment under inhumane conditions, or rape leading to lifelong physical, mental, and social effects). He argued that the promotion and protection of health are inextricably linked to the promotion and protection of human rights and dignity. The interrelatedness and interconnectedness of health and development were prominently recognized in the Millennium Development Goals through enumeration of specific, measurable health targets.

At the roots of today's health deficits is absolute poverty.[22] At all times and in all societies of the world, "men and women were sick because they were poor, they became poorer because they were sick, and sicker because they were poorer."[23] Poor people lack education; access to adequate nutrition, safe water, and sanitation; and the purchasing power to buy basic health services. Four broad mechanisms are responsible for and contribute to the perpetuation of health disparities[24]:

social stratification—the very fact that people are poor

differential exposure—a greater exposure to multiple health risks (malnourishment, unsafe water, lack of health knowledge, etc.)

differential susceptibility—greater vulnerability due to the interactions among multiple health risks

differential consequences of disease—potentially catastrophic loss of income, of land, or of livestock; school dropouts; or other illness-

produced disadvantages that keep the vicious poverty-illness circle
intact

Not one of these factors can be influenced by corporate responsibility endeavors of "Big Pharma"—at least not to any significant extent. The realization of the *right to health*—however defined—is interrelated with and
interconnected to progress in the realization of all other civil and political
as well as economic, social, and cultural rights covered by the UDHR,
particularly "the right to food, housing, work, education, human dignity,
life, non-discrimination, equality, the prohibition of torture, privacy, access to information, and the freedoms of association, assembly and movement."[25] A meaningful discussion of rights must deal with the respective
duty bearers. As with all rights formulated in the Universal Declaration
of Human Rights, states are the primary bearers of duties. States have
clear and binding obligations under human rights law. As a matter of fact,
all human rights are *above all* incumbent on states and their institutions;
the state has the prime responsibility to respect, protect, and fulfill its
people's right to health, including the following obligations:

> *Obligations to respect* include, among other considerations, refraining
> from denying or limiting equal access for all persons to preventive,
> curative, and palliative health services, as well as refraining from
> prohibiting or impeding traditional preventive care, healing prac
> tices, and medicines
>
> *Obligations to protect* include, among other considerations, the duties of
> states to ensure that privatization of the health sector does not con
> stitute a threat to the availability, accessibility, acceptability, and
> quality of health facilities, goods, and service
>
> *Obligations to fulfill* require states to, among other things, adopt a na
> tional health policy with a detailed plan for realizing the right to
> health; ensure provision of health care, including immunization
> programs against the major infectious diseases; ensure equal access
> to all the underlying determinants of health (safe food, potable
> water, basic sanitation, and so on); and ensure the provision of a
> sufficient number of hospitals, clinics, and other health facilities as
> well as the provision of a public, private, or mixed health insurance
> system that is affordable for all

To start with, states and their institutions must do away with torture, violence against children, and harmful traditional practices that violate human rights and the health of the victims.[26] Once these basics have been achieved, continuous national efforts toward the realization of health rights must follow on at least three different fronts[27]:

  nonhealth interventions that have health benefits, such as respecting the right to food, providing clean water, improving sanitation, offering better primary education, and improving governance and basic infrastructure, including that for health purposes

  medical interventions, such as vaccinations and drug therapies, medical examinations, tests, and cost effective treatment—especially for poor people; most benefits from public spending on curative health services do *not* go to the poorest but to wealthier people[28]

  nonmedical health interventions, such as training medical personnel, building better health information systems, and strengthening systems for procuring and storing medicines and other medical equipment; the health policy impact depends on the efficacy of the public sector and the incentive structures of the given institutional arrangements

In situations where the primary duty of the state is neglected—whether due to a lack of resources (incapability) or deficits in governance (unwillingness)—the international community ought to be called to account. With development assistance in the case of incapability and with a mixture of pressure and incentives in the case of unwillingness, the international community is expected to take joint action to achieve the progressive realization of the right to health. Richer nations, in particular, are called on to facilitate access to essential health facilities, goods, and services in poor countries wherever possible and to provide the necessary aid when required.[29] Calling to account those who are the primary duty bearers of the respect, protection, and fulfillment of the right to health is not a mean dialectic attempt to evade corporate responsibilities but is necessary at least for two reasons: (1) to avoid this important debate from becoming mired in side issues and wrong priorities; and (2) to avoid the development of unrealistic expectations about sustainable deliverables from the private sector, especially pharmaceutical corporations.

    Access to medicine forms an important part of the right to health; enhancing access to medicines is also part of the Millennium Development

Goals. While states have the primary responsibility to ensure access, the Millennium Development Goals recognize this as a *shared responsibility*—that is, other national and international actors have to play a role. Amongst these actors are pharmaceutical companies. The question then is, What exactly must a pharmaceutical company do in order to be a responsible corporate citizen? Activists may find it easy to make demands on corporations because they will not have to pay the respective bills. Sincere corporate commitments to help realize health rights for the poor do require financial resources in addition to those necessary to run the corporation's normal activities. The spending of such resources may have a negative impact on profitability in a highly competitive environment. Thus, private enterprises—being market-oriented and profit-driven—run up against limits in cases of market failure; things become even worse if market failure and state failure come together and create negative synergies for the poor, leaving them defenseless and exposed to premature death and preventable sickness. On the other hand, to shrug off the "corporate shoulder" and do nothing in the face of the biggest social problem of humankind is neither a socially nor a morally acceptable option. The situation presents a challenge and an opportunity for moral leadership and corporate vision. What, then, is corporate responsibility within an environment of mass poverty, market failure, and failing states?

A FAIR-MINDED APPROACH TO CORPORATE RESPONSIBILITY

The most respected common denominator for responsible corporate conduct today is compliance with the ten principles of the United Nations Global Compact (UNGC).[30] The Global Compact covers internationally accepted norms in the areas of human rights, labor standards, environmental care, and anticorruption. Companies committed to these norms will incorporate them into their corporate policies and management processes and will require third parties within their sphere of influence to adhere to relevant policies.[31] To associate the term *corporate responsibility* with pragmatic, reasonable content I have suggested a Dahrendorf model with three levels of classification: the "*must* dimension," the "*ought to* dimension," and the "*can* dimension"—each with its specific moral quality and contributions to society.[32]

The "*must* dimension" covers nonnegotiable corporate duties, which include, for example, compliance with national law and regulations and not engaging in deception or fraud. The protection of the environment as well as of the life, health, and safety of employees, customers, and neighbors are other imperative obligations of the company. Shareholders expect a fair return on their investments and employees expect fair wages. Within this dimension, corporations fulfill their societal responsibilities through the creation of jobs, tax payments, and contributions to insurance and pension funds. If companies also provide training and further education on the job, employees improve their employability and value on the job market. Companies add further value to society and the national economy through products and services that meet immediate customer needs or enhance their quality of life. Innovative medicines, for example, help accelerate the cure of diseases, alleviate their symptoms, avoid chronic disability, shorten hospitalization, and reduce overall health care costs by allowing patients to return to work.[33]

While legal compliance covers much of the road to responsible corporate conduct in countries where the quality of law is state-of-the-art and enforced, "legality" is an insufficient criterion for corporate conduct in countries where this is not the case[34]—thus the "*ought to* dimension" of corporation responsibility. Responsible companies will go beyond legal minimums by applying higher corporate norms, *even if* local law would allow lower standards. Examples include paying "living wages" instead of legally prescribed "minimum wages" that in many cases do not cover the basic needs of a worker and his core family.[35] Other examples are the provision of free or heavily subsidized meals, corporate health services for employees and their families, and nursery schools for single working mothers. Free training opportunities using company infrastructure, scholarship programs for the children of low-income employees, and similar programs are further benefits not only to corporate staff but also to the company in that they help attract the best employees and enhance corporate morale. Companies competing with integrity[36] will also strive to avoid benefiting from unhealthy or otherwise unfair working conditions of third parties and bring their influence to bear wherever possible.

The "*can* dimension" covers philanthropic corporate social investments, such as pro bono research, community and neighborhood programs, volunteerism, and donations. Although such corporate deliverables can have very beneficial outcomes for underprivileged communities—and are therefore often given a high profile in corporate communications—this dimension of the corporate responsibility portfolio will always be voluntary in the sense of "nice to have." It would in no way compensate for a lack of responsible conduct as determined by the "must" and "ought to" dimensions (see figure 1).

The process by which a corporation reflects on what to do and where to set limits will raise a variety of highly specific issues that probably would not otherwise be discussed without an explicit reflection on global corporate obligations. The issues include the following:

What is a reasonable definition of "living wage?"
What should the according basic needs basket include?
Which parts of a social package considered "normal" in the corporation's home country (for example, a pension fund) should a company "export" to its business in a developing country that has a very different average income level and institutional setting?

Other issues will be very general, for example,

How far beyond an insufficient legal framework should a company go with regard to environmental investments?
Should a company have philanthropy in its corporate responsibility portfolio? And if so, to what extent?

Figure 9.1 The Hierarchy of Corporate Responsibilities

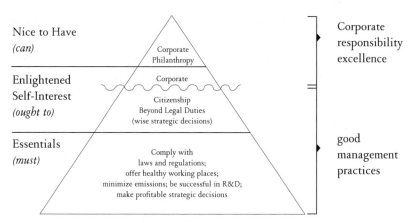

While a company has no option other than to adhere to given laws and regulations, perceptions of how far beyond legal requirements a corporation should go are subject to great pluralism of opinion—and hence the discretion of management. From an economic point of view, one could argue that every dollar spent on corporate responsibility beyond legal requirements and standards of decency, such as the UNGC principles, is a dollar not spent on potentially profit-generating activity. In other words, there *are* opportunity costs associated with corporate responsibilities that extend beyond conventional *good management practices*—mainly in the form of benefits not realized through alternative investments. And there are those who question whether companies should go out of their way to define and promote wider self-chosen objectives.[37]

Every company has to draw the line of corporate responsibility somewhere, even those that "contribute to a better society and a cleaner environment . . . [by] not only fulfilling legal expectations, but also going beyond compliance and investing 'more' into human capital, the environment and the relations with stakeholders."[38] While dialogue with fair-minded stakeholders will help to sharpen awareness about social, political, and environmental problems, the ultimate decision on how far a company extends its "responsibility borderlines" remains the duty of a well-informed top management.

RETURNS ON CORPORATE RESPONSIBILITY INVESTMENTS

As mentioned above, the corporate responsibility literature suggests two sets of reasons for corporations to apply standards higher than the legal minimum: *intrinsic rightness* (morality) and the *business case* (reputation and profit). Both reasons are valid. It is intrinsically right not to accept in one's sphere of influence the violation of human rights, the exposure of employees to unhealthy and unfair working conditions, the infliction of damage on the environment, or corruption as a means to promote business or avoid regulation. This is a simple matter of course and indisputable.[39]

The second set of reasons seen to encourage higher corporate responsibility is of an instrumental nature as it entails strategic business advantages, such as prevention or at least reduction of legal, financial, and reputation risks and often significant punitive damage costs; attraction, retention, and motivation of above average employees as well as enhanced corporate morale; enhanced corporate reputation and corporate branding; creation of goodwill among ethically minded investors and consumers;[40] and, eventually, preservation of corporate freedom.[41] For some observers, the discussion is closed. In 2004 Marjory Kelly announced the discovery of the statistical "Holy Grail"—eagerly sought but previously never found. Kelly argues that *socially responsible companies perform better financially.*[42] The manner in which Kelly summarizes the meta-analysis done by Orlitzky, Schmidt, and Rynes is plausible. Indeed, the authors were able to answer affirmatively the question posed by *Business Week* in 1999: "Can business meet new social, environmental and financial expectations and still win?"[43] A closer look, however, reveals that a number of issues are left unresolved, and those issues remain of great significance for corporate stakeholder strategy, and thus for the corporate response to stakeholder demands and eventually the extent of social responsibility deliverables.[44] Kelly's meta-analysis is unclear concerning whether the positive statistical correlation is explained by good management practices—that is, cutting-edge managers taking corporate responsibilities seriously and therefore anticipating and solving problems before they have an impact on the bottom line—or a result of superior financial performance, allowing for more, deeper, and broader corporate responsibility investments.

While there is a high plausibility for the *business case* for corporate responsibility, it is not easy to establish it empirically. Margolis and Walsh found in their analysis that the "clear signal that emerges from thirty years of academic research—indicating that a positive relationship exists between social performance and financial performance—must be treated with caution."[45] And according to the Institute of Business Ethics, "the relationship between good financial performance and other indicators of corporate responsibility . . . is (at best) positive but not definitive."[46] Nikolay Dentchev found "various positive and negative effects" of initiatives that are meant to contribute to society and the natural environment. The relationship between financial performance and corporate responsibilities extending beyond legal compliance, however, was found to be "inconclusive, complex and nuanced."[47] This is not a surprise. If the correlation between excellent corporate responsibility and excellence in economic results were obvious, it would not be debated.

So it seems that whereas the "costs" of corporate responsibility efforts beyond the legal minimums can in most cases be quite clearly quantified as additional investments,[48] and in some cases also be measured in terms of foregoing sales at the borderline of legitimacy, the "return" on corporate responsibility is difficult to establish, at least in the short term. The avoided costs of accidents, labor disputes, negative media exposure, unpleasant public criticism, or additional political regulation is equally inaccessible to measurement as the opportunity benefits due to environmental pollution not occurring because of investments made to prevent it. Fluctuations of share prices, too, usually can be explained more by general bullish or bearish movements on financial markets and sector-specific preferences than by the moral quality of a specific corporate activity. Of course, "wild" cases such as Enron, Arthur Andersen, WorldCom, Tyco, or others could support the argument that noncompliance potentially is more expensive than compliance with responsibility criteria. Such negative examples are not the rule, however, but the exception. As value premises determine the point of view from which reality is studied, we are back to Margaret Wolfe Hungerford's famous observation that with respect to the business case of corporate responsibility, like art, "Beauty is in the eye of the beholder."

Indeed, innovation, efficiency, effectiveness, the ability to make the most of market potential and interpret the signs of the times correctly, as well as the art of saving unnecessary costs and spending available resources at the right place and at the right time will retain their overriding importance in the future as preconditions for business success. But there is much plausibility in the argument that corporations that assume responsibility beyond the legal minimum (the "must" dimension) by applying good management practice well into the "ought to" dimension are likely to run lower risks and fare better with their employees, investors, and customers. It also seems logical that companies that are considered by the public to "be part of the solution" will better be able to argue for entrepreneurial freedom than those who are considered to be "part of the problem."

Corporate responsibility investments along these lines—and up to a certain limit (represented by the "wavy line" in figure 1)—are therefore likely to create a win-win situation for society and the corporation. The societal benefits of higher incomes, better health, education, training, and employability are matched by corporate benefits such as, for example, increased motivation, higher productivity, and lower absenteeism. Investments up to the point where none of the participating subjects (or institutions) can be made better off without another subject being made worse off (in absolute terms) are, therefore, good managed practices. Economists refer to this point as the "Pareto Optimum." Thus far, I have presented a fairly uncontroversial line of reasoning, but this is not the cutting edge of today's corporate responsibility debate.

TOWARD A NEW DEFINITION OF CORPORATE RESPONSIBILITIES?

An issue that was discussed early in the corporate responsibility debate by Archie Carroll has gained significant momentum in recent years.[49] Society's expectations of the performance of a business vis-à-vis the big social problems are far removed from actual corporate performance. Given the scale and complexity of global poverty, a majority of people in most modern societies expect (and most NGOs demand) that large (and multinational) companies will become much more involved in seeking solutions to broader societal problems—such as alleviating poverty or improving health—*outside* companies' direct sphere of influence.

In addition, a growing amount of academic literature promotes a concept of corporate responsibility that represents a totally new dimension. The notion that corporations (especially large, multinational corporations) are as powerful, if not actually more powerful, than governments (of poor countries) leads to the expectation that companies will assume additional quasi-governmental responsibilities.[50] Therefore, companies are seen to have an obligation not only to do responsible business but increasingly to step outside the boundaries of conventional corporate activities:

- "A (large) company is expected to take action to influence an outcome where it is *capable* and not "only" where there is either proximity to the problem to be solved or a causal link between the problem and the corporation."[51] While John Kline restricts his arguments, for the time being, to "political actions," a growing acceptance of a *"capability, not causality or proximity,"* approach would be a paradigm change in corporate responsibility thinking.

- "Corporations enter the arena of citizenship at the point of government failure in the protection of citizenship. More precisely, they are *expected to partly take over those functions with regard to the protection, facilitation and enabling citizen's rights—formerly an expectation placed solely on governments.* . . . If a term such as 'corporate citizenship' makes any sense in the proper meaning of the term, 'corporations' and 'citizenship' in modern society come together at exactly the point where the state ceases to be the only guarantor of citizenship any longer."[52]

- Under certain conditions transnational corporations are seen to have a (moral) "duty of assistance" to people in "burdened societies," where socioeconomic circumstances make it difficult or impossible to live decent lives.[53]

This gap between societal expectations and concrete corporate responsibility deliverables poses an issue of societal acceptance of whatever a company is doing. Just as with temperature, where there is a "felt" and "measurable" temperature, there is a "measurable" corporate responsibility (expressed by what is actually delivered) and a "felt" corporate responsibility (a comparison of what is done with what is expected). The solution to this problem offered by some—change the CSR "game" through "focused commitment to reaching a goal that exceeds societal expectations"[54]—is easier articulated than fulfilled.

Potentially open-ended extensions of the definition of *corporate responsibility* raise many valid and vexing questions for even the most enlightened management. Is the assumption that "citizenship," and therefore also "corporate citizenship," are normative concepts, implying not only economic rights but also social duties, an acceptable basis from which corporations to work? Would a corporate management that refuses to accept such a concept by definition be acting irresponsibly? Or would this extended definition represent a waste of corporate resources and bad management practices? Should corporate executives who feel impelled to assume such responsibilities not do so with corporate resources but instead devote part of their personal income to causes they personally regard as worthy?[55] Is there a middle course if and when certain societal preconditions are met?

Corporate Responsibility Endeavors Beyond Good Management
Practices

Clearly, there are a number of potentially valuable corporate responsibility "deliverables" well beyond good management practices, that is,
above the wavy line of the "ought to" and including the "can" dimensions
of the corporate responsibility pyramid (figure 1). While accepting the imperative of profitability, professional experience suggests a wide discretionary freedom—Donaldson and Dunfee call it "moral free space"—for
managerial decisions to include corporate responsibility deliverables beyond the direct strategic business case in their portfolio.[56] Within that
space corporate expenditures are still likely to increase societal benefits
but will have increasingly lower, and eventually no, returns on investment for the company. In order to explore this issue in depth, let us look
again at a pharmaceutical company's contributions toward respecting,
supporting, and fulfilling the "right to health" of poor people through
corporate philanthropy.

As outlined above, the prime responsibility to respect, protect, and
contribute toward the fulfillment of the human right to health lies primarily with the state and secondarily with the international community.
Business enterprises—as "organs of society"—are widely seen to have human rights responsibilities arising from the wording of the preamble of
the Universal Declaration of Human Rights: that "every individual and
every organ of society, keeping this Declaration constantly in mind, shall
strive by teaching and education to promote respect for these rights and
freedoms and by progressive measures, national and international, to secure their universal and effective recognition and observance."[57]

Today many concerned citizens see the pharmaceutical industry as
having special responsibilities toward the fulfillment of the "right to
health" based on article 25 of the Universal Declaration of Human Rights.
To these citizens it is not sufficient to point to the fact that the most important corporate contributions toward the common good result from the
normal business activities and the core competencies of a pharmaceutical
corporation, that is, research, development, production, and sale of safe
and effective medicines. No doubt, a profitable pharmaceutical corporation is able to contribute additionally by, for example, making donations,
offering differential pricing, or doing pro-bono-research,[58] among other

activities.[59] Such contributions, although not legally demanded, are certainly *morally desirable*. But where should the line be drawn between what is essential and what is beyond this?

While the corporate willingness to engage in *differential pricing* of drugs included on the WHO's essential medicines list for the world's poorest may be considered by some as within the "ought to" dimension, other benefits such as donations, pro bono research, and corporate philanthropy activities to support broader health and development goals are clearly beyond normal business obligations and what is conventionally considered good management practice. Why should companies engage in such activities—beyond the reason that they are *morally* desirable?

Given the background of mass poverty and the correspondingly high mortality and morbidity in poor countries, even generous individual corporate activity can make only a small difference. But at the same time, a number of other questions have to be answered. Because the "access to medicine" or even "right to health" issues comprise much more than just availability of inexpensive drugs, what else should a corporation get involved in?[60] Even with differential pricing, people living in absolute poverty cannot afford complex therapies over a long period of time. And even if such drugs are donated, problems remain—be they with sustainability, with patient compliance, or with drug safety.

If drugs can only be donated in a responsible way following investments in health infrastructure (for example, hospitals, health centers, doctors, nurses) and efforts to train and educate health personnel and patients, but the government of a donation-receiving country is not willing or able to allocate the necessary funds to fulfill these preconditions, should the corporate sector jump in and do what the government—the primary duty bearer—is not able or willing to do? Considering this question from a business point of view, the answer is clear and simple: Beyond a certain threshold, additional corporate responsibility investments may be good for society in the short term but have greatly diminishing, if any, return on corporate investment.

For market-oriented and profit-driven enterprises, the limits of "normal business" are reached when markets fail. A concerned public, however, increasingly questions this definition of "normal business." The potential expectation of corporate deliverables deduced from an extended definition of a "duty of assistance" for individuals in "burdened societies" is immense. For the 2.5 billion people with a daily per capita income of less than US$2, *any* drug researched, developed, and manufactured in Switzerland is beyond their purchasing power. The case is even clearer for states where political failures have resulted either in internal warfare (for example, "outlaw states" in the Rawlsian terminology,[61] such as Somalia) or misallocation of scarce resources for military expenditures instead of health care.

It is these two categories of failure that leave the poorest of the poor exposed to premature death and otherwise preventable sickness. Not accepting *any* responsibilities in the face of the biggest social problem of contemporary humankind may be rational from a simplistic but myopic "business point of view." Such an attitude, however, is not a morally acceptable option for a "good" company. The corporate question to be answered, therefore, is not "Are we doing something or nothing?" but rather "What are we doing, in what areas, for whom and in partnership with whom, over what period of time and how much?"[62] One strategic option for answering such questions is corporate philanthropy.

Corporate Philanthropy

Corporate philanthropy should not be confused with corporate responsibility per se and certainly does not substitute for a "corporate house" not being in order.[63] Yet it is part of corporate responsibility portfolios—in the "can" dimension—and, if properly done, can result in significant contributions to solutions for poverty-related problems.

A number of enlightened companies with a good business performance invest part of their revenues to make the world a better place.[64] For nearly thirty years Novartis has invested through its Foundation for Sustainable Development and made significant contributions to projects and programs concerned with development cooperation and humanitarian assistance, helping to increase the effectiveness, efficiency, and significance of aid.[65] The Novartis Institute for Tropical Diseases is engaged in not-for-profit research, addressing neglected diseases such as tuberculosis and dengue fever and applying cutting-edge scientific know-how and technologies.[66] It goes without saying that once management has decided in favor of corporate philanthropy, the programs and projects following from this decision have to be managed in a sustainable and professional way so that they can deliver superior results with the resources made available. Professional corporate philanthropy is not a playground for a top management's "fashion of the month good-doerism." It has to be focused, cost effective, and sustainable and strive for the highest return on philanthropic investment in a manner that is measurable with clear indicators.

There are, however, two distinctly different strategies by which corporate philanthropy can be structured. One strategy is to work *needs oriented* and focus on the most destitute. Another strategic approach is to focus on areas that influence *the competitive context of the company.*

Corporate Philanthropy in a Long-Term Competitive Context
There are a number of convincing arguments in support of corporate philanthropy focusing on areas that influence the competitive context of a company.[67] Michael Porter and Mark Kramer stress the importance of at least four elements of the competitive context:

> *Factor conditions,* for example, availability of high-quality, specialized inputs such as human resources, physical infrastructure, administrative infrastructure, etc. Hence, charitable giving to improve education and technological institutions, efforts to make administrative processes more transparent and efficient, and philanthropy supporting environmental efforts can improve the quality of factor conditions upon which corporate success depends in the long run.
>
> *Demand conditions,* for example, presence of sophisticated and demanding local customers and recognition of customer needs that anticipate similar needs elsewhere. Hence, philanthropy contributing to the improvement of the size and quality of the local market creates a win-win situation for both the communities and the company.
>
> *Context for strategy and rivalry,* for example, presence of local policies and incentives, presence of rules and norms governing competition, reducing corruption, etc. Hence, philanthropy that helps to create a more productive and transparent environment for competition and other factors that create a more attractive market serve the community and are also beneficial to the company in the long term.
>
> *Related and supporting industries,* for example, presence of capable, locally based suppliers and clusters of industries. Hence, by fostering the development of clusters and strengthening and supporting industries, philanthropy can make a difference for the communities and at the same time serve the company in the long run.

According to Porter and Kramer, this kind of philanthropy "can often be the most cost-effective way—and sometimes the only way—to improve competitive context. It enables companies to leverage not only their own resources but also the existing efforts and infrastructure of nonprofits and other institutions . . . Leading companies will be best positioned to make substantial contributions and will in turn reap a major share of the benefits."[68] In addition, Porter and Kramer see "disproportionate benefits because of the superior reputation and relationship [corporate philanthropy] builds."[69] Under such circumstances they see no inherent contradiction between corporate philanthropy improving the competitive context and delivering goods and services to make the world a better place.

There may be, however, an inherent logical consequence to this kind of corporate philanthropy that is not likely to be in the interest of the world's poor. Strategic corporate philanthropy does not extend to environments of absolute poverty. For the sake of simplifying the following discussion and to make the point clear, we will differentiate between "upper-class," "middle-class," and "lower-class" poor. Corporate philanthropy intended to improve the long-term competitive context will almost never focus on the poorest countries and the most destitute citizens. Its legitimate focus will be "upper-middle-class" and "upper-class" poor. Because these groups constitute the markets of the near future, such investments are not only good for those communities that benefit but also are in the medium- and long-term interest of the shareholder.

The poorest of the poor suffer from much more than just "income poverty." Their lives are burdened by many additional deprivations with regard to access to services, personal safety, freedom of choice, exposure to risks, or perceptions of powerlessness and voicelessness.[70] More than one billion "lower-class poor" are caught in a vicious circle of poverty and hence are most in need of help—including needs-based corporate philanthropy.

Needs-Based, Poverty-Oriented Corporate Philanthropy

The analysis of the state of the world's health continues to show striking problems. The *WHO World Health Report 2005* reports that

each year 3.3 million babies—or may be even more—are stillborn; more than 4 million die within 28 days of coming into the world;

and a further 6.6 million young children die before their fifth birthday. Maternal deaths also continue unabated. The annual total now stands at 529,000—often sudden, unpredicted deaths which occur during pregnancy itself (an estimated 68,000 as a consequence of unsafe abortion), during childbirth, or after the baby has been born—leaving behind devastated families, often pushed into poverty because of the cost of health care that came too late or was ineffective.[71]

While a baby girl born in Japan today can expect to live for about eighty-five years, a girl born at the same moment in Sierra Leone has a life expectancy of only thirty-six years. In some countries the situation actually worsened in the 1990s, and worrying reversals in newborn, child, and maternal mortality have taken place. Overall, 35 percent of Africa's children are at higher risk of death today than they were ten years ago. Every hour, more than five hundred African mothers lose a small child; in 2002 alone, more than four million African children died. Those who do make it past childhood are confronted with adult death rates that exceed those of thirty years ago. Life expectancy, always shorter in sub-Saharan Africa than elsewhere around the globe, is shrinking. In some African countries it has been cut by twenty years, and life expectancy for men is less than forty-six years.

Programs to tackle vaccine-preventable diseases, malnutrition, diarrhea, or respiratory infections still have a long way to go. Immunization is stagnating in many countries at levels between 50 and 70 percent. Overall, progress has slowed and is increasingly uneven, leaving large disparities between countries, as well as between the rich and poor within countries. The main causes of death among children are perinatal conditions closely associated with poverty, diarrhea, pneumonia and other lower respiratory tract conditions, and malaria. HIV/AIDS is now the world's leading cause of death in adults aged fifteen to fifty-nine; almost five thousand men and women in this age group and almost one thousand of their children are killed by HIV/AIDS every twenty-four hours in sub-Saharan Africa. Because mortality statistics alone substantially underestimate the burden of disease, the WHO's picture of the disease burden using "disability-adjusted life years" (DALYs) gives an even more dramatic picture.[72] The reaction of the international community fails to be commensurate. Development assistance is far less than what is needed and affordable—and commitments made are often not fulfilled.[73]

Upon reflection on this tragedy, corporate management may opt for needs-oriented corporate philanthropy and focus on the poorest because it appears to be the right thing to do. This will result in programs and projects that lack any connection with markets and hence the corporate competitive context for years to come. The single most decisive factor for such engagements will be the value-based conviction of top management that the company as a corporate citizen should make a contribution to the fight against human misery.

Because poverty is the main cause for lack of access to health services and medicines, and because of their natural affinity to health issues, a pharmaceutical company willing to engage in corporate philanthropy should focus on poverty-related health issues. A sustained engagement in poverty-related corporate philanthropy will have a substantial impact. While small within the context of global misery, the work of the Novartis Foundation for Sustainable Development, for example, has contributed to many positive outcomes over the past twenty-five years, including the following:

> the cure of several million leprosy patients—nearly five million alone since Novartis started distributing all medicines for multidrug therapy free of charge in the year 2000
>
> more than five million people in rural sub-Saharan Africa being able to live better lives by providing better seed varieties and promoting improved agricultural practices
>
> empowering hundreds of thousands of people in poor communities, enhancing their opportunities to cope with the challenges of their daily lives and prevent illness
>
> saving thousands of lives, mainly children under the age of five, as a result of the foundation's commitment to poor communities in sub-Saharan Africa and Southeast Asia
>
> supporting the development of strategies and good practices (for example, for the psychosocial care of AIDS orphans and vulnerable young people; social marketing in leprosy campaigns and patient-centered tuberculosis treatment; and innovative approaches to sustainable health care such as informal health insurance for sub-Saharan rural areas) in collaboration with local stakeholders,

resulting in tangible successes for poor people and leveraging existing efforts of other institutions engaged in the same sector.

But activities of this sort raise another issue: While legitimate business standards are easily accepted as good management practice, the legitimacy of programs that go well beyond the "normal business corridor" with corporate funds for needs-oriented philanthropy cannot be determined in business terms. As humanitarian objectives are not part of normal business terminology, difficulties in justifying corporate philanthropy focused on destitute people may arise. Such difficulties could be reduced if and when companies receive appropriate positive feedback from civil society.

CIVIL SOCIETY'S FEEDBACK ON EXCELLENCE IN CORPORATE RESPONSIBILITY

Mainstream stakeholder theory suggests that maintaining dialogues with a great variety of corporate stakeholder groups, and eventually satisfying their demands to the highest possible degree, will yield positive results for the company.[74] The main reasons supporting this theory are of a strategic nature:

closer contact with diverse stakeholders and NGO networks deepens understanding of societal expectations in the context of social, political, and ecological issues

dialogue enhances the efficiency of a corporation's adaptation to societal demands

dialogue provides direct knowledge of constituencies and their opinion leaders

dialogue fosters a higher sensitivity for broader societal goals through a willingness to weigh and address the multiple claims of civil society

Therefore, stakeholder relations are perceived as advantageous to the company because they serve as an "early warning system" about societal expectation trends and help the company develop social competence. Social competence, in turn, makes a company's top management better able to anticipate external changes and deal with them before they have a negative impact on the business environment. Last but not least, accepting and eventually fulfilling stakeholder demands through additional investments of corporate resources can have a positive effect on corporate reputation. According to this argument, commitments beyond the "wavy line,"—that is, excellence in corporate responsibility—should result in an even better reputation for the company, which could be beneficial with regard to customer loyalty, employee recruitment and retention, investments by ethical investment funds, and a company's standing within the political landscape. But stakeholder theory and corporate praxis are not exactly the same.

On the one hand, there is no doubt that today's world is a better place due to many highly committed people working in dedicated civil society groups to induce changes in corporate policies. Despite the wide and distinct diversity of these groups and movements, for simplicity's sake they will be categorized here under the term *nongovernmental organizations.* It is a fact that NGO initiatives have contributed toward improvement in the social, environmental, and political quality of corporate conduct (for example, Reverend Leon Sullivan's Principles, the Global Reporting Initiative, the Valdez Principles, or, more recently, the Clean Clothes Campaign, the Equator Principles, the Extractive Industry Transparency Initiative, and the Business Leadership Initiative for Human Rights [BLIHR]). In many cases these initiatives came from small enlightened groups who, in order to draw as much attention as possible to their cases, adopted highly unorthodox methods and innovative actions. Many of the causes that NGOs were fighting for thirty years ago have become standard procedure in enlightened corporations today. Seen from this perspective one could say that those who do similar things today are simply enlightened citizens who are forced to make their (valid) points by unorthodox means because of a stubborn lack of acceptance by corporations.

No company (or any other institution) is perfect, and any management can take undue risks and make mistakes about which—with the benefit of hindsight—nobody can be proud. No single actor has all the answers to all important questions. In addition, the rules of the "legitimacy game" change over time. Heightened sensitivity and enhanced social competence can help to correct policies and procedures that while implemented with the best of intentions and according to the leading theories at the time, were not successful or perhaps were harmful to communities. From this point of view, NGOs that expose corporations and their perceived or actual misdeeds can be regarded as part of a creative societal conflict that eventually brings about changes for the better. Therefore, engaging in strategic stakeholder relations can be a good investment of corporate time and resources, even if the process is sometimes a difficult one.

On the other hand, for many NGOs globalization per se is not a desirable process because it seems to encourage a "race to the bottom" with regard to social and ecological standards. Multinational corporations (MNCs), viewed as the main drivers of globalization, are closely associated with a negative perception of globalization that triggers worries and fears among many groups. In addition, such companies are commonly seen as being too big and—because size is often equated with power—excessively powerful as well.[75] Against this background and based on generalizations of the "worst case" performances of a few companies, many NGOs portray multinational corporations in general as *the* parties responsible for virtually all political, social, and ecological evils. NGOs insinuate that multinational companies are run by immoral, unscrupulous, and exceedingly greedy managers who enrich themselves at the expense of the common good and the human development opportunities of the world's poor.

As a matter of fact, companies who compete with integrity and put their "house" in order by filling potential gaps between legality and legitimacy are usually not excluded from such criticism. On the contrary, "good" companies sometimes are even more the focus of suspicion and insinuation.[76] According to the mind set of many NGOs, who deny "earned reputation" for responsible conduct, even corporate philanthropy activities are not positively acknowledged, or the respective motives are questioned (for example, corporations are charged with having a hidden market agenda, improving public relations under the disguise of charity, diverting the public's attention from shady corporate conduct, or promoting the same old tainted profit motive masquerading as altruism). This is particularly true in Europe.[77]

Of course, NGOs always need to have a critical distance from the corporate sector and demand more and better corporate responsibility—and in pluralistic societies it is normal that perceptions with regard to "how much is enough" differ to some extent. It is also understood that there is a fine line that NGOs must tread in their dealings with the corporate world if they want to maintain their countervailing power and not be absorbed into a corporate public relations embrace. In an imperfect corporate world, NGOs risk their own credibility by appearing to be too close to the institutions they set out to monitor and hold accountable according to their public role as watchdogs and whistle-blowers. After all, the media prefer "scandals," the most controversial arguments, and the most accusatory language—and media attention is helpful in NGOs' fight for financial contributions. Given the high sophistication of activists in managing the media, the tragic result of this phenomenon is that the media presence of "accusing" NGOs is much higher than that of "moderate" institutions that advocate their cases in a balanced or differentiated style.

However, justified criticism of reckless corporate behavior for an informed public debate is quite another thing than general MNC bashing on ideological grounds.[78] Some of the fair-minded NGOs silently condone being perceived as part of the fundamentalist faction; others signal semi-public support for selected critical positions as long as it helps to raise their profile. Still other public interest groups tolerate "accusers" within their organization and selectively send them to high visibility events—while maintaining a more "moderate" position in their published contributions. And perhaps most importantly, far too few fair-minded public interest groups, or other actors within civil society, publicly support a contrasting view concerning the issues discussed here or distance themselves from unfair criticism of corporate responsibility.

Due to fierce competition in fundraising markets it might look attractive for an NGO to position itself as a sort of "Robin Hood" and generate media attention; however, the inherent need to cultivate, or sometimes to invent, the corresponding "Sheriff of Nottingham" as an adversary will backfire by weakening the willingness of corporations to do better and more in the realm of corporate responsibility deliverables beyond the "wavy line." An attitude of this sort not only reflects a lack of intellectual integrity but as a matter of course destroys the precondition for corporate representatives to strive to be dialogue partners in deliberative processes, which by definition are never easy. Strategies that nurture the perception that (multinational) corporations and their managers are not only obsessed by pathological greed but also systematically cheat, bend the law, and subvert politics will result in resignation and cynicism rather than pioneering commitment and will lead to "corporate responsibility fatigue" and a return to a legal compliance–oriented approach.[79]

Running the risk of being perceived as patronizing critical NGOs, I think it is legitimate to ask NGOS to adhere to some minimum civilized rules, such as the following:

- avoid generalizing known examples of breaches of corporate responsibility and using those cases as the basis for sweeping accusations directed at *all* MNCs
- be aware of a fair division of responsibility in modern societies by acknowledging the core contribution to the common good that results from conventional business activities and the fact that the private sector cannot be expected to remove or remedy all social evils; be open to debates on dilemmas arising from this division of responsibility
- apart from outlining ideals, also try to define a reasonable pace for companies seeking to expand and improve their responsibility portfolio and avoid the reflex to ask for "more" regardless of what is done, which spurs suspicions within the corporate sector that expectations are insatiable[80]
- be "concrete solution"–driven instead of simply "moral identity"–driven and avoid statements on the political metalevel (like "End globalization!") as well as moralizing or ideological overtones

Besides encouraging a holistic definition of corporate responsibility, a very important effect of following such rules is the possibility of bringing fair-minded managements into the necessary debate on pragmatic solutions for a number of complex issues arising from "failing markets" or "failing states." Neither companies nor NGOs—and even less the governments of poor countries—will be able to implement sustainable solutions to today's complex social problems without intelligently engaging with each other and developing an innovative kind of symbiosis that does not discredit the legitimate objectives of structurally different institutions.

The significance of differentiated—that is, where justified negative *but also* positive—feedback for companies is underlined by the fact that few companies are fortunate enough to have a socially sensitive management that will do the right thing regardless of external appreciation simply as a result of its deep-rooted value premises. Corporate managers who allocate resources strictly according to return on narrow financial investment criteria are in a clear majority today, and they will remain so in the foreseeable future. For these managers there are currently few or no incentives to do more than what the law, the market, and decency demand. Hence, they will not invest in programs resulting from a holistic definition of corporate responsibility and certainly not in poverty-oriented corporate philanthropy. The fact that human nature responds to positive incentives is likely to have positive effects from the perspective of individual senior managers and motivate allocation of more resources for corporate responsibility deliverables beyond the "normal business case."[81]

Using traditional macroeconomic language, the conditions defining the "Pareto Optimum"[82] need to be changed (see figure 2). If fair-minded observers, NGOs, media, and other actors of civil society would be more appreciative of corporate endeavors beyond the "normal business case" or at least go on record with a differentiating judgment, they could create "reputation capital" for "good" corporations and change the equation for the business case.[83] This would create a new dimension of competition

Figure 9.2   Reputation Capital and Societal Benefits

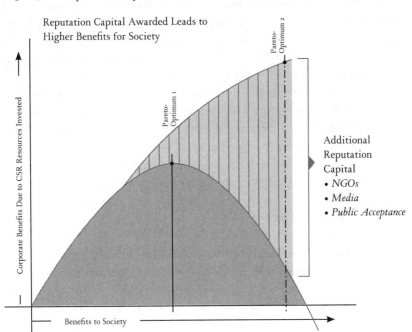

between companies operating with integrity and lead to more and better corporate responsibility deliverables beyond the "normal business case."

Business can play a significant role in the solution of major global issues. But it can neither do it alone nor in the context of a conventional, conservative business model. Sustainable successes are best achieved within a framework of good governance and in harmony with the expectations of society. Increasingly enlightened NGOs engage with corporations in coping with major challenges. In the cases where such joint ventures have yielded good results—in the sense of bringing complex issues closer to a broadly accepted solution—interaction was characterized by a constructively critical cooperation between civil society actors and the corporate sector. The MNC-NGO collaboration paradigm—that is, combining and pooling skills, experiences, and resources beyond those of any individual actor—has led in a few selected cases to an improved state of societal affairs, without calling into question the identity of the involved parties and the particularity of their interests. All participating actors perceived "ownership" in the reciprocal relationship, in the explicit negotiation process, and in the results achieved—allowing constructive changes to be implemented or, at the very least, areas of dissent to be reduced. Today, best practices in this respect are reflected by the World Wildlife Fund, Transparency International, and the Amnesty International Business Group. Public interest groups and other civil society institutions that are willing to apply a (reciprocal) fairness principle in relations with the private sector are likely to play an increasingly important role. While maintaining their identity, integrity, and independent profile, NGOs partnering with corporations can help to find new and better approaches to preventing the descent of planet Earth into environmental disaster and social degradation.

Beyond a critical threshold additional corporate resources spent on corporate responsibility above the "wavy line" will increase the benefit to society but not to the company (Pareto Optimum 1). A new Pareto Optimum could be reached by the *reputation capital* given by civil society, the media, and the wider public—with much higher benefits for the world's poor (Pareto Optimum 2). Because reputation ranks high on the corporate agenda, public appreciation of efforts beyond the "normal business case" is likely to motivate even hard-nosed business managers to do more and better. Looking at the resources that are spent today for corporate reputation purposes, the potential for diversion into, for example, corporate philanthropy is significant. Assuming that the total market for advertising is more than US$400 million,[84] and making the (modest) assumption that only 5 percent is channeled into general corporate advertising or investments in corporate branding, about US$20 billion could become available to stretch the limits of corporate responsibility.

NOTES

1. See http://www.un.org/News/Press/docs/2004/sgsm9387.doc.htm.

2. See the World Bank's World Development Reports of all recent years, especially the one of 2000/2001, *Attacking Poverty* (New York: Oxford University Press, 2001). For more information on poverty and its multiple dimensions, see the UNDP Human Development Reports, especially UNDP, *Human Development Report 2003. Millennium Development Goals—A Compact among Nations to End Human Poverty* (New York: Oxford University Press, 2003), as well as http://www.un.org/largerfreedom/contents.htm. For information on DALYs, see the World Health Organization's *Global Burden of Disease Estimates for 2002,* http://www.who.int/healthinfo/bod/en/index.html.

3. See http://www.prb.org/Publications/Datasheets/2006/2006WorldPopulationDataSheet.aspx.

4. The Millennium Development Goals are to reduce by half the proportion of people living on less than a dollar a day, to reduce by half the proportion of people who suffer from hunger, to reduce by two-thirds the mortality rate among children under five and by three-quarters the maternal mortality ratio. See http://www.un.org/millenniumgoals.

5. See Global Compact/Global Public Policy Institute, *Business UNusual: Facilitating United Nations Reform through Partnerships* (New York: Global Compact/Global Public Policy Institute, 2005); and UN General Assembly, *In Larger Freedom: Towards Development, Security and Human Rights for All* (Report of the Secretary-General, New York, 2005).

6. See K. M. Leisinger, "Overcoming Poverty and Respecting Human Rights: Ten Points for Serious Consideration," *International Social Science Journal* 56 (2004): 313–20.

7. See, for example, the Corporate Crime Reporter, who compiled a list of "The Top 100 Corporate Criminals of the 1990s" (http://www.corporatecrimereporter.com/top100.html) using "the most narrow and conservative of definitions—corporations that have pled guilty or no contest to crimes and have been criminally fined." The "100 Corporate Criminals" fell into fourteen categories of crime: environmental (38), antitrust (20), fraud (13), campaign finance (7), food and drug (6), financial (4), false statements (3), illegal exports (3), illegal boycott (1), worker death (1), bribery (1), obstruction of justice (1), public

corruption (1), and tax evasion (1). A list that reflects that modern corporate governance is not just about avoiding crimes but about participating in an open debate about legitimate courses of action is currently updated by the Business and Human Rights Resource Centre (see http://www.business-humanrights.org/Documents/Chart-Responses.doc).

8. See GlobeScan, *Voice of the People* (Toronto: GlobeScan, 2002). The survey "The Voice of the People" was conducted by Gallup and GlobeScan (formerly Environics) first in 2002 and has been repeated annually since then, including focus questions on the respective themes of the World Economic Forum. See http://www.bizcommunity.com/PressOffice/PressRelease.aspx?i=170&ai=5231.

9. M. Keeley, *A Social Contract Theory of Organization* (Notre Dame, IN: University of Notre Dame Press, 1988), 216ff. Keeley argues that this implies looking for harm and dealing with it preventatively (222ff).

10. J. M. Clark, "The Changing Basis of Economic Responsibility," *Journal of Political Economy* 24, no. 3 (1916): 209–29, reprinted in M. B. E. Clarkson, ed., *The Corporation and Its Stakeholders: Classic and Contemporary Readings* (Toronto: University of Toronto Press, 1998), 28.

11. L. Whitehouse, "Corporate Social Responsibility: Views from the Frontline," *Journal of Business Ethics* 63, no. 3 (2006): 279.

12. GlobeScan, *The GlobeScan Survey of Sustainability Experts. 2004-5 Highlights Report* (Toronto: GlobeScan, 2005), 15.

13. From the title of an interview with Michael Porter by Mette Morsig, in *European Business Forum* 15 (Autumn 2003).

14. European Commission, *Promoting a European Framework for Corporate Social Responsibility,* Green Paper (Luxembourg: European Commission, 2001), 4.

15. Ibid., 8.

16. A. Smith, *The Theory of Moral Sentiments* (Indianapolis: Liberty Fund, 1984), 135. Close to this "theoretical" observer's view comes surveys or polls such as the *Environics/GlobeScan Millennium Poll* (1999) or expert surveys such as the *GlobeScan Survey of Sustainability Experts* (2005).

17. *Swiss CSR Monitor* (Zurich: Institute of Sustainable Development of the Zurich University of Applied Sciences Winterthur, 2006).

18. A. Attaran, "How Do Patents and Economic Policies Affect Access to Essential Medicines in Developing Countries?" *Health Affairs* 23, no. 3 (May/June 2004): 155–66.

19. IBLF, *The Buck Stops Where? Managing the Boundaries of Business Engagement in Global Development Challenges,* http://www.iblf.org/resources/general.jsp?id=57.

20. Article 25.1 of the Universal Declaration of Human Rights (1948) affirms that "everyone has the right to a standard of living adequate for the health of himself and of his family, including food, clothing, housing and medical care and necessary social services." The International Covenant on Economic, Social,

and Cultural Rights (1966) interprets this in article 12.1. as "the right of everyone to the enjoyment of the highest attainable standard of physical and mental health." A similar statement—"the enjoyment of the highest attainable standard of health as a fundamental right of every human being"—was enshrined in the WHO's constitution over fifty years ago and is part of numerous international treaties and conventions (see "25 Questions and Answers on Health and Human Rights," in *WHO Health & Human Rights Publication Series,* no. 1 [July 2002]). Last but not least, the General Comment No. 14 (2000) on "Substantive Issues Arising in the Implementation of the International Covenant on Economic, Social and Cultural Rights" reaffirms the "right to the highest attainable standard of health" (United Nations Economic and Social Council, E/C.12/2000/4, November 8, 2000).

    21. J. Mann, "Health and Human Rights," *Health and Human Rights: An International Journal* 1, no. 1 (1994): 1–2.

    22. See K. M. Leisinger, "Health Policy for Least Developed Countries," *Social Strategies* 16 (1985).

    23. C.-E. A. Winslow, *The Cost of Sickness and the Price of Health* (Geneva: WHO, 1951), 9. The French sociologist Louis René Villermé was one of the first to look for and find a clear correlation between poverty and mortality in his neighborhood studies in Paris at the beginning of the nineteenth century.

    24. See D. Carr, "Improving the Health of the World's Poorest People," *Population Reference Bureau: Health Bulletin* 1, no. 1 (2004): 14.

    25. In this way the according Article 25 in the Universal Declaration on Human Rights is spelled out by the General Comment No. 14, para. 3. The General Comment is written by the Committee on Economic, Social, and Cultural Rights, a group of experts nominated by the countries that have ratified the International Covenant on Economic, Social, and Cultural Rights.

    26. WHO, "25 Questions and Answers on Health and Human Rights," 10.

    27. D. E. Bloom and D. Canning, "A New Health Opportunity," *Development* 44, no. 1 (2001): 36ff.

    28. See, for example, F. Castro-Leal et al., "Public Spending on Health Care in Africa: Do the Poor Benefit?" *Bulletin of the World Health Organization* 78, no. 1 (2000): 70.

    29. General Comment No. 14, para. 39.

    30. See K. M. Leisinger, "Capitalism with a Human Face: The UN Global Compact," *Journal of Corporate Citizenship,* no. 28 (December 2007); and http://www.unglobalcompact.org for the great variety of concepts behind the term *responsible corporate conduct.* See also *Economist Intelligence Unit: The Importance of Corporate Responsibility,* White Paper (London: Oracle, Economist Intelligence Unit, 2005). Interestingly enough the tenor of this *Economist* publication is much more positive toward corporate responsibility than the "Good Company" series.

31. See, for example, K. M. Leisinger, "Opportunities and Risks of the United Nations Global Compact: The Novartis Case Study," *Journal for Corporate Citizenship* (Fall 2003): 113–31.

32. For the approach used to distinguish social norms according to different degrees of obligation, see R. Dahrendorf, *Homo Sociologicus* (Cologne: Opladen, 1959), 24; for a similar differentiation of corporate responsibilities, see A. B. Carroll, *Business and Society: Ethics and Stakeholder Management,* 2nd ed. (Cincinnati: South-Western Publishing, 1993), 35.

33. See, for example, *Epidemiology and End Results Program, 1975-2000* (Division of Cancer Control and Population Sciences, National Cancer Institute, 2003); and American Cancer Society, "Cancer Facts and Figures 2004," *Journal of Pediatric Oncology Nursing* 21, no. 3 (2004): 160–64.

34. In this context see the old Kantian differentiation between "legality" and "morality," as discussed in Kant's "Introduction into the Metaphysic of Morals": "The laws of freedom, as distinguished from the laws of nature, are moral laws. So far as they refer only to external actions and their lawfulness, they are called juridical; but if they also require that, as laws, they shall themselves be the determining principles of our actions, they are ethical. The agreement of an action with juridical laws is its legality; the agreement of an action with ethical laws is its morality" (http://etext.library.adelaide.edu.au/k/kant/immanuel/k16m/k16m6.html).

35. *Living wages,* even if defined in a dynamic concept, refer to a "basic needs" basket, which again is defined in a relatively narrow manner. Whatever remuneration goes beyond these parameters must be justifiable by the corporate desire to hire better than average workers and employees and not by social idealism. Despite critics who argue otherwise, several UN World Investment Reports have established that as a rule, transnational corporations with their headquarters in Europe or the United States pay much higher salaries and wages and give substantially more benefits. This could also be viewed as a problem, as it attracts the best national talents and hence puts native firms up against a competitive disadvantage. Another argument to be taken seriously in this context is the fact that most workplaces in the industrial sector pay substantially higher salaries than any within subsistence agriculture or local handicraft—hence caution must be applied when comparing remuneration packages.

36. R. De George, *Competing with Integrity in International Business* (New York: Oxford University Press, 1993).

37. Milton Friedman's famous phrase, "the business of business is business," is frequently quoted in this respect ("The Social Responsibility of Business Is to Increase Its Profits," *New York Times Magazine,* September 13, 1970).

38. European Commission, *Promoting a European Framework for Corporate Social Responsibility,* 5 and 8.

39. See K. M. Leisinger, "Holzwege für den aufrechten Gang. Christliche Werte als Handlungsorientierung für unternehmerische Entscheidungen," *Freiburger Zeitschrift für Philosophie und Theologie* 52, no. 3 (2005): 628–79.

40. This argument is only valid under the assumption that consumers and investors have sufficient information about the corporate responsibility policy to make informed purchasing and investment decisions, the validity of which is not clearly established. See Whitehouse, "Corporate Social Responsibility," 280.

41. See K. M. Leisinger and K. M. Schmitt, *Corporate Ethics in a Time of Globalization* (Colombo: Sarvodaya Vishva Lekha Printing, 2003), 154–63.

42. M. Kelly, "Holy Grail Found: Absolute, Positive, Definitive Proof CSR Pays Off Financially," *Business Ethics: Corporate Social Responsibility Report* 18, no. 4 (Winter 2004): 4ff.

43. M. Orlitzky, F. L. Schmidt, and S. L. Rynes, "Corporate Social and Financial Performance: A Meta-Analysis," *Organization Studies* 24, no. 3 (2003): 403–41.

44. Ibid.

45. J. D. Margolis and J. P. Walsh, *People and Profits: The Search for a Link between a Company's Social and Financial Performance* (Mahwah, NJ: Lawrence Erlbaum, 2001), 13. For the methodological difficulties, see also J. D. Margolis and J. P. Walsh, "Misery Loves Companies: Whither Social Initiatives by Business?" *Harvard Business School Social Enterprise Series,* no. 19 (2001): 9ff.

46. See Institute of Business Ethics, *Does Business Ethics Pay?* (London: Institute of Business Ethics, 2003), 9.

47. N. A. Dentchev, "Corporate Social Performance as a Business Strategy," *Journal of Business Ethics* 55 (2004): 398.

48. For example, due to additional training of employees, management processes around corporate guidelines, improvement of corporate social services, more comprehensive systems or environmental protection, etc.

49. Carroll, *Business and Society,* 14.

50. For an interesting discussion of this approach, see F. Wettstein, "From Causality to Capability: Towards a New Understanding of the Multinational Corporation's Enlarged Global Responsibilities," *Journal of Corporate Citizenship* 19 (Fall 2005): 105–17.

51. See J. M. Kline, "Political Activities by Transnational Corporations: Bright Lines versus Grey Boundaries," *Transnational Corporations* 12, no. 1 (2003): 1–26.

52. D. Matten, A. Crane, and W. Chapple, "Behind the Mask: Revealing the True Face of Corporate Citizenship," *Journal of Business Ethics* 25, nos. 1–2 (2003): 116; emphasis added by the author.

53. N. Hsieh, "The Obligations of Transnational Corporations: Rawlsian Justice and the Duty of Assistance," *Business Ethics Quarterly* 14, no. 4 (2004): 643–61. Hsieh is building his arguments on John Rawls's account of the "Law of

the People." See J. Rawls, *The Law of Peoples* (Cambridge, MA: Harvard University Press, 1999).

54. See Mark Kramer and John Kania of FSG Social Impact Advisors (www. fsg-impact.org) on the occasion of a Corporate Philanthropy Summit in New York, June 6–7, 2006 (http://www.corporatephilanthropy.org/summit).

55. Milton Friedman made use of this argument in his famous article "The Social Responsibility of Business Is to Increase Its Profits." He concluded that one could refer to some of these responsibilities as "social responsibilities"—but as those of individuals and with their personal resources, not of business with shareholders' money. See http://www.colorado.edu/studentgroups/libertarians/issues/friedman-soc-resp-business.html. See also a special section on "The Good Company" in the *Economist* (January 22, 2005).

56. See T. Donaldson and T. W. Dunfee, *Ties That Bind: A Social Contracts Approach to Business Ethics* (Boston: Harvard Business School Press, 1999), 36 and 38ff; see also Carroll, *Business and Society,* 33ff.

57. For a more in-depth discussion, see K. M. Leisinger, "On Corporate Responsibilities for Human Rights" (contribution of the Special Advisor of the UN Secretary-General on the Global Compact, New York, 2006, http://www.unglobalcompact.org/NewsAndEvents/articles_and_papers/index.html).

58. For example, Novartis donated the multidrug therapy cure for leprosy until this biblical disease was eliminated (see http://www.novartisfoundation. com/en/health_cooperation/leprosy/index.htm); offered differential pricing on antimalarial Coartem (see http://www.novartis.com/corporate_citizenship/ en/01_2005_fighting_malaria.shtml); and undertook pro bono research at the Novartis Institute for Tropical Diseases (see http://www.nitd.novartis.com).

59. Department for International Development, *Increasing People's Access to Essential Medicines in Developing Countries: A Framework for Good Practices in the Pharmaceutical Industry* (London, UK Government Policy Paper, March 2005).

60. See K. M. Leisinger, "The Right to Health—A Duty for Whom?" *UN Global Compact Quarterly* (April 2005), http://www.enewsbuilder.net/global compact/e_article000375786.cfm?x=b4J1cSV,b3hPgoVQ. For the huge complexity of the health issue, see also L. P. Freedman, "Achieving the MDGs: Health Systems as Core Social Institutions," *Development* 48, no. 1 (March 2005): 19–24.

61. "Burdened societies," "duty of assistance," or "outlaw states" are all terms and concepts used by John Rawls in *The Law of the Peoples.*

62. See http://www.novartisfoundation.org/page/content/index.asp?Menu ID=257&ID=587&Menu=3&Item=45.6 for a comprehensive discussion. The proceedings of this symposium can be ordered from the Novartis Foundation for Sustainable Development, P.O. Box CH-4002, Basel, Switzerland.

63. More comprehensively see K. M. Leisinger, "Corporate Philanthropy: The Top of the Pyramid," *Business and Society Review* 112, no. 3. (September 2007): 315–42.

64. See http://www.corporatephilanthropy.org.

65. See http://www.novartisfoundation.com.

66. See http://www.nitd.novartis.com.

67. M. E. Porter and M. R. Kramer, "The Competitive Advantage of Corporate Philanthropy," *Harvard Business Review* (2002). See also http://www.fsg-impact.org/app/content/ideas/item/293.

68. Ibid., 7ff.

69. Ibid., 9.

70. See Voices of the Poor, http://www1.worldbank.org/prem/poverty/voices/index.htm. See also World Bank, *World Development Report 2000/2001. Attacking Poverty*, 15ff.

71. World Health Organization, *The World Health Report 2005. Make Every Mother and Child Count* (Geneva: WHO, 2005), xiv.

72. For details, see http://www.who.int/healthinfo/boddaly/en/.

73. See, for example, J. Sachs, "The Development Challenge," *Foreign Affairs* 84, no. 2 (March/April 2005): 78–90.

74. A subjective selection of the most important literature in this respect includes E. R. Freeman, *Strategic Management: A Stakeholder Approach* (Boston: Pitman, 1984); Donaldson and Dunfee, *Ties that Bind;* Clarkson, *The Corporation and Its Stakeholders;* Carroll, *Business and Society;* J. E. Post, L. E. Preston, and S. Sachs, *Redefining the Corporation, Stakeholder Management and Organizational Wealth* (Stanford, CA: Stanford University Press, 2002); R. Phillips, *Stakeholder Theory and Organizational Ethics* (San Francisco: Berret-Koehler, 2003).

75. For example, "Business interests . . . have been antagonistic to human rights" (S. Swithern: "From Bhopal to Doha: Business and the Right to Health," *New Academy Review* 2, no. 1 [2003]: 50); or "MNCs . . . also undermine the ability of individual states to protect people from human rights abuses" (D. Kinley et al., "Australia: Casten Centre for Human Rights Law," *New Academy Review* 2, no. 1 [2003]: 92).

76. A telling example concerns the four chemical companies in Basel, Switzerland. Only one of them has pledged support to the UN Global Compact (Novartis). The other three companies are not being questioned about why they do not have the courage to commit to global corporate citizenship guidelines; however, Novartis faces insinuations of "blue-washing"—that is, abusing the UN logo for public relations purposes.

77. The picture is different in the United States, where corporate philanthropy enjoys a high degree of appreciation and is accompanied by much goodwill, with the result of substantially higher amounts of resources dedicated to corporate philanthropy than in Europe. See http://www.corporatephilanthropy.org.

78. Of course, generalized corporate prejudices about NGOs is equally unhelpful and intellectually shoddy.

79. There are already developments that could be interpreted as signs of corporate responsibility fatigue. A number of companies that for years made special efforts in sustainability reporting are changing their attitude and going back to a legal compliance–based approach (personal communication with members of the Hertie School of Governance Research Team, Berlin, August 29, 2006).

80. The bar is raised until it is eventually knocked down in a vicious circle of self-fulfilling prophesies from groups most critical of multinationals, resulting in an inversion of proof. For example, Médecins sans Frontières did so with respect to Novartis offering antimalarial Coartem at production cost to WHO for distribution to poor societies. Médecins sans Frontière attacked the company publicly for not following through on its promises when Novartis announced problems with the production of the surprisingly high quantities needed—well beyond the initial forecast of the World Health Organization. The problems developed due to issues beyond corporate control; one component of the combination product Coartem is a plant whose production depends on a long agricultural cycle. Disappointingly, there were no public corrections made by those who accused the company when—after substantial additional investments and efforts to overcome the bottlenecks—the production targets were eventually surpassed and, incidentally, finally were much higher than the real demand.

81. This argument is not meant to insinuate that people only act morally if there are strong incentives to do so. Our argument is based on Amitai Etzioni's theory that people's behavior is influenced by two factors: first, by what they perceive to be their moral obligation and, secondly, by what they perceive to be in their interest. Etzioni acknowledges significant differences with regard to the extent to which each of these factors works with different personalities. Amitai Etzioni, *The Moral Dimension: Towards a New Economics* (New York: Free Press, 1988).

82. Named after Vilfredo Pareto, the Italian economist and sociologist, this is an allocation pattern beyond which it is not possible to make a subject better off without making another subject worse off.

83. In addition to reputation capital of civil society, other "rewards" could be thought of, such as price differentials in public tenders, preference given by international/institutional purchasing, etc.

84. See http://www.zenithoptimedia.com/gff/pdf/Adspend%20forecasts%20July%202006.pdf.

PART V

Some Case Studies

CHAPTER 10

A Public-Private Partnership for Enterprise Development

The Case of the Angola Enterprise Program

Ofelia C. Eugenio

In today's world, the private sector is the dominant engine of growth. If the private sector does not deliver economic growth and economic opportunity—equitable and sustainable—around the world, then peace will remain fragile and social justice a distant dream. That is why, I call today for a new partnership amongst governments, the private sector and the international community.

—Former UN Secretary-General Kofi Annan

INTRODUCTION

The private sector plays a vital role in alleviating the prevalence of poverty in most developing countries. There are many encouraging results all over the world that demonstrate that the private sector has contributed significantly to economic growth, job creation, increasing incomes for the poor, and, ultimately, poverty reduction. The private sector includes multinational corporations (MNCs) as well as micro, small, and medium enterprises (MSMEs). It encompasses both formal and informal sectors. Even the poor entrepreneur in a village is an important and integral part of the private sector. In the developing world MSMEs, on average, make up over 90 percent of enterprises and account for 50–60 percent of employment. The prevalence of MSMEs is more pronounced at the lower-income levels. In fact, many poor households rely on micro and small enterprises as their only source of income. Against this background, the promotion of MSMEs is considered essential for making progress toward achieving the Millennium Development Goal of halving the fifth of the planet's population living on less than a US$1 per day by the year 2015.

Despite its important role in the development of a country, especially for poor countries, the private sector (particularly MSMEs) is confronted with various issues and constraints that hinder its growth, including the following:

lack of an enabling environment, with restrictive laws and regulations adversely affecting MSMEs and unsupportive or biased policies favoring bigger and formal businesses
macroeconomic impediments (for example, political instability, lack of transparency and accountability, unsound macroeconomic policies)
lack of access to credit, training, and other support services
cultural and gender issues
a negative attitude toward the informal business sector

The Commission on Private Sector Development[1] cited three major structural challenges that confront, to varying degrees, the private sector in all developing countries: micro enterprises and many small and medium enterprises operate informally; many small and medium enterprises have barriers to growth; and a lack of competitive pressure shields larger firms from market forces and the need to innovate and become more productive. The constraints faced by the private sector are multifarious, and multifaceted approaches are required to overcome them. The commission recommends that addressing these constraints in order to unleash the potential of the private sector will require programs tailored to the needs of individual countries.

Harnessing the development potential of the private sector can lead to sustained and equitable growth and development. Doing so requires deliberate and concerted efforts by players within and outside of the private sector. Business linkages between big/formal enterprises with small/informal enterprises should be fully explored. Continuing support to the sector also should be provided by the government, donors, NGOs, and civil society. The development of the private sector also requires exploiting and maximizing the resources already available. The managerial, organizational, and technological innovations that reside in the private sector should be used to improve the lives of the poor.

In recent years increased attention has been given to public-private partnerships within the framework of corporate responsibility. These partnerships are viewed as a new model for collaboration and cooperation between public and private players working toward private sector development and other development initiatives. It is against this background that the United Nations Development Program (UNDP) in Angola has engaged in a public-private partnership—the Angola Enterprise Programme (AEP)—intended to promote enterprise development and help reduce poverty in Angola. The remainder of this chapter will focus on AEP, beginning with some background information about Angola and its private enterprise sector, in particular MSMEs.

AN OVERVIEW OF ANGOLA

The Country Profile

Angola is a beautiful, diverse, and vast country endowed with an enviable plethora of natural resources. It has the potential to be one of the richest countries in Africa given its abundant mineral resources, mainly oil and diamonds. It is also rich in water resources. Angola is a large country, with a total land area of 481,353 square miles, almost twice the size of Texas. In 2005 the total population was estimated at 16.5 million, with 4.5 million people residing in the capital city of Luanda.

But like many developing countries, Angola presents a stark contrast between wealth and poverty. The development of the country has been stunted by over three decades of civil war that ended in April 2002. Angola is now in the process of reconstruction; the country is achieving rapid economic growth, with GDP increasing by over 10 percent per year and expected to rise over the next couple of years. Despite these economic gains, Angola ranked 160 out of 177 countries in the *Human Development Report 2005,* with a Human Development Index (HDI) of 0.445. It is estimated that 68 percent of the estimated 16.5 million residents live below the poverty line (less than US$1.70/day) and 26 percent live in extreme poverty (less than US$0.75/day). Health indicators in Angola are among the worst in the world, with 260 of every 1,000 children dying before the age of five. The maternal mortality rate is also high, at 1,700 deaths per 100,000 births, which is estimated to be 100 times the rate in the United States. There is widespread malnutrition, although the number at risk for malnutrition has been cut in half since 2003. Thirty-two percent of people in Angola lack access to safe drinking water. Life expectancy at birth is roughly forty-two years.[2]

HIV/AIDS and malaria remain the greatest public health challenges to Angola. The HIV/AIDS prevalence rate was officially estimated at 5.5 percent in 2004,[3] although incidence could have been higher due to lack of statistical information and a limited number of surveillance centers. It is estimated that 22 percent of the population has been affected by malaria. The incidence of tuberculosis, however, another fatal disease affecting many Angolans, has been drastically reduced, with many recovering from the disease since Angola has built a successful national monitoring and treatment system over the past four years. The population is generally young, with 60 percent under the age of twenty. The government has made huge strides in providing access to education, registering gross enrollment rates of over 91 percent in 2003. Nevertheless, the government is faced with the challenge of improving the quality of education and decreasing gender disparity; 83 percent of men and 54 percent of women are illiterate.

Angola is still heavily dependent on imports because little has been achieved in attempts to revive agricultural and industrial production. The country's enormous agricultural potential remains largely untapped and restricted due to land mine contamination, although smallhold farmers are slowly starting to return to the land in the interior of the country. Absence of effective land titles hinders efforts to expand agricultural production, which is also exacerbated by deplorable conditions or even absence of physical infrastructures to facilitate trade, especially in provinces and remote areas.

As in many developing countries, unemployment is high in Angola, particularly among women and youth. According to the UNDP *National Human Development Report of 2004,* the unemployment rate is estimated to be between 45 and 49 percent. The IMF Intelligence Report, however, has higher estimates of 60 percent in 2004 and 58 percent in 2005. Fifty percent of the population is surviving on informal sector businesses.[4] Farming, livestock, and artisanal fishing employ two-thirds of the country's workforce, yet agriculture accounts for a mere 8 percent of the GDP. Manufacturing contributes only 4 percent to the GDP, compared to 25 percent in 1975,[5] while oil represents 55 percent of the GDP and 90 percent of exports.[6]

Angolans will soon be heading to the election polls for the first time after the long civil conflict. Election registration has been ongoing since 2006. Various organizations, including UNDP, are helping the government to hold a free and fair election and strengthen the rule of law in the country. The challenge is rebuilding Angola after three decades of war. Clearly, the rebuilding process necessitates diversification of the economy and reinvigoration of productive sectors other than oil and diamonds through necessary reforms. Equally important—given the limited employment opportunities in the formal sector—is the need to promote private sector development and stimulate micro, small, and medium enterprises in order to create new sources of employment and, most importantly, reduce poverty.

The Micro, Small, and Medium Enterprise Sector in Angola

Angola's history of colonialism, conflict, and fifteen years of a highly centralized economy did not favor the development of entrepreneurial culture and spirit. However, due to economic pressures and lack of employment opportunities in the formal sector, the majority of the people engage in various forms of small businesses to earn income. There is an absence of reliable statistics on MSMEs in Angola. According to the survey of businesses conducted by Angola National Statistics in 2004, it is estimated that the bulk (80 percent) of enterprises are micro and small. Owing to the absence of an official definition of MSMEs, micro enterprises include those with 0 to 4 workers, small from 5 to 9 workers, and medium from 10 to 20 workers. The only criterion used to define MSMEs in Angola is the number of workers; in other countries, however, other criteria are sometimes used, including amount of capitalization, amount of sales turnover, registration, and frequency of operation (continuous and intermittent), among others. MSMEs, especially in the informal sector, have become the major source of consumer goods and are the largest source of employment in Angola.

Table 10.1   Participation Rates in MSMEs

Gender	Overall	Micro	Small	Medium
Male	62%	50%	75%	87%
Female	38%	42%	25%	13%
Total	100%	100%	100%	100%

Results of the 2005 diagnostic study on MSMEs conducted by the Catholic University (also referred to as UCAN) as part of the Angola Enterprise Programme—which covered a total of 1,000 entrepreneur respondents, with 500 from the capital city of Luanda, 200 from the industrial city of Benguela, and 300 from rural Huambo—revealed the following demographic information about Angolan entrepreneurs. Men dominate MSMEs, with 62 percent participation compared to 38 percent among women. The same trend is true in all three geographical locations and for all enterprise categories (micro, small, and medium). The participation of men increases as enterprises grow bigger, but the opposite is true for women, as illustrated in table 1. Bigger businesses are owned by men. Male entrepreneurs also are economically better off than their female counterparts. The entrepreneur-respondents were young—almost half between the ages of twenty and forty. The bigger the business, the older the entrepreneur, suggesting a very high correlation between age and size of business. About 75 percent of the respondents have reached at least the first level of secondary education, although, again, men usually attained a higher level of education than women. Only 5 percent of women attended university and 7 percent are illiterate. As with age, there is a high correlation between the size of the business and level of education of the entrepreneur. Entrepreneurs in Luanda have attained the highest level of education, followed by Benguela and then Huambo. Only 18 percent of the respondents worked in the formal sector before joining the MSME sector. Although there were diverse reasons why entrepreneurs wanted to start a business, the most frequent response was to secure financing, while a few wanted to own a business instead of working for others.

With regard to the entrepreneurs' households, for over half of the total (56 percent), their business is the main source of income, with the highest percentage in Luanda at 76 percent, followed by Benguela at 26 percent and Huambo at 6 percent. As the business grows, the household becomes dependent on it as the main source of income. About 50 percent of households have four to six members, including other relatives outside of the nuclear family unit. About half of the respondents own their houses, but the bulk of those who own houses are from the provinces. In the capital city of Luanda, over half of the respondents rent or stay with relatives. Entrepreneurs from Luanda have better living conditions; their houses are made of permanent materials such as cement or bricks, and they have access to water and light. In contrast, the majority of the entrepreneurs in Benguela and Huambo have poor living conditions, with houses made of adobe and no access to water and light. The bigger the enterprise, the greater the access to water and light. As with education, male entrepreneurs are better off than females, with most men having access to water and light. Over half of the entrepreneurs (56 percent) have migrated from other provinces, with the percentage of migrants highest in Luanda (62 percent). In Benguela only a few have migrated (36 percent), and fewer still in Huambo (13 percent).

Commerce is the most common type of business among these entrepreneurs, with 74 percent of respondents engaged in an enterprise of this sort. This coincides with the results of a survey of businesses undertaken by Angola National Statistics, which found that 70 percent were involved in commerce. A few entrepreneurs are involved in providing services, and a negligible portion of MSMEs are in transport, construction, and other service-related enterprises. In Luanda, over half of the respondents (64 percent) do business in urban areas and only 34 percent in peri-urban areas. In Benguela 44 percent operate their businesses in urban areas and only 12 percent in rural areas. In Huambo the majority operate in peri-urban areas (71 percent), with 27 percent in urban areas and 1 percent in rural areas. On average, businesses in Luanda are eight months old. This short period of operation could be attributed to ease of entry of migrants to the city. However, it could also be an indication of the instability of business, where business fail frequently due to high competition, low capitalization, and low income. Enterprises in Benguela and Huambo have been operating longer—between eleven and thirty months, indicating less competition and more stability. Over half of the enterprises covered in the survey (51 percent) have been registered as individual/single proprietorship and none as a limited company. About 20 percent preferred to stay informal; only 17 percent did not register because of the expense or lack of knowledge about the process. Bigger businesses are usually registered, and registration is highest in Luanda. For about 75 percent of the enterprises, daily sales amount to $125. This sales amount should be approached with caution, however, because many entrepreneurs do not maintain sales records. The initial investments for these businesses ranged from $125 to $3,125. Over half (54 percent) have initial investment of $125, and this is primarily the case in Huambo. Those with higher investments of $3,000 or more (a quarter of the respondents) are from Luanda. The enterprises operating in urban areas are located within a building (shops or offices), while those operating in peri-urban and rural areas are mainly ambulant and no do not operate in fixed or permanent locations. The 1,000 enterprises that were surveyed reported employment of 4,916 workers, or an average of 5 workers per enterprise, with most working in commerce. All of the businesses could be categorized as micro or small enterprises.

A market study of the Business Development Services (BDS), commissioned by UNDP as part of the AEP and undertaken by Hans Posthumus Consultancy in April 2006, observed that there is a huge diversity of enterprises, each influenced by numerous factors, including their maturity (in terms of growth), the sector in which they operate and other contextual factors such as geographical location. The study further found that most entrepreneurs do not have natural models or examples of how enterprises should operate, and they often lack the "innovative thinking" that distinguishes them from their competitors. Many of the present entrepreneurs are not entrepreneurs by choice but by circumstance. They were unemployed and had few alternatives; in response, they set up their own income-generating activities, which in some cases have grown into small enterprises.

Few of the enterprises operate in the manufacturing sector, and if they do, they use outdated equipment and technology. Their competitive advantage has been the use of cheap labor, yet it is doubtful that this will remain an advantage in the near future. The application of modern technology is, in general, also absent from the trade and services sectors, resulting in labor-intensive and often less-efficient operations.

The market study further noted that many entrepreneurs, when beginning their businesses, are rather formalistic and often have unrealistic expectations or plans. Feasibility plans are written that require considerable borrowing, yet their own equity is limited. Start-ups often assume that all assets need to be in place and leave little room for improvising and step-by-step growth. Many business owners indicate that growth of their undertaking is only possible with additional financial injections, and they ignore the fact that natural growth also can be obtained through improved business operations (cost reduction, productivity improvements, differentiating margins, increasing turnover, etc.).

It is a common observation that the MSME sector in Angola, as in many developing countries, lacks dynamism, particularly with the bulk of activities being in commerce. Productivity is low, with only few entrepreneurs engaging in manufacturing enterprises and some providing services in transport, catering, and restaurants, among others. The informal sector has become the "sector of last resort" for survival of a large proportion of the population in the cities. Although economic data on this sector is scarce, a 2003 study financed by the UNDP on urban micro enterprises in Angola provides some interesting information on this sector. It is estimated that more than half of the population survives through informal sector businesses. Around 82 percent of operators in the informal sector are self-employed, which indicates that the sector is in its early stages of development. Approximately 74 percent of the informal sector is involved in commerce (petty trading), while barely a tenth of informal sector operators are involved in traditional productive activities such as baking, carpentry, or welding. Another significant feature is the predominance of women—47 percent of women worked in the informal sector in comparison with 27 percent of men.[7]

Constraints to and Recommendations for MSME Development

Angolan MSMEs face tremendous difficulties as they fight to survive and grow in this volatile economy. The formally registered enterprises are being squeezed between the officially limited profit margins and high taxes. The economic police dictate that customers are charged no more than a 25 percent mark-up, while a combination of monthly and annual taxes produce an effective tax rate on profits of 47 percent, which leaves little for the owner of the business.[8]

Angola is one of the most difficult countries in which to establish a business, according to a World Bank study on doing business.[9] Angola ranked 156 out of 175 countries in terms of ease of doing business and ranked 170 out of 175 countries in ease of starting a business. As shown in table 2, there are thirteen procedural steps that must be taken in order to start a business, which necessitate 124 days and cost the equivalent of 486.7 percent of gross national income (GNI) per capita. It is noteworthy that the government is trying to implement various reforms to facilitate the establishment of businesses. In 2003 the government established Guiche Unico, a one-stop shop for business registration, mainly for use by partnerships and companies. It has drastically reduced the time, cost, and bureaucratic hurdles to registering a business, but only for partnerships and companies.

The top three problems cited by the 1,000 micro, small, and medium entrepreneurs in the UCAN survey were lack of clients, lack of credit, and lack of raw materials. The problem of access to loans/credit is more pro-

Table 10.2   Comparative Analysis of Starting a Business by Region or Economy, 2007

Region or Economy	Procedures (Number)	Duration (Days)	Cost(% of GNI per capita)	Minimum Capital (% of GNI per capita)
East Asia and Pacific	8.2	46.3	42.8	60.3
Europe and Central Asia	9.4	32	14.1	53.9
Latin America and Caribbean	10.2	73.3	48.1	18.1
Middle East and North Africa	10.3	40.9	74.5	744.5
OECD	6.2	16.6	5.3	36.1
South Asia	7.9	32.5	46.6	0.8
Sub-Saharan Africa	11.1	61.8	162.8	209.9
Angola	13	124	486.7	74.1
Botswana	11	108	10.6	0.0
Malawi	10	37	134.7	0.0
Mozambique	13	113	85.7	10.4
South Africa	9	35	6.9	0.0
United States	5	5	.07	0.0

Source: www.doingbusiness.org

nounced in Luanda than in Benguela and Huambo. The BDS market study, on the other hand, noted the following problems and constraints of MSMEs (some of the observations are drawn from the results of the UCAN study as well). Angolan MSMEs lack services that could support their development and growth, and the services that are available are concentrated in Luanda and focused on larger clients. MSMEs have limited access to credit. Similarly, access to business development services is limited, and the design and structure of such services, when available, do not sufficiently take into account the needs and realities of doing business at the lower end of the market.

Most enterprises have limited access to capital and operate with little working capital. Access to financial assistance is still very restricted and obtaining investment capital is cumbersome, with commercial loans more often than not having relatively short repayment periods. Interest rates do not stimulate investments in manufacturing, and microfinance is mainly intended for trading activities with high gains and over short time periods. This observation is also drawn from the results of the entrepreneurs surveyed by UCAN, where it was revealed that only one-fifth of the enterprises ever benefited from a loan (with medium enterprises benefiting relatively more). Complicated procedures and high costs were cited as the main reasons for business owners not taking a loan.

Many of the entrepreneurs and their staff have completed primary education, but most have gained their "business skills" in real life. Vocational training centers, both private and public, appear to focus on technical skills, and little attention is given to business or entrepreneurial skills. It is believed that only 12 percent of the entrepreneurs have ever participated in professional training. Thus, when entrepreneurs were asked what they needed most, training ranked second (28 percent), after access to financial assistance (43 percent). Given the extremely limited exposure to successful and nontraditional business operations, many skills and businesses are simply copying from others.

Lack of access to financial resources for working and investment capital is prevalent and is one of the major causes hindering growth of the enterprises. Although there are some indications that access to capital is improving, many entrepreneurs still find it difficult. Few banks are willing to take a risk on the client's future, but they take a retrospective approach by looking at the client's record and guarantees. Only recently have banks started to demand feasibility studies, which serve as loan applications but not necessarily as business plans. Most of the entrepreneurs are not able to develop such plans and hire the services of others to do so. It should be noted that the resulting plan is not a joint product but often a financial plan developed by the expert with little involvement by the client. In fact, few entrepreneurs work on a business plan at all, be it on paper or in their minds.

Some entrepreneurs find it difficult to register their business, while others are not concerned with formalization at all. Respondents indicated that registration is an expensive and cumbersome procedure, although in various provinces these difficulties were said to be easier to overcome. In some instances, business associations assist (and in fact demand) that their members register their businesses. Other entrepreneurs had difficulty procuring goods, mainly because of their weak position as a small buyer vis-à-vis a large seller but also due to the fact that few have a range of reliable suppliers. Some also expressed concern that wholesalers and retailers were encroaching on their business by also offering goods in smaller units, which is typically a service provided by micro entrepreneurs. The respondents need to develop alternative procurement and marketing strategies that give them (another) competitive advantage.

Unreliability of basic services such as electricity and water was also mentioned frequently since it seriously affected the enterprises' productivity. More often than not, problems with electricity or water result in production stoppages, or businesses have to revert to alternative supplies (such as a generator) with all the added costs, again affecting profitability. Access to affordable and reliable services was high on the entrepreneurs' list. This issue could become part of the public agenda if the entrepreneurs organized to lobby or influence the government. In the short term, they might consider sharing the costs when they procure water and electricity (sources) jointly, or when a leasing company provides expensive equipment to them.

In general, there seems to be a rather limited market, and many entrepreneurs find it difficult to compete. Many entrepreneurs expressed a need "to sell more," but they had few ideas on how that could be achieved, except through financial injections and advertising. When asked how these injections would then be used to increase turnover, most of them remained puzzled. Several entrepreneurs indicated that they had difficulty analyzing their operations in terms of financial results. They expressed a need to learn how to record their business transactions in order to understand their business better.

Most entrepreneurs had difficulty explaining their needs, and that might be the most crucial issue: how to identify and specify their needs. Most reverted to mentioning topics such as "how to manage better," "how to calculate costs and prices," and "how to adhere to government requirements" (like tax declaration). In most cases, the entrepreneurs suggested that these topics would be best addressed by training courses. Most entrepreneurs had heard of or even frequented such one-week courses. Even though many of these courses were given free of charge, the entrepreneurs expressed a willingness to pay for training if necessary.

There was a general reluctance toward using the services of consultants; most entrepreneurs considered them to be providing inadequate services at rather high costs. However, that reputation seems to be based upon secondhand information, since few had actually hired consultants for specific jobs. On the other hand, business owners often operate in isolation, and there were indications that some entrepreneurs actively sought advice. These advisors were usually people they respected and were members of their own "circles," and the entrepreneurs did not pay for services provided directly.

Meanwhile, the UNDP micro enterprise study cited earlier found that most productive micro enterprises operate in dilapidated premises and are hampered by poor infrastructure and public utilities. They are undercapitalized and have very limited access to credit and business services. The micro enterprise owners in the study were unable to pay their workers regular wages and had underdeveloped entrepreneurial skills, although those in the service sector were found to be more successful and possess good business sense, despite lacking more conventional business skills. The main constraint to expansion of these businesses was the lack of financial resources.

Other constraints to MSME development can include the following:

limited entrepreneurial skills and competencies
very limited access to credit—there are nine banks in Luanda and 1.7
    billion business deposits, with only $338 million in business credit
    given in 2002

little experience with microcredit—there are no professional micro-finance institutions and DW, Banco Sol, and MINFAMU have less than 10,000 clients combined

a large number of potential clients do not have access to financial services—500,000 bankable MSMEs do not have access to credit

vocational training is supply driven and concentrated in Luanda, while most centers have depleted and antiquated assets and few market linkages

lack of physical infrastructure to facilitate business (for example, poor road network, limited cold storage warehouses, etc.)

Because of these constraints, MSMEs have remained marginalized, and many owners prefer to continue operating informally. Consequently, their huge potential to become engines of economic growth and development in Angola has remained untapped.

Surprisingly, despite these constraints, MSMEs are growing in Angola and in other developing countries. This phenomenon can perhaps be attributed to the following factors:

lack of employment opportunities in the formal sector

low level of incomes, even for those working in the formal sector

migration of people to urban areas

retrenchment and retirement of employees

increasing process of globalization and growth of multinational companies

growing acceptance of free market philosophies emphasizing private initiative and enterprise as the mainspring of economic progress

economic growth and economic pressures to earn more money in order to achieve better standards of living

THE ANGOLA ENTERPRISE PROGRAMME

Rationale and Background

The government of Angola, UNDP, and Chevron, in collaboration with various stakeholders, were convinced that they could contribute to the reconstruction of Angola by jointly embarking on an Angola Enterprise

Programme, which aims to reduce poverty through private sector development, in particular support of MSME entrepreneurs. The AEP is aligned with the government's national development priorities, especially those for economic growth, private sector development, and poverty alleviation. By generating employment and raising people's incomes, the AEP can make significant contributions to Angola's national poverty reduction strategy and economic growth strategy. It will also help Angola come closer to achieving the Millennium Development Goals.

The AEP supports the overall vision of UNDP, which is poverty reduction for sustainable human development, and is in line with the UNDP *Country Cooperation Framework 2001-2003*. Similarly, the AEP supports UNDP's mission to build a coalition of partners on the ground to support Angola's efforts to reduce extreme poverty and is aligned with efforts to support the achievement of Millennium Goal 1—Eradicate Extreme Poverty. The UNDP will provide support to the overall strategic direction of the program and will play a critical role in the areas of policy support, regulation, legal frameworks, and institutional building.

For Chevron, the AEP forms part of the US$25 million Angola Partnership Initiative (API) launched by Chevron to support the diversification of the Angolan economy, the national poverty reduction strategy, and creation of employment. It also helps raise the company profile of Chevron and other private sector partners in Angola and helps promote corporate social responsibility (CSR).

UNDP and Chevron created the partnership in November 2002 as part of the framework of the API, ChevronTexaco's Sustainable Development Company. The AEP project document was signed and approved by the government through the Ministry of Planning on December 2003. Full implementation of the AEP commenced in mid-June 2004; it was initially intended to run for three years, ending in June 2007, and has since been extended.

Program Description

The Angola Enterprise Programme is a public-private partnership that seeks the cooperation and support of various organizations within the government, the private sector, academia, and civil society, as well as donors and NGOs, in the creation of a vibrant Angolan private enterprise sector, especially the micro, small, and medium enterprise sector. The

AEP's mission is to contribute to the development of a conducive private enterprise sector and to build the capacity of local institutions to provide sustainable and quality services to Angola's private enterprises.

The AEP is focused on three key areas: microfinance, business development services (BDS), and the creation of an environment conducive to business. Microfinance is aimed at expanding access to financial services for MSMEs by building and strengthening the capacity of banks and other financial institutions to provide sustainable microfinance services. The AEP hopes to introduce new models of BDS by strengthening existing centers that provide sustainable and quality services to entrepreneurs. Creation of a supportive and conducive environment for small enterprise development is facilitated through formulation of appropriate policies and legislative reforms as a result of public debates and policy recommendations and from studies/research that establish a knowledge base on MSMEs.

The guiding elements of the program strategy are the following:

- Build consensus around a medium-term vision through frequent dialogue between all stakeholders, especially public and private sector representatives as part of a national strategy and action plan for private sector development
- Promote the development of MSMEs in all regions of Angola based on pilot experiences in one or two provinces
- Develop local capacity as part of a strategy to promote sustainable institutions, which through competition and working toward cost recovery, will continue to provide services to the MSME sector long after the AEP has ended
- Emphasize the role of women, particularly given their importance in the development of the family and their prevalence in the micro enterprise sector
- Make market-oriented investments that encourage the most effective use of resources and, through the strengthening of market mechanisms, ensure that future resources will be invested in an efficient manner
- Work with a venture capital approach based upon pilot projects that will use a variety of mechanisms and institutions to deliver services; positive results should mobilize resources to expand the success of the program over time

The direct clients of the AEP are the locally based institutions supporting MSMEs, making the enterprises themselves the indirect clients of the AEP.

The initial three-year project had an original budget amounting to US$4 million ($3 million from Chevron and $1 million from UNDP). It was the intention that UNDP would undertake resource mobilization activities to attract more partners and leverage more funds. As of November 2006, the budget was increased to US$4.439 million, with an additional US$100,000 provided by the World Bank's Information for Development Program for the establishment of a business incubator, and additional funds from UNDP for the establishment of a Small Business Resource Center.

The AEP and Development

The relevance and pertinence of the AEP to Angola's socioeconomic development is quite high for a variety of reasons. First, it is aligned with government national development priorities, especially for economic growth, private sector development, and poverty alleviation. MSMEs can provide much-needed income and employment opportunities given the high incidence of poverty, high unemployment, and the importance of informal sector businesses. Second, the majority of the stakeholders that participated in the AEP midterm review recognized the project as having facilitated broader awareness and understanding of MSMEs and microfinance—an issue that previously had been underplayed or perhaps ignored despite its importance. The AEP has organized forums, advocacy activities, and first-ever comprehensive studies about MSMEs. All of these initiatives have contributed to the establishment of a knowledge base on MSMEs, which can provide valuable information for formulation of appropriate MSME policy and legislative reforms and enable other MSME initiatives to have a greater likelihood for success.

Third, the AEP has introduced innovative models of business development services, such as one-stop BDS centers in Luanda and Benguela, a business incubator, and, recently, a small business information center that provides updated information and other services to entrepreneurs. Fourth, the AEP has established broad partnerships with local and international donors, UN agencies, the private sector, academia, and organizations within civil society, including NGOs. This broadened public-private partnership was one of the first initiatives of UNDP in Angola and the first in the attempt to promote MSMEs within the country. It has demonstrated that cooperation and collaboration between and among various stakeholders can create synergies, promote complementary resources, and avoid duplication of efforts.

Milestone Achievements as of October 2006

In the area of microfinance, since 2004 the AEP has assisted in expanding the supply of credit, especially to poor entrepreneurs, by building the capacity of the two biggest and longest-running microfinance providers in Angola: Banco Sol (a commercial bank) and Development Workshop (an NGO). Through an international technical service provider (ACCION International) and with support from the United Nations Capital Development Fund (UNCDF), a series of training and study tours were provided to the officers and staff of these two organizations to help them gain a better understanding of the best practices of microfinance and to help improve the performance and delivery of their microfinance services. Stakeholders had the opportunity to visit leading international microfinance institutions and learn from their business models. AEP support has helped improve the quality portfolio of both microfinance institutions and resulted in wider client outreach. Both institutions were able to collectively provide sustainable microfinance services to over 22,000 clients. It should be recognized, however, that other organizations also have provided capacity-building support to both Banco Sol and Development Workshop.

The AEP also facilitated the establishment of the Microfinance Unit within the Banco Nacional de Angola (Central Bank) in 2004. The unit, which was integrated with the Supervision Unit within the Central Bank in October 2006, had organized various microfinance seminars, workshops, and national forums to disseminate international best practices in the development of microfinance, to ensure greater policy coherence, and to guide the formulation of the National Microfinance Policy and Strategy. Before its transfer in October 2006, the Microfinance Unit organized a series of training sessions in microfinance that led to the creation of the first network of microfinance professionals in Angola. Moreover, the Microfinance Unit, in collaboration with the AEP, commissioned a microfinance baseline study, which is regarded as the first comprehensive study of microfinance in Angola. On October 7, 2006, NovoBanco, a newly established commercial bank devoted to provision of microfinance services, in collaboration with the AEP, launched a project to promote a savings culture among children. The program is targeting the participation of twenty-one schools and two thousand elementary students.

With respect to BDS, the AEP has facilitated greater access to business training, advice, and other support services necessary to turn a good idea into a great business. This has been achieved by supporting the founding of two independent business development service centers (one in Luanda and one in Benguela) and the establishment of the business incubator in Luanda. The AEP provided start-up funds and technical assistance to the two BDS centers and the business incubator. Both BDS centers have provided a wide range of services to entrepreneurs, including entrepreneurship and enterprise development training, business diagnosis, business plan preparation, and credit facilitation. The AEP midterm review has recommended terminating the AEP's direct financial support to these two centers and instead broadening AEP support of other BDS providers for greater client outreach and impact. Through September 2006, the two BDS centers have collectively provided services to a total of 334 entrepreneur-clients. Currently, both BDS centers are operating on their own with minimal support from AEP.

In collaboration with the National Institute for Employment and Vocational Training and the Information for Development Program, the AEP has helped establish the first business incubator in the city of Luanda. The incubator provides a building, common business facilities, and continuing business support services to approximately thirty clients (eight pre-incubation or with business ideas, ten incubation or start-up businesses, and twelve virtual or existing businesses). In addition, the AEP is currently undertaking preparatory activities for the establishment of the first small business resource/information center in Angola to provide updated information necessary to start, operate, and expand businesses, as well as provide important information for policy makers, students, researchers, and other stakeholders.

In working toward creation of an environment conducive to businesses, the AEP commissioned the Catholic University to carry out a diagnostic study of the MSME sector in Angola in 2005, with the intention of establishing a knowledge base on small businesses. Through the dissemination of the information gathered and resulting analysis, the study has contributed to informed public policy design. This information—what businesses need and want—serves as the basis for AEP work.

In order to overcome the barriers to establishing a business (with Angola holding the dubious distinction of being the most difficult country in the world in which to start a business), the AEP has been working to reduce excessive regulation and to give businesses a voice in the policy process. So far, the AEP has undertaken a consultative process to review the registration process and other constraints to business. This information served as the basis of discussion at a forum in early 2007, which recommended some political measures to simplify business registration.

Apart from studies and forums on MSMEs in general and microfinance, the AEP also has conducted an in-depth national study on the vocational training sector. In collaboration with the National Institute for Employment and Vocational Training, the AEP organized a national forum on vocational training with the aim of reaching a consensus on how to strengthen the sector and provide market-driven vocational training and courses. In addition to providing important information to prospective entrepreneurs, the AEP has helped open a dialogue among business, government, and civil society that can help ensure the new policies take the needs of all into account.

Lessons Learned

The success of the AEP is in part a result of the combination of UN development goals and private sector profit-oriented goals, with the fusion made possible through the promotion of corporate social responsibility toward achieving the shared goal of contributing to the reduction of poverty in Angola. The AEP experience has demonstrated that cooperation among various stakeholders, although a difficult process, is possible. Other lessons learned include the following:

- Investing sufficient time and effort in understanding the situation of the country, especially the MSME sector and related sectors, is necessary for identifying appropriate interventions and the various stakeholders and potential synergies among them.
- Public-private partnership modalities such as those within the AEP should enjoin broader participation of productive sectors other than

major industries and encourage greater collaboration, coordination of efforts, and pooling of resources and expertise for greater impact.

- Partnerships should be managed through clearly defined roles and responsibilities. Donors, as members of the project board, should be responsible for strategic decisions and should be discouraged from micro-managing. The executing agency should be given flexibility to implement the program within agreed parameters.

- Partners and beneficiaries should be equally represented on the project board so that strategic decisions will take into consideration their interests.

- Donors and partners should be committed to the long process of institutional capacity building and should provide continuous and long-term support, including provision of adequate resources, to achieve desired results and outcomes. Given the low human and institutional capacity and the nascent civil society organizations and private sector in Angola, the process for institutional capacity building and strengthening should involve an evolution from individual capacity development to institutional capacity, which takes longer than the usual three to five years required in more developed countries with more mature MSME sectors.

- An exit strategy should be defined from the beginning so that donors, partners, and other stakeholders are aware of the long-term approach for developing the MSME sector and building institutional capacity and discouraged from looking for "quick fixes."

- Partners should have a clear understanding of expected outcomes and deliverables and should commit to their achievement; changes in outcomes and work plans should be minimized. Proposed changes should be carefully analyzed to ensure that they will lead to the achievement of the expected outcomes.

- Interventions should be designed to promote integration and synergies that will be cost-efficient while achieving better results and greater impact to beneficiaries.

- It is important to clearly define beneficiaries through client segmentation and mapping and have a good understanding of their profiles, needs, and constraints in order to ensure that interventions will be responsive to the specific needs of clients/beneficiaries. Do not treat MSMEs as a homogenous group.

THE WAY FORWARD

After almost three years, the AEP has made some headway in improving the business climate in Angola. However, much work remains to be done. The UNDP in Angola and the AEP team are now searching for new partners in their efforts to continue the project. A vigorous resource mobilization effort is continuously undertaken both internationally and locally to identify new partners and leverage more funds. New partners will be brought into the planning process as UNDP charts the way forward.

NOTES

1. This commission was convened in June 2003 upon the order of the then UN Secretary-General Kofi Annan. Its main task is to answer two questions: How can the potential of the private sector and entrepreneurship be unleashed in developing countries? How can the existing private sector be engaged in meeting that challenge? In 2004 the commission produced a report entitled *Unleashing Entrepreneurship: Making Business Work for the Poor*. See also Kiendel Burritt, *Expanding Access to Financial Services in Malawi* (New York: UNCDF, 2006); CGAP, *Building Inclusive Financial Systems—Donor Guidelines on Good Practice in Microfinance* (New York: CGAP/World Bank, 2004), http://www.uncdf.org/english/microfinance/sectorDev/index.php; and IFC, *Simplification of Business Regulations at the Sub-National Level: A Reform Implementation Toolkit for Project Teams* (Washington, DC: IFC, 2006).

2. *Angola Millennium Goals Report Summary 2005* (Luanda: Government of Angola and UNDP, 2005), 6.

3. UNDP, *Defusing the Remnants of War: Economic Report on Angola 2002-2004,* prepared by Bernard Ouandji (Luanda: UNDP, 2005), 4.

4. UNDP, *Promoting the Urban Micro-Enterprise Sector in Angola,* prepared by Fion de Vletter (Luanda: UNDP, 2002).

5. UNDP, *Economic Report on Angola 2002-2004* (Luanda: UNDP, 2004).

6. UNDP, *Angola Millennium Goals Report Summary 2005.*

7. UNDP, *Promoting the Urban Micro-Enterprise Sector in Angola;* also cited UNDP, *Project Document ANG/03/011—Angola Enterprise Programme—Support to the Development of the Micro Enterprise Sector in Angola, Luanda* (Luanda: UNDP, 2003).

8. UNDP, *Project Document ANG/03/011.*

9. See http://www.doingbusiness.org/

CHAPTER 11

Producing Generic Medicines in Afghanistan
Opportunities and Challenges of a Multistakeholder Partnership

Brigitte Hélène Scherrer

INTRODUCTION

The German philosopher Immanuel Kant was probably one of the first to see the benefits of nations cooperating through commercial relationships, thereby avoiding armed conflicts and, in particular, wars between two or more nations.[1] People have spread throughout the Earth and have been forced to develop lawful relations with each other. States were formed for defense against violations, and people have been forced to abide by laws to keep the peace for the sake of others. Although differences of language and religion have kept states separate, competition nevertheless maintains an equilibrium and commerce has made peace far preferable to war.

Throughout the following centuries, the idea of achieving peace through commerce has been taken over, extended, and at least partly translated into reality by a multitude of persons, states, and/or organizations. In a speech inspired by Jean Monnet, the French foreign minister Robert Schuman proposed integrating the coal and steel industries of western Europe in May 1950. In April 1951 the six west European states (Belgium, France, Germany, Italy, Luxembourg, and the Netherlands) signed the Treaty of Paris establishing the European Coal and Steel Community (ECSC). That treaty was the start of a unique idea that gradually has evolved over the past fifty-five years and culminated in today's largest supranational

organization—the European Union (EU). The EU, grouping and representing twenty-five European states in an independent political entity
without borders and using a common currency, is probably the most striking example of the conviction that peace can indeed be achieved through
commerce. Or, to state it simply, the EU has kept its promise: there has
been more than half a century of peace among European states.

Through the changed pattern of national and/or potentially international conflicts shifting from interstate to intrastate conflicts, the international "peacekeeping" agenda equally has evolved and been adapted.
In 1999 then–United Nations Secretary-General Kofi Annan formulated
the United Nations Global Compact with the aim to bring companies together with UN agencies, labor, and civil society in order to support universal environmental and social principles. Through the power of
collective action, the Global Compact seeks to promote responsible corporate citizenship so that business can be part of the solution to the challenges of globalization. In this way, the private sector—in partnership
with other social actors—can help realize the UN's vision: a more sustainable and inclusive global economy.[2] A remarkable number and variety of
partnerships between large transnational companies (TNCs), NGOs,
and/or the public sector have emerged since the Global Compact was initiated, and today it is obvious that the concerned actors have recognized
the necessity, not to say the imperative, of cooperating with each other in
order to achieve effective and sustainable results in achieving peace in its
very broad sense.

This chapter focuses on a very practical case related to a concrete
peace-building effort in a post-conflict setting: a multistakeholder partnership aiming to establish a generic medicines factory in Kabul, Afghanistan. The project was initiated by the Business Humanitarian Forum
(BHF), a Swiss-based international nonprofit association, in early 2002.
The BHF's overall goal is to broker and facilitate linkages between large
businesses, potential investors, and local partners; to strengthen and expand the local micro, small, and medium enterprises (MSME); and to facilitate the development of new products and services that addresses the
needs of the poor in post-conflict and/or developing countries.[3]

In the first section of this chapter the importance of private sector development in post-conflict and/or developing countries will be high-

lighted. The second section will analyze the different crucial phases of the partnering process in theory, in order to be able to examine the partnering process in practice in the next section. The third section will focus exclusively on the generic medicines factory in Kabul. The final section will evaluate the outcomes, challenges, and opportunities of this multi-stakeholder partnership and draw lessons learned for future similar undertakings. For semantic clarification, the term *peace* is used in this chapter to mean "the absence of war and other hostilities," and the term *commerce* is defined as "the buying and selling of products and services between firms, usually in different states or countries."[4]

POST-CONFLICT RECONSTRUCTION: IMPORTANCE OF PRIVATE SECTOR DEVELOPMENT AND ENGAGEMENT

As Mr. Suleman Fatimie, former vice president of the Afghanistan Investment Support Agency (AISA), stated in October 2006, "The private sector is the engine of growth for Afghanistan! Private sector development is key in reducing poverty, improving the living standards of people, and eliminating poppy cultivation and production!"[5] Development of the local private sector also was defined as one of the four reconstruction priorities by the Afghan government in 2003. According to International Alert, "There can be no successful business in an unsuccessful society and there can be no successful society without successful business. Prosperity requires peace."[6] Poverty reduction through economic growth has become the overarching goal of international development.[7] The literature and international practice demonstrate that creating jobs and increasing locally produced products and services is the only long-term solution for creating a sustainable local economy, economic welfare, and, ultimately, peace. The importance of economic growth as a means for poverty eradication also was recognized and defined by the international community in the framework of the Millennium Development Goals (MDGs) in the year 2000. The security environment, however, directly affects businesses by impacting on their operations, investments, and, ultimately, their profits. Currently, the greatest challenge and obstacle to attracting investors in Afghanistan is the deteriorating security situation.[8]

The private sector can contribute to creation of a sustainable local economy in a variety of ways, including, and in particular, through its core function of stimulating economic growth, providing jobs, and generating wealth. The private sector increasingly is seen as the key to job creation, particularly in immediate post-conflict environments, where the need is greatest. By offering jobs and demanding that people participate in an economic activity, the domestic private sector does significantly contribute to a country's reconstruction efforts and to the strengthening of civil society. A strengthened civil society can resist illegitimate leaders and can withstand changes in the government. A weak civil society, with high unemployment, is at the mercy of illegal "employers" and prone to violent activities. A society in which people are gainfully employed is also better prepared for democracy building and sustainable peace. Most importantly, strengthening the local private sector and creating sustainable employment prevents the recurrence of the violence that caused so much suffering in the past.

The private sector has vast resources, energy, and creativity and can make a significant difference in meeting the most pressing humanitarian problems. Business already plays an important role in humanitarian work through its corporate philanthropy donations, direct support for specific humanitarian programs, and the funding of many business foundations. The challenge of attracting business support for humanitarian work is not so much a matter of convincing corporations to play a role but rather of encouraging greater involvement, providing guidance concerning the most constructive business support, demonstrating alignment with business objectives, and facilitating their support. The aim must be to make humanitarian support very simple for a company so that it can do something that is clearly worthwhile, aligned with the company's business objectives, limited in scope, and easy.[9]

Newly established firms or aspiring entrepreneurs in developing and/ or post-conflict countries often lack the skills and experience to organize, finance, manage, and market their products or services effectively. In many poor and developing countries, the business services that are provided by accounting, law, and consulting firms are limited and very expensive. Training in and advice concerning production and information technologies also can be difficult to find.[10] It is in this area that the private sector can become involved through capacity building and training and provision of needed technology.

THE CIVIL SOCIETY SECTOR'S LIMITED CAPACITY AND THE ROLE FOR BUSINESS IN POST-CONFLICT RECONSTRUCTION: THE BHF MODEL

The civil society sector, composed of international organizations, international nonprofit organizations, and other associations, has proved to be very effective in resolving humanitarian problems. The international community seeks to improve post-conflict situations by assisting the affected country in reestablishing conditions in which business and other aspects of economic life can function normally. There is also no doubt that the primary responsibility for the preservation and restoration of peace has to remain with the public sector.[11] Only the public sector can formulate conflict prevention policies and gain political legitimacy for their implementation. However, when it comes to the socioeconomic aspect of peace building, the business sector should play a role both in planning and in implementing preventive operations. The case for business to become involved in conflict prevention is supported not only by the manifest corporate stake in international stability. The growing criticism and pressure that corporations face today concerning their role and power in a globalized economy is a second imperative to their involvement. Therefore, creating partnerships that include the public, civil society, and business sectors and that seek to advance sustainable conditions of peace must be the long-term goal. Collective solutions can achieve a scale and impact that cannot be matched by the actions of one of the actors alone.

In Afghanistan the BHF has developed a program based on partnerships with companies to help rebuild local production facilities in basic sectors, including food, medicines, housing, and construction materials. Projects developed by the BHF identify urgent humanitarian needs in post-conflict situations, take advantage of corporate philanthropy and interest in corporate social responsibility, recruit local investors to establish local ownership, and make use of the credibility of UN agencies and the interest of local authorities to see early economic regeneration.

The BHF works in harmony with the UN Global Compact. The objectives of the program are to promote stability through creating employment opportunities and strengthening local productive capacity, which will help the country move away from dependency on aid and build a vibrant indigenous private sector. If a post-conflict society rebuilds privately owned factories and thereby starts to produce goods locally, it succeeds in taking an important step toward independence.[12] The BHF model draws particularly on the technical expertise and specialized resources of the business sector and brings them to bear where they are needed most. The BHF itself fulfills many specific roles: finding, selecting, and recruiting private sector contributors; putting together project proposals; negotiating partnering agreements and other necessary documentation; finding necessary funding; stimulating interest and providing a continuing catalyst for success; and managing the overall development of the project.[13]

The BHF pilot project for Afghanistan, likely to be the first one to actually reach the production stage, is for creation of a generic medicine production facility to help fill the country's desperate need for medicines of all kinds. This project resulted from an offer by the European Generic Medicines Association (EGA)—an alliance of more than five hundred European generic pharmaceutical companies—to donate their business expertise, production equipment, training, and initial raw materials to help an Afghan doctor and businessman build a small generic medicines factory in an industrial park on the outskirts of Kabul. The factory will produce essential antibiotics and analgesics and provide Afghan children currently dying of easily curable infectious diseases with the means to survive. This project and its partners will be explained in detail below.

There are several ways business can become involved in private sector development in post-conflict/developing countries. The following section briefly examines three of these: commercial, semicommercial, and noncommercial. This specific distinction has been established by Andreas Wenger and Daniel Moeckli in their study *Conflict Prevention: The Untapped Potential of the Business Sector,* their findings are presented below.

Commercial

The role of the commercial corporate peace builder is most easily associated with the profit-oriented nature of companies. Business opportunity is the major driving force for companies to become commercially involved in conflict prevention. Adopting this role, corporate actors offer their commercial services and products to local parties, or, especially, to international actors involved in prevention and/or post-conflict reconstruction. This kind of commercial partnership is already well established in the fields of humanitarian disaster relief and military peace support operations. There are innumerable contractual agreements with actors such as the UN, with business supplying equipment, relief products, and many other services. Such public-private partnerships (PPPs) typically revolve around logistics, engineering, and transport.

The impact of commercial corporate action on conflict prevention has obvious limits, however, and the potential for corporate action is relatively modest. Many requirements of private sector development cannot be achieved with commercial services. The role of the contractor is undeniably an important one, but it cannot generate the kind of balanced approach and vigor that is lacking today in conflict prevention.

Semicommercial

This semicommercial role requires business leaders to combine the profit motive of their business operations with the willingness to take on additional risk for the cause of conflict prevention. Thus, semicommercial measures link the commercial interests of business with a distinctive notion of corporate social responsibility (CSR). Doing well while doing good, in terms of economic peace building, means that companies foster efforts for private sector development through business activities that are not related to contractual work. Activities may include portfolio investment or trade, in particular buying goods processed responsibly by local factories in conflict-prone countries. But foreign direct investment undoubtedly achieves the most substantial and sustainable effect for peace building. As recognized by the U.S. Agency for International Development (USAID) and formalized through the Global Development Alliance (GDA) in 2001, foreign-backed industrial projects make up an essential part of any private sector development strategy in post-conflict and/or developing countries.

Semicommercial corporate peace building is an option worth considering for enterprises. Going into a country early—that is, immediately after a peace agreement has been established or even while troubles continue—can allow companies to establish an advantageous market position before their competitors arrive: the so-called first-mover advantage. Early investment often means greater short-term risks, but in the long run it might well bring high returns. Also, early investment sends an important signal to other investors. And, probably most important, the presence of transnational companies in conflict areas is an important catalyst for building or enhancing local business capacity. Spillovers usually occur through direct links between transnational companies and local suppliers or buyers. By providing economic opportunity regardless of people's ethnicity, religion, or color, foreign companies can also make an important contribution to attempts at overcoming hostile perceptions and cultural stereotypes within local communities.

Companies considering investment in a difficult and possibly hostile environment must, however, carefully assess the cause and nature of the conflict in order to fully apprehend potential risks and opportunities. Semicommercial corporate peace builders must carefully coordinate their actions with other actors already present on the ground. Partnerships between business and nonbusiness actors is, again, the key to success, from both a commercial and a peace-building point of view.

Noncommercial

Finally, enterprises can contribute to economic peace building by bringing a genuine business perspective to private sector development as noncommercial actors of conflict prevention. Companies that take this role offer their extensive economic experience and know-how to any actor seeking to create economic opportunities in a conflict-prone country. The business sector may advise other international peace builders on private sector development–related issues, work directly with local governments and NGOs, or support and empower local companies and entrepreneurs in a business-to-business approach. Enhancing the capacity of the local business sector is an area where international business action can be particularly useful. Such an approach allows companies to empower local entrepreneurs and develop indigenous private sector growth.

The case for corporate know-how transfer and assistance is particularly compelling in view of the limited capabilities and poor performance of current actors in economic peace building. Corporations as noncommercial peace builders significantly impact the advancement of peace and stability without taking high business risks. Therefore, noncommercial peace building might well become the most prominent role of corporate conflict prevention in the future.

THE PARTNERING PROCESS IN THEORY: GENERAL PRINCIPLES

Rationale for Cooperation

In 2000, with the establishment of the UN Global Compact, then–UN Secretary-General Kofi Annan emphasized the importance of partnerships among governments, the private sector, and civil society in order to achieve sustainable development. The rationale for cooperation is neither new—throughout the past twenty years, various kinds of partnerships between different actors on the international scene have emerged and proved to be a very effective tool in trying to deal with peace-building issues—nor unknown. Reasons for cooperation among different actors working on peace-building efforts are obvious: mutual interests and benefits, different perceptions and motivations of risk assessment, and profit-making and reconstruction efforts are only a few examples that call for cooperation among the private sector, international organizations, and civil society organizations. The most beneficial partnership is one in which each actor has different core competencies, technical knowledge, and experience in specific issues.

The Different Phases in the Partnering Process

It is not the aim of this chapter to show each partner's contribution, but it is important to review very briefly the basic steps in any partnering process:

1. Identify project opportunities and potential project partners
2. Agree on goals, objectives, expected outcomes, and core principles
3. Plan program activities and responsibilities of each partner
4. Mobilize cash and noncash contributions
5. Manage the partnership *and* the project
6. Implement the project on the ground, according to the preset objectives
7. Measure the effectiveness, impact, and outcomes of the project
8. Review the partnership; allow for partners to leave and new ones to join

9. Terminate the partnership if appropriate or build on a sustainable solution

While these nine phases of a partnering process might appear very basic and obvious, it is paramount to keep them in mind throughout the lifetime of a partnership. In difficult and rapidly changing environments such as in a post-conflict country like Afghanistan, it is normal for the nature of a partnership to change; therefore, it has to be reviewed constantly and adjusted accordingly. If one partner has accomplished its role, it should either leave and allow the partners to move ahead without it or allow the partners to look for a new, relevant partner for the new situation.

THE PARTNERING PROCESS IN PRACTICE:
AFGHAN GENERIC MEDICINES—
A MULTISTAKEHOLDER PARTNERSHIP

The Look Ahead in 2002: Enthusiasm and Dynamism

After the Afghan conflict ended in late 2001, the BHF gathered its informal contact group of humanitarian organizations to ask how it could help them in the task of post-conflict reconstruction in Afghanistan. The unanimous answer was that they would benefit from informal dialogue sessions with the business sectors that could contribute to the reconstruction effort. The reasoning, objectives, and considerations of business people are quite different from the logic followed by international civil servants, and the dialogue between the two groups can be very fruitful.

At one of the first of these meetings in February 2002, the BHF invited the World Health Organization (WHO) to give a presentation on the availability of medicines in Afghanistan. A WHO staff doctor who had just returned from Afghanistan gave a presentation that included pictures of the empty central warehouse in Kabul where medical supplies are stored for dispersal throughout the country. In view of the isolated communities scattered throughout much of Afghanistan, the central government maintains dispensaries in many rural areas and supplies medicines for use in local communities. The WHO presentation on this occasion was particularly striking; there were simply no stocks of medicines available for the medical dispensary system in Afghanistan. Years of inactivity and the general deterioration of the medical supply system under Taliban rule had left the system in virtual abandonment. The BHF set out to interest the pharmaceutical industry in this problem.

At the suggestion of several of the BHF's regular contacts, in March 2002 the organization invited to Geneva Rory O'Riordan, CEO of Clonmel Healthcare, an Irish generic medicines company, and chairman of the European Generic Medicines Association, which groups together all generic medicine production companies operating in Europe. The EGA is based in Brussels and had recently started a program entitled Access to Medicines, the objectives of which fit well with what the BHF had in mind. During informal brainstorming at the time of his visit to Geneva in 2002, O'Riordan indicated that many generic medicine companies had recently replaced their production machinery with computer-controlled machines and that the replaced machinery was still in good condition and in storage. The idea of using this machinery as the central donation to make possible the creation of an Afghan production facility was hatched.

The EGA later confirmed its offer to donate surplus manufacturing equipment for the Afghanistan project and added that it would train Afghan technicians in European generic medicine plants at no cost so that they could operate the equipment effectively. Surplus machinery is usually kept in storage, requiring the owner to pay ongoing warehousing costs; thus, using it as a charitable donation has advantages for the owner as well. The EGA agreed that it would also supply the ingredients for the most-needed medicines free of charge for the period of one year from the start of production. Later the EGA volunteered to supply some medicine stocks even before completion of the manufacturing plant in order to develop supply patterns.

At the end of 2002 the BHF asked the Afghan Ministry of Public Health to identify a number of Afghans who were medical professionals, had impeccable backgrounds, and would be interested in leading a project of this kind. After considerable research was undertaken with the help of the United Nations Development Programme (UNDP) Country Office in Afghanistan, in 2003 the BHF and UNDP identified Dr. Karim Baz as the central local investor and entrepreneur for this purpose. Dr. Baz is a respected figure with a medical practice of his own, and he has made a substantial personal investment in the project. In July 2003 the

"Infrastructure Rehabilitation Agreement for a Generic Medicines Production Plant in Kabul, Afghanistan" was signed by the BHF, Dr. Karim Baz, EGA, and UNDP in Geneva.

Project History: Overview, 2003–2006

During the summer of 2003 a problem arose concerning the issue of locating and purchasing land for the project. Land ownership is still a big problem in Afghanistan and can hinder many projects and investments even today. The problem was solved with the understanding and support of the mayor of Kabul, who met with the BHF in Geneva to receive a briefing on the project. The cornerstone of the building was then laid in June 2004 with the participation of the former Afghan minister of public health, Dr. Suheila Siddiq.

Another challenge that came up in 2004 was how to manage the delivery of the manufacturing equipment to Kabul. The equipment, donated by a U.S.-based member of the EGA, was located in a warehouse in New Jersey and needed to be transported by ship from the East Coast of the United States to a port from where it could be sent by air to Kabul. Storage in Kabul was not safe, so delivery could only be made when the factory building was complete and ready to receive the machinery.

At the beginning of 2004 the BHF approached its contacts at DHL, the express delivery company, and asked if they would undertake responsibility for the delivery. DHL responded positively, though the challenges in such an undertaking were considerable, especially in view of the size and weight of the donated equipment. DHL, having been actively engaged in various kinds of commercial and noncommercial humanitarian relief operations in the past, was certainly one of the most professional partners for this undertaking. Since the Afghan generic medicines project was not a typical commercial project, DHL agreed to enter into the partnership through its corporate social responsibility activities. During 2004 DHL was bought by the German company Deutsche Post (the German post office), and the company became Deutsche Post World Net (DPWN).

In summer 2004 the pharmaceutical company was officially registered at the Afghanistan Investment Support Agency (AISA) under the name of "Baz International Pharmaceutical Company" (BIPC). During late 2004 and early 2005, the partners in the project were able to obtain financing from the German government through the German Investment and Development Corporation (DEG) for the transport of the equipment from the United States to Kabul. The financial support was given in the form of a DEG grant and was formalized in a PPP agreement among all the partners in April 2005.

Also during 2005 the BHF procured insurance for political risk for the transport of the equipment and the start-up of the factory so that the equipment would be insured at the time of its arrival in Kabul in the summer of 2005. DPWN/DHL transported the machinery from the United States first by ship to a port near Dubai and then flew the equipment to Afghanistan on July 5, 2005, using two specially chartered cargo planes. During the remainder of 2005 the medicines factory was under construction in Kabul—built entirely by Afghan construction workers and engineers—and was completed in early 2006, with the exception of the electrical wiring system and a heating and ventilation (HVAC) system.

During 2005 the BHF encountered a fairly large hurdle that would prove to delay the project for nearly one year. This issue was related to the start-up of the production equipment and machinery. Given the fact that the American machines came from different machinery producers, and that they had been in storage prior to transport to Kabul, there was work that needed to be done to get these machines in good working condition, particularly to produce high-quality medicines. Afghanistan had witnessed a great "brain drain" over the nearly twenty-five years of war, and it was impossible to find any local Afghan engineers or mechanics who knew these machines and could fix them. Also, the BHF could not persuade any American or European engineers to travel to Kabul because they felt the risk of traveling to Afghanistan was too high. Eventually, the BHF found some engineers from a country in the region who knew how to fix these machines and who were not hesitant to travel to Afghanistan. Under the instruction of two EGA representatives who traveled to Kabul in 2005, these engineers repaired and installed the machines at the factory. Also, a first training session on "Good Manufacturing Practice" (GMP) and "Standing Operating Procedure" (SOP) was given to previously identified future employees at the factory site by an EGA representative in summer 2005. In the past Afghanistan has had one important pharmaceutical manufacturing company in Kabul, led by the former German pharmaceutical company Hoechst (which since 2004 has been part of the Sanofi-Aventis Group). There is, therefore, a knowledgeable workforce available in the pharmaceutical sector in Afghanistan, which has been recognized as a significant advantage for this challenging venture. During 2006 Dr. Karim Baz and the BHF held several interviews with potential production and quality control employees for the factory.

While the machines were being repaired and electrical issues were resolved through the purchase of two new generators for the factory, the BHF undertook several business advisory tasks. In October 2005 a BHF representative led a market study on the pharmaceutical market in Afghanistan. This included several interviews and visits to the WHO office in Kabul, with international and national NGOs in Afghanistan, and visits to the "Bazar" for medical products near Kabul and a couple of wholesalers that are mainly importing their products from Pakistan, China, and India. This study did considerably help the project partners to better understand the rather nontransparent pharmaceutical market in Afghanistan and also to raise awareness of the tremendous problem of counterfeit and bad-quality medicines being imported and sold in Afghanistan.

BHF representatives actively promoted this project among the generic medicines industry in Europe and the United States. The project was presented at the 9th International Generic Pharmaceutical Alliance (IGPA) Conference in Monaco in June 2006. In September 2006 the EGA presented its Annual Award for 2006 to the BHF in recognition of its "work to ensure access to medicines in Afghanistan." Ambassador John J. Maresca, BHF's president, accepted the award on behalf of the organization at the 12th Annual Conference of the EGA in Budapest.

As of the end of 2006, all the machines that have been repaired are running correctly. Two missing tablet compressing machines were sent from Ireland to Kabul and were installed at the factory in December 2006. When completed, the factory will employ ten to fifteen trained Afghan technicians plus another fifty Afghan workers and will produce 300 to 400 million direct compression tablets per year for the seriously undersupplied medicines market in and around Kabul. Initially, it will produce widely used basic medicines such as analgesics and antibiotics. The product range will later be expanded up to thirteen medicines identified as essential by WHO.[14]

The Look Behind in 2006–2007: Open Challenges

The next and final steps prior to the opening of the factory are the formal hiring and training of the staff to produce the medicines; training of BIPC management; handover of medicine recipes and procedures for production to BIPC from the EGA; and production of several test batches and trial testing in BIPC's in-house, state-of-the-art laboratory to ensure the quality of the products that will be sold in Afghanistan. Though a marketing strategy has been discussed and many market contacts have already been established, the BIPC management will need to organize several marketing and public relations events to communicate to wholesale buyers and to the public the opening of BIPC and the list of products it will produce. This will improve the chances of strong initial sales and help BIPC management to develop distribution channels. Related to the BIPC physical structure, the wiring of the factory needs to be completed as well as finalization of some of the plumbing and other low-cost building elements. BIPC management would also like to hire an engineering firm to install a HVAC-system in early 2007.

The target date for the official opening was spring 2007. Given that there has been wide local coverage of this project, with inquiries on the start date even from President Karzai, and given that there is still an urgent need for quality medical supplies in Afghanistan, the BHF, EGA, Dr. Baz, and the UNDP hoped to be able to finish all remaining work in early 2007 and meet this start-up goal. The successful start-up of this project will lead to an improved and brighter future for all of Afghanistan. Unfortunately, I left BHF in November 2006, and therefore I am not able to provide an update on the project. As far as I know, the factory is still not up and running.

Evaluation and Lessons Learned

When it comes to evaluating a multistakeholder partnership in such a challenging country as Afghanistan, probably the most striking lesson learned is to try to move away from a purely humanitarian approach of wanting to help the local population and toward adopting a real business approach. Working in a country like Afghanistan involves several inherent difficulties and uncertainties—such as political instability and lack of basic infrastructure (roads, electricity, water supply, etc.)—that can seriously delay any project on the ground.

It is, therefore, of paramount importance to identify and select potential partners according to the degree to which they can significantly add value to the partnership, be it financially, in kind, or through technical assistance. Their respective roles and deliverables have to be clearly identified and contractually agreed upon. The following section highlights six considerations that have been identified as being critical in this particular multistakeholder partnership.

Nature, Objective, and Goals of the Partnership

First, it is important to define the nature of the partnership and the overall goal that has to be achieved. Second, each partner's role has to be clearly defined from the beginning of the partnership. In fact, this is the most crucial and important prepartnering activity, and it should be evaluated very carefully. Each partner needs to clearly and realistically define its commitment—and, in particular, the limits of it. It does not help anyone if commitments are stretched too far on paper and then are not able to be implemented on the ground. These specific commitments, to be defined for every phase of the project, have to be evaluated and adjusted, if necessary, as the project moves along.

Regarding multistakeholder partnerships in particular, the partners have to define a project manager who takes the lead in day-to-day project activities, who is present on the ground, and who constantly maintains open and transparent communication among all the project partners throughout every project phase. The project manager also acts as the formal representative for the entire partnership. Project management is even more important in a noncommercial business engagement. CSR departments are often very small and do not have the necessary human resources to closely follow these kinds of projects. Also, multinational companies that engage in a multitude of CSR partnerships simply cannot afford to follow and/or oversee each partnership's activities in detail. Furthermore, there should be regular board meetings at which the partners can exchange views about progress, identify potential project-delaying factors or problems, and determine corrective actions.

Presence on the Ground

It is crucial for the designated project manager to have a strong and constant presence on the ground where the project is being implemented. This is even more important if the project is being implemented in a difficult environment like Afghanistan, where circumstances can change daily. The project manager needs to be in constant contact with the local partner; other international organizations, donors, and/or funders; and of course the government and its relevant ministries.

Of course, the presence needed on the ground does vary depending on the project. However, experience shows that a full-time and 100 percent presence/work time is required for the management of a multistakeholder partnership. In addition, regular communication between the headquarters and the responsible project manager on the ground is indispensable, and representatives from headquarters should regularly undertake working missions in order to maintain awareness of potential difficulties or project-delaying factors. There is often a gap in clear understanding and grasping of apparently small and irrelevant technical or human resources–related details between the headquarters and the project manager on the ground. A profound understanding and good management of these very important day-to-day decisions can only be done if someone is present on the ground. Additionally, a professional and constant presence on the ground obviously generates and fosters trust among the project partners involved.

Potential and Limits of CSR Activities

As previously mentioned, when defining the nature of the partnership, the potentials and—more importantly—the limits of CSR activities have to be clearly defined among the partners. CSR activities are often non-commercial activities and therefore might not be entirely measurable and quantifiable. However, a clear definition of the nature and scope of such an activity is the start of a promising and successful undertaking.

Time Horizon: Importance of Long-Term Commitments

Time is an issue that is often perceived in a different way by each partner involved. Again, the project manager who is present on the ground often has a more realistic and rather long-term vision of development and the outcomes of the project, while the private sector partners are usually more concerned with a rapid and effective outcome.

This mix of differences in time frames and perspectives can become an obstacle in the functioning of a partnership; however, the issue can be overcome by partnering with an experienced organization that has already been working in the country in question for a significant period of time. Every developing and/or post-conflict country has different speeds and dynamics that allow for a different implementation of development projects at a different pace. "Working in partnership takes time" is the unanimous comment made by all the project partners of the Afghan generic medicine project. Consequently, increased communication and transparency throughout the project phases are both crucially important factors that improve with time and through regular evaluation of lessons learned.

Financial/Budgetary Considerations

Another critical issue multistakeholder partnerships often face is the challenge of finding suitable and long-term funding for the project in question. It is not enough to assemble enthusiastic project partners with excellent ideas and technical know-how but without any funding available to implement these ideas. Therefore, it is very important to establish a professional business plan and a financial/cash-flow analysis for the entire duration of the project. Any financial shortfall will unnecessarily delay the project and might even damage the project and the project partners' reputations.

Hostile Context

Working in a post-conflict country certainly means different challenges than working in a peaceful and/or developing country. A profound and well-established feasibility study for the country in question needs to be done and understood by all the project partners before even agreeing on a project/partnership. The partners need to be made aware of potential difficulties and obstacles that might extend the time frame of a partnership.

Other country-specific considerations that have to be taken into account include the local component: project partners have to agree on whom they want to deal with in case there is no legitimate government in place yet. Dealing with corruption is also a major challenge in most post-conflict/developing countries, and the project partners have to agree upon a clear and transparent strategy on how to address this challenge. In addition, international security warnings should be taken very seriously. Any security arrangements need to be managed by the project managers' headquarters and the project manager on the ground, who is certainly the most qualified person to judge the appropriateness of a specific measure in question. Last but not least, in a war-torn country like Afghanistan, tremendous work needs to be done in trying to rebuild trust among the entire society in order not to increase social and/or ethnic discrepancies and distrust. Creating cross-sector dialogue and partnerships and open communication with local representatives of partner organizations are certainly worthwhile activities in this respect.

CONCLUSION

The multistakeholder partnership involved in established a generic medicines factory in Kabul is providing evidence that these kinds of partnerships can work effectively and that civil society organizations, such as the BHF, can become a bridge linking the Western business sector with international organizations and/or local entrepreneurs in post-conflict and/or developing countries. In addition, projects of this sort can aid in development of the local private sector and, more importantly, in creation of badly needed jobs and production of needed products and/or services.

Even more important, however, is that this project has demonstrated the multiple roles the private sector can play in trying to achieve and foster peace in post-conflict or developing countries. There are various ways for the private sector to become involved, and it is by no means limited to large investments and/or high-risk undertakings. On the contrary, under specific circumstances even short-term technical assistance can be highly beneficial for the project in question.

We must not forget, though, that building and working on partnerships does take time—and considerably more time in very difficult and unstable post-conflict environments. And we must also consider that we have a duty and responsibility to work on improving the state of the world and to achieve the MDGs to which the international community is committed. We are almost halfway to the deadline for achieving the MDGs, but we are far from being halfway to meeting the goals themselves. Therefore, it is time to seriously join forces and keep the goals very straight in mind so that we can proudly look back on what we—the international community as a whole—have achieved.

NOTES

This chapter reflects the views of the author alone and cannot be associated in any form with the Business Humanitarian Forum.

1. Immanuel Kant, *The Perpetual Peace* (1795), in *Perpetual Peace and Other Essays on Politics, History, and Morals,* ed. Ted Humphreys (Indianapolis: Hackett Publishing, 1983). See also Sanderson Beck, *Peace Plans of Rousseau, Bentham, and Kant* (available at http://san.beck.org/GPJ15-Rousseau,Kant.html).

2. See http://www.unglobalcompact.org.

3. The Business Humanitarian Forum was established in 1999 at a round-table discussion in Geneva attended by senior business and humanitarian leaders, including Sadako Ogata, Cornelio Sommaruga, John Whitehead, George Russell, Peter Bell, and Robert Zoellick. Former UN Secretary-General Kofi Annan encouraged the group to pursue the matter since "expanding markets and human security and well-being go hand in hand" (Kofi Annan, "Who We Are: Message to the Business-Humanitarian Forum," January 27, 1999, http://www. bhforum.org. For several years the organization has been calling attention to the need for greater business involvement in humanitarian work and the positive potential of partnerships between businesses and international organizations.

4. See http://www.investorwords.com.

5. Personal discussion between Mr. Suleman Fatimie and the author, October 2006, Kabul, Afghanistan.

6. International Alert, *Local Business and the Economic Dimensions of Peacebuilding* (London: International Alert, 2006).

7. M. Forstater, J. MacDonald, and P. Raynard, *Business and Poverty: Bridging the Gap* (London: Prince of Wales International Business Leaders' Forum, 2002).

8. Personal discusion with Suleman Fatimie.

9. John J. Maresca, "Post-Conflict Reconstruction: Developing Public-Private Partnerships," *UN Chronicle,* no. 3 (2003): 14, http://www.un.org/Pubs/chronicle/2003/issue3/0303p14.asp.

10. C. Lancaster, K. Nuamah, M. Lieber, and T. Johnson, *Foreign Aid and Private Sector Development* (Providence, RI: Watson Institute for International Studies, 2006), http://www.watsoninstitute.org/pub/ForeignAid.pdf.

11. Andreas Wenger and Daniel Moeckli, *Conflict Prevention: The Untapped Potential of the Business Sector* (Boulder, CO: Lynne Rienner, 2003).

12. Eleonore Kopera, "Business and Post-Conflict Reconstruction in Afghanistan," in *The Aid and Trade Review* (2004).

13. John J. Maresca, "Bringing Generic Medicine Production to Afghanistan: The Business Humanitarian Forum's Cooperative Project with the European Generic Medicines Association," *Journal of Generic Medicines* 2, no. 3 (April 2005): 256.

14. WHO, *Model List of Essential Medicines, 13th ed.* (April 2003), http://www.who.int/medicines/publications/essentialmedicines/en/.

CHAPTER 12

Grassroots Enterprise Development in Post-Conflict Southern Sudan and Darfur

Preliminary Observations

Samer Abdelnour, Babiker Badri, Oana Branzei, Susan McGrath, and David Wheeler

INTRODUCTION

In this chapter we describe the development of a research program aimed at discovering what assets and approaches may be mobilized to optimize the conditions for self-reliant grassroots enterprise development in post-conflict Southern Sudan and Darfur. We also present the results of preliminary fieldwork conducted in Sudan in 2006 and provide some thoughts on "next steps" for successful private sector development in Sudan in coming years, with a particular focus on women-led enterprises.

THE SUDANESE CONTEXT

Central to this study is the identification of effective models for private sector development approaches for self-reliant economic development in post-conflict Sudan. First, an understanding of the postwar development strategies of the Government of National Unity in Sudan (GNU) and the Government of South Sudan (GoSS) is critical to the study. We are especially interested in contrasting experiences in enterprise development in Southern Sudan (post-conflict) with those in Darfur (continued conflict).

On January 9, 2005, Africa's longest-running civil war ended with the signing of the Comprehensive Peace Agreement (CPA) between the Government of Sudan (GoS) and the Southern Sudan People's Liberation Army/Movement (SPLA/M). The CPA laid the foundation for the creation of the presidency of Sudan's GNU, officially established in Khartoum on July 9, 2005. The interim national constitution established the GoSS and provided for a six-year interim period after which the GoSS will hold a referendum in Southern Sudan exercising an option of secession and creation of a new and independent country.[1]

In 1983 the GoS attempted to reduce the administrative autonomy of the South, marking the start of the second Sudan civil war. The conflict continued until the signing of the CPA.[2] The conflict between the GoS and Southern Sudan rebels and among Southern rebels themselves, combined with famine and disease, killed over 2 million people, created an estimated 400,000 refugees in neighboring countries, and created the world's largest internally displaced person (IDP) population, estimated at over 4 million.[3] Meanwhile, Janjaweed and other militias have been at the center of a growing humanitarian emergency in Darfur, affecting millions of people, including an additional 1.8 million IDPs and more than 200,000 refugees in Chad.

The complex humanitarian emergency in Darfur, the fragile nature of the CPA, as well as the ongoing potential for conflict to emerge in eastern Sudan give cause for grave concern regarding the establishment of an early, sustained peace in Sudan. However, given the international community's support for the disarmament, demobilization, and reintegration (DDR) processes in Southern Sudan, and given mounting international pressure regarding the crisis in Darfur, there always remain possibilities for positive developments and transitions to peaceful coexistence in the country.

According to Weiss et al.,[4] postintervention obligations to rebuild wartorn societies fall under three main categories: peace building, security, and justice and reconciliation. Taken broadly, these themes remind us that DDR processes alone do not represent a panacea. Development is an important and often difficult task for nations emerging from war, as relief aid often overshadows efforts devoted to postwar development. Many international development agencies strictly adhere to nondevelopment relief activities during and immediately after active conflict. In the case of Sudan, where there exists multiple and varying degrees of ongoing conflict, post-conflict economic development is of critical concern.

There is growing evidence that as market economies become more widespread and as business and trade become central factors in economies around the world, the role of enterprise in the maintenance of peace and security is of increasing importance. Moreover, there are growing numbers of success stories outlining the innovative and effective ways in which micro, small, and large businesses have been able to contribute to crisis prevention and conflict resolution around the world and support sets of tools and resources—for example, the International Labour Office's (ILO) *Guidelines for Employment and Skills Training in Conflict-Affected Countries.* The ILO has catalogued specific experiences related to entrepreneurship development programs for refugee and IDP groups in Sudan, Somalia, and South Africa.[5] Before we examine the detailed case for enterprise in conflict and post-conflict zones with regard to Southern Sudan and Darfur, we will discuss the emerging discourse surrounding the role of the private sector in international development.

THE ROLE OF THE PRIVATE SECTOR IN INTERNATIONAL DEVELOPMENT

There is increasing general interest in exploring the role of the private sector in international development. The intellectual arguments for market-based approaches to development owe much to the work of Sen.[6] This has legitimized the activities of international agencies like the World Bank and the United Nations in this domain.[7] And a growing recognition of the failure of traditional development models has even permitted bilateral agencies, nongovernmental organizations, and foundations to articulate a private sector–based approach.[8]

In response to the increased role envisaged for the private sector by international organizations and policy makers, the management literature has begun to reflect a business-based approach to development, leveraging the capabilities of multinational corporations (MNCs) and their partners in developing countries. The argument is that MNCs and their partners may bring the poor into the global economy by providing goods and services to those at the bottom of the economic pyramid (BOP).[9] This approach, predicated on a combination of conventional strategic management theory and neo-Schumpeterian economics, seeks to provide a framework for selling consumer goods to the world's 4 billion people living on less than US$1,500 per annum. Profits are made in the normal way, albeit with creative approaches to partnerships and margins.

Although this articulation is not without its critics,[10] BOP proponents argue that multinational corporations and their larger domestic partners have a special role to play because they can mobilize resources (for example, in distribution and communications); leverage between international markets; more easily build partnerships and commercial infrastructure; and transfer products and services between developed and developing countries with relative ease.[11] Thus, today it is not uncommon for business leaders and international business organizations to argue for a special role for large domestic and international businesses in development, both in peaceful and less peaceful situations.[12]

However, there is a complementary method to the "top down" approach of the BOP theorists, one that seeks to draw attention to the potential for self-reliant entrepreneurship, which may or may not require the presence of large domestic or international firms.[13] In this "sustainable local enterprise" approach, it is argued that indigenous human, social, economic, and natural resources capital may be harnessed effectively for economic development with or without external intervention, although the regulatory, political, social, and security conditions for self-reliant enterprise may not always be present.

One of the situations in which sustainable local enterprise may not be expected to flourish is in war zones and post-conflict economies dominated by centralized power structures and an absence of goodwill (social capital). And yet, as noted above, international agencies like the ILO as well as international development and social entrepreneurship scholars suggest that micro enterprises may play a very important role in post-conflict rehabilitation and peace building by gradually reconstructing the social fabric of the affected communities.[14] It is precisely this phenomenon, and how it arises, that our research aims to address.

Private Sector Development in Zones of Conflict

The objective of our research in Sudan is to discover the processes by which grassroots micro and small enterprises—in particular enterprises pursued by women—may contribute to poverty alleviation and improved security in post-conflict Southern Sudan and Darfur. Understandably, given some of the human rights and environmental abuses that have been associated with the role of international business in developing countries,[15] international development researchers have devoted substantial attention to the economic incentives that prompt the initiation and perpetuation of conflict and violence.[16] From an economic perspective, the risk of conflict often is heightened by greed rather than grievances[17]: "civil wars are less likely the higher is their opportunity cost, the fewer the lootable resources, and the more substantial are the obstacles to collective action. The variable which is insignificant is the demand for justice."[18] Korf notes that the "war (or shadow) economies of combatants and the survival economies of civilians are intertwined . . . greed produces grievances, which in turn stabilize the war economy and offer economic opportunities for greedy entrepreneurs of violence."[19] But rebellion-as-business can be stalled.[20]

Limiting access to lootable resources, such as diamonds, helps in the short term.[21] A long-term solution requires a combination of local and legitimate economic development alternatives that raise the opportunity cost of conflict and facilitate collective action.[22] Entrepreneurial actions involving the community can help accomplish both goals.[23] However, our understanding of what types of entrepreneurship may effectively stabilize local communities and counterbalance rebellion-as-business, and how such entrepreneurship comes to emerge and succeed under such challenging conditions, remains limited to a small number of recent academic studies.[24] Taken together these studies suggest that micro enterprises may play an initial trigger role in stimulating positive cycles of change. Scaling up gradually involves family and then community members, signals lucrative economic opportunities, and involves actively mentoring new generations of entrepreneurs.

International development research also shows that a lack of economic opportunity often exacerbates conflict.[25] And war often devastates entire generations of legitimate entrepreneurs, replacing them with "entrepreneurs of insecurity" who exploit structural upheaval and political uncertainty for factional or personal enrichment.[26] Yet conflict also can promote an "entrepreneurship of coping," which has contributed to post-conflict rehabilitation in war-torn areas such as Rwanda and Uganda.[27] Studies conducted by Honig and Thakur[28] show that entrepreneurs subject to economic, social, or political upheavals are more successful at launching enterprises under extreme adversity, more resilient in the face of external shocks, and more likely to yield equitable economic opportunities for marginalized groups in their local communities. With a few exceptions,[29] however, most of the insights into this "entrepreneurship of coping" remain limited to contextually bound success stories or criticisms of existing development initiatives.[30]

Women entrepreneurs often emerge under conditions of hardship. Many would have never been allowed to work if their communities were not in turmoil, and the majority never even considered starting a venture until their spouses were displaced, killed, or maimed during conflicts.[31] Yet by creatively combining local social capital and pooling the few natural, financial, and human capital resources available, they quickly manage to compensate for their lack of education and prior experience.[32] The phenomenon is not restricted to the African continent. From Peru to the West Bank, Iraq, Afghanistan, and northeast Sri Lanka, repeated waves of structural upheaval have produced highly resilient female entrepreneurs.[33] They have replaced traditional businesses with adaptive small ventures that involve their communities, and their launch, survival, and success rates compare favorably to ventures in developed countries.

The handful of studies that document the emergence and growth of these female entrepreneurs note that "they are a different breed of women; women who have been subjected to war and who have come out stronger than most women entrepreneurs in society."[34] Studies emphasize the role of individual characteristics—especially motivations and goals and informal personal contacts.[35] But with the exception of a few studies that analyze a host of individual and contextual factors influencing business start-up and performance[36] under challenging circumstances, our understanding concerning the dynamic interplay between these women-led enterprises and their communities remains limited.[37]

METHODOLOGY

In this research program we are seeking to understand under what circumstances grassroots enterprises may help reverse the downward spiral of poverty and social unrest by creating positive cycles of equitable and sustainable economic opportunities for marginalized communities in post-conflict and existing conflict zones. Our chosen settings of Southern Sudan and Darfur allow for real-time observation and comparison of the emergence of entrepreneurship in the spectrum of war-torn and post-conflict zones in two specific geographic regions. We wish to discover which forms of entrepreneurial activity are most beneficial and sustainable for local communities in conflict and post-conflict zones. We are especially—but not exclusively—interested in exploring the enabling and balancing forces that facilitate the emergence of women-led enterprises. The reasoning for this focus is that women often emerge as entrepreneurs during periods of turmoil. Their businesses have immediate positive effects for their extended families and local communities and contribute to post-conflict stabilization, gender equalization, and empowerment—potentially creating a more stable basis for development than traditional, male-run ventures.[38]

This study is a collaborative effort between Ahfad University for Women (Sudan), York University and Dalhousie University (Canada), and a large number of other academic, governmental, and civil society partners. As noted previously, the main goal of the study is to investigate private sector, post-conflict economic development opportunities for particular communities within Southern Sudan and Darfur most marginalized by conflict. These communities include IDPs and families of ex-combatants from Southern Sudan, who will be demilitarized and reintegrated into society as part of official DDR processes in the South; and women IDPs in Darfur. Our research takes a qualitative approach and employs a combination of participative action research[39] and case study methods.[40] In the initial stages, in order to establish the scope of post-conflict enterprise development in Sudan, participative action research methods are being employed. In due course this will be followed by a grounded approach in order to elucidate models describing the emergence and development of enterprise in conflict and post-conflict zones. This will be done through the development of case studies systematically exploring the life cycle stages, enablers, and inhibitors of launch and success of enterprises across different levels and types of conflict and post-conflict communities. Particular attention will be paid to case studies of women-led enterprises.

Our research seeks to provide at least a partial response to the still-unanswered questions of how women and other groups emerge as successful entrepreneurs under conditions of turmoil and hardship and how the growth of their ventures yields positive benefits for their war-torn and post-conflict communities—in terms of improved livelihoods, stability, equity, and empowerment.[41] Our inquiry focuses especially on the potentially symbiotic relationship between women-led enterprises and the community for several reasons. First, social capital represents a central and necessary resource for business start-ups, both in terms of mobilizing human talent and for piecing together innovative networks that help channel the necessary human, financial, and ecological resources for economic development.[42] Second, women entrepreneurs' primary goal for starting and operating a business is often to provide for their immediate and extended family—their enterprises are driven by a social purpose. Women entrepreneurs are, simply put, a combination of "hungry" but largely altruistic entrepreneurs.[43] This paradoxical duality may increase their chances of survival by tightening feedback cycles, increasing their understanding of and adaptation to shifting external demands, and thus speeding up their own personal learning journeys as entrepreneurs.[44] It also may unleash a positive cycle by supporting the education and formation of future entrepreneurs in the household and the community. Third, the scaling up of micro enterprise is the outcome of successful collective action; venture success hinges on the buy-in by the community and at the same time gives back to the community.[45] Finally, nurturing a symbiotic relationship with the community gets to the heart of the disruptive relationships that perpetuate conflict.

In contemporary conflicts, "the community" represents the focal point of conflict. "It is at the community level where contending claims for people's hearts and minds' are fought and where most of the physical violence and suffering occurs. Today's battlefield is the city or the village . . . Conflict entrepreneurs have a sophisticated understanding of community level dynamics and institutions and exploit this knowledge to achieve their objectives."[46] In order for peace builders to construct viable community-level capabilities for peace, a detailed understanding of the communities in which they operate is essential.

PRELIMINARY FIELDWORK

In preparation for our broader study, we conducted fieldwork in Southern Sudan and Darfur between April and June 2006. In undertaking this initial scan we employed a participatory social assessment (PSA) methodology. Such an approach is qualitative in nature and falls within the realm of participative action research. This approach is consistent with the participatory rural approach (PRA), which, according to Chambers, is the local facilitation of investigation, analysis, presentation, and learning, ensuring that local people present and own the outcomes and also share in the learning process.[47] In this approach, facilitators are self-critical and continuously examine their behaviors and beliefs while accepting personal responsibility for errors and embracing them as an opportunity to improve learning. Information and ideas also must be shared among local people, between local people and facilitators, and among facilitators themselves.[48] Key to using the PSA approach is the legitimization of local indigenous knowledge by local representation in the community, ownership of research, and empowerment of local communities and agencies.

In our fieldwork there was extensive reliance on local Sudanese institutions in the planning and completion of the fieldwork. The Government of Sudan and Government of South Sudan provided security clearance and support in the collection of data in their respective constituencies; Ahfad University for Women provided logistical support and allowed the researchers to have the benefit of its strong and long-standing social and institutional connections; and many Sudanese academic organizations provided technical and logistical support as well as access to the local communities they serve.

Focus groups were conducted with IDP communities and interviews were conducted with government officials, NGOs, and individuals. Participatory techniques such as pile ranking and proportional piling were used during focus group sessions to encourage the communities to conduct their own analysis of the questions and then present them to the researchers, who acted as facilitators. Transparency was imperative to the fieldwork; thus, each individual interviewed was given an explanation of the research actors and purpose. As many of the focus group participants were illiterate, and verbal authorization is custom, the researchers verbally explained the research purpose and actors to tribal leaders and focus group participants in order to gain acceptance. Each group had the opportunity to ask clarification questions.

All fieldwork with IDP communities was conducted through local institutions with the assistance of local research teams, making this a truly Sudanese research initiative. Detailed training in techniques and approaches was provided to all interviewer-facilitators by Ahfad University. Reliance on local institutions and research teams provided a bridge for overcoming diverse language and cultural gaps found in Sudan and also created an important opportunity for the forming of linkages among local Sudanese institutions in an often institutionally fragmented situation. It is hoped that linkages formed between various collaborating Sudanese institutions will provide support and access for future research initiatives that will follow as a result of the fieldwork.

SELECTED COMMENTARY FROM PRELIMINARY FIELDWORK

Research preparation, including the development of focus group and interview questionnaires, occurred primarily during the months of March through April 2006. As noted above, the fieldwork was conducted between April and June 2006, with some follow-up field activities occurring in July 2006. Four locations and communities or organizations were visited: in Juba, South Sudan, focus groups were conducted in the Lobonok camp and interviews were conducted with the GoSS, NGOs, and the United Nations Development Programme (UNDP) workers; in Malakal, South Sudan, focus groups were convened in the Obel camp; in El Fashir, Darfur, the Abu Shoke and Dar es Salaam camps were visited and a focus group with blacksmiths was conducted; finally, in Nyala Darfur, a focus group was conducted in the Seref camp.

Lobonok IDP Camp, Juba, South Sudan

The IDPs at Lobonok are of Eastern Baria ethnicity and originate from the East and Central Equatoria regions. They were displaced in 1997 by fighting between GoS forces and the SPLA. Intrusions by the Ugandan Lord's Resistance Army (LRA), who at the time of the study still occupied lands close to their areas of origin as well as lands close to the present location of the IDPs, have also contributed to their displacement. During the conflict, the GoS encouraged the IDPs to remain in urban Juba in order to prevent their recruitment by SPLA forces. Post-CPA, the LRA remains the major obstacle for the return of the IDPs to their homeland.

Many of the IDPs told us of rape, murder, and murder by rape. Formerly pastoralists, the IDPs survived initially by collecting and selling grasses and firewood. This quickly became unsafe due to attacks on the

IDPs, especially women, as they travelled further away from the camp as resources became scarce. Now, all members of the family, from young children to the elderly, sit on the ground all day, breaking large rocks into smaller ones. For our research team, the sight of an entire community doing such strenuous work was redolent of hard labor in a prison camp. No tools or gloves are used and many injuries result. The rocks are collected in large bags, each selling for less than US$1 per day. Thus, a person in the camp might earn around US$1 per day after a full day of breaking the rocks. Ironically, their labor serves the international development community, as middlemen who buy the rocks sell them to builders constructing buildings for international nongovernmental and multilateral agencies. The same group of IDPs told the researchers that the location of the camp was being considered for another tent compound, and thus they would be relocated again. Their second displacement would also serve the interests of development agencies, who would house their staff in the new tent compound. Once relocated, each family will again have to construct their *tukuls*.

For the IDPs of Lobonok camp, the primary prewar livelihood was farming, with a minority participating in hunting and gathering activities during the off-season. Their activities were primarily subsistence in nature, with surplus taken to markets for sale. This is not surprising as the Baria are traditionally a pastoral tribe. Immediately after being displaced, postwar livelihoods included collecting firewood, charcoal, dry grass, and other building materials as well as crushing stones and providing cheap labor to the local marketplace. Due to resource depletion and the activities of the LRA in the region, grass and firewood collection has since become a high-risk option; thus, the current livelihood strategy of the IDPs has been reduced primarily to crushing stones, which are sold to the local construction industry. Although men were previously involved in wood collection, there has been a shift in roles in the community due to violence by the LRA. One elderly female focus group participant argued that "women are subjected to physical violence and rape by the LRA, yet it is better than having the men killed."

When asked which livelihoods they would like to adopt, many of the IDPs stated that they would like to return to farming and agriculture, yet with improved skills and technology that would allow them to become more productive so that they could increase the available surplus for sale in the market. Some, especially youth, were interested in business and trade activities. Honey making was also a popular desired livelihood, as well as tailoring. Some IDPs stated that if they had to continue crushing stones, the use of basic tools or machinery might assist with their work, for example, hammers and stone crushers.

Although not mentioned in the context of prewar or postwar livelihoods, some IDPs stated that there are women in the camp who brew a traditional beer called *marissa*. The brew, usually made from sorghum and high in vitamin B and protein, has a long history within the communities of Southern Sudan and the Nuba Mountains. The researchers are not aware of how the conflict has affected the production of the brew. At Akot, outside of Rumbek, the researchers discovered that one of the IDPs participating in a focus group produced and sold her beer to the local community and was able to provide a slightly higher standard of living for herself. Remittances played a role in the IDPs sustenance when they first arrived at Juba. Relatives in the area provided food, small amounts of money, and clothing, until IDPs were able to begin collecting charcoal and cutting firewood and grass. The IDPs stated that they do still possess assets in their places of origin.

The main concern of the Lobonok IDPs is the issue of security if they return to their villages. They are very afraid of the LRA. Access to food and water, health care, and education are also major concerns. One IDP stated that without food, all people do is think about their losses and their children are constantly crying from hunger. The youth expressed that education is a major concern for them. They are tired of heavy labor associated with gathering and breaking rocks and are aware that their abilities are being wasted. Children are going without education and social services.

The IDPs at Lobonok believe that the GoSS should begin helping them immediately, prior to their return to their homes. During the focus group, it was mentioned that UNICEF had trained thirty IDPs—twenty men and ten women—to maintain water pumps. A few of the focus group participants stated that they would have preferred training in digging and constructing pumps as well as maintenance. Some of the women participating stated that they were able to produce the traditional beer *marissa*. The focus group indicated that carpentry and building skills are lacking in the community. Indeed, the IDPs stated repeatedly that they do not have any skills. The researchers felt very strongly that their displacement and complete removal from traditional livelihoods has led to a severe lack of confidence in their real abilities.

The IDPs at Lobonok have a general understanding of the terminology of entrepreneurship, and they support enterprise development as a tool to improve livelihoods. They believe that enterprise can lead to gradual improvements in income, which in turn would be spent on food, health care, the building of schools to improve education for their children, and clothing. These improvements would help them to feel human again.

At one point a local NGO, the Nile Community Development Organization (NICODO), provided five men and five women from the camp with small loans and business training. They were able to open a small *kushuk* in the market, selling biscuits, dry goods, etc. Unfortunately, the market was bombed, and the IDP merchants were not able to repay their loans. Although the program appeared to assist with income generation for the participants, NICODO did not continue their activities at Lobonok after the IDPs defaulted on their loans. The women in the focus group stated that they would use loans to sell goods at the market or start a bakery to make and sell bread if there was enough demand to sustain a business.

Relief aid is received from the GoSS in the form of sorghum and nonfood items such as utensils. The IDPs feel very strongly that until they have returned to their place of origin, they will require assistance to sustain their lives. Once they return, however, they will be wholly self-sufficient. If there is a cessation in the support they receive, they would starve unless they were able to find employment in the market or with the GoSS.

Obel IDP Camp, Malakal, South Sudan

Obel camp is an interesting case for many reasons: it is a long-term encampment where residents have been practicing a variety of livelihood strategies; there are a number of different tribal communities living together in one area; IDPs have access to diverse resources, such as land and the Sobat river; and there is clear tension between the traditional or tribal authority of the camp and youth (possibly ex-combatants) in the camp. Obel camp is located approximately one hour by bus from the town of Malakal, in the Upper Nile Province, along the lower Sobat River. The camp is divided into four sections: Obel 1, 2, 3, and 4. It is a mixed IDP camp, with people from Baria, Farqack, and other locations of the South. The IDPs have lived in Obel for approximately twenty-one years, since 1985. Tribes living in the camp include Shuluck, Nuer, Aljwack, Marle, and Dinkas. The Nuer and Shuluck are, however, the dominant tribes.

After having met the tribal authority at Obel and commencing supervision of the research in teams across the camps, the researchers were confronted by a number of youths. The group clearly considered themselves security for the camp. The fact that the researchers had received authorization from the tribal leaders of the camp did not seem to interest them. They were well-dressed, requested funds, spoke excellent English, appeared to be very well-organized, and had a clear system of authority or rank. These youth are likely ex-combatants who returned to Obel after the signing of the CPA. After much discussion, the group accepted the researchers and the research agenda and began to discuss the topic of livelihoods at the camp.

In this impromptu focus group the youth described the various livelihoods traditionally practiced by the tribes—Nuer were basically herders, with some farmers; Shuluck were the majority of the camp, and were primarily fishermen, then farmers, and finally herders. In the past, if there was stability in their places of origin, the community might have returned. However, the situation is not clear now, and this has caused conflict with the owners of the land on which the camp rests.

Pre-conflict livelihood strategies included herding (greater than half), fishing, farming, and the collection of grass and firewood. Due to the location and availability of land and the river, post-conflict livelihood strategies still include the same, but with the added option of the production of *marissa,* coffee and tea making, and other small-scale enterprise.

Major demands of the youth include electricity, roads, and a safe water supply. Improved infrastructure and tools or equipment (such as machinery or nets) would help increase productivity. Some people in Obel are ready for entrepreneurial activity, and some require training in investment, planning, and management. Brick making, using the abundant supply of cattle dung, was suggested as a potential enterprise activity addressing the construction needs of the community. Irrigation systems for farming were also discussed as important in improving productivity.

Remittances are transferred through the *hawala* system, and these are promoted by word of mouth. Still, the number of people in Obel receiving remittances is very few. Microfinance, banks, and revolving funds are topics that were discussed with great interest, although it appears that past loan schemes with fishermen were not successful because—it was reported—the fishermen defaulted on their loans. International NGOs do not provide training, services, or water to Obel. The World Food Programme (WFP) delivers food twice annually, but the dates are not fixed. Furthermore, the youths mentioned to the researchers that the WFP is moving from provision of food for IDPs to provision to those who are returning to their places of origin.

The researchers witnessed a variety of livelihoods being practiced, many of which appeared to be traditional in nature. Women collecting grass, fishermen in small boats in the Sobat River, livestock grazing in the field on the opposite bank of the river, to name a few. There is also a very active market at Obel, where a wide variety of products and services are sold.

Blacksmiths IDP Collective, El Fashir, Darfur

In El Fashir, the researchers met with a group of displaced blacksmiths who had formed a collective with the assistance of Practical Action Sudan (formerly known as the Intermediate Technology Development Group [ITDG]). In 1990 Practical Action began to work with blacksmiths in the Kokabia locality of El Fashir to help build capacity for their trade. This included the formation of a blacksmiths society. The blacksmiths faced numerous challenges. Furthermore, blacksmiths are a traditionally neglected group, associated with the lower castes of Darfur society.

Practical Action works to provide technical and managerial support, including official registration and recognition of the collective, shelter for blacksmiths that require it, and space for office work, storage, and training. Training covers areas of design, manufacturing, production, and quality control. Practical Action also assists with the negotiation of large contracts and has helped facilitate a revolving fund consisting of credit in the form of steel. Almost all of the raw material used is scrap metal shipped from Khartoum—old oil drums, automotive parts, and anything else that can be salvaged. Inputs primarily consisting of scrap and tools are primitive; thus, products tend to be basic and unrefined.

As a collective, the blacksmiths produce mainly agricultural tools and have been producing more than 90,000 tools annually for various agriculture-related NGOs. According to Practical Action senior staff in

El Fashir, these collective contracts are worth upwards of 500 million Sudanese pounds annually. Individually, the blacksmiths operate as independent entrepreneurs and produce a wide variety of goods. Examples include desks made from old oil drums, traditional handicrafts and tools such as daggers, and innovative traps to catch coyotes. A similar collective was started by Practical Action in Kanang, and currently the two societies contain over 160 members. In 2003, when conflict erupted in Korma and Taweeleh, blacksmiths in this area scattered. Most came to El Fashir and were sheltered by their counterparts. The blacksmiths collective has also been replicated in other cities, including Dar es Salaam and Kutum. The researchers spoke with a number of blacksmiths and heard their stories of struggle and success. One blacksmith interviewed has been able to purchase a small property and provide stability to his family. Others also have found success, although to varying degrees. Some members are struggling financially but find security and opportunity in the collective.

Although not a women-run enterprise, the case of the blacksmiths collective is of interest for a number of reasons: it highlights a unique and successful cooperation between an NGO and individual entrepreneurs; it incorporates a mechanism of credit available to its members; the blacksmiths are a marginalized group—due both to their displacement and the discrimination associated with their caste/trade; and the social capital intensive, collective model appears to be resilient. The blacksmiths expressed a long-term goal of constructing a communal manufacturing facility complete with electricity, smelting capability, heavy machinery, and storage. This would serve the purpose of improved variety and quality of production and training. Members of the collective mentioned that they are beginning to save for such an investment. On the demand side, the collective hopes to improve their marketing. Approximately 50 percent of their current production is sold to Kasala, Kutum, Karang, Dar es Salaam, Ocar, Lagaua, and Kordofan. The collective hopes that marketing efforts could create access to Khartoum and regional and, perhaps, international markets.

El Seref Camp, Nyala, Darfur

El Seref camp has been in operation since October 2004 and is located on the southern outskirts of Nyala. It is home to IDPs from North, East, and

South Darfur. According to the tribal leaders representing the IDPs at El Seref camp, the following international NGOs are present and operating: CARE, International Medical Corps (IMC), Humedica (Germany), and World Vision. Relief aid is only addressing about 50 percent of the IDPs' needs, and water scarcity is a huge problem in the camp. However, the researchers observed small plots of land next to some tents in the IDP camp, as well as some larger plots at the edges of the camp. This is a testament to the survival instinct of the Darfur tribes, who, even in times of stability, live on inhospitable land. Due to the political tension among IDPs in Darfur, the issue of return was not discussed during the focus groups at the request of the Government of Sudan humanitarian staff.

The livelihoods practiced by the IDPs at El Seref camp prior to the conflict were mainly farming, trade, animal husbandry, and herding, and to a lesser degree tailoring, building, handicraft production, and mechanic work. After displacement, approximately 70 percent of the IDPs are unemployed. The 30 percent that are employed work mainly as laborers but also in handicrafts, food, coffee, or tea preparation, baking, collecting firewood, building, tailoring and needlework, trade, random and irregular labor, butchering, clothes washing, farming, and mechanic work. Women are engaged mainly in food, coffee, or tea preparation, collecting firewood, and as clothes washers in El Fashir.

The IDPs at El Seref wish to adopt livelihoods in trade and farming and to a lesser degree in animal husbandry and livestock, construction, handicraft production, and tailoring. Obstacles to achieving their desired livelihoods include no access to credit or cash, robbery/theft of assets, and lack of transportation. Participants in the focus group stated that they are not aware of any remittances being received by the residents of El Seref camp. The main concerns of the IDPs are scarcity of food and water, inadequate relief and limited access to relief cards, lack of firewood, theft of donkeys and goods, and robbery between residents of Nyala and IDPs.

The IDPs at El Seref have experience primarily in trade and animal husbandry. In order to fully utilize their existing skills, they require money, goods, scales for trade, carts for donkeys, and vehicles to transport goods. Alternative fields that could generate income include brick making, porters (carrying things from place to place) and general labor. The IDPs at this camp view enterprise as a good way to improve livelihoods. Enterprises do exist in the camps according to the focus group participants. Entrepreneurs often work alone or in groups. Some are involved in trading of goods from Nyala or handicraft production. When asked what capacity is needed for starting and sustaining a small enterprise, a group of women IDPs overwhelmingly exclaimed that credit was the main enabler required.

Food is received solely through relief aid. Food relief consists of wheat, sorghum, oil, *bisselah* (beans), lentils, and salt. Sugar is not received. The IDPs feel that they will be able to become independent of aid once the conflict has subsided (implying return to their lands). Although the IDPs stated that food is currently received from aid only, it was evident that some IDPs are attempting to sow land in and around the camp and that food was also sold in the adjacent market, which serves camp residents.

OBSERVATIONS

The above data are partial and preliminary. Therefore, it is difficult to draw universal conclusions from our fieldwork at this time. However, some preliminary observations can be made from our research to date in both Southern Sudan and Darfur. In Southern Sudan there exists a wealth of natural resources that can enable enterprise and self-reliance when access to resources is not prevented by social, political, or security reasons. Currently, access to markets is limiting the development and growth of enterprise at Obel. And even though Lobonok IDP camp is in close proximity to Juba markets, IDPs are not able to access local resources any longer. It appears that both camps face challenges due to their location in relation to urban areas, which may be a determining factor in access to (or interference with) resources and markets. It appears that in South Sudan long-term displacement has increased dependence on aid and in some locations has excluded an entire generation from self-reliance. Nevertheless, the requisite resources for enterprise exist and indeed should increase as the Comprehensive Peace Agreement allows for new opportunities for commercial activity in a developing postwar economy.

At the time of writing, the conflict in Darfur had not subsided. Logistically, it is more challenging to travel and conduct fieldwork in Darfur today than when this research was undertaken. However, even here the researchers found strong potential for enterprise development. The case of the blacksmiths IDP collective showed that there are resilient enterprise models that are succeeding and allowing members to access business enablers such as training and certain forms of credit. The residents of El Seref camp have been displaced relatively recently and are living in tents with no access to resources. Still, they are determined to become self-reliant and have a strong skill set and understanding of enterprise enablers. Even in the difficult political and environmental climate they faced, Darfur IDPs are participating in the large markets that have developed at the camps, and many are working in adjacent towns.

Perhaps the most challenging factor for sustainable enterprise development in Darfur and Southern Sudan will be the new mind sets that will be required on the part of those with power over resource allocation to allow the development and launch of enterprise-based activities in complex environments. Currently, many international organizations choose to overlook local actors—including IDPs—in the provision of relief aid and associated services. Unfortunately, an understandable focus on relief aid completely overlooks existing capabilities for self-reliance and may even work to undermine the self-confidence of those who are bypassed. Working with local actors to build in-country capacity may require extra effort, but it could provide access, legitimacy, and opportunity and build human and social capital, which may result in longer-term potential for economic self-reliance. Engagement of researchers, especially local academia, could ensure that opportunities for replication of successful enterprise are better understood and may advance knowledge dissemination on grassroots enterprise development and the opportunity for postwar reconstruction and peace building.

NEXT STEPS

Based on the preliminary fieldwork, we are now in a position to convene a broad range of stakeholders to explore opportunities for further identification of entrepreneurial activity that is surviving in conflict and postconflict zones in Sudan. This will then allow for the second phase of qualitative research, during which "what works" may be described and modeled using grounded methods. Thereafter the potential exists for larger-scale research programs based on knowledge sharing and replication of such models.

NOTES

The authors are deeply grateful to Foreign Affairs Canada and the International Development Research Centre for funding the research described in this chapter.

1. USAID, *Sudan—Complex Emergency,* Situation Report no. 11 (Washington, DC: USAID, 2006).

2. H. Ruiz, "The Sudan: Cradle of Displacement," in *The Forsaken People,* ed. F. Deng and R. Cohen (Washington, DC: Brookings Institution, 1998).

3. USAID, *Sudan—Complex Emergency.*

4. T. G. Weiss et al., "The Responsibility to Protect: Research, Bibliography, Background," in *Supplementary Volume to the Report of the International Commission on Intervention and State Sovereignty* (Ottawa: IDRC, 2001), 39–45.

5. International Labour Office, *Guidelines for Employment and Skills Training in Conflict-Affected Countries* (Geneva: ILO, 1998).

6. A. Sen, *Development as Freedom* (New York: Anchor Books, 1999).

7. Commission on the Private Sector and Development, *Unleashing Entrepreneurship: Making Business Work for the Poor,* Report to the Secretary-General of the United Nations (New York: United Nations, 2004), http://www.undp.org/cpsd/documents/report/english/fullreport.pdf; International Finance Corporation, *Paths Out of Poverty: The Role of Private Enterprise in Developing Countries* (Washington, DC: IFC, 2005).

8. CARE Canada, *Making Markets Work for the Poor: CARE Canada's Strategy for Helping the Poor through Enterprise* (Ottawa: CARE Canada, 2005), http://www.idrc.ca/uploads/user-S/11231718621CARE_-_Making_Markets_Work.pdf; K. Hoffman, *Aid Industry Reform and the Role of Enterprise* (London: Shell Foundation, 2005); SIDA, *Making Markets Work for the Poor: Challenges to SIDA's Support to Private Sector Development* (Stockholm: SIDA, 2003).

9. See C. K. Prahalad and A. Hammond, "Serving the Poor, Profitably," *Harvard Business Review* 80, no. 9 (September 2002): 48–57; C. K. Prahalad and S. L. Hart, "The Fortune at the Bottom of the Pyramid," *Strategy + Business* 26 (2002): 2–14; C. K. Prahalad, *The Fortune at the Bottom of the Pyramid: Eradicating Poverty Through Profits* (Upper Saddle River, NJ: Wharton School Publishing, 2005), and S. Hart, *Capitalism at the Crossroads: The Unlimited Business Opportunities in Solving the World's Most Difficult Problems* (Upper Saddle River, NJ: Wharton School Publishing, 2005).

10. A. G. Karnani, "The Fortune at the Bottom of the Pyramid: A Mirage," Ross School of Business Paper No. 1035 (2006), http://ssrn.com/abstract=914518.

11. Prahalad and Hart, "The Fortune at the Bottom."

12. J. Nelson, "The Business of Peace—The Private Sector as a Partner in Conflict Prevention and Resolution" (The Prince of Wales Business Leaders Forum, International Alert, Council on Economic Priorities, 2000); World Business Council for Sustainable Development, *Doing Business with the Poor: A Field Guide* (Geneva: WBCSD, 2004).

13. D. Wheeler, K. McKague, J. Thomson, R. Davies, J. Medalye, and M. Prada, "Creating Sustainable Local Enterprise Networks," *MIT Sloan Management Review* 47, no. 1 (2005): 33–40.

14. J. Goodhand and D. Hulme, "From Wars to Complex Political Emergencies: Understanding Conflict and Peace-Building in the New World Disorder," *Third World Quarterly* 20, no. 1 (1999): 13–26.

15. D. Wheeler, H. Fabig, and R. Boele, "Paradoxes and Dilemmas for Stakeholder Responsive Firms in the Extractive Sector: Lessons from the Case of Shell and the Ogoni," *Journal of Business Ethics* 39, no. 3 (2002): 297–318.

16. J. Herbst, "Economic Incentives, Natural Resources and Conflict in Africa," *Journal of African Economies* 9, no. 3 (2000): 270–94; M. I. Lichbach, *The Rebel's Dilemma* (Ann Arbor: University of Michigan Press, 1995); T. M. Shaw, "Regional Dimensions of Conflict and Peace-Building in Contemporary Africa," *Journal of International Development* 15, no. 4 (2003): 487–98.

17. P. Collier, "Doing Well Out of War," in *Greed and Grievance: Economic Agendas in Civil Wars,* ed. M. Berdal and D. M. Malone (Boulder, CO: Lynne Rienner, 2000).

18. P. Collier and A. Hoeffler, *Justice-Seeking and Loot-Seeking in Civil War* (Oxford: World Bank and CSAE, 1999), 15.

19. B. Korf, "Rethinking the Greed-Grievance Nexus: Property Rights and the Political Economy of War in Sri Lanka," *Journal of Peace Research* 42, no. 2 (2005): 202

20. P. Collier, A. Hoeffler, and M. Söderbom, "On the Duration of Civil War," *Journal of Peace Research,* 41 no. 3 (2004): 253–73.

21. D. Keen, "Incentives and Disincentives for Violence," in *Greed and Grievances: Economic Agendas in Civil Wars,* ed. M. Berdal and D. M. Malone (Boulder, CO: Lynne Rienner, 2000), 19–42.

22. Shaw, "Regional Dimensions"; I. de Soysa, "The Resource Curse: Are Civil Wars Driven by Rapacity or Paucity?" in *Greed and Grievance: Economic Agendas in Civil Wars,* ed. M. Berdal and D. M. Malone (Boulder CO: Lynne Rienner, 2000).

23. A. M. Peredo and J. J. Chrisman, "Toward a Theory of Community Based Enterprise," *Academy of Management Review* 31, no. 2 (2006): 309–28.

24. See A. Fadahunsi and P. Rosa, "Entrepreneurship and Illegality: Insights from the Nigeria Cross-Border Trade," *Journal of Business Venturing* 17 (2002): 397–429; B. Honig, "Human Capital and Structural Upheaval: A Study of Manufacturing Firms in the West Bank," *Journal of Business Venturing* 16 (2001): 575–94;

M. Nest, "Ambitions, Profits and Loss: Zimbabwean Economic Involvement in the Democratic Republic of the Congo," *African Affairs* 100, no. 400, (2001): 469–90. See also a set of accounts of isolated cases of success or failure: S. Ayudurai and M. S. Sohail, "Profile of Women Entrepreneurs in a War-Torn Area: Case Study of North Sri Lanka," *Journal of Developmental Entrepreneurship* 11, no. 1 (2006): 3–17; S. D. Barwa, "Impact of Start Your Business (SYB) Training on Women Entrepreneurs in Vietman," ILO Vietnam Working Paper Series no. 1 (Vietnam: ILO Office, 2003); P. D. Hookoomsing and V. Essoo, "Promoting Female Entrepreneurship in Mauritius: Strategies in Training and Development," SEED Working Paper no. 58, Series on Women Entrepreneurship Development and Gender Equality (Geneva: International Labour Office and ILO Antananarivo, 2003); N. A. Karim, "Jobs, Gender and Small Enterprises in Bangladesh: Factors Affecting Women in Small and Cottage Industries in Bangladesh," SEED Working Paper no. 14, Series on Women Entrepreneurship Development and Gender Equality (Geneva: International Labour Office, 2001); G. Finnegan and K. Danielsen, "Promoting the Development of Women Entrepreneurs—Means and Ends in Women's Entrepreneurship Development," in *First Inter-Cultural Micro-Enterprise Development Summit* (Colombo, Sri Lanka: ILO, 1997); and R. Richardson, R. Howarth, and G. Finnegan, "The Challenges of Growing Small Businesses: Insights from Women Entrepreneurs in Africa," SEED Working Paper no. 47, Series on Women Entrepreneurship Development and Gender Equality (Geneva: International Labour Office, 2004).

25. Goodhand and Hulme, "From Wars."

26. L. P. Dana and N. France, "Small Business in Mozambique after the War," *Journal of Small Business Management* 34, no. 4 (1996): 67–71; F. Reyntjens, "The Privatisation and Criminalisation of Public Space in the Geopolitics of the Great Lakes Region," *Journal of Modern African Studies* 43, no. 4 (2005): 587–98; Shaw, "Regional Dimensions"; and D. Zaitch, "The Ambiguity of Violence, Secrecy, and Trust among Colombian Drug Entrepreneurs," *Journal of Drug Issues* 35, no. 1 (2005): 201–27.

27. R. H. Green and I. I. Ahmed, "Rehabilitation, Sustainable Peace and Development: Towards Reconceptualization," *Third World Quarterly* 20, no. 1 (1999): 186–206.

28. Honig, "Human Capital"; and S. P. Thakur, "Size of Investment, Opportunity Choice and Human Resources in New Venture Growth: Some Typologies," *Journal of Business Venturing* 14 (1998): 283–309.

29. Honig, "Human Capital"; P. Jackson, "What Is the Enabling State? The Views of Textiles and Garments Entrepreneurs in Zimbabwe," *Journal of International Development* 16 (2004): 769–83; D. Olomi, "Entrepreneur Characteristics and Small Firm Performance: A Literature Review and Priority Research Issues in the African Context," in *African Entrepreneurship and Small Business Development,* ed. L. K. Rutashobya and D. R. Olomi (Dar es Salaam: DUP Ltd., 1999);

M. A. Roy and D. Wheeler, "A Survey of Micro-Enterprise in Urban West Africa: Drivers Shaping the Sector," *Development in Practice* 16, no. 5 (2006): 452–64; Peredo and Chrisman, "Toward a Theory."

30. For success stories see Barwa, "Impact of Start"; and Hookoomsing and Essoo, "Promoting Female Entrepreneurship." For critical studies see Nest, "Ambitions"; and D. Moore, "Levelling the Playing Fields and Embedding Illusions: 'Post-Conflict' Discourse and Neo-Liberal 'Development' in War-Torn Africa," *Review of African Political Economy* 27, no. 83 (2000): 11–28.

31. Ayudurai and Sohail, "Profile of Women"; Barwa, "Impact of Start"; Karim, "Jobs"; Richardson et al., "The Challenges."

32. See R. Ruzibuka, "Entrepreneurs' Social Network Influences on Performance," *IDM Small Business and Entrepreneurship Cluster Compendium of Case Studies* (2001); R. Ruzibuka, "Transformation of Micro-Finance Schemes from Subsistence Living to Small Scale Enterprises: An Analysis of Policies for Integration of Science and Technology into the Clients' Activities, The Case of Rwanda" (research report presented at the UNESCO Expert Group Meeting on Transformation of Micro-Finance Schemes from Subsistence Living to Small-Scale Enterprises, Mombasa, July 11–14, 2005).

33. A. M. Peredo, "Emerging Strategies Against Poverty: The Road Less Traveled," *Journal of Management Inquiry* 12, no. 2 (2003): 155–66; R. Looney, "The Business of Insurgency: The Expansion of Iraq's Shadow Economy," *National Interest*, no. 81 (Fall 2005): 67–72.

34. Ayudurai and Sohail, "Profiles of Women," 4.

35. D. Olomi and L. K. Rutashobya, *African Entrepreneurship and Small Business Development* (Dar es Salaam: DUP Ltd, 1999); A. Shabbir and S. di Gregorio, "An Examination of the Relationship Between Women's Personal Goals and Structural Factors Influencing their Decision to Start a Business: The Case of Pakistan," *Journal of Business Venturing* 11 (1996): 507–29; and Ruzibuka, "Entrepreneurs' Social Network."

36. Shabbir and Gregorio, "An Examination"; and Honig, "Human Capital."

37. Peredo and Chrisman, "Toward a Theory."

38. Ayudurai and Sohail, "Profiles of Women."

39. K. Lewin, "Action Research and Minority Problems," *Journal of Social Issues* 2 (1946): 34–46; G. I. Susman, "Action Research: A Sociotechnical Systems Perspective," in *Beyond Method: Strategies for Social Research,* ed. G. Morgan (Newbury Park, CA: Sage, 1983).

40. B. Glaser and A. Strauss, *The Discovery of Grounded Theory: Strategies for Qualitative Research* (Chicago: Aldine, 1967); J. Corbin and A. L. Strauss, "Grounded Theory Research: Procedures, Canons, and Evaluative Criteria," *Qualitative Sociology* 13, no. 19 (1990): 3–19; and K. M. Eisenhardt, "Building Theories from Case Study Research," *Academy of Management Review* 14, no. 4 (1989): 532–50.

41. Goodhand and Hulme, "From Wars."

42. Wheeler et al., "Creating Sustainable."

43. A. P. Fiske, *Structures of Social Life: The Four Elementary Forms of Human Relation* (New York: Free Press, 1991).

44. S. D. Sarasvathy, *Effectuation: Elements of Entrepreneurial Expertise* (Northampton, MA: Edward Elgar, 2008).

45. Peredo and Chrisman, "Toward a Theory."

46. Goodhand and Hulme, "From Wars," 18.

47. R. Chambers, "Rural: Rapid, Relaxed and Participatory," Discussion Paper no. 331 (Brighton: University of Sussex, Institute of Development Studies, 1992).

48. Ibid.

CHAPTER 13

Ford Motor Company, Human Rights, and Environmental Integrity

Gerald F. Cavanagh, S.J., Mary Ann Hazen, Brad Simmons, and David Berdish

INTRODUCTION

Ford Motor Company and its leaders are committed to providing long-term, sustainable prosperity for both their firm and society as a whole. People today and future generations need mobility, jobs, family income, and a natural environment that will support them.[1] Ford cooperates with many nongovernmental organizations to achieve greater prosperity and peace for both present and future generations.

Ford Motor Company employed 300,000 people worldwide and manufactured and sold 6.8 million vehicles in 200 countries in 2005. Ford is a globally recognized brand. Its reputation as a firm is vital to its success in selling vehicles. Therefore, in addition to financial goals, Ford has developed many social and environmental policies and programs aimed at sustaining future generations around the world; Ford also provides data on their progress. Ford Motor has documented these policies, programs, and results in the firm's corporate citizenship reports, which have been published annually since 1999. In their two most recent *Sustainability Reports,* Ford examined fewer issues but did so in greater detail than in earlier reports.[2] The issues were chosen because (1) they have a significant impact on the company, (2) they are of significant concern to stakeholders, and (3) Ford has a reasonable degree of control over them. Ford also provided a separate report in 2005 concerning its impact on climate change.[3] It was published after shareholders representing the NGOs Interfaith Center for Corporate Responsibility (ICCR) and the Coalition for Responsible Economies (CERES) filed a shareholder resolution with Ford in November 2004 asking for more information on Ford's greenhouse gas emissions.[4]

These recent reports provide substantial comparable data on Ford's efforts to address these issues. This presentation of policies, actions, and results, and the transparency with which they are presented, benefits both Ford and the firm's many stakeholders, who have asked for and deserve such information. Ford's programs on social and environmental issues are noteworthy since these activities are undertaken in spite of adverse business conditions that have increased costs, reduced profits, and generated some financial losses. These unfavorable business conditions stem in part from strong global competition, excess production capacity, uncertainty of oil availability and prices, and the large costs Ford bears for pensions and health care for its hundreds of thousands of workers and retirees.[5] In this chapter we will examine three specific social and environmental Ford programs and their results: (1) human rights and working conditions, (2) greenhouse gas emissions, and (3) material use and recycling.

HUMAN RIGHTS AND WORKING CONDITIONS AT FORD FACILITIES AND SUPPLIERS

In order to better understand stakeholder needs and perceptions, in the year 2000 Ford held a "summit" with representatives of a broad range of stakeholder groups, including NGOs. This gathering identified human rights as a key issue for multinational companies.[6] Ford managers were surprised by this result since they had not thought of human rights and working conditions as a major issue for either Ford or the auto industry. Apparel and toy manufacturers, along with mining and petroleum firms, are faced with violations of human rights, such as excessive work hours, child labor, physical punishment, and using local police to discipline workers. Nevertheless, Ford recognized that human rights and working conditions, especially for its suppliers, was an issue that required their attention. There is additional evidence that supporting human rights and good working conditions provide a foundation for a lessening of global violence.[7]

Ford managers identified potential human rights problems in the workplace, such as discrimination, forced labor, child labor, excessive working hours, unfair compensation, health and safety issues, and lack of freedom of association.[8] Moreover, these issues are receiving increased attention around the world, and Ford wanted to take the initiative. Therefore, in 2003 Ford developed its own Code of Basic Working Conditions and joined more than one thousand multinational firms that have adopted codes of conduct on working conditions.[9] The Ford Code prohibits harassment, discrimination, forced labor, and employment of children below the age of fifteen. The Code also pledges competitive compensation, a safe and healthy work environment, observing local law on working hours and overtime, and recognizing the right of employees to organize. Ford asked the NGO Business for Social Responsibility for help in developing the Code. The Code was also reviewed by leading human rights experts, including those from other NGOs, the Interfaith Center for Corporate Responsibility, Human Rights First, Amnesty International, Human Rights Watch, and the Prince of Wales International Business Leaders Forum. The Ford Code covers much of the same material as the United Nations Global Compact with Business, but Ford goes further when they commit specifically to worker health, safety, reasonable work hours, and fair compensation. However, Ford Motor Company has not signed the United Nations Global Compact with Business.

Ford is a member of the NGOs Coalition on Environmental Responsible Economies (CERES) and Global Reporting Initiative (GRI) and uses their criteria for reporting human rights issues, working conditions, and compliance with their own Code. Ford reports according to the GRI standards and provides its results on their reporting Website.[10] Using these standard reporting profiles enables us to compare Ford's year-to-year activities to the activities of other firms. Furthermore, Ford has integrated this social and environmental reporting into the annual assessment of individual facilities; the Ford Production System (FPS) helps to organize production in Ford facilities globally. FPS provides a rating for each facility, which includes productivity, environment, health and safety, community engagement, human rights, and working conditions. Each facility must prepare a report that follows the CERES Facility Reporting Initiative format. When Ford first did such an assessment in 2004, they found that they were complying with the Code in their wholly owned or majority owned facilities. This is not surprising since they have control over these facilities; however, Ford has less control further down the supply chain.[11]

Ford managers decided to extend their Code to their suppliers. However, applying the Code of Basic Working Conditions to suppliers is more difficult. Ford has more than 2,000 suppliers that are located at 7,500 sites, which, in turn, manufacture 130,000 different parts for Ford vehicles. Of the 60 countries in which these suppliers are located, 17 are in emerging market countries that often have substandard working conditions. Nevertheless, the Code was extended to all suppliers as part of purchasing contracts with suppliers in 2004.[12] Ford also has established a new high-level position to oversee human rights and workplace issues in supplier's contracts and plans outside monitoring and verification of suppliers' compliance with the Code.

China is an outsourcing destination for many manufacturers because it has low wages and a large workforce. China has comprehensive labor laws on the books. If these laws were evenly enforced, it would lessen human rights and workplace violations, but China does not adequately enforce these laws. For example, while the work week is legally restricted to sixty hours, this limit is often overlooked because factories are pressed to lower costs and fill orders with very little lead time. In addition, some young women coming from villages to work in cities are expected to bribe or provide sexual favors to the person that hires them.[13] The Ford code tries to bring stability and fairness to the work place.[14] Assessment of these efforts will be discussed later in this chapter. Let us now turn to Ford's actions with regard to one of the most important environmental problems facing the globe: greenhouse gases and global climate change.

GREENHOUSE GAS EMISSIONS FROM PRODUCTION FACILITIES AND VEHICLES

A second major issue that concerns Ford and its many stakeholders is the firm's contribution to greenhouse gas emissions and to global climate change. Carbon dioxide emissions are the principal contributor to the greenhouse effect (hence the term *greenhouse gas [GHG]* emissions). Carbon dioxide in the atmosphere reflects the earth's heat, resulting in gradually rising temperatures.[15]

Greenhouse gas emissions are continuing to increase, as is the temperature of the earth.[16] Glaciers the world over are melting at an increasing rate; recent studies show that much more ice is melting into the seas than models had predicted. "The apparent sensitivity of ice sheets to a warmer world could prove disastrous. The greenhouse gases that people are spewing into the atmosphere this century might guarantee enough warming to destroy the West Antarctic and Greenland ice sheets," which would drive up sea levels at rates not seen since the end of the last ice age.[17] Scientists note that this melting of the world's glaciers and the rising sea levels will likely inundate many low-lying cities and countries and also turn some presently arable land into desert.[18] Since 1994 Swiss Re, a large reinsurance firm, has recognized the new dangers from storms, hurricanes, and rising sea levels and has urged governments and firms to act to reduce greenhouse gas emissions. It is also increasing insurance rates in vulnerable areas.[19] The United States contributes more greenhouse gas per person than any other country; the United States contains about 5 percent of the world's population but generates about 25 percent of the world's greenhouse gases. About 12 percent of the greenhouse gas emissions worldwide stem from burning fossil fuels in cars and trucks.[20]

Global climate change, in the context of energy needs and development, was the subject of the 14th Session of the United Nations Commission on Sustainable Development (UNCSD 14) in May 2006. Present at this meeting were ministers and high-level officials from China, Egypt, the Netherlands, South Africa, the United States, and Qatar. In addition, business representatives from some of the largest energy-producing and -consuming firms were present, including Alcan, Enel (Italy's largest utility), Eskom, and Shell. The International Chamber of Commerce (ICC), the World Business Council for Sustainable Development (WBCSD), and the World Energy Council (WEC) were also represented. At this 2006 meeting of the UNCSD, Valli Moosa, chairman of Eskom (a major South African utility) and chair of the Business Action for Energy Initiative, said "There is no reason on earth today why anyone should live without access to correctly priced energy. But it requires a proper financial strategy. Governments should make a global concerted effort to put the necessary frameworks in place to meet important goals on access, availability and affordability of energy." WBCSD president Bjorn Stigson moderated the panel on energy and development and commented that it was sobering to realize that the gap between what is needed and what can be achieved today remains vast. WBCSD chair Travis Enger added that "uncertainty about the future framework is a barrier for business to invest in clean energy infrastructure."[21] Shortly after this meeting, at the annual EU-U.S. summit meeting in Vienna in June 2006, President George Bush and EU president Manuel Barroso promised in a joint statement to "act with resolve to reduce greenhouse gas emissions."[22]

As the above account shows, concern for clean energy is paramount in most of the nations of the world. Rapidly developing nations pose their own problems. However, if all the world's people lived like the average person in China or India lives now, there would be no global warming problem. The average American is responsible for twenty times as many carbon dioxide emissions as the average Indian. Making reference to this, Sunita Narain, director of the Center for Science and Environment in New Delhi, India, says that it is unacceptable and immoral that the United States does not take the lead on climate change. On the other hand, China and India have a total population of 2.4 billion people. Many of them would like to heat their homes and have automobiles, as do people in the United States, Europe, and Japan. The Kyoto Treaty did not include China and India, but both nations are aware of the climate problem and are trying to utilize technologies that could potentially reduce greenhouse gases. The outcome of their efforts is uncertain.[23]

Adding to the urgency, competition for petroleum and other natural resources is a potential source of future global conflict. China, India, and other developing countries are rapidly increasing their use of fossil fuels, which are finite. Many expect future wars to take place over diminishing supplies of petroleum.[24]

FORD MOTOR'S RESPONSE TO CARBON DIOXIDE EMISSIONS

Automobiles require much energy, and most models generate proportionate greenhouse gases. Ford Motor recognized as early as 2001 the threat of global climate change and its own responsibility in dealing with it.[25] Ford, along with other vehicle manufacturers, requires major capital investment and has long product development times. Thus, vehicle makers require more predictability and lead time with regard to new regulations than do most other industries. In addition, Ford points out that GHG emissions from vehicles are influenced by many factors. To illustrate this, they demonstrate that GHG emissions can be characterized by the following shorthand formula : GHG emissions = fuel + vehicle + driver. That is, greenhouse gas emissions are a result of (1) the type of fuel used, (2) fuel efficiency of the vehicle, and (3) the driver's choice of vehicle, fuel, and driving behavior.

While the fuel efficiency of a vehicle is determined by an automobile manufacturer, the other two elements are not under the control of Ford. Each of the contributing elements is heavily influenced by personal choices, which in turn are affected by government regulations and the resulting rewards and sanctions. Hence, a case can be made that national governments have the principal responsibility for overall fuel efficiency through such devices as taxes and mileage standards. Moreover, a primary responsibility of government is the long-term good of all its citizens, including future generations. When government fails in this, however, as is currently the case in the United States,[26] the problem becomes more difficult. In a democracy, parties and individuals are voted in and out of office and new laws and regulations are passed. So automobile manufacturers face the uncertain prospect of both changing government regulations and shifting consumer demand. Thus, planning future products is more difficult than it would be otherwise. Nevertheless, when government fails to act, a heavier responsibility falls on business and individual citizens.

The need for a reduction of GHG emissions coincides with a call for energy security. Analysts point out that the immense amount of petroleum that the United States imports from Iran, Saudi Arabia, Venezuela, and Russia puts the country in a position of funding autocratic regimes. In each of these cases, billions of U.S. petroleum dollars enable these countries to be more powerful enemies of democracy and freedom and also give autocratic leaders more resources to repress their own citizens. Thus, the massive U.S. imports of petroleum not only undermine U.S. security but also subvert democracy and freedom around the world.

In light of these business, national, and world priorities, Ford has committed itself to continuing to (1) reduce the GHG emissions and energy use in production operations; (2) develop the capability to build and sell lower-GHG-emission vehicles; and (3) cooperate with industry partners, oil companies, and government policy makers to establish more certain and stable policies and regulations for reducing mobile GHG emissions.

ENVIRONMENTAL GROUPS AND FORD

Ford Motor and CEO Bill Ford have been criticized publicly by several environmental groups for their gas-guzzling vehicles. The Sierra Club, Bluewater Network, Rainforest Action Network, U.S. Pirg, and Global Exchange have sponsored full-page advertisements in the *New York Times* and other leading newspapers proclaiming their accusations. The ads feature Chairman Bill Ford and his pledge to increase the overall fuel economy of Ford vehicles and the acknowledgment of Ford's *Global Climate Report* that "global warming is one of the greatest challenges facing the company." The above NGOs charge that "Ford's fleet continues to produce more global warming pollution on average than any other major automaker." Another charge is that Ford has joined with the other major automakers in a suit to prevent California from implementing a law requiring reductions in global warming pollution.[27]

Environmentalists acknowledge that General Motors, with its huge Hummer, along with DaimlerChrysler, Toyota, and Honda, with their new, bigger SUVs and pickup trucks, all deliver poor fuel economy as well. However, the environmental groups chose to target Ford because Bill Ford has been an outspoken advocate of the environment and had pledged to increase fuel economy of Ford's pickup and SUV by 25 percent by 2005. However, the U.S. enthusiasm for larger and heavier vehicles followed in the wake of Bill Ford's announcement. Moreover, these vehicles also generated larger profit margins for Ford. The SUV fashion has now faded because of the increased price of gasoline, and Ford now faces slower sales and increased cost pressure. In addition to their concern for the customer and the environment, Ford also has responsibilities to their other stakeholders, including employees, dealers, and shareholders.[28]

Ford responds to the criticism of their environmental record by demonstrating that they have developed technologies to increase fuel economy and lower emissions of their vehicles. Some of these vehicles, such as the hybrid and flexible fuel vehicles, are now on the road. Ford also has new power sources in test vehicles, such as the hydrogen-fueled internal combustion engine and the hydrogen fuel cell. In their special report on Ford's impact on climate change, the firm presents important summary data on their goals and accomplishments. However, they acknowledge, "we know that many of our stakeholders expect this report to spell out specific targets and milestones for improvements in the fleet fuel efficiency of our products. It will not do that. In our highly competitive industry, there continue to be too wide a range of possible futures for technologies, markets, and regulatory frameworks for our company to set unilateral targets on the in-use performance of our products."[29]

In June 2006 Ford again was criticized by environmentalists when the firm backed away from a September 2005 commitment to build capacity to manufacture 250,000 hybrid vehicles a year by 2010. After the heads of U.S. automakers met with President George Bush, Ford chair Bill Ford announced that fuel economy strategies should not focus on a single solution like hybrids but should also include a flexible array of options, including hybrids, clean diesels, biodiesels, advanced engine technologies, and E85 ethanol.[30] A month later Ford became the first automaker to begin production of a commercially practical hydrogen motor. The motor is a hydrogen-powered internal combustion engine that emits little but water vapor into the air. The engine is designed for shuttle buses, and it was delivered in Florida in late 2006. Ford places greenhouse gas emissions in the broader context of mobility. They define *mobility* as the free flow of information, people, and goods: "We are beginning to think about how our business might evolve if we conceived our Company as a provider of mobility solutions rather a manufacturer of cars and trucks."[31] In addition to the efforts noted above, Ford also is working to reduce environmental impact through material use and recycling.

MATERIAL USE AND RECYCLING

Ford has recycling programs for their products, processes, and facilities. For example, in Germany Ford recycles their products by offering incentives through their "Clean and Safe" program to encourage those who own older, usually high-emission, vehicles to retire or recycle them to obtain new Ford products. Air quality is improved, and more than 300,000 cars and trucks have been recycled into 290,000 tons of metal by certified dismantlers.[32] It is not difficult to recycle metal, which makes up about

75 percent of a vehicle, because a mature infrastructure for doing so is in place. However, the European Union passed legislation requiring that by 2015, 95 percent of a car must be recyclable; other countries, including Japan and Korea, are considering similar laws.[33] So Ford, along with other manufacturers, must find ways to recycle materials in addition to metal.

One effort by Ford includes the use of natural products or biomaterials in their products and facilities. Such materials can return to a natural state and act as nutrients to the earth.[34] This is not a new concept to Ford: Henry Ford experimented in the early 1940s with a soy-based material for a trunk lid. More recently, a Ford manager said, "we're looking to replace glass fiber with natural fiber such as hemp. We're looking at soy-based foam materials. In addition to enhancing recyclability, biomaterials also offer the environmentally friendly possibility of composting at the end-of-vehicle life."[35] Such biomaterials are being studied in Ford's concept car the Model U. For example, a polyester fabric, which can be recycled and reprocessed into fiber again and again without losing any performance qualities, is used on the seats, dash, steering wheel, headrests, door trim, and armrests of the Model U. The Model U's canvas roof and carpet mats consist of a fabric made from polylactide or PLA, a biopolymer that Cargill Dow derived from corn. This fabric is a potential "biological nutrient" made to safely return to the soil. Also as part of its Model U efforts, Ford is testing a lubricant made from sunflower seeds in conjunction with Shell Global Solutions.[36]

In addition to innovations in the materials used in its products, Ford is applying its "reduce, reuse, recycle" philosophy in its manufacturing processes and facilities. For example, in the development of the Model U, Ford is "addressing flexible manufacturing processes that reduce energy use and parts complexity."[37] In two high-profile venues, Ford has employed recycled and recyclable materials. The first, the Rouge Center in Dearborn, Michigan, built in the early twentieth century, is an intimate part of the history of Ford Motor Company—it is the site of the founder's dream of vertical integration and the home of the Model A. Today, it is the country's largest former industrial brownfield project that was revived using green technology; it includes the assembly plant with a 10.4 acre "living" roof planted with sedum and the restoration of natural habitats. The roof provides natural insulation in both winter and summer; the sedum absorbs the rain water so that less flows to the sewers. Sunlight is converted to energy, and shallow ditches (swales) collect rainwater and thus allow it to go into the ground rather than sewers.[38] Five miles away,

Ford Field, the home of the Detroit Lions, was built using recycled materials. Recycled glass is part of the terrazzo flooring and crumb rubber from recycled tires acts as a shock absorber underneath the playing surface.[39]

RATIONALE FOR FORD'S SOCIAL AND ENVIRONMENTAL PROGRAMS

Since 1999 Ford Motor has provided its stakeholders with an annual *Corporate Citizenship Report*. In the first issue Chairman Bill Ford described the aspirations of Ford Motor Company: "we see no conflict between business goals and social and environmental goals. I believe the distinction between a good company and a great company is this: A good company delivers excellent products and services; a great one delivers excellent products and services and strives to make the world a better place."[40]

Making the world a better place includes providing prosperity, stability, and peace to countries around the world.[41] Peace benefits all peoples and also provides an environment in which cars and trucks can more readily be made and purchased. Therefore, it is important to Ford to support peace between nations and among peoples. These ambitions were made more explicit in 2002 when the firm developed the Ford Business Principles. Two of the seven principles are especially relevant to the issues we discuss here: "Accountability: We will be honest and open and model our highest standards of corporate integrity," and "Environment: We will respect the natural environment and help preserve it for future generations." In the same report Bill Ford says that "The Principles embody our ambitions. Gaps do exist between these aspirations and current reality. But I am personally committed—as I know our Company is committed—to work to close these gaps and deliver the spirit of the Principles in our day-to-day work."[42]

ASSESSMENT OF FORD'S SOCIAL AND ENVIRONMENTAL PROGRAMS

Ford committed itself to human rights and better working conditions when they developed their own Code of Basic Working Conditions.[43] The firm audited all of its facilities with regard to human rights and working conditions and is now monitoring the working conditions in all of its suppliers. From 2003 through 2005, Ford commissioned pilot assessments of working conditions at ninety supplier facilities in China and Mexico. The evaluations were conducted by third parties. Each assessment drew upon reviews of employee documents—including timekeeping and wage records—a plant inspection, interviews with management, and confidential on-site interviews with randomly selected workers.

In seventy-six supplier facilities in China and fourteen in Mexico, Ford found cases of poor timekeeping systems that resulted in incorrect overtime wages, a need for more clearly defined policies on discrimination and harassment, and some safety and health problems. No instances of forced labor and only one instance of an underage worker (the legal working age in China is sixteen) were found. There were an average of 11.2 problem issues per site in China and 6 per site in Mexico. In each instance, Ford presented the problems to the supplier, and the supplier was given six months to correct the situation. Follow-up visits verified that 98 percent of the issues were corrected within that six-month period in China, and 55 percent were corrected in Mexico.[44] Assessment has had an impact on the working conditions at supplier facilities in China and Mexico. For example, "Facilities that did not have fire exits now have them. Workers at one facility no longer live in a dormitory above a warehouse full of hazardous chemicals. Workers are now provided the required wage and social insurance benefits, including paid time off and maternity leave. Facilities now have provided the proper personal protection and safety equipment for workers."[45] Ford also conducted training sessions for more than four hundred managers from supplier firms in China and Mexico. The training sessions focused on Ford's expectations derived from their Code of Basic Working Conditions. These training sessions were done in conjunction with the NGO Business for Social Responsibility. The ultimate sanction for supplier noncompliance was, of course, withdrawing the purchasing contract.

The combination of training sessions and assessments have clarified expectations and improved business relationships between Ford and its suppliers. However, some large suppliers have undergone assessments from several different automobile manufacturers; this is redundant and time-consuming.[46] Therefore, it would be more efficient if national governments assumed the enforcement of their own working conditions and human rights regulations and responsible third-party NGOs undertook the required supplemental assessments.[47] In the meantime, Ford plans to expand its training and assessment to its suppliers in fifteen additional countries over the next three years.

Concerning global climate change and greenhouse gas emissions, over the last five years Ford has improved the energy efficiency of its worldwide production facilities by more than 18 percent and the emissions of carbon dioxide by 15 percent, compensating for changes in production. For example, wind turbines produce all the electricity used at Ford's Dagenham diesel engine plant in England.[48] In spite of these successes, the operation of vehicles generate up to nine times more carbon dioxide emissions than their manufacture.

With regard to developing and selling vehicles that emit less GHG emissions, in Europe, Japan, and Canada public awareness and resulting government regulations have reduced carbon dioxide emissions. These governments have enacted a combination of high fuel taxes, vehicle labeling, and higher taxes on vehicles that produce more carbon dioxide. These regulations have brought a reduction of greenhouse gas emissions from vehicles. Since 1995 Ford has reduced the average GHG emissions of vehicles they sell in Europe by 11 to 37 percent.[49]

In the United States during the past decade Ford has sold 1.5 million flexible fuel vehicles (FFV) that can operate on up to 85 percent bioethanol. Most current U.S. biofuel technology uses corn. Hence, it does not save much energy when one considers the energy required for planting, fertilizing, harvesting, and producing the corn biofuel. Nevertheless, additional use of biofuels would (1) reduce GHG emissions, (2) reduce our balance of payments deficit, and (3) reduce our dependence on and, hence, support of oil-producing countries. Use of biofuels will be a short-term step while additional clean energy options are pursued.

Ford also has joined several emission trading groups. For example, Ford participates in the Chicago Climate Exchange (CXX). Begun in 2003, CXX includes 177 member firms, including Dupont, Motorola, IBM, Amtrak, and American Electric Power.[50] This trading scheme will be more effective when the United States imposes limits on carbon emissions. In addition, Ford is the only auto manufacturer participating in the United Kingdom emissions trading scheme.[51] Ford also sponsored eco-driving programs in Europe, Canada, and the United States to demonstrate how driving habits can save fuel and GHG emissions. Drivers can save up to 20–25 percent of their fuel, money, and GHG emissions by driving in a more careful and environmentally responsible way.

With regard to material use and recycling, Ford points to several successful initiatives. Total Waste Management is a Ford process whereby a single, professional waste management supplier for each of eighty Ford facilities worldwide is offered incentives for reducing waste. The St. Thomas Assembly Plant in Ontario, Canada, reduced its solid waste by 90 percent; the plant won the Recycling Council of Ontario's Gold Award for outstanding waste reduction, reuse, and recycling efforts. The plan included replacing disposable packaging with returnable containers, increasing metal scrap recovery, and placing recycling stations along the assembly line.[52] Landfill gases are used to provide energy to the Wayne Michigan Stamping and Assembly Plants and surplus electricity to Detroit Edison. A program to reclaim paint solvent in a closed-loop recycling effort that began in 1984 is now practiced in all nineteen North American Ford assembly plants. Solid paint and solvent waste are removed and used as fuel, and liquids are distilled, refined, and reused in the plants.[53] At the Dearborn assembly plant Ford converts hydrocarbons from paint fumes into electricity; this process will be modified and applied in two other North American plants.[54]

When reporting on social and environmental programs, Ford asked an outside committee to review their programs and disclosure. The committee praised Ford's "leadership and commitment to transparently communicate with its stakeholders." In the area of human rights, the committee noted that the Ford report is particularly strong on human rights and the application of Ford's Code of Basic Working Conditions, even with its suppliers. The committee urged Ford to undertake future reports to examine "the concerns of communities and workers and provid[e] greater detail on working conditions."[55] However, the social and environmental programs employed by Ford and all publicly held firms often are limited by pressures from shareholders for short-term financial performance.

INFLUENCE OF THE MULTINATIONAL CORPORATION AND THE NATION-STATE

The intentions, influence, and actions of Ford Motor can be compared with those of the United States and viewed as examples of the global influence of the multinational corporation (MNC) and the nation-state. The traditional goal of the nation-state is to pursue the common good, but that goal is generally defined with regard to its own citizens. The MNC's traditional goal is to serve the interests of its stakeholders and to generate a profit, but today's large MNC has stakeholders in scores of countries—in the case of Ford in two hundred countries. Hence, in order to serve its many stakeholders, the MNC has a principal interest in promoting stability, peace, and prosperity for peoples in those many nations. Recall that it was Henry Ford who famously provided the first 5-dollar-a-day jobs in the United States for Ford employees so that working people would be able to buy Ford products. Today most MNCs (with the exception of arms manufacturers) cannot effectively develop or sell products or services in a country that is not stable, peaceful, and to some extent prosperous. This goal of promoting stability, peace, and prosperity for peoples around the world prevails for Ford and most other large MNCs (see table 1).

On the other hand, the United States, as an example of the nation-state, has resorted to force on several occasions to pursue its interests. Force generally does not serve the interests of most communities, especially when people are injured, killed, or displaced and properties are destroyed. Hence, we note the paradox that the nation-state, which has the responsibility to pursue the common good, often views that good in narrow, national terms and acts accordingly. On the other hand, the interests of the large MNC are more closely tied to the peace and prosperity of the many nations in which it does business. This relationship encourages the MNC to actively work for stability, peace, and prosperity in those countries and globally.

While Ford's actions have generally supported stability and peace in other countries, other firms have overthrown elected presidents (ITT in Chile), profited from sweatshops (Nike), and abused local peoples to obtain natural resources (ExxonMobil, Freeport McMoRan). In many of these instances, the MNC's concern for stability was at the expense of the human rights of local peoples. While some of these self-centered actions occurred in the past, MNCs' record of promoting stability and peace is not as unblemished as one might wish.

UNITED NATIONS PRINCIPLES
FOR RESPONSIBLE INVESTMENT

Investors often pressure firms to cut corners on environmental, social, and other long-term issues. Customers want their goods at the lowest price,

Table 13.1 Peace Makers: Nation State vs. Multinational Corporation

	U.S (as Nation-State)	Ford Motor (as Multinational Firm)
Traditional Goal	Common good of U.S. citizens	Profits for Ford's shareholders
Responsibility	Promote and defend interests of U.S. and its citizens	Provide products and services that customers want and can depend upon
Stakeholders	Citizens of U.S. and others	Shareholders, customers, employees, suppliers, dealers, and communities in 200 countries
Accountable to	Voters of U.S. and other nations through treaties	Shareholders, customers, employees, suppliers, dealers, and communities in 200 countries
Multinational oversight	Not responsible to any non-U.S. party	Responsible to governments, agencies, states, and localities wherever operates
Means of protecting own global interests	Negotiation, treaties, and military force	Laws, courts of host nation, and World Trade Organization
Works for stability and peace	Yes, if in, and not opposed to, U.S. interests	Ford has sales and operations in 200 nations, so it is in its interest to promote stability and peace

and most investors want firms to generate more short-term profits. To provide support for responsible business policies and actions, the United Nations Environment Program Finance Initiative sponsors Principles for Responsible Investment. These Principles incorporate the environmental, social, and governance issues that have been discussed throughout this chapter. The UN has enlisted more than fifty institutional investors representing more than $4 trillion to observe the Principles in their investment activities.[56] The investment firms that sign the six Principles pledge to incorporate environmental, social, and corporate governance issues into investment analysis and decision-making processes. This new initiative has the potential to succeed in changing investment and corporate behavior because it seeks to influence stockholders, who often have the greatest influence of all the stakeholders in management decisions.

SUMMARY AND CONCLUSIONS

Ford has been certified by third parties that its own facilities meet the standards set out in its Code of Basic Working Conditions, and it is doing a similar audit of the facilities of its two thousand suppliers. Its audit of supplier facilities in China and Mexico resulted in considerable improvement of working conditions. Ford has reduced GHG emissions from its production facilities by 15 percent; the firm recognizes, however, that nine times as much GHG emissions comes from its vehicles. Ford has produced 1.5 million vehicles that can operate on 85 percent ethanol. In 2004 Ford introduced the Ford Escape hybrid SUV, which gets 50 percent better fuel economy. However, Chairman Bill Ford backed off his 2001 pledge to increase the firm's pickup and SUV fuel economy by 25 percent. And in June 2006 Ford backed away from a commitment made in fall 2005 to build capacity to make 250,000 hybrid vehicles by the end of the decade. Ford's rationale for this change was the need to focus on other alternative fuel vehicles. Ford Motor attempts to use materials that can either be recycled or will biodegrade. This is especially true in its European operations, where governments mandate recycling. Its $2 billion investment in an environmental state-of-the-art factory complex in Dearborn, Michigan, has received international attention.

Ford works with many NGOs regularly; in 2000 they invited leaders of various NGOs to a "summit" in order to gather key concerns of various stakeholders. Moreover, Ford uses GRI and CERES standards for annual measurement and reporting of social and environmental progress. Ford Motor Company chair Bill Ford's goals are clear: to provide quality vehicles that produce fewer greenhouse gas emissions and provide good wages and support humane working conditions for Ford's and its suppliers' employees around the world. Ford is working with various stakeholders to reach these goals.

NOTES

1. See Sandra Waddock, *Leading Corporate Citizens: Visions, Values, Value Added,* 2nd ed. (New York: McGraw-Hill, 2006).

2. *Our Route to Sustainability: Connecting with Society—Ford Sustainability Report 2004/5,* and *Our Route to Sustainability 2005/6.* Both reports are available at http://www.ford.com/go/sustainability.

3. *Ford Report on Business Impact of Climate Change, 2005,* http://www.ford.com/go/sustainability.

4. "Ford Publishes Climate Change Report," *Business and the Environment,* March 17, 2006, 6.

5. *Our Route to Sustainability 2004/5,* 5.

6. Philip Mirvis and Bradley Googins, "Stages of Corporate Citizenship," *California Management Review* 48 (Winter 2006): 104–26. Mirvis and Googins find that this meeting and its results place Ford Motor in their "innovative" category among corporations, which is category 3 of 5. Most other firms fall within the first two categories—elementary and engaged.

7. Timothy L. Fort and Cindy A. Schipani, *The Role of Business in Fostering Peaceful Societies* (Cambridge: Cambridge University Press, 2004), 143–82.

8. These are economic, social, and cultural rights, as distinguished from political rights. See John M. Kline, *Ethics for International Business* (London: Routledge, 2005), 27; Patricia H. Werhane and Tara J. Radin, *Employment and Employee Rights* (Malden, MA: Blackwell, 2004); Laura P. Hartman, Denis G. Arnold, and Richard E. Wokutch, *Rising Above Sweatshops: Innovative Approaches to Global Labor Challenges* (Westport, CT: Praeger, 2003); and Salad Meckled-Garcia and Basak Cali, *The Legalization of Human Rights: Multidisciplinary Perspectives on Human Rights and Human Rights Law* (London: Routledge, 2006), 9–31.

9. David Vogel, "Corporate Responsibility for Working Conditions in Developing Countries," in *The Market for Virtue: The Potential and Limits of Corporate*

Social Responsibility (Washington, DC: Brookings Institution Press, 2005), 75–109. See also Oliver F. Williams, C.S.C., ed., *Global Codes of Conduct: An Idea Whose Time Has Come* (Notre Dame, IN: University of Notre Dame Press, 2000).

10. See http://www.ford.com/aboutford/microsites/sustainability-report-2006-07/gri.htm.

11. However, Ford is in a stronger position than many manufacturers that outsource since it has more stable and better relations with its suppliers than do makers of shoes, clothing, toys, and other low-cost goods. See additional data in Vogel, *The Market for Virtue,* 82–87.

12. See the letter from Ford president James Padilla in *Our Route to Sustainability 2004/5,* 5.

13. Fort and Schipani, *The Role of Business,* 155.

14. Congressional-Executive Commission on China, *Codes of Conduct: U.S. Corporate Compliance Programs and Working Conditions in Chinese Factories* (Washington, DC: U.S. Government Printing Office, 2003). See current reports on China's working conditions and labor law by the Congressional-Executive Commission on China at http://www.cecc.gov/.

15. See Richard P. Turco, *Earth under Siege: From Air Pollution to Global Change* (New York: Oxford University Press, 2002), 365–405; also Ross Gelbspan, *Boiling Point: How Politicians, Big Oil and Coal, Journalists, and Activists Are Fueling the Climate Crisis* (New York: Basic Books, 2004).

16. The U.S. Congress asked the National Academy of Sciences to evaluate global warming: "There is sufficient evidence . . . that the last few decades of the 20th Century were warmer than any comparable period in the last 400 years" (National Research Council, *High Confidence that Planet Is Warmest in 400 Years,* June 22, 2006). In 2004, the latest year for which we have data, U.S. emissions of greenhouse gases grew 2 percent from the previous year and 16 percent from 1990. See Department of Energy, *Emissions of Greenhouse Gases in the United States 2004,* Report #DOE/EIA-0573 (Washington, DC: DOE, 2006).

17. Richard A. Kerr, "A Worrying Trend of Less Ice, Higher Seas," *Science,* March 24, 2006, 1698–1701.

18. Lester R. Brown, *Plan B 2.0: Rescuing a Planet Under Stress and a Civilization in Trouble* (New York: W.W. Norton, 2006), esp. chap. 2, "Beyond the Oil Peak" and chap. 4, "Rising Temperatures and Rising Seas."

19. Leaders Group of the World Business Council for Sustainable Development, *From Challenge to Opportunity: The Role of Business in Tomorrow's Society* (2006, http://www.wbcsd.org/plugins/DocSearch/details.asp?type=DocDet&ObjectId=MTgyMTM). Sponsors of and participants in this report include BP, Procter & Gamble, Swiss Re, Adidas, and Storebrand.

20. "Greenhouse Gas Emissions Increased in 2005: US Study," *Space and Earth Science,* May 2, 2006, 26. See also U.S. Environmental Protection Agency,

"U.S. Inventory of Greenhouse Gas Emissions and Sinks" (2007, http://www.epa.gov/globalwarming/publications/emissions).

21. World Business Council for Sustainable Development, "Business Debates the Energy Challenges with Ministers at UNCSD" (2006, http://www.wbcsd.org/plugins/DocSearch/details.asp?type=DocDet&ObjectId=MTkxNDc).

22. World Business Council for Sustainable Development, "US, EU Agree to High-Level Talks on Climate Change" (2006, http://www.wbcsd.org/plugins/DocSearch/details.asp?type=DocDet&ObjectId=MTk1MDM).

23. Bryan Walsh, "The Impact of Asia's Giants: How China and India Could Save the Planet—Or Destroy It," *Time*, April 3, 2006, 60–62.

24. Fort and Schipani, *The Role of Business*, 183–222.

25. Ford Motor Co., "Greenhouse Gases and Fuel Economy," *Connecting with Society: 1999 Corporate Citizenship Report*, 59–68; see also Ford Motor Co., *2001 Corporate Citizenship Report*, 6–9, 45–47, 50–51; *2002 Corporate Citizenship Report*, 16–19, 26–29, 36–39; *Ford Report on Business Impact of Climate Change, 2005*, 2. For a third-party assessment, see Vogel, *The Market for Virtue*, 121–23.

26. There is also a lack of international standards and control, some of which is due to the lack of cooperation by the United States. See Kline, *Ethics for International Business*, 27.

27. Ann Job, "Ford Can't Escape the Crosshairs of Green Groups: For Environmental Activists, Automaker Is No. 1 Target for Its Low Fuel Economy," *Detroit News*, January 2, 2005, C1. An ad to this effect ran in the *New York Times* on March 21, 2006, A15.

28. See the criticism of GM for providing subsidies for gas guzzling vehicles by Thomas L. Friedman, "A Quick Fix for the Gas Addicts," *New York Times*, May 31, 2006, A23.

29. *Our Route Sustainability, 2005/6*, 3.

30. Bryce Hoffman and Deb Price, "Ford Bails Out on Hybrid Promise," *Detroit News*, June 29, 2006, 8.

31. *Our Route to Sustainability 2004/5*, 10 and 14.

32. See http://www.ford.com/about-ford/news-announcements/featured-stories/featured-stories-detail/ford-recycling.

33. John Teresko, "Green Machines," *Industry Week* 254, no. 2 (February 2005): 40-45.

34. William McDonough and Michael Braumgart, *Cradle to Cradle: Remaking the Way We Make Things* (New York: North Point Press, 2002), and P. Mahoney, "Design Goes 'Green,'" *Machine Design* 77, no. 12 (July 2005): 64–71.

35. Paul C. Killgoar Jr., Director of Environment, Physical Science, and Safety at Ford's Research and Advanced Engineering, as cited in Teresko, "Green Machines," 44.

36. See http://www.ford.com/about-ford/news-announcements/featured-stories/featured-stories-detail/ford-recycling.

37. Ibid.

38. Mahoney, "Design."

39. See http://www.ford.com/about-ford/news-announcements/featured-stories/featured-stories-detail/ford-recycling.

40. Ford Motor Co., Letter from Bill Ford, in *Connecting with Society—1999 Corporate Citizenship Report,* 3.

41. For excellent background on this, see Helen O. P. Alford, Charles Clark, S. A. Cortright, and Michael Naughton, eds., *Rediscovering Abundance: Interdisciplinary Essays on Wealth, Income, and Their Distribution in the Catholic Social Tradition* (Notre Dame, IN: University of Notre Dame Press, 2006).

42. Ford Motor Co., *2002 Corporate Citizenship Report,* 2, 6–7.

43. Ford Motor Co., *2003/4 Corporate Citizenship Report,* 78–79.

44. See Table B, "Working Conditions Assessment Status for Supply Chain," in *Our Route to Sustainability 2004/5,* 41. Ford's concern for human rights and working conditions is also chronicled in their *2001 Corporate Citizenship Report,* 10–11, 24–25; and the Ford *2002 Corporate Citizenship Report,* 52.

45. For Motor Company, *Our Route to Sustainability 2004/5,* 33–34.

46. Aaron Chatterji and David Levine, "Breaking Down the Wall of Codes: Evaluating Non-Financial Performance Measurement," *California Management Review* 48, no. 2 (Winter 2006): 29–51.

47. For additional information on monitoring corporate codes, see S. Prakash Sethi, *Setting Global Standards: Guidelines for Creating Codes of Conduct in Multinational Corporations* (Hoboken, NJ: John Wiley, 2003); and S. Prakash Sethi and Oliver F. Williams, C.S.C., *Economic Imperatives and Ethical Values in Global Business: The South African Experience and International Codes Today* (Dordrecht: Kluwer, 2001).

48. Ford Motor Company, *Our Route to Sustainability 2005/6,* 5.

49. Ibid.

50. World Council for Sustainable Business "Persistence Starts to Pay Off for Chicago Emissions Market" (2006, http://www.wbcsd.org/plugins/DocSearch/details.asp?type=DocDet&ObjectId=MTkyMDM).

51. For a full list of these commitments, see Appendix 2 of *Ford Report on Climate Change 2005,* 11.

52. See http://www.ford.com/about-ford/news-announcements/featured-stories/featured-stories-detail/ford-recycling.

53. J. Johnson, "Automatic Recycling," *Waste News* 10, no. 9 (August 2004): 5; see also http://www.ford.com/about-ford/news-announcements/featured-stories/featured-stories-detail/ford-recycling.

54. K. Crawford, "Turning Waste into Watts," *Business 2.0 Magazine,* October 1, 2005, http://money.cnn.com/magazines/business2/business2_archive/2005/10/01/8359240/index.htm.

55. *Our Route to Sustainability 2004/5,* 46–47.

56. The Principles for Responsible Investment are available at http://www. unpri.org/principles. For a list of the investment firms that have signed the Principles, see http://www.wbcsd.org/templates/TemplateWBCSD5/layout.asp? MenuID=NjA&doOpen=1&ClickMenu=LeftMenu#. On the importance of investment in both poverty reduction and sustainable development in developing countries, see Jeffery D. Sachs and Walter V. Reid, "Investments Toward Sustainable Development," *Science,* May 19, 2006, 1002.

CHAPTER 14

Creating Shared Value

Nestlé S.A. in Developing Nations

Lisa Newton and John Bee

This chapter is divided into three parts. A brief introduction will provide the moral platform for the efforts that Nestlé S.A. has undertaken in the developing world. A survey of several of the projects that are part of those efforts will show the connections among the creation of markets, the achievement of human benefit, and the journey to world peace. Finally, a more detailed presentation of one of the projects aims not only to tell a good story but also to identify the elements of success in corporate endeavors to do real and sustainable good in the world.

THE ETHICAL BASIS FOR CORPORATE WORK FOR THE LEAST ADVANTAGED

From the presidential podium of the Society for Business Ethics meeting in 1999, President John Boatright delivered his parting thought: "Does Business Ethics Rest on a Mistake?"[1] His argument was intriguing: business ethics, he pointed out, tries to create moral managers: it judges the actions of corporate officers against a standard of "promotion of the common good," or "adherence to the moral law," or some such accepted rubric of philosophical ethics. The burden of every critique of corporate activity is that the corporation has, or has failed to, "put ethical behavior before profits." The purpose of ethics seems always, and only, to be the limiting of profit seeking, which is understood as motivated by greed—a deadly sin. But the corporate officer already has a moral obligation, Boatright pointed out. He has a quasi-fiduciary obligation to the shareholders (of a publicly held company) or the owners (of a privately held company) to make the business operate at the highest profit that prudence will allow. Of course, he must not break the law, or allow the factory to operate in an unsafe manner—not because he is a good citizen and a nice guy but because such practices regularly result in much higher costs at several levels. But he may not decide to limit profitable activity, or incur costs, beyond such prudence because the money at his disposal technically is not his. He has accepted stewardship of the property of others, and he has promised to protect it. So to ask a corporate officer to support local causes, or undertake environmentally conservative practices, at great expense to the company when not required to by law is to ask him to break a very serious promise, and it cannot be morally right to break a promise. We may criticize his actions designed to increase shareholder wealth on any grounds we choose—but not on moral grounds. A "business ethics" that sets "morally correct behavior" in opposition to "profit seeking" is, therefore, very seriously flawed. Boatright is not constitutionally opposed to ethical outcomes; but he wants those outcomes to arise from the normal operations of markets. If we want ethical outcomes, Boatright suggests that we shape the law and the institutions to create moral markets—markets that yield profit and allow the corporate officer to keep his promises to the shareholders while also producing good outcomes for all concerned, especially the least advantaged.

Several objections have been raised to Boatright's thesis, none of which can be considered as feasible in reality. Of course corporations can and do simply give to charity—that is, donate the shareholders money to help the poor—especially when disasters strike; we will see some examples of such giving in what follows. But charity is not sustainable. No business practice is sustainable unless it will yield economic reward as well as a warm fuzzy feeling in the heart. The shareholders will not stand for it, but more importantly, it amounts to the breaking of a promise, a promise institutionalized in our society as standard business practice and on which our economy depends. Boatright is going to have to be taken seriously, whether we like it or not.

What is *sustainability*? Let us start with a definition: Any business practice is sustainable if it yields economic reward, respects and protects the people involved in it at any level, and leaves the natural environment just the way it found it. These three criteria of sustainability—the economic, the ethical, and the environmental—have been codified by John Elkington (and many others) as "the Triple Bottom Line," a triple test of acceptability for the long term.[2] Note that violations of the noneconomic rubric, through abuse of workers (or defrauding consumers) or through degrading the environment, will bring the enterprise to an end sooner or later, no matter how good the numbers look to Wall Street in the short term. In the presentation that follows, we will see several examples of one company, Nestlé S.A., weaving the three strands together for the common good and for the peace of the world in the long term.

NESTLÉ'S APPROACH TO CORPORATE BENEFICENCE

Prior to the developments outlined here, Nestlé had a tradition of corporate giving, just as did most major corporations of the developed world, particularly in the United States and Europe. But this practice was not sustainable for either Nestlé or the recipients of the aid: the recipients of the charity were not settling into a pattern of production that would sustain them over the long run, and Nestlé was in perpetual danger of alienating enough shareholders to force any "giving away" of funds to halt. Over time, the notion of "partnerships" came to replace the notion of "charity": in a true partnership, all parties benefit, and each is committed to the success of the other at least in part out of self-interest. There are several examples of partnerships that have brought success to some of the poorest people of the world.

Pakistan is one of the least developed and most dangerous nations in the world. Its infrastructure, while excellent in the cities, is all but absent in the mountainous rural regions. It is very difficult to govern, with a mix of religious and secular communities and traditions, and it is prone to earthquakes. Above all, armed conflict brings danger: Pakistan is one of the few nations in the world with the capability of delivering nuclear weapons, so any conflict—for instance, with its traditional adversary, nuclear-capable India—brings the possibility of the first nuclear conflagration since 1945.

Pakistan's tendency to violence is intimately linked to the state of the economy in many parts of the country: there is little possibility for sustainable industry, social customs that bar women from the workplace make it difficult for families to remain economically viable, and a flagging educational system fails to provide an educated workforce. In partnership with NGOs and governments, Nestlé refurbished schools, built housing for the poor, and provided a veritable mountain of earthquake relief in the wake of the Kashmir earthquake. Most important, however, is its partnership with dairy farmers in the Punjab, a region near India.

Nestlé gave start-up assistance to farmers, who were to provide high-quality milk for Nestlé's milk product operations. The farming techniques required were unfamiliar to the Pakistani farmers and not easy to maintain and improve, and the farms were scattered widely, making it difficult to assemble farmers for instructional meetings. So Nestlé trained agricultural extension workers—in particular, *female* agricultural extension workers, who were easily available for training because of the limited employment opportunities for women. They also were acceptable to the farmers because of their advanced technical expertise. Where necessary, Nestlé sent crews to the villages to erect barns or dig wells in order to get the farmers started. As a result of these efforts, the partnership has empowered women, who can set a silent example to the next generation without the need for open attack against traditional social institutions; a steady source of high-quality milk is available for Nestlé, whose partnership with Nestlé-Milkpak aims to become Pakistan's largest food company; and above all there is now a peaceful and profitable dairy industry where there was none before, as well as a powerful motivation for Pakistanis in that area to at least maintain the peace.

Many of the same initiatives are at work in Colombia. Nestlé makes milk products in South America as well, in particular cocoa and powdered milk. For reasons of business strategy alone, it aims to increase market share and market penetration in nontraditional areas, while continuing to ensure the high quality of its products. In Colombia the climate is appropriate for dairy farming, and Colombia, like Pakistan, has a history of violence. At the time Nestlé approached the Colombian government about the possibility of setting up a dairy industry in the region of Caqueta, a truce had been declared in a bloody civil war marked by atrocities on both sides. Many of the fighters had done nothing but fight for the last ten years, and they had no economic background in any trade but farming. The preferred farm product was coca—the basis for cocaine, an industry that has made Colombia infamous in the developed world. Nestlé introduced sustainable farming methods in many places in the country and in some locations, Caqueta in particular, assisted farmers in entering the dairy industry. This operation is considerably more extensive, and of longer duration, than the Pakistan project, but it has the same objectives: to create a viable and sustainable livelihood for the people; to give residents an alternative to conflict and a powerful motivation to avoid conflict in the future; and to provide Nestlé with a steady supply of milk, a steady market for its products, and an equally powerful motivation to continue to support the enterprise.[3]

Across the ocean in Nigeria, Nestlé also introduced sustainable farming methods and simple projects to help farmers, such as the installation of mechanical threshers, which saves hours of backbreaking labor for many crops. The company became a major food distributor, an activity that rapidly drew them into the health care field: as in many places in Africa, Nigeria was riddled with HIV/AIDS, and the disease had rendered the workforce entirely unreliable. Through no fault of their own, workers simply would not show up for work—because they were sick; because they had to take care of someone who was sick; because they had to make arrangements for children whose caregiver was too sick to take care of them anymore; and, all too often, because they had to participate in or attend village funerals for those who had died of the disease. HIV/AIDS is peculiar in this way: most of the infectious diseases that ravage the poorer countries of the world prey first on the very young and the very old, but HIV/AIDS attacks the young adults—those in the prime of life and the workforce of the nation. One of Nestlé's first projects, done in cooperation with the International Red Cross, was to educate the people of Nigeria, adults and youth alike, on the ways to protect themselves from HIV/AIDS. Such education was especially necessary in regions where there was no access to drugs and health care of the kind that makes it possible for those suffering from the disease in the United States to lead relatively normal and productive lives. Another major health problem, universal in sub-Saharan Africa, is malnutrition. In all the regions where it has manufacturing facilities, Nestlé generously contributes to food supplies and to education on nutrition. Again, Nestlé is acting out of simple self-interest: if the workers have enough to eat, they will work better than if they do not. At the same time, of course, such contributions are good for the people.

THE PROJECT FOR PEACE IN NIGERIA

One project in particular stands out, both because of its ingenuity and success and because of features that can be replicated in other projects, companies, and countries. Tribal conflicts have been part of Nigerian history as far back as we can trace. (At one point in the late 1960s, Hausa and Ibo tribes actually split into two warring nations, and the Ibo people seceded and formed the republic of Biafra. After Biafra was defeated in the resulting civil war, the country has been one, at least officially, ever since.) The discovery of oil, and the influx of oil money, did nothing to calm the violence. As a matter of fact, it has made it worse, since there is now more to fight about. Yet the Nigerians are not systematically geographically divided; members of all tribal groups live together in the cities. Observers suggest that one of the major problems bedeviling Nigeria is that with no history of civil society, Nigerians have no way to negotiate or resolve natural conflict. Nestlé asked if there was any way to teach Nigerians peaceful conflict resolution techniques.

Here Nestlé paired up with the NGO Search for Common Ground (SCG), which specializes in making films oriented toward the promotion of peace. They conceived a television series—sort of a reality TV experience in which a small number of Nigerian actors would confront, address, and demonstrate possible resolutions to the type of conflict situations that afflict the society. The benefits from the project were unusually varied. First, if the series did its job as projected, Nigeria might be on its way to finding peace among its warring factions. Second, conflict or not, Nigeria had a small but expanding middle class and, thus, an increasing audience for television. Actors would be needed for television shows, and SCG was prepared to seek out and train actors, not only those that it would need for the series but also an acting corps for the nation's future in all fields. That corps, in turn, would also be trained in conflict resolution and hopefully would take its place among the nation's leadership within civil society. Third, in the course of training the actors, SCG would found a drama school that would outlive the project; this institution would be in a position to develop additional series along the same lines. Fourth, SCG would have a showpiece that it could translate and use as a model for other nations in which it was working. And fifth, Nestlé, which along with the Nigerian government was underwriting the cost of the training of the actors and the series itself, could place its advertisements on the show and reach an audience that otherwise would never know anything about its products.

In the end, Nestlé made two video series. The first, "The Academy," was about the recruitment and the training of the actors for the project. Twenty actors were chosen from about 59,000 applications—these were very bright and ambitious students—and the series followed them from their homes (an education in itself for a Western audience), through transportation to the school and the learning process, including learning the discipline of following directions and working through an entire day. The other series, "The Station," constitutes the first ten episodes of the show itself.[4]

Did the project bring peace to the world, or at least to Nigeria? We will not know for many years. However, the major advantage of the partnership was that it laid the groundwork for many future projects of this type, proving that companies in the private sector can work with both governments and NGOs on worthwhile enterprises, that profit is not incompatible with genuine benefit to the health and welfare of the people of a developing nation, and that many inventive minds can collaborate on work that will benefit many. Perhaps that is all we can ask for at this point.

NOTES

1. John Boatright, "Does Business Ethics Rest on a Mistake?" *Business Ethics Quarterly* 9, no. 4 (1999): 583–91.

2. John Elkington, *Cannibals with Forks: The Triple Bottom Line of 21st Century Business* (Gabriola Island, BC: New Society Publishers, 1998).

3. Incidentally, an excellent video is available from Nestlé that details the start of the operations and the manner of carrying on the business.

4. Videos of both of these series are available from Nestlé at http://www.nestle.com.

CHAPTER 15

IBM and Corporate Citizenship

Stanley Litow

Corporate citizenship describes a company's total dealings with the community—local, regional, national, or global. It encompasses traditional corporate philanthropy as well as activities far beyond the traditional. A company's record of social responsibility is a critical component of its brand value, and if properly planned and delivered, it can provide a significant competitive advantage in the marketplace. Corporate citizenship, therefore, is of material benefit to the company and essential to a business's success wherever it operates, including emerging markets. Corporate citizenship exists at the nexus between a company's business and community interests. While there are certainly inherent conflicts between these elements, and natural tensions that need to be balanced and resolved, it is possible to resolve these conflicts satisfactorily and for a business to be successful as both an economic and social enterprise.

To be effective as a business, it is vital that a company fully understand the global communities where its employees and customers reside and where it does its business; this is true both of the local and international communities. It is impossible to do this well without engaging and interacting comprehensively with neighboring institutions—public, private, and voluntary—through sustained civic activity. Polls, grants, studies, committees, or third parties are not enough for building this type of relationship; rather, direct participation and engagement by the company, its employees, and its leadership is necessary. To understand the value of corporate citizenship, a firm needs comprehensive and effective ways to benchmark and measure performance; as with any other element of business, corporations must learn what works and what does not and how to improve through innovation. It is for these reasons that IBM helped to form the Global Leadership Network (GLN), which consists of nearly two dozen world-class companies seeking to identify how high to set the bar for performance and how to measure their performance using a framework that lends itself to both benchmarking and continuous improvement.[1]

In the best sense, private sector resources both build and sustain communities. Their employment rolls and taxes support community infrastructure, government, and schools. Company employees participate as voters, parents, and taxpayers and support the civic and community sector financially and by offering stewardship and full participation. In this scenario, the community and its businesses are not adversaries but full partners. Through its labor practices and behavior, a company can contribute to the community work life, and company practices can promote safer, cleaner, and sounder environments and the ethical behavior critical to community health and vitality. At IBM and many other companies—but certainly not all—a code of ethics is embedded into the expectations set for every employee on a global basis. IBM's code of ethics is part and parcel of all company business practices.

While companies must meet their commitments as full partners, it is also true that communities must do the same. The manner by which a community or a company approaches issues such as regulation, taxation, energy costs, transportation, and labor practices impacts the ability of a company or a community to succeed. Local schools, social welfare infrastructure, and the arts are vital to business success and contribute to decisions concerning a business location, expansion, or contraction. Because of the interdependency of business and community, no one business or sector can "go it alone." Collaboration and partnership across all sectors of the economy is critical and essential for community stability.

Progressive companies see their social investments and policies as being intrinsically linked to their core values. Sustaining values requires that these values be linked closely to the company's business strategy. Without a link to values and principles, it is impossible to initiate broad strategic efforts or to respond to crises. Great companies—and real leaders—have a set of core beliefs that defines the corporate culture and a company's behavior. They are able to sustain those beliefs or values over time, beginning with the quality of a company's goods or services and the way it treats its employees and customers and extending to how it treats the broader community. A corporate culture of this kind encompasses business ethics, environmental actions, and fiscal and labor policy. Great companies prize the core values of integrity and trust. They have high aspirations for their products and services and enduring values that set them apart. They consistently do some things better than anyone else, delivering products of value and sustained financial performance. They are "long distance runners" who understand the needs of their customers, their investors, and their employees and deliver sustained value to all of them over the long term. But just as significant, they view communities as their full partners, and they are committed to delivering value to them as well.

At IBM one of our core beliefs is that we provide the best-quality technology and innovation for our customers and the world in general. This is something that goes to the very core of our company and is part of our business model. Progressive business leadership committed to high values is needed today more than ever before, and it may fall to leaders who exercised it in the past to do so again. Let me offer some examples. In the 1950s our then CEO, Tom Watson Jr., released a policy letter explaining publicly IBM's policy of hiring new employees regardless of race, color, or creed. In 1956 Watson and IBM acted on that policy when he announced plans to build a manufacturing plant in Kentucky that would employ nearly two thousand people. When the plant opened it was the first fully racially integrated manufacturing plant south of the "Mason-Dixon Line" dividing the segregated South from the integrated North. His decision clearly contributed to the advancement of race relations in the United States and a shift in American social and economic policy. It was courageous to be sure, but it was also good business, providing for IBM a competitive edge as a diverse employer that sustains itself today. A 2004 *Harvard Business Review* article profiled the IBM diversity program as a model for corporate behavior. David Thomas, the Harvard Business School professor who wrote the article, documents the depth and reach of IBM's global efforts and highlights the executive-level and board leadership that helps drive the program more than fifty years after Watson's efforts in Kentucky.[2]

IBM was one of the first companies to prepare an annual environmental impact report and an annual report on diversity and one of the first to provide paid vacations, health insurance, sick leave, job sharing, and domestic partner benefits. These actions, taken by one company, not only influenced actions taken by other companies but also supported and, in some cases, helped to shape public policy. In 2007 we issued the company's third comprehensive social report. It profiles IBM's leadership across the panoply of issues that encompass social responsibility: supply chain practices, corporate philanthropy, business ethics, diversity, fiscal transparency, security and privacy, etc. In particular, the report highlights the company's efforts to harness the power of innovation in service to the social and educational goals of the broader society.

With regard to IBM's leadership, the last three U.S. National Education Summits, in 1996, 1999, and 2001, were led by IBM's CEO, just as in 1962 when our then CEO led the White House's Economic Summit for President Kennedy. Now our CEO, Sam Palmisano, leads the National Innovation Initiative (NII) and the collaborative effort to produce a Global Innovation Outlook (GIO), working with a range of stakeholders in business, academia, government, and the nongovernmental sector. This is a global effort to understand the promise of innovation. This kind of leadership parallels the leadership of CEOs in the past, from a commitment to diversity in the United States and worldwide to the innovation, in partnership with NASA, that fueled the space program and put a man on the moon in the 1960s. These practices go hand in hand with the company's focus on innovation and leadership, with benefits for both our customers and the community. Other companies such as GE, Pfizer, and American Express have enviable performances in these areas as well. Pfizer's CEO, working in collaboration with the UN and the Business Roundtable, has organized and led the private sector response to disaster relief, as just one example.

In 1969 IBM's then CEO, Tom Watson Jr., put it well in an internal IBM speech and publication: "We accept our responsibilities as a corporate citizen in community, national and world affairs; we serve our interests best when we serve the public interest. We acknowledge our obligation as a business institution to help improve the society we are part of." This is why citizenship efforts are focused on sharing our technology innovations with communities, just as we do with our customers. In 2005 well over five hundred software patents were made available, free of charge, to anyone working on open source projects. Open source technology is critical to fueling opportunity in an open society globally. And, as a globally integrated enterprise, we take our international obligations seriously.

After all, since 1987 most of our revenue has come from non-U.S. operations. In corporate philanthropy, more than one-third, and rising, of our resources are targeted to communities outside of the United States, the largest percentage by any U.S. company. And this is a long-standing practice; in a Conference Board publication from the 1980s that charted the extent of international contributions by U.S. headquartered companies, they marveled at the fact that fully half of all the international contributions made that year came from one U.S. company: IBM.

Corporate philanthropy is still a large part of corporate citizenship. We have always understood that without quality schools, we cannot have stable communities or stable businesses. Thus, it is no surprise that 80 percent of IBM's philanthropy efforts support education. Through the Reinventing Education Initiative, launched at IBM in 1994, we develop cutting-edge tools that have resulted in direct improvement in student achievement. The global Reinventing Education program now serves over 80,000 teachers and over 8 million children globally. Reinventing Education was recently launched in India and China as well as Vietnam, Mexico, and urban and rural areas across the United States. We also have developed a new way to teach nonliterate children how to read using innovative voice recognition software and developed new tools to improve teacher quality by allowing teachers to build best practices databases and provide mentorship to other teachers. We have developed a new early childhood computer center and donated over 40,000 centers worldwide. These computer centers exist throughout Africa, Latin America, Asia, and the Middle East. We also have developed a means to automatically translate Web pages from English to Spanish and incorporate bilingual email to promote communication between teachers, students, and parents.

For the last decade we have invested in independent evaluative studies to both document the success of our efforts and, even more importantly, to identify ways to improve our initiatives. The Center for Children and Technology has documented improvements in a variety of academic disciplines and across grade levels. Evaluators at the University of Texas and from Jobs for the Future have documented gains in reading and pronunciation, and global evaluation studies in the United States by Bank Street College and similar studies in other countries have documented the value of our early learning programs to a sound basic education. Our clear focus on education and systemic improvement in education recognizes the value of education to society as well as its centrality to global businesses and economic opportunity.

In 2005 IBM announced the Transition to Teaching program to encourage senior IBM employees to consider second careers as K–12 teachers; company support is given in the form of free tuition and leaves of absence for teacher certification activities. This innovative program, planned and operated in full partnership and cooperation with educators from school systems and colleges and universities across the United States, has proved very popular with employees, with school leaders, and with the public. A major focus of our education work has been in the developing world. Among the sites around the world for Reinventing Education, in addition to some of the most troubled urban and rural school districts in the Unites States, is the state of Hidalgo in Mexico, the state of Rio in Brazil, and rural areas in Vietnam, China, and India. In addition, Kidsmart early learning centers that we have contributed worldwide are now prevalent throughout the United States, Europe, Latin America, Asia, and Africa. A recent evaluation study in South Africa demonstrated the value of the Kidsmart program to early literacy and numeracy. In India, the early literacy centers have been installed and supported throughout the most disadvantaged villages in a partnership with the Byrraju Foundation. In each of these cases, the Kidsmart program is delivered via collaboration with key NGOs: in South Africa with the Centre for Early Childhood Development (CECD), and in India with the Byrraju Foundation.

IBM's partnership in India with Byrraju focuses primarily on rural areas. In Andhra Pradesh, for example, as part of IBM's commitment to donate 1,500 computer centers worldwide, some 300 early learning computer centers have been donated across 54 locations, which were selected by Byrraju because of the existence of core health care and other services and the presence of committed staff. Working with Byrraju on site selection and teacher training has allowed us to mobilize and deliver the programs more quickly and to ensure higher-quality services for children, teachers, and parents. Likewise, in South Africa the partnership with CECD, a highly regarded national NGO, has allowed us to work collaboratively on site selection, teacher and parent training, and assessment since the program began there in 1999. Working together in all nine South African provinces—Western Cape, Gauteng, Free State, Eastern Cape, Northern Cape, Limpopo, Mpumalanga, North West, and KwaZulu Natal—some five hundred learning centers have been contributed by

IBM. Recently, we have expanded into Ghana and Namibia as well. CECD's independent evaluation was able to document increased English proficiency by student learners, eased instruction for teachers, increased learner confidence, and improved parent and teacher engagement. Working together, IBM and CECD established a practitioner network to promote best practices and ease teacher isolation.

In November of 2004 IBM launched World Community Grid,[3] making powerful grid technology available to address the most critical health and environmental issues facing society. World Community Grid harnesses the unused cycle time of hundreds of thousands of PCs and donates the resulting "supercomputer" power to researchers trying to find a cure for AIDS and Alzheimer's. Initially, the power of this humanitarian grid was made available to the Institute for Systems Biology's Human Proteome Folding Project and then to Scripps Institute's Fighting AIDS at Home initiative. Because of the power of the grid, innovation researchers were able to make significantly greater progress on their work. In 2006 IBM added a cancer research project sponsored by the New Jersey Cancer Institute and Rutgers University, and in 2007 we added a project to complete a new climate model in Africa sponsored by the University of Cape Town in South Africa. In 2008 a project to end global hunger via a rice DNA project, sponsored by the University of Washington, was initiated. By creating a permanent humanitarian grid—a virtual supercomputer— we can provide a permanent source of supercomputer power at no cost for literally dozens of high-yield health and environmental research projects worldwide. With over 65 million PCs in the world, the potential impact of grid technology on society is staggering. In the early part of 2007, in partnership with the World Bank's International Finance Corporation (IFC), we launched a free site on the Internet that offers assistance in business growth, development, and job generation to small businesses in the developing world.[4]

Programs like these have helped solve education, economic, and social problems but have also built the value of the IBM brand, leading directly to new patents, products, and a host of services for use in education and other fields. For example, to the delight of educators and art historians, IBM digitally restored Michelangelo's *Pietà* while also developing new telemedicine applications. It is this dual benefit that has led to our use of the Web and innovative technology to advance knowledge of Egyptian culture through our Eternal Egypt Website[5] and has led us to do similar work in China on a project dubbed "Beyond the Forbidden City," with the Smithsonian's new Museum of African American History and Culture, with the Vatican Library, with the Museum of Modern Art in New York, and with the Hermitage Museum in Russia. Beta testing of technology in efforts to benefit communities helps build better products for our customers but also provides a public good. It helps train our consultants and researchers and builds employee morale, but it also adds value to communities. From a company and shareholder perspective, it adds to the overall value of the IBM brand, which is also enhanced by environmental leadership and supply chain practices. When tensions develop between a community beta test and a product or service for our customers, a supply chain, or environmental practices, it is difficult but vital to consider community interests side-by-side with business interests in order to be fully consistent with our core values.

A study by Hillard Fleischman found that 87 percent of employees surveyed felt a greater sense of dedication to a socially involved employer, and Turban and Greening found a direct correlation between a firm's social responsibility and its attractiveness as an employer to new employees.[6] We find this to be the case at IBM, where the engagement of employees in the community builds skills and relationships, helping us to find and keep the best talent. Companies such as Timberland or Home Depot can make similar claims.

In a recent year, 25 percent of IBM's U.S. media coverage dealt with community relations, and its ability to positively influence media and government officials has been palpable. The two media stories concerning IBM that garnered the most publicity were on the Transition to Teaching program and the World Community Grid. Recent research has demonstrated that a large and growing percentage of a company's market value is comprised of so-called intangible assets—reputation, brand equity, strategic positioning, alliances, and knowledge. Interbrand, an international branding consulting agency, says that 25 percent of the world's total financial wealth is tied up in these intangible assets.[7] According to some estimates, the reputation capital of IBM is worth nearly $55 billion. What percentage of that wealth and value emanates from our corporate citizenship? It should be clear that strategic efforts at corporate citizenship pay off in brand value, research, publicity, stock purchases, improved employee morale, opportunity, and advantage. And for this reason, corporate citizenship needs to be understood and advanced at corporations worldwide.

Through the Global Leadership Network we hope to find out how high to set the bar for citizenship and how to measure our performance against this standard, going beyond compliance and moving forward to improvement. In addition to IBM, the GLN consists of companies like GE, GM, Cargill, 3M, FedEx, Diageo, Omron, Cemex, Pfizer, Xerox, Prudential, Nokia, and Manpower, representing over $500 billion in revenue and nearly 9.5 million employees. IBM helped to found this network of likeminded companies because we know that quality corporate citizenship cannot consist solely of reporting what a company has done in the past but also what it can do better in the future. We are aided by expert technical help from Accountability, a key NGO in the United Kingdom, and the Boston College Center for Corporate Citizenship in the United States. We firmly believe that such activity is part of building the long-term economic value of the company, and it must be managed with the same seriousness of purpose as any other core element of the business. We encourage other companies to learn from and hopefully join the GLN as they seek to improve their performance. To this end, we have prepared an interactive online tool that helps companies to benchmark performance against other companies with a goal of continuous improvement.[8]

At IBM and for our current CEO, Sam Palmisano, the past is prologue to the future. Building on the tradition of IBM's exemplary citizenship, in 2003 we launched the On Demand Community to use On Demand Computing to fuel a next-generation approach to community relations, allowing all our employees and retirees to engage in community service. On an intranet site, designed to appeal to our over 300,000 employees worldwide, employees find a host of technology tools created to improve schools and community organizations, including online lectures and tutorials and lists of best practices. In one year 37,000 employees signed up and performed nearly 1.4 million hours of community service; we now have well over 100,000 employees and retirees who have performed over 6.2 million hours of service, making the IBM On Demand Community the largest corporate community volunteer program on the planet. This program is equally popular and valuable in places like India and China as it is in the United States. Its value is measured not only in the number of employees involved but in the impact they have made worldwide. They have promoted business transformation in soup kitchens, schools, community centers, and programs for the aged and for people with disabilities. One Internet-based tool constructed with the Community Resource

Exchange (CRE) in the United States allows IBM employees to work on developing quality assessments and measurements of nonprofit agency performance.

In 2003 IBM's CEO launched a major company-wide effort to define the company's values. Since our inception nearly a century ago, our company has been grounded in strongly held beliefs. Thomas Watson Sr. and Jr. came to call these IBM's "Basic Beliefs," and they committed the company to a broad definition of leadership. But in the twenty-first-century world our technology allows us to engage our employees worldwide in setting these values through use of an IBM Web-enabled "values jam"— an electronic "conversation" using social networking tools pioneered by IBM research. IBM's core beliefs include being a trusted partner for customers, a reliable long-term investment, and a progressive employer and responsible corporate citizen. Over time, these beliefs grew into practices and approaches and became the qualities that people began to expect of IBM and its employees. They also helped us become a model for other businesses, guiding us through decades of extraordinary progress and change. In July of 2003, via the "values jam," we invited IBM employees in 170 countries to participate in a bold seventy-two-hour experiment in which they would discuss and determine just what we represent to ourselves and the rest of the world. This was an opportunity to validate and refine our values. What emerged was a twenty-first-century view of IBM's core values, which describe the company and what the people who work for it stand for: dedication to every client's success, innovation that matters for our company and for the world; and trust and personal responsibility in all relationships.

Here is one example of IBM's values in practice: On December 26, 2004, a tsunami hit in the Indian Ocean. IBM's response was swift and certain. Similar to the way we mobilized after the 9/11 attacks on New York, we quickly assembled a group from our Crisis Response Team (CRT), moving them into affected areas in Indonesia, India, Thailand, and Sri Lanka. Working closely with local government officials and NGOs in the four countries, a team of two dozen CRT members provided an organization registry to allow for the rapid registration and collection of information about nongovernmental, government, and multinational organizations; a request management system to coordinate and track relief requests; a people registry to support tracking of those missing or deceased; a camp registry to track location, numbers of individuals, and operations information; and an assistance database, damage tracking system, burial information system, health and incident management system, and a logistics management system. Following that experience, we were able to mobilize even more resources to respond to the devastation of Hurricane Katrina in the Gulf Coast. Additionally, in Pakistan we have developed a set of resources that resemble "Disaster Relief in a Box," a solution featuring open source software tools dubbed "Sahana" that can be deployed quickly to any disaster worldwide. Sahana had its first test after the 2002 earthquake in Indonesia; IBM employees were on the ground within twenty-four hours of the quake. We are now working with a range of NGOs so that Sahana can be deployed more widely.

Among the company's new efforts will be an automatic translation and social networking project to ease the division between the Arabic- and English-speaking worlds, and as mentioned above, a portal on the Internet for small women- and minority-owned businesses, better literacy tools for children and adults, and expansion of efforts to improve the teaching of math and science. We hope to advance the bridge between those that have and those that have not through deployment of open source software tools for people with disabilities, with language problems, and in remote locations. We will continue to engage our employees and business partners in these global efforts through the On Demand Community and to respond to societal needs as they develop. To advance common understanding we will continue our efforts with National Geographic to plot the history of mankind on the planet through the Genographic Research Project.

A critical component of our work is the close alliance we have developed with a number of stakeholders. In education, we have partnered with school systems, states, ministries of education, and, of course, with parents and teachers. On a broader level, partnerships have been established with NGOs around the world. In 2005 our work with stakeholders was exemplified in the Global Innovation Outlook, which was constructed with the active involvement and collaboration of customers, universities, governments, and NGOs

Corporate responsibility, though practiced at IBM since the inception of the company nearly one hundred years ago, is still a relatively new concept and much misunderstood, as has been shown by some recent, high-profile cases of poor corporate behavior. For example, Enron and MCI, before their fall from grace, both showed up on a list of one hundred top companies compiled by *Business Ethics Magazine,* demonstrating how little we know and how much we have to learn about true corporate social responsibility. A cursory review of the companies that comply with the Global Reporting Initiative or the UN Global Compact and those that do not reveals the inherent flaws in social reporting or in signing on to a variety of compacts. It is difficult to know, however, what to measure and how to measure it, particularly for entities outside of business. Working together, business, NGOs, and government can address gaps in both expectations and performance.

IBM employees have been generous with their time and talent, and the company has been generous with its resources. From a philanthropic standpoint, our annual contributions budget exceeds $150 million. Our employees in the United States alone also have contributed financially to philanthropic activities. In 2005 over $35 million went toward the company's charitable campaign, and IBM's matching grants program added another $20 million to the total. Employee giving outside the United States, though not tracked in the same way, is certainly considerable. Add to this the value of IBM employees' 3.5 million hours of volunteer service—which according to the Points of Light Foundation can be valued at about $15 per hour—and that represents another $50 million or more. In the near future we expect the company's financial contributions and that of our employees, both directly and through volunteerism, to equate to a contribution of a quarter of a billion dollars worldwide. This is a level of commitment few, if any, other companies could match.

A company cannot be successful unless the communities in which it operates are as well. We have a shared responsibility to ensure our mutual well-being. Globally integrated companies have unique opportunities to set the bar high for quality business practices. We cannot do this in only one way and judge it through philanthropy or generosity alone. A company needs to be judged on how it made its money in the first place, not on how much extra money it gives away. Rosabeth Moss Kanter, of the Harvard Business School, characterized the IBM approach as going from "spare change to real change."[9] Strong social performance and citizenship cannot be advanced via the creation of a social report or via signatory on one or a number of pledges or compacts. It must stem from a commitment to values, principles, and ethics that exist at the very intersection of business and society.

NOTES

1. See http://www.globalleadershipnetwork.org/.

2. David A. Thomas, "Diversity as Strategy," *Harvard Business Review* 82, no. 9 (September 2004): 107–17.

3. See http://www.worldcommunitygrid.org.

4. See http://www.smetoolkit.org/smetoolkit/en.

5. See http://www.eternalegypt.org/EternalEgyptWebsiteWeb/Home Servlet.

6. Hillard Fleischman, "Consumers Demand Companies with a Conscience" (out of print report in possession of the author, 1999); D. W. Greening and D. B. Turban, "Corporate Social Performance as a Competitive Advantage in Attracting a Quality Workforce," *Business and Society* 39 no. 3 (2000): 254–80; and D. B. Turban and D. W. Greening, "Corporate Social Performance and Organizational Attractiveness to Prospective Employees," *Academy of Management Journal* 40, no. 3 (1996): 658–72.

7. See http://www.interbrand.com.

8. See https://globalleadershipnetwork.org/.

9. Rosabeth M. Kanter, "From Spare Change to Real Change: The Social Sector as Beta Site for Business Innovation," *Harvard Business Review* 77, no. 3 (May 1999): 122–32.

CHAPTER 16

General Electric and Corporate Citizenship
Improving the Health of the Poor in Africa

Marshall Greenhut with Bob Corcoran

POVERTY IN AFRICA

Africa is, by far, the most impoverished continent in the world. Thirty-five out of the bottom thirty-eight ranked nations, including the bottom twenty-two, on the 2006 United Nations Human Development Index were African nations.[1] Additionally, thirty-four of the least developed nations in the world are in Africa.[2] Africa was the only region of the world where per capita GDP fell in the last two decades of the twentieth century. Worldwide, poverty has declined significantly in the last twenty years. In China alone 400 million people were lifted out of absolute poverty. Yet progress has been almost nonexistent in Africa, particularly sub-Saharan Africa. In 1980 one out of every ten poor people lived in sub-Saharan Africa; by 2000 that number had jumped to one out of three. The World Bank estimates that the ratio will jump to one out of two in the near future.[3] From 1980 to 2001 the percentage of the population in sub-Saharan Africa living on less than US$1 per day rose from 43 percent to 46 percent. In real numbers it was a rise from 164 million to 314 million people. Per capita GDP in the region actually fell 14 percent in real terms.[4] Africa's health conditions are by far the worst in the world. HIV/AIDS has lowered life expectancy and tuberculosis has become endemic. Malaria kills thousands of children each day. Other tropical diseases coupled with poor health care cause the loss of billions of dollars in production each year.

Traditional direct aid has not been effective in curing Africa's ills. Despite over $400 billion in aid since World War II, little progress has been made. Poor governance has been cited as the primary reason for this lack of development. While corruption has certainly been a major issue, it alone is not a sufficient explanation for the problems in Africa. Jeffrey Sachs of Columbia University's Earth Institute posits that Africa, even in well-governed areas, is stuck in a "poverty trap, too poor to achieve robust, high levels of economic growth (and in many places too poor to grow at all)."[5] Thus, fundamental changes must be made in order to improve quality of life in Africa. Sachs identifies several key factors contributing to Africa's poverty trap. These include very high transportation costs and small market size; low productivity in agriculture; a very high disease burden; adverse geopolitics; and very slow diffusion of technology from abroad. These factors combine to make Africa the most likely region of the world to fall into a poverty trap.[6]

High Transportation Costs and Small Market Size

Africans tend to live in the interior of the continent. Shipping goods between the coastal ports and where the population lives and works is expensive. Transportation costs are much higher in Africa than in Asia. Estimates put the rate per ton mile at two and half times that in Asia. If transportation costs were halved, the volume of goods transported could increase by as much as 500 percent. Additionally, sub-Saharan Africa is effectively cut off from Europe, its major industrialized trade partner, by the Sahara. Africans tend to live inland for a variety of reasons. The soil tends to be better and the rains more constant in the interior highland regions.[7] Centuries of slave trade also discouraged people from living near the coasts. This creates a problem in Africa because the rivers are generally not navigable by ocean-going vessels. In *The Wealth of Nations* Adam Smith discussed this problem:

> There are in Africa none of those great inlets, such as the Baltic and Adriatic seas in Europe, the Mediterranean and Euxine [Black] seas in both Europe and Asia, and the gulphs of Arabia, Persia, India, Bengal, and Siam, in Asia, to carry maritime commerce into the interior parts of that great continent; and the great rivers of Africa are at too great a distance from one another to give occasion to any considerable inland navigation.[8]

Isolation problems are exacerbated by small market size. Africa lacks the modern road system required for high-intensity trade.[9] Africa needs an extensive road system connecting the exterior to the interior and within the interior itself. However, such road systems are expensive to build and maintain.

Low Productivity in Agriculture

Most Africans live in regions where irrigation is difficult or impossible. Thus, Africa has the lowest percentage of food crops produced on irrigated land of any region in the developing world. The high transportation costs of fertilizer and erratic rainfall also negatively impact African food production.[10] In a meeting with African villagers, Jeffrey Sachs found that only two out of two hundred farmers currently were using fertilizer, yet all had used it in the past. About one quarter of them were using fallows with nitrogen fixing trees, an advanced technique taught by the World Agroforestry Center that reintroduces nutrients to the soil. The rest were farming soils depleted of nutrients because they were too poor to purchase either fertilizer or nitrogen-fixing trees.[11] This created something of a feedback loop. If the farmers had enough money to plant nitrogen-fixing trees, they would be able to feed themselves and likely have excess crops to sell. But because they do not have enough money to buy either, they are unable to produce a large enough yield to either feed themselves or sell for profit. Finally, Africans have been slow to utilize improved seeds from the developed world.

Very High Disease Burden

Sub-Saharan Africa has the highest HIV infection rate in the world. An estimated 24.5 million sub-Saharan Africans were living with HIV at the end of 2005, with 2.7 million having contracted the disease that year alone. The adult prevalence rate has shown a slight decline (6.2 percent to 6.1 percent), but the epidemic is growing in absolute numbers. The rate has stabilized as the number dying from AIDS-related illnesses roughly equals the number newly infected. Nearly two-thirds of the people infected with HIV live in sub-Saharan Africa. Among women and children the situation is even worse. Three-quarters of the women living with HIV reside in sub-Saharan Africa, as do nearly 90 percent of the children.[12]

Tuberculosis (TB) is spreading along with HIV throughout Africa. An HIV positive individual with TB is far more likely to become sick and succumb to the disease. While declining in all other parts of the world, TB is growing in Africa. An estimated 400 new cases per 100,000 people occur in sub-Saharan Africa, nearly double anywhere else in the world.[13] Inconsistent and inadequate treatment can lead to the development of drug resistant strains, which exacerbate treatment issues.

Finally, many vector-borne parasites cause massive problems throughout Africa. Onchocerciasis, better known as river blindness, affects 18 million people in Africa. Though rarely fatal, hookworm (Necatur americanus) affects hundreds of millions and is a leading cause of child morbidity. It can cause low birth weight in newborns and physical and neurological retardation among children. Schistosomiasis affects 200 million people worldwide, 85 percent of whom reside in sub-Saharan Africa. Caused by a helminthic parasite in the genus *Schisosoma,* the disease is contracted from the water supply. Bathing, washing, or collecting water in rivers, streams, and standing water is enough to expose people to the parasite. While generally considered to have a fairly low mortality rate, new research by the World Health Organization (WHO) suggests that Schistosomiasis may be responsible for as many as 200,000 deaths per year.[14] It is second only to malaria among tropical diseases in terms of morbidity.

Malaria is an infection caused by parasitic protozoa in the genus *Plasmodium.* It is both preventable and treatable, but it remains a disease that is both caused by, and a cause of, poverty. Of the more than 1 million yearly deaths caused by malaria worldwide, 90 percent occur in Africa, mostly among small children.[15] Malaria is an example of the poverty trap. With enough investment, malaria could be controlled (though not eliminated) in Africa. However, Africa lacks the resources to make such investments, and as the disease lowers productivity, the continent is impoverished further.

Adverse Geopolitics

Africa certainly suffered at the hands of both European and Arab powers. The slave trade was followed by direct colonial rule. Even after independence, African dictators often added to the problems. Wars have continued to rage across many portions of the continent and political stability has been rare. Many of the governments that have survived are corrupt and authoritarian. During the Cold War the major powers often propped up such governments for reasons of their own.

Slow Diffusion of Technology

Africa has been slow to take up technological advances, especially in agriculture and health. While much of the world has seen a large increase in crop yields over the past thirty years, gains in Africa have been minimal. The high-yield varietals created for the developed world, Latin America, and Asia do not suit the agronomics of Africa. Research into high-yield varietals did not include crops grown in Africa. As a result, in 1998 only 27 percent of crops planted in sub-Saharan Africa were high-yield varietals, compared to 82 percent in Asia, 52 percent in Latin America, and 58 percent in the Middle East and North Africa. This has resulted in a sub-Saharan African cereal yield of less than half of the other regions.

THE UN MILLENNIUM DEVELOPMENT GOALS

In September 2000 world leaders met at the United Nations Millennium Summit. There they agreed to a set of time-bound, measurable goals for combating extreme poverty. These goals, which came to be known as the Millennium Development Goals (MDGs), provide a framework for the UN system to work together toward a common end. Each of the goals has quantified targets that are to be reached by 2015.

> Goal 1: Eradicate Extreme Poverty and Hunger. The first target is to halve, between 1990 and 2015, the proportion of people living on less than US$1 per day. The second target is to similarly halve, in the same time period, the proportion of people who suffer from hunger.
>
> Goal 2: Achieve Universal Primary Education. Ensure that all children, regardless of sex, will be able to complete a full course of primary schooling.

Goal 3: Promote Gender Equality and Empower Women. Eliminate gender disparity in primary and secondary education, preferably by 2005, and in all levels of education no later than 2015.

Goal 4: Reduce Child Mortality. Reduce by two-thirds, between 1990 and 2015, the under-five mortality rate.

Goal 5: Improve Maternal Health. Reduce by three-quarters, between 1990 and 2015, the maternal mortality ratio.

Goal 6: Combat HIV/AIDS, Malaria, and Other Diseases. Halt and begin to reverse the spread of HIV/AIDS by 2015. Halt and reverse the incidence of malaria and other major diseases by 2015.

Goal 7: Ensure Environmental Sustainability. Integrate the principles of sustainable development into country policies and programs and reverse the loss of environmental resources. Halve, by 2015, the proportion of people without sustainable access to safe drinking water and basic sanitation. Achieve by 2020 a significant improvement in the lives of at least 100 million slum dwellers as measured by the proportion of households with access to secure tenure, that is, a secure environment, including such things as safe housing, access to potable water, etc. (UN-HABITAT).

Goal 8: Global Partnership for Development. Develop further an open, rule-based, predictable, nondiscriminatory trading and financial system. Address the special needs of the least-developed countries (including debt relief and more generous development assistance for countries committed to poverty reduction). Address the special needs of landlocked developing countries and small island states. Deal comprehensively with the debt problems of developing countries through national and international measures in order to make debt sustainable in the long term. Develop and implement, in cooperation with developing countries, strategies for decent and productive work for youth. In cooperation with pharmaceutical companies, provide access to affordable essential drugs in developing countries. In cooperation with the private sector, make available the benefits of new technologies, especially information and communications technology.

The UN MDGs are ambitious yet achievable goals. The world has made significant progress toward many of the goals, yet Africa lags behind. In 2005 developed nations pledged to double aid to Africa. Aid alone, however, may not be sufficient.

THE MILLENNIUM VILLAGE PROJECT

In 2002 United Nations Secretary-General Kofi Annan commissioned the Millennium Project to develop a concrete action plan for the world to meet the Millennium Development Goals. Jeffrey Sachs was chosen to lead the project. In 2005 the project presented its final recommendations to the secretary-general.

At the Earth Institute Sachs developed the idea of the Millennium Villages Project (MVP). The project is an attempt to show how rural African communities can lift themselves out of poverty. Earth Institute scientists and experts work with local communities, national governments, and nongovernmental agencies to provide a proven package of technologies that can improve agricultural production, health, education, and access to markets. As the villages successfully raise themselves out of poverty, the project will work with national governments to scale up the poverty-reducing measures. The UN Millennium Project and the Earth Institute at Columbia University have three main goals in this project:

> to (i) provide rigorous proof of concept for integrated, community-based, low-cost interventions to meet the Millennium Development Goals in rural Africa, (ii) identify mechanisms for national-level scaling up of community-based interventions to support the design of national MDG-based development strategies, and (iii) engage governments and donors in a 10-year scaling-up effort across Africa and other hunger hotspots in Latin America and Asia.[16]

In meeting these goals, the MVP is committed to the principle of community empowerment through participation and leadership in design and implementation.

All interventions are to be based on scientifically proven biophysical and socioeconomic research coupled with local knowledge and implemented within the budget estimates of the Millennium Project—approximately $110 per person per year. The villages are to be built in conjunction with existing community, government, and NGO programs in the area. The MVP will work to strengthen local institutions and build capacity and empowerment at the local level. Beneficiaries must pay for part costs either in cash or in-kind. This will add buy-in capabilities and further increase empowerment.[17]

The project intends for villages to become self-sustaining after five years of involvement. All interventions must include an exit strategy in which local governments take over provision of public services. The project will attempt to scale up services by spreading the advances from village to village, district to district, and finally country to country. The MVP is dedicated to the principle that "bottom-up" approaches can work with "top-down" ones provided they are properly linked. Together they are more productive than the sum of their parts.[18]

In the short term, the Millennium villagers will be living in an environmentally sustainable manner in five years. The project will produce methods and manuals for implementing and scaling up the various activities in the Millennium Villages. The project will train and equip thousands of villagers and government agents with the requisite knowledge and expertise to allow them to train other villages in order to scale up the program and meet the MDGs. In order to facilitate scaling up, there will be three types of Millennium Villages. The Millennium Research Village (or Type 1 Millennium Village) is the core of the project. In these villages interventions will be rigorously monitored and outcomes quantified in order to establish proof of concept. Each village of approximately 5,000 people will serve as a demonstration model for achieving the MDGs. Type I Villages have been established in a variety of agro-ecological zones. Sites for research villages were selected according to a number of criteria. Each selected village had a high prevalence of hunger and deep poverty, generally accompanied by poor health, sanitation, and water. The villages were not connected to electrical, telephone, water, or sewage grids. Each village was located in a stable, reasonably well-governed country with cooperative regimes. Finally, each village was chosen to represent a key representative agro-ecological zone of sub-Saharan Africa. The project selected villages in an attempt to encompass the diversity of not only farming systems but infrastructure, social structure, and environments as well.

Type 2 Millennium Villages will consist of about ten villages surrounding the Type 1 Villages. These "cluster" villages will focus on implementing the communities-based strategies for achieving the MDGs. The goal of the Type 2 Villages will be to integrate village-level interventions across an entire district. These villages will help researchers, governments, and NGOs understand and demonstrate how community-based improvements can be coordinated, implemented, and financed on a larger scale. They also will aid in the understanding of what needs to be provided at the district level. Referral hospitals, transportation infrastructure, power generation, and water treatment facilities potentially could benefit from the economies of scale at the district level. Both types of villages will serve to attract public and private donors by showing practical, results-based, measured, and monitored results at the village and district levels. Finally, the Type 3 Millennium Villages will replicate the successes of the other villages in areas outside of the vicinity of Type 1 and Type 2 Villages. The Millennium Project will support these villages by making training, manuals, and other tools from the core villages available. The project will maintain the emphasis on community-based implementation.

GE AND THE FUNDAMENTALS
OF CORPORATE CITIZENSHIP

In 2002 Jeffrey Immelt, chairman and chief executive officer of GE, appointed GE's first vice president for corporate citizenship. Bob Corcoran, who currently holds the position, stated that a company needs three things in order to be a good corporate citizen: (1) strong economic performance and stakeholder impact; (2) rigorous compliance with fundamental accounting and legal requirements; and (3) going beyond compliance by supporting ethical actions. Sustained economic performance provides benefits to shareholders, employees, and communities. But economic performance must be built upon a foundation of compliance with all financial and legal rules. Corcoran also states that compliance systems and a compliance culture are vital.[19]

As a result, GE audits its suppliers in the developing world to ensure compliance with labor, safety, health, and environmental standards. Through their Company Supplier's Policy, GE employs a team of 430 auditors who assess more than 3,000 suppliers. Suppliers are required to provide employees with a safe and healthy workplace, comply with laws and regulations regarding minimum wages and maximum hours, and comply with local environmental regulations. Further, they must not use forced or compulsory labor, employ child workers, or adversely affect the local environment. While these may not seem like stringent standards, they do establish a base level of citizenship for all companies with which

GE does business. GE has terminated several hundred supplier relationships due to poor performance with regard to these standards. Further,
many other suppliers have addressed problems due to the program.[20]

GE aspires to leadership in four major areas: their ecomagination program, emerging markets, compliance and governance, and environmental
health and safety.[21] Ecomagination refers to the development and marketing of products designed to address pressing environmental issues. GE
recognizes the need to include citizenship in emerging markets from the
first day of business in a community in order to meet the needs and solve
the problems of local communities. Compliance and governance must be
included at all levels of the organization, not merely the financial and
legal departments. Finally, GE's environment, health, and safety (EHS)
system is designed to "establish global standards, promote business leadership, responsibility and accountability for performance."[22]

GE and Africa

GE first became involved in Africa in response to a request from their
African-American Forum (AAF) affinity group to increase the company's
presence in Africa. After careful consideration, executives at GE decided
that the company could not profitably operate in sub-Saharan Africa. It
could, however, become involved as a donor. In October 2004 General
Electric announced a five-year, $20 million initiative to bring improved
health care and infrastructure to hospitals in Africa. GE Healthcare, GE
Energy, GE Infrastructure, and GE Consumer and Industrial pledged to
donate a combination of power generation and health care equipment,
water filtration systems, and appliances to assist African families and
hospitals. The announced goals were to reduce infant mortality rates and
provide cleaner water, wider access to medical treatment, and sustainable
power. The program, known as Project Impact, was piloted in Ghana.

GE saw donation of equipment to hospitals and clinics as a way to improve the region in a strategic and sustainable way. GE laid down several
important ground rules before giving any donations.[23] First, there would
be no cash donations of any kind. Second, large, expensive machines
would not be included in the program. This decision was simply a matter
of GE getting the most bang for their buck. A single highly capable, million dollar MRI machine could only treat a very limited number of patients per year. For the same money a rural clinic could be transformed

into a district hospital that could service 100,000 people. Therefore, simple but effective X-ray, anesthesia, baby warmer, and incubation equipment was donated. Local involvement and ownership are crucial to the project's sustainability. GE worked with local governments, NGOs, and local tribal leaders to ensure their support and buy-in for the initiative. It was vital that beneficiaries be part of the process.

In addition to in-kind donations, GE provided training support to guarantee maximum efficiency. GE combined their technology with training and management skills in an attempt to ensure sustainable service to the communities in Africa. AAF volunteers were selected by GE for individual two- to four-week projects in Africa. Each proposed project had to meet several core requirements. The objectives and outcomes had to be stated along with the skills and competencies required. Additionally, after a site was launched, it was "adopted" by a GE business-based AAF chapter. In doing so, an ongoing relationship was formed between members of the affinity group and community members in Africa. Senior business leaders were engaged to track progress and initiate benchmarking studies.[24]

GE's first projects in Africa were located in Ghana. There, GE transformed a rural clinic into a district hospital. In addition to the equipment donations mentioned above, GE provided a new electrical power system, including emergency power, and a new water system. GE also donated a new critical care monitoring system to Ghana's central teaching hospital, including thirteen monitors and a central desktop station for monitoring cardiothoracic patients. GE also donated two anesthesia/ventilators for surgical teams. By 2006, GE had four sites operating in Ghana with the assistance of AAF sustainability partners. Five additional sites came online and were commissioned in the fourth quarter of 2006.

GE and the Millennium Village Project

While GE leaders were aware of the Millennium Village Project, they believed the goals of the GE initiatives were different from the MVP. GE worked with higher-level hospitals, while the MVP worked at the village level. However, in 2006 the two organizations formed an alliance. The Millennium Village Project began to design their medical system using a hub and spoke model. Each research village would have a village cluster clinic to provide for outpatient care and simple baby deliveries, along with nutrition, dispensary, and family planning needs. A subdistrict hospital would service a number of clusters and provide for simple surgeries and complex deliveries. Additionally, it would be responsible for all inpatient procedures. Finally, complex procedures and scheduled surgeries would be performed at a referral hospital. Through the partnership GE would focus on providing clinics with equipment and upgrading the subdistrict hospitals. GE also would seek out select opportunities for upgrading referral hospitals. By late 2006 GE had begun to deploy equipment in clinics in Sauri, Kenya, and Mayange, Rwanda. In November 2006 GE personnel traveled to Potou, Senegal, and Mwandama, Malawi, in preparation for deployment in those two research villages.

CORPORATE AID VERSUS GOVERNMENT AID

GE has seen immediate successes as a result of its actions in Africa. Given the well-documented difficulties on the continent, why has GE been able to achieve such success in so short a period of time? Corporations often have greater freedom in choosing beneficiaries than governmental agencies or even NGOs (who are beholden to their donors). This freedom allows companies to be more selective in choosing communities in which they can do good. Furthermore, GE was able to bring its well-documented managerial expertise to task in Africa. Nonprofit and governmental employees generally do not have the degree of managerial skills possessed by seasoned business leaders. GE treats its philanthropic efforts like a business. Objective deliverables and a long-term plan are demanded before any product is donated. Obviously, there is a need and a place for government aid to Africa. GE has provided an example of how to effectively spend resources on the continent.

Good Citizenship Is Good Business

How did General Electric come to decide to commit such a large amount to Africa? GE certainly is not the first company that comes to mind when corporate responsibility is discussed. Under Jack Welch GE had a record of compliance and integrity, but he, like many in his generation, tended not to think of a company as having an overt moral duty to take action in this manner. Traditionally, the purpose of a company has been to provide jobs and wealth, to make a profit, to pay taxes, and to obey laws. Social responsibility has generally been left up to the government and individuals. But ideas are changing.

In May 1999 the Environics Institute (now called GlobeScan) conducted the Millennium Poll on Corporate Social Responsibility. Through 25,000 interviews the poll showed dramatic evidence of the shifting ideas consumers have about companies. Two in three respondents wanted companies to go beyond their historic economic goals and contribute to society as well. Furthermore, simply contributing to charities and community projects does not satisfy people's expectations of social accountability. Fully half of the surveyed population claimed to be paying attention to the social behavior of companies, and one in five consumers reported rewarding or punishing companies based on their perception of the companies' social performance. When asked an open-ended question about how they form impressions of companies, consumers most frequently mentioned social responsibilities.[25]

GE CEO Jeffrey Immelt recognized the changing realities. In 2004 virtue was foremost on the list of things he told two hundred corporate officers were necessary for GE to stay on top. As Immelt said in a *Fortune* interview, "The reason people come to work for GE is that they want to be about something that is bigger than themselves. People want to work hard, they want to get promoted, they want stock options. But they also want to work for a company that makes a difference, a company that's doing great things in the world."[26]

Philanthropy and Talent

It has become almost to a cliché to state that a company's most important asset is its employees. But cliché or not, talent recruitment and retention is absolutely vital for a modern high-tech company. Good corporate citizenship and philanthropy can aid greatly in both. According to research done by Walker Information and the Council on Foundations, employees with a favorable impression of their company's giving program are far more likely to remain loyal to their employer. Furthermore, they are much more likely to feel a strong personal attachment to their firm and to think of their company's problems as their own. Additionally, they are twice as likely to recommend the company as a place to work. Finally, employees who rate their company's corporate citizenship high are 23 percent more likely to intend on staying with the firm.[27] Given the high costs of recruit-ment and training, many donor programs might actually save companies money. This is especially the case for a high-tech firm.

Corporate Citizenship and Marketing

Charitable giving can increase exposure and enhance a company's image in the eyes of consumers, and image enhancement can lead to greater sales. Furthermore, a company with a well-established record of reputa-ble dealings is less likely to be punished by consumers for mistakes. A firm also can increase sales by linking a product or service to a well-respected charity or organization that also provides access to a new mar-ket. Strategic alliances between for-profit and not-for-profit corporations abound in the marketplace.

Corporate Citizenship and New Product Development

When developing low-cost products intended for donation to Africa, GE was able to develop technology that was potentially profitable in other markets. For example, while Africans could not afford the low-cost ultra-sound equipment at any price, it is possible to sell such devices in China and India. A more telling example is GE's billion dollar ecomagination initiative designed to create environmentally friendly technology. GE is not spending money on this program out of selflessness. Clearly, the lead-ers at GE believe that there is much money to be made in environmentally friendly products and services. The firm has become active in the debate on climate change, even going so far as to lobby the U.S. government to crack down on carbon emissions. Is this the right thing to do morally? Very likely it is. Yet GE produces emission-free nuclear plants and has in-vested heavily in wind technology. Clearly, GE sees a curb on emissions as being in its own best interests financially as well.

Altruism and the Corporation

Much of corporate giving can be seen as enlightened self-interest. The cynic might take this to imply that there is no true corporate altruism. When considering this, it is vital to keep in mind that companies have no motivations of their own. After all, they are merely legal entities—but they are run by human beings. Corporations are collections of men and women who have joined together to accomplish something that they could not achieve on their own. Corporate culture is created by thinking, feeling people. Clearly some people in the corporate world are deeply committed to personal values, but while good citizenship can be good business, it is not always so.

An argument could easily be made that many of GE's recent initiatives are in their own self-interest. And such an argument would contain a great deal of truth. Yet the fact remains that it was a change in leadership that prompted the increase in General Electric's philanthropy. Certainly GE benefits to some degree from good corporate citizenship, but the firm did not face any definite requirements to go as far as it has. Starbucks and Costco are both willing to accept a lower return on investment in order to provide their part-time employees with the option for full medical coverage. Their direct competitors generally do not offer this benefit, yet they still are able to attract employees. Why, then, do Starbucks and Costco adhere to his policy? Because the founder of each company is deeply committed to the well-being of his employees.

Do Motives Matter?

We can conclude, then, that some companies might practice good corporate citizenship for purely self-interested, economic reasons, while others may be deeply committed to a set of positive values. The obvious question raised is, Does the motive matter? Should a company that gives for purely self-interested reasons be valued any lower than a truly selfless one? Complicating the question is the difficulty in determining motives on both the individual and corporate levels. A biochemist may choose to work in a pharmaceutical company both because his income is higher than it would be in academia and because he wants to work on life-saving drugs. Are his motives pragmatic or altruistic? Similarly, GE may be choosing to research low-carbon power generation because its leaders believe that it is the right thing to do and because they see the opportunity for financial profit.

However, for the sake of argument, let us suppose that motives can be divined. Do we care about a company's intentions or its actions? As long as a company is benefiting its community, should we even ask about motives? Motives may matter largely because they are a predictor of future behavior. If a company is providing for its employees solely because it needs to in order to retain them, then if the labor market changes the company may well discontinue the benefits. Similarly, if a company practices good environmental stewardship simply to enhance its image, can it be trusted when no one is looking? Possibly not, but if the same company was motivated by sincere values, then regulation and observation are unlikely to be necessary.

On the other hand, sometimes doing the right thing for the wrong reason can lead to the greater good. People who feel pressured to volunteer often find great fulfillment in helping others. Furthermore, if given the choice between a company creating positive change for a selfish reason and a well-intentioned firm causing harm, would not virtually everyone opt for the former? If so, then it seems that actions matter more than motives. In the end, many people might say, "I do not care why they did the right thing, just that they did it." Yet if actions matter more than motives, why are we so concerned with motives when companies do harm? If a drug company rushes a product to market that causes untimely deaths, the public is deeply interested in motive. If the drug was a cancer drug fast-tracked in an attempt to save lives, people tend not to blame the company. On the other hand, if the reason for the rush is perceived as financial, the company will be pilloried.

Motive matters legally as well. Punitive damages are awarded on the basis of motive in many civil cases. To be guilty of most crimes the perpetrator must have committed the criminal act (the *actus reus*) with criminal intent (*mens rea*)—that is, with malevolent motives. The very terms *corporate malfeasance* and *corporate wrongdoing* imply a malicious motive. Motives are no easier to detect with regard to negative corporate behavior than they are for positive behavior. Yet in the former case, the motives seem vital. It seems paradoxical that we should care so much about motive in cases of malfeasance if we do not in cases of philanthropy. In the end, the initial question has no easy answer. Most people want companies to be a positive force in the world. It would seem to be preferable, though perhaps not necessary, for companies to be motivated by positive values rather than merely pragmatism.

CONCLUSION

Abject poverty remains endemic to sub-Saharan Africa despite a decline in poverty elsewhere in every other region of the world. The causes are myriad: low productivity in agriculture, high transportation costs, massive disease, and adverse geopolitics. Together these elements add up to a poverty trap from which Africans cannot escape without outside assistance. The Millennium Village Project has sought a means of breaking the trap and allowing rural Africans to pull themselves up out of poverty. In order to do so, rural Africans and the MVP need contributions from the developed world. Corporations like General Electric may be the best suited to provide much of the needed help. Together with NGOs and local governments, GE has been able to make positive changes in Africa that far exceed the value of the money invested. In doing so, GE's leaders have helped more than the people of Africa. They have improved the lives of their own employees and strengthened their company.

NOTES

1. See http://hdr.undp.org/en/media/hdr06-complete.pdf.

2. See http://www.un.org/special-rep/ohrlls/ldc/ldc%20criteria.htm.

3. See http://web.worldbank.org/WBSITE/EXTERNAL/TOPICS/EXT POVERTY/0,,contentMDK:20195240~pagePK:148956~piPK:216618~theSiteP K:336992,00.html.

4. Ibid.

5. Gordon McCord, Jeffrey Sachs, and Wing Thye Woo, "Understanding African Poverty: Beyond the Washington Consensus to the Millennium Development Goals Approach," in *Africa in the World Economy: The National, Regional and International Challenges,* ed. Jan Joost Teunissen and Age Akkerman (The Hague: FONDAD, 2005), 5.

6. Jeffrey Sachs et al., "Ending Africa's Poverty Trap," *Brookings Papers on Economic Activity* 1 (2004): 130–31.

7. Ibid., 133.

8. Adam Smith, *The Wealth of Nations* (1776; New York: Modern Library, 1985), book I, chap. 3, para. 8.

9. Sachs, "Ending Africa's Poverty Trap," 131–32.

10. McCord, Sachs, and Woo, "Understanding African Poverty," 28.

11. Jeffrey Sachs, "The End of Poverty," *Time,* March 14, 2005, 49.

12. UNAIDS, *UN Report on Global AIDS Epidemic* (New York: United Nations, 2006), 17, http://www.unaids.org/en/KnowledgeCentre/HIVData/GlobalReport/default.asp.

13. WHO Fact Sheet no. 104, revised March 2007, http://www.who.int/mediacentre/factsheets/fs104/en/.

14. *Prevention and Control of Schistosomiasis and Soil-Transmitted Helminthiasis,* WHO Technical Report Series 912 (Geneva: WHO, 2002).

15. "Malaria in Africa," Roll Back Malaria Website, http://www.rbm.who.int/cmc_upload/0/000/015/370/RBMInfosheet_3.htm.

16. See http://unmalawi.org/reports/m_village_scalling.pdf and http://www.millenniumvillages.org/progress/index.htm.

17. Ibid.

18. Ibid.

19. Bob Corcoran, interview with the author, November 2006.

20. See http://www.ge.com/company/citizenship/suppliers/index.html.

21. Bob Corcoran, "On Human Rights: A Letter from Bob Corcoran, GE Vice President of Corporate Citizenship," http://www.ge.com/files/usa/citizenship/pdf/GE_2006_citizen_bcorcoran.pdf.

22. Ibid.

23. Bob Corcoran, interview with the author, November 2006.

24. Jeffrey Immelt, "Putting GE's Resources to Work in Africa," *CECP New Century Philanthropy* (Fall 2006): 8.

25. The poll discussed here is available at http://www.iblf.org/docs/MillenniumPoll.pdf.

26. Marc Gunther, "Money and Morals at GE," *Fortune,* November 1, 2004, 1.

27. See http://www.measuringphilanthropy.com/us_studies/docs/nat_study_ employee.pdf.

CHAPTER 17

From Being Apart to Being Partners

The Experience of Barloworld

Daniel Malan

BEING APART

In 1871 a gentleman by the name of Cecil John Rhodes arrived at the South African diamond fields. He acquired a few claims for himself and then started to buy up the claims of those who failed around him. Slowly he built an empire that today still dominates the world diamond industry in the form of De Beers. At the time, Rhodes established the British South African Company and started a process of moving northwards into Africa in order to "extend the sphere of influence" of the British government. This process received the blessing of Her Majesty's government and was supported by the British South African Company's own army, police force, and flag. The logo of the company displayed its motto: "Justice, Commerce, Freedom."

"Commerce" was certainly appropriate—Rhodes traded effectively and became a very rich man. He also found time to become prime minister of the Cape Colony and openly declared that he required this political position in order to speed up the process of extending the sphere of influence of His Majesty's government. Certainly one cannot criticize him for a lack of transparency! Perhaps a bit more problematic are the "Justice" and "Freedom" components of the motto. In Rhodes's own words: "Africa awaits us . . . it is our duty to seize every opportunity of acquiring more territory . . . [that] means more of the Anglo-Saxon race . . . the most human, most honorable race the world possesses."[1] Some would argue that the treaties that were signed with local communities depended more on deceit than justice, in particular the one that resulted in the acquisition of the land that was later named after Rhodes himself—Rhodesia (today Zimbabwe).

The company that was founded by Rhodes—De Beers—is a well-respected company today, along with many other large local companies and subsidiaries of multinational corporations. Many of these companies are listed on the South African stock exchange (JSE Limited), the fifteenth largest stock exchange in the world. The JSE established a Socially Responsible Investment (SRI) Index in 2004 to identify listed companies that have integrated the principles of the triple bottom line into their business activities. Through a voluntary process, listed companies can apply to be assessed for inclusion on the Index based on their governance and social, environmental, and economic performance. In 2006, 58 companies were included on the Index out of a total of 62 participating companies (in 2005 and 2004 respectively, 49 out of 58 and 51 out of 74 participating companies were successful in their bid to be included in the Index).[2] However, many companies today are still dealing—indirectly—with the legacy of Cecil John Rhodes. This could perhaps be attributed to two reasons: the perception that whites still control the South African economy, and the fact that the South African economy is by far the dominant one on the African continent.

First, despite many attempts by the private sector to transform itself, in part supported by governmental interventions[3] in terms of black economic empowerment, the face of corporate South Africa remains relatively white. This is exacerbated by the fact that many companies require their black managers to remain in South Africa to fulfill employment equity targets; therefore, expatriates in other parts of Africa are predominantly white (and male). Second, the dominance of the South African economy has resulted in some resentment of South Africa and—in particular—of South African companies in the rest of Africa. Figure 1 portrays the sizes of the ten biggest economies in Africa, clearly illustrating the dominance of the South African economy.

This chapter examines the historical case study of one company—Barloworld—that dealt effectively with many of these challenges several years ago. It is presented as an example of a success story, one from which

Figure 17.1 Top Ten Economies in Africa

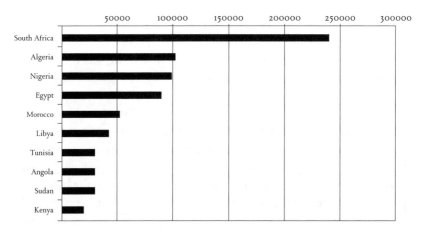

Source: World Development Indicators Database, World Bank, July 1, 2006.

many companies today may be able to learn. Ironically, the same company recently has been shrouded in controversy for its perceived lack of transformation. This serves as an important reminder that dealing with these issues remains an ongoing challenge for any company operating in the complex South African environment.

CITIZENS, COLONIALISTS, TOURISTS, AND ACTIVISTS

In a previous article[4] I outlined the following descriptions to define the relationships between the social and political roles that multinational corporations (MNCs) can fulfill in host countries (see figure 2).

Corporate citizens are viewed as responsible corporations who want to make a real and lasting contribution to the countries and communities within which they operate; they are sustainable corporations with a commitment to social responsibility as well as environmental integrity. Corporate citizens are defined by Michael Hopkins as companies who are "concerned with treating the stakeholders of the firm ethically or in a socially responsible manner." Hopkins further states that "the aim of social responsibility is to create higher and higher standards of living, while preserving the profitability of the corporation, for its stakeholders both within and outside the corporation."[5] Corporate citizens have high levels of social involvement but avoid involvement in the political process. Their intention is to profit from new markets, but they enter into such markets with a sense of humility and respect for local customs, traditions, and even competitors.

Corporate colonialists follow strategies similar to the doctrine of economic colonialism—that is, acquiring "colonies" or regions as a source of profit, without any real regard for the well-being of those regions. Economic colonialism has been defined as an attempt "to control another nation's economy. States can directly exert influence through economic policy and economic aid; however, economic colonialism may be most effective when applied indirectly through multinational corporations that invest in the key industries of targeted nations."[6] One of the best examples of economic colonialism is the approach of Cecil John Rhodes, as described above.

Figure 17.2   Social and Political Roles of Corporations

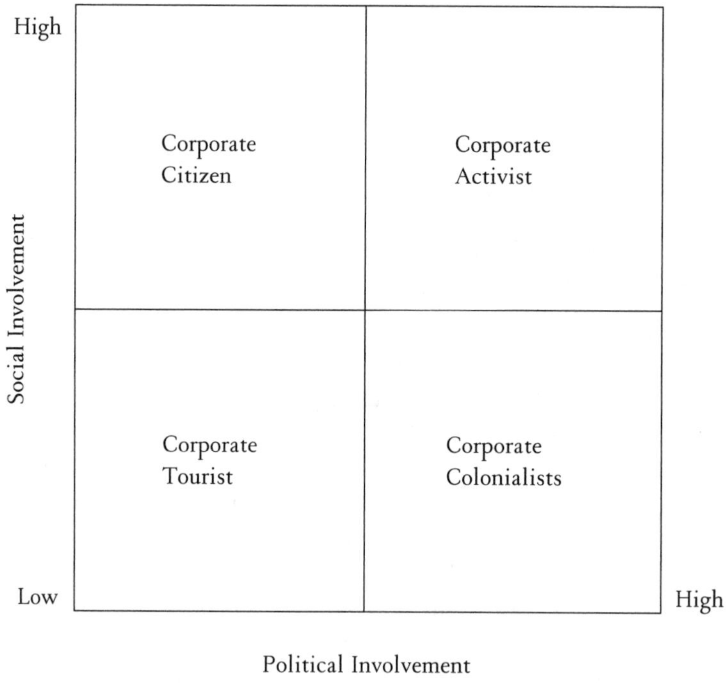

Source: Daniel Malan, "Corporate Citizens, Colonialists, Tourists or Activists? Ethical Challenges Facing South African Corporations in Africa," *Journal of Corporate Citizenship* 18 (Summer 2005): figure 4.

Corporate tourists are companies that establish a quiet presence in host countries without much social or political involvement. This approach could be the result of a specific conservative strategy to ensure an easy exit if things go wrong or a result of a lack of strategy altogether. Either way, the position resembles that of a tourist who is there to look around and stay awhile but can easily pack his or her bags at the slightest hint of trouble.

Corporate activists have the most problematic position on the grid. This is illustrated by the fact that the concept of an "activist" evokes both positive and negative emotions, depending on the audience. Actively participating in both the social and political components of a host country seems problematic, and the gut reaction to this type of participation is negative: the rule of thumb seems to be that corporations should become involved at the social level but should refrain from playing a political role. One of the interesting historical examples of a corporate activist has been Body Shop International, which has played an active roll in support of a range of political and social issues, including human rights and animal testing campaigns.

INTEGRATED SOCIAL CONTRACTS

One way for companies to make sense of these complexities is through the application of Integrated Social Contracts Theory (ISCT), as developed by Tom Donaldson and Thomas Dunfee.[7] This theory is particularly suited to provide guidance on ethical issues in international business (including social and political activities of corporations) and in essence suggests the following:

- There is an absolute moral threshold (so-called hyper norms) that apply anywhere in the world.
- Large corporations should have respect for local customs and traditions without transgressing this moral threshold.
- Context matters when deciding between right and wrong. Although this might seem like a relativist escape clause, it highlights the fact that there are ethical decisions in the complex global marketplace that are rarely easy to make. If applied in conjunction with respect for hyper norms and local customs, it does not lead to relativism.

ISCT has been described as a position that lies midway on the spectrum of moral belief, separating relativism from absolutism.[8] This approach assumes that there is something called "moral free space" where stakeholders—for example, South African corporations and their host countries and communities—can negotiate micro social contracts that would determine what should be regarded as ethical and unethical behavior. One of the consequences of "moral free space" is that sometimes two conflicting conceptions of ethics can both be valid, depending on the situation. Therefore, if there is no absolute right or wrong (absolutism), and if relativism is to be avoided, what is the solution? ISCT combines two types of contract theory: micro contracts can be negotiated between or within specific groups or communities, while a universal macro contract ensures a level of consistency in the sense of providing the absolute moral threshold mentioned earlier. According to Donaldson and Dunfee, this approach holds fundamental truths to be relevant while allowing for legitimate differences within business communities and between historical theories. It also avoids the difficulty of the vagueness of macro contracts while at the same time avoiding the problem that a micro contract may be morally out of bounds, for example, when a local community comes together and develops a contract that excludes members of a certain race or religion from that particular community.[9]

Using the same thought experiment as the traditional social contract arguments of Locke, Rousseau, Hobbes, and Rawls, the question posed by Donaldson and Dunfee focuses on how economic participants define business ethics, rather than the classical question of what citizens require of the government and how they define political justice. The experiment assumes a group of imaginary contractors who are rational and knowledgeable. Departing from the classical social contract, Donaldson and Dunfee do not assume that these contractors are ignorant of all facts about themselves—they (the contractors) simply do not know in what economic communities they are members, and they do not know their own level of personal wealth. It also is assumed that the contractors have an underlying sense of right and wrong instilled in them from their upbringing. It is argued that these imaginary contractors will soon confront the fact that it is impossible to obtain consensus on a *single* morality as the framework for global economic ethics. The question then remains: How will they find a basis for agreement? Donaldson and Dunfee argue that the following core assumptions will be accepted by all contractors:

All humans are constrained by bounded moral rationality—that is, humans are constrained by physical and psychological limits. They make mistakes, and existing ethical theories are not always sufficient to resolve difficult ethical dilemmas.

Higher-quality and more efficient economic interactions are preferable to lower-quality and less-efficient economic interactions.

All things being equal, economic activity that is consistent with the cultural, philosophical, or religious attitudes of economic actors is preferable to economic activity that is not. [10]

Given these assumptions, Donaldson and Dunfee argue that the hypothetical contractors will agree on the following macro social contract as the minimum terms for economic ethics:

Local economic communities have moral free space in which they may generate ethical norms for their members through micro social contracts.

Micro social contracts must be grounded in consent; individual members should have the right to exit. For example, a disgruntled employee who objects to a corporation's human rights policies in developing countries has the right to resign and find employment elsewhere. [11]

In order to become obligatory (legitimate), micro social contracts must be compatible with hyper norms.

In cases of conflicts among norms, priority must be established through the application of rules consistent with the spirit and letter of the macro social contract.

Hyper norms are defined as "key limits on moral free space," constituting principles so fundamental that they are discoverable in a "convergence of religious, political and philosophical thought." [12] Donaldson and Dunfee identify three categories of hyper norms: structural (for example, the duty to develop and fulfill obligations in connection with social structures that are efficient in achieving social goods), procedural (for example, rights of voice and exit), and substantive (for example, promise keeping and respect for human dignity). Evidence in support of hyper norm status includes widespread consensus that a principle is universal, the principle in question is a component of a well-known global industry standard or supported by major NGOs, or the principle is known to be consistent with major religions or philosophies and supported by the laws of many different countries.[13] Using international bribery as an example, Donaldson and Dunfee demonstrate the process of identifying hyper norms:

> A manager for an airplane manufacturer makes/is considering a payment of $5 million to go personally to the Minister of Defence of a developing country to "win" a contract for jet fighters.
>
> It is not necessary to identify the full range of hyper norms applicable to all forms of bribery. The question instead is whether a hyper norm applies to this particularly egregious form of the practice. Transparency International, the OECD, the OAS, the Caux Principles, laws in numerous countries . . . leaders of major accounting firms . . . major religions . . . and major philosophies all support a presumption that this practice violates a hyper norm.[14]

Finally, in applying ISCT to the ethical decision-making process, the following steps should be followed:

- Identify all the relevant stakeholders
- Identify the relevant hyper norms (there is not a definitive list of hyper norms—the quest for such a list would resemble an absolutist approach)
- Determine that the key norms are *authentic*—that is, there must be evidence that the norms are supported by a clear majority
- Determine that the authentic norms are *legitimate*—that is, not in conflict with any hyper norm
- Resolve conflicts if and when they arise through rules consistent with the spirit and letter of the macro social contract

BARLOWORLD

Barloworld is a diversified industrial company that was founded in South Africa in 1902. The company manufactures, markets, and distributes products and services and markets and distributes leading international brands on behalf of principals (including Caterpillar and Daimler-Chrysler). It is also a licensee for Avis in southern Africa, Sweden, Denmark, and Norway. During 2006 the company had operations in thirty-one countries around the world, with approximately 50 percent of its 25,000 employees working in South Africa.

The company subscribes to a philosophy of value-based management (VBM), which provides a behavioral framework for employees and the company. According to the Barloworld Website, the company is striving to sustainably create value for all its stakeholders, which are identified as shareholders, customers, principals and suppliers, employees, and the communities and environment within which the company operates: "The implementation of VBM is a key driver of increased cash flow, profit and value creation. VBM makes every management team within Barloworld focus on creating value for all our stakeholders and is a long-term strategic program. The benefits of the many VBM-driven initiatives within the organization will continue to grow value as we expand our asset base."[15]

THE MIDDELBURG FORUM

This chapter focuses on the experience of one of Barloworld's subsidiaries, Middelburg Steel and Alloys (MSA), in the late 1980s. The interpretation of events has been provided by Mark Drewell, currently a Barloworld group executive and at the time the public affairs manager at MSA.

During the mid- to late 1980s South Africa was going through a sustained period of violent repression by the Nationalist Party government under the leadership of President P. W. Botha. The result was increasing resistance from the African National Congress–led Mass Democratic Movement. The African National Congress (ANC) was still a banned organization and severe apartheid laws were in effect, for example, laws prohibiting interracial marriages and the existence of separate "group areas" for different races The Mass Democratic Movement was comprised of a combination of nonprofit organizations, community-based organizations, and coalitions such as the United Democratic Front, trade unions such as the Congress of South African Trade Unions (Cosatu), and underground members of the ANC. Consumer boycotts and worker protests were commonplace, international sanctions were in place, and the government found itself in an increasingly isolated situation. The town of Middelburg was run by a Conservative Party council—a party to the right of the National Party on the South African political spectrum. The

Conservative Party wanted to reintroduce even the petty apartheid laws that had been repealed, albeit reluctantly, by the National Party. The town was crippled by a lights and water boycott in the black township of Mhluzi, where the council had switched off the lights and turned off the water as a result of nonpayment for these services. As was the case in the rest of South Africa at the time, intimidation and killings were not unusual on a day-to-day basis.

It was within this complex and difficult context that Middelburg Steel and Alloys had to conduct its business. Regardless of how it responded to the moral issues surrounding apartheid, it was facing a real business problem. The high number of political stay-aways—that is, employees refusing to work in order to make a political statement—meant that the company was no longer in a position to produce sufficient quantities of their product. It was on the verge of losing a major Japanese customer, who would simply go somewhere else if MSA could not deliver on their contractual obligations.

At the time, MSA had a Barloworld Group Code of Employment Practice in place. The company had integrated its facilities, and specific programs were in place to ensure improved opportunities for black staff. The company had an excellent human resources system in place and a supportive workforce; yet the external conditions threatened the continued existence of the company. MSA decided to convene a community forum, which transformed the nature of the company and the conservative town of Middelburg.

The establishment of the Middelburg Forum was not without its problems. All stakeholders had their own problems to contend with: the white council was in financial trouble as a result of nonpayment for services; the black councillors from the township did not have any legitimacy in their own community; the comrades (a term for activists within the Mass Democratic Movement) were facing intimidation and threats from the security forces; and the trade union leaders were branded as sellouts by many comrades as a result of their participation in the Forum. To break the deadlock, MSA offered to pay the money owed by the township to the council if all parties agreed to talk. This strategy proved successful, and when the lights were switched on all parties agreed to meet. According to Mark Drewell, however, the first meeting of this fragile alliance lasted only a few minutes before some of the participants walked out.[16] Tensions were running high, and at a subsequent meeting some participants refused to drink tea while their comrades were starving in the township. As the facilitator of the Middelburg Forum, MSA applied the theory of Spiral Dynamics, which is described by its originator as one that "reveals the hidden complexity codes that shape human nature, create global diversities, and drive evolutionary change. These dynamic Spiral forces attract and repel individuals, form the webs and meshes that connect people within groups, communities and organizations, and forge the rise and fall of nations and cultures."[17] The results were phenomenal. Over time, people joined hands and started transforming the town. Businesses across the board became involved in the donation of materials and skills to establish crèches and libraries, while local people in the townships donated their labor. People from the white community of Middelburg visited the township to clean up and repair damaged sanitation facilities. The establishment of small black-owned businesses was encouraged and supported, and over time the violence and aggression came to an end.

The impact of the Middelburg Forum and the successful way in which it managed to bring opposing parties together to solve problems were noticed elsewhere. In the words of Mark Drewell,

> It was during a full meeting of councillors, church leaders, business leaders and comrades from the township that we heard a knock on the door, and in walked Anglican Archbishop Desmond Tutu. We were obviously surprised, but he asked us to carry on while he sat at the back and listened. Later, he asked if he could say a few words. He started with a prayer and then said that if what was happening in Middelburg could be repeated throughout the country, then South Africa would have a great future ahead of it.[18]

This sentiment was echoed by John Gommersal, at the time the managing director of MSA, who said, "If harmony, success and incredible growth is possible within an equal opportunity company such as Middelburg Steel and Alloys, why can't it be extended to the town, region and country as a whole?"[19] Eventually, the Middelburg Forum became the blue print for the South African National Peace Accord. The National Peace Accord was signed on September 14, 1991, by twenty-six organizations and political parties, who all committed themselves to the promotion of "peace, harmony and prosperity in violence-stricken communities."

LESSONS FROM THE MIDDELBURG FORUM CASE

Today, the Middelburg Forum and our interpretation of the events should be considered within their proper historical context. However, there are important lessons relating to the issues raised earlier in this chapter. The Middelburg Forum is an excellent example of a micro contract between different stakeholders. The participants in this contract made their own rules at a *local* level while adhering to a set of hyper norms (respect for the individual, commitment to "a better town for all," etc.). The identification of stakeholders, and agreement amongst the stakeholders on hyper norms that were both authentic and legitimate, provide a classical example of how micro contracts can be negotiated and implemented.

Middelburg Steel and Alloys—and by extension Barloworld—also displayed all the characteristics of a corporate activist. The company deliberately disobeyed some of the immoral apartheid laws in place at the time and made a conscious decision to get involved in the political process. Although there were commercial benefits to be enjoyed as a result of this involvement, it is reasonably clear that at least some of these decisions and actions were based purely on moral grounds. Finally, the case study provides a very good example of the power of effective stakeholder engagement. It is reasonable to believe that the political views of MSA and Barloworld did not coincide with either the conservative town council or those of the comrades in the townships. Yet the company was able to identify the key stakeholders and was willing to step in and facilitate a process that could lead to real solutions without merely highlighting the problems.

CONCLUSION

Ironically, Barloworld received a lot of bad press early in 2007. Criticism was leveled against the company by the South African Public Investment Corporation (PIC) for its lack of transformation and its lack of black executive directors. Subsequently, the company announced the appointment of its first black executive director, Isaac Shongwe. Its chairman, Warren Clewlow, also announced his resignation after corporate governance concerns were raised about his independence. Clewlow's son-in-law was appointed as the company's CEO.

Recent events highlight the fact that no organization is immune to criticism and that earlier success stories do not necessarily guarantee continued success in different time frames or contexts. Thirteen years after the first democratic elections in South Africa, large corporations are facing new challenges, although many of these challenges still relate to an inability to deal with issues from the past. At the same time, current problems should not take anything away from the fact that Barloworld played a critical role in the transition to democracy in South Africa. It is clear that self-interest played an important role in the actions taken by the company—almost twenty years after the fact, it is difficult to determine whether moral outrage at apartheid or the threat of losing a lucrative Japanese contract was the more important factor in the establishment of the Middelburg Forum. Regardless, the Forum remains an excellent example of an innovative partnership and one that organizations can learn from today. The issues and the context may be different, but the model remains robust and relevant.

Today, every MNC faces challenges that are not unlike those faced by Barloworld in South Africa in the late 1980s. Instead of moral outrage about apartheid, however, there are new concerns about issues such as the spread of HIV/AIDS, growing inequality, international terrorism, and climate change. Instead of comrades in the townships, there are activists who protest—often violently—on the streets of major cities around the world. The South African experience clearly demonstrates that banning dissident voices and trying to suppress popular opinion with violence are recipes for disaster. Partnerships and dialogue between opposing parties are the most effective solutions, and micro contracts, activism, and stakeholder engagement are the critical factors that will determine long-term success.

NOTES

1. A. Davidson, *Cecil Rhodes and His Time* (Pretoria: Protea Book House, 2003), 9.

2. More information is available at http://www.jse.co.za/sri.

3. Examples include the Employment Equity Act (55 of 1998) and the Broad-Based Black Economic Empowerment Act (53 of 2003), as well as the Codes of Good Practice on Broad-Based Black Economic Empowerment. These documents and more information can be found at http://www.gov.za.

4. Daniel Malan, "Corporate Citizens, Colonialists, Tourists or Activists? Ethical Challenges Facing South African Corporations in Africa," *Journal of Corporate Citizenship* 18 (Summer 2005): 49–60. The next two sections contain extracts from the original article.

5. Michael Hopkins, "A Planetary Bargain and the Bottom Line: Corporate Citizenship, Financial Performance and Staying Power," ILO Enterprise Forum (Geneva: ILO, 1999).

6. See http://encyclopedia.thefreedictionary.com/Economic%20 colonialism.

7. T. Donaldson and T. Dunfee, *Ties that Bind: A Social Contracts Approach to Business Ethics* (Boston: Harvard Business School Press, 1999).

8. Ibid. Donaldson and Dunfee describe the full spectrum as ranging from extreme relativism through cultural relativism, pluralism (ISCT), and modified universalism to extreme universalism (absolutism).

9. Donaldson and Dunfee, "Ties that Bind."

10. Ibid., 46.

11. Given high levels of unemployment in both developed and developing countries, this right is clearly more complicated than it appears initially. Especially in developing countries, employees are quite often in a position where they have many dependents and no job security. It would, therefore, be extremely idealistic to expect them to resign from a job for moral reasons when they know they are unlikely to find alternative employment.

12. Ibid., 49, 50.

13. Ibid., 60.

14. Ibid., 61.

15. More information can be accessed on the company Website, http://www.barloworld.co.za.

16. Mark Drewell, interview with the author, Johannesburg, January 29, 2007.

17. More information can be found at http://www.spiraldynamics.net.

18. Drewell, interview.

19. Ibid.

CHAPTER 18

Occidental Petroleum, Cerrejón, and NGO Partnerships in Colombia

Lessons Learned

Alexandra Guáqueta

INTRODUCTION

One theme in the ongoing debate about the role of business in the new global setting is whether multinational corporations (MNCs) can act as a source of positive influence in weak governance zones. In other words, can MNCs conduct operations in ways that promote democracy and human rights, that do not exacerbate armed conflict, and that support sustainable peace? Companies may be committed to good behavior, but this does not necessarily mean engaging actively in such a complex and politicized terrain. What drives companies to expand the scope of their corporate social responsibility mandates so as to address conflict and peace issues in a constructive manner? What does it mean in practical terms for business to engage in peace-related activities? What can NGOs and others do to encourage companies to be conflict-sensitive?

This chapter explores these issues by reflecting on the preliminary findings from the implementation of a human rights, conflict-sensitive corporate code of conduct, the 2000 Voluntary Principles on Security and Human Rights (VPs). In 2005 Fundación Ideas para la Paz (FIP), a Bogotá-based think tank looking at conflict and peace issues in Colombia, agreed to help Occidental Petroleum and Cerrejón, the largest open pit coal mine in Latin America and owned by

BHP Billiton, Anglo American, and X-strata, implement the VPs under the condition that lessons learned could be shared publicly.

During 2005 and 2006 FIP and the companies carried out various activities, including the piloting and testing of a VPs-compatible risk and impact assessment methodology, the Conflict Sensitive Business Practice (CSBP). CSBP is a guide for extractive businesses that was developed by International Alert (hereafter referred to as Alert), a London-based peace-building NGO involved in the VPs process.[1] While the codes of conduct and most actors involved in the projects were global, the exercise was mainly local. Thus, the story and findings presented here add a special dimension to the analysis: the necessity of building bridges between international and domestic settings as a key element in promoting Peace through Commerce.

At the time of the collaborative work between FIP, Alert, and the companies, Colombia's forty-year-old conflict posed vexing challenges for business. Public disenchantment with past peace processes and growing perceptions of local illegal armed groups being greed-driven had tilted the balance in favor of using more stick and less carrot in ending the conflict. This allowed President Álvaro Uribe, who proposed tougher security measures, to be elected in 2002 and re-elected in 2006. His government launched, with help from the United States, an unprecedented military offensive against the left-wing Marxist guerrilla group FARC (Revolutionary Armed Forces of Colombia), which had expanded considerably by resorting to extortion, kidnapping, and drug money. The ELN (National Liberation Army), a smaller rebel organization, already had suffered important losses to right-wing illegal armed forces, the so-called paramilitary, and was considering holding peace talks. However, it still continued to carry out attacks, illegal fundraising, and political work in rural areas. The armed confrontation between state forces, rebels, and illegal paramilitary groups had displaced over one million people in recent years, who were now in need of humanitarian attention and jobs. The internally displaced were not the only ones seeking help. Military pressure on guerrillas and the general deterioration of the conflict had driven more than 11,000 rebels out of their groups, and they, too, sought state help in the form of reintegration packages. In addition, the Uribe government had convinced paramilitary groups, totaling about 30,000 combatants, to demobilize, and their reintegration had become a national priority. Society, however, was divided on whether to help with this process. The armed group was notorious for perpetrating brutal massacres, for directly running a good part of the drug business, for engaging in widespread extortion, for manipulating local politics, and for having ties with public security forces. Uribe's peace offer, the 2005 Justice and Peace Law, was thus seen as extremely lenient. Besides, there was increasing evidence that many were betraying the agreements and re-organizing as criminal networks. All this had attracted unusual international attention, and the international community was strongly divided as to whether they should support Uribe's policies or not. U.S. backing of Colombia's own "war on terror" only politicized the issue further.

The remainder of this chapter is divided into three parts. The first part provides nonspecialists with a brief background of the VPs and the CSBP risk and impact assessment tools. The second section describes some of the activities carried out by the companies, FIP, and Alert to implement the VPs and to introduce CSBP. The third section presents the preliminary findings of the project. It identifies the incentives that drove companies to work on these issues through collaboration with FIP and Alert and discusses the challenges of changing corporate ideas and behavior.

THE TOOLS AND THEIR PURPOSE

The Voluntary Principles on Security and Human Rights

In December 2000, after a long year of arduous discussions, some of the major multinational oil and mining companies; Amnesty International, Human Rights Watch, and other NGOs with global reach; and the U.S. and UK governments committed to the VPs.[2] The code of conduct was a response to various predicaments. Companies with operations in countries with authoritarian regimes or affected by armed conflict, poverty, and deep social tensions—the so-called weak governance zones—faced violent attacks and kidnappings, social investment with little impact, difficult relations with corrupt public officials and with military forces involved in human rights violations, tensions with local communities, and even massive protests. By operating under such circumstances, companies had become easy targets for northern-based advocacy NGOs, who maintained that investments were only fuelling poverty, corruption, and violence. NGOs sought divestment, compensation, or substantial changes in

corporate conduct, and their strategies included the publication of reports harmful to companies' reputations and financial integrity as well as
helping local victims sue the MNCs in U.S. and European courts.[3] Corporate bad press, on the other hand, had placed home governments in an un-
comfortable situation. They, too, were under the limelight, criticized by
NGOs for benefiting from oil production at the expense of human rights
and for undermining democratic foreign policy goals.

This was how the VPs emerged after the mid-1990s scandals involving
BP, Shell, Occidental Petroleum (Oxy) and others in Nigeria, Colombia,
and Indonesia.[4] Companies, NGOs, and home governments reached basic
understandings on the need for oil revenues to achieve development, a
role for business in promoting human rights, and companies' right to
protect themselves as long as they observed international human rights
norms and certain best practices in managing security and political risks.
The text of the VPs identifies such best practices in the form of recommendations on how to conduct risk and impact analyses and how to
manage relations with public and private security forces on the ground.
Concerning the former, the code asks companies to assess the direct and
indirect effects of their operations, including their security policies, on
existing or potential conflicts and human rights; to consult a wide range
of sources to better understand conflict dynamics; and to consider the
ability of local authorities to enforce the law. Concerning the latter, they
encourage closer monitoring of money and equipment provided to the security forces; better due diligence with regard to the past and present
human rights performance of the security forces that protect them; proactive responses in cases of violations; restraint in the use of force; and explicit support for human rights and international humanitarian law when
interacting with security forces and host governments.[5] The code does not
address peace as such, but the explicit references to human rights and the
expectations of company conduct vis-à-vis security providers effectively
makes it a pro-peace code. It prevents the exacerbation of conflict ("doing
no harm") and promotes underlying values of peace.

The Conflict-Sensitive Business Practice Toolkit

Something the code does not address is the role of participant NGOs in
implementation, monitoring, and governance. Therefore, NGOs involved
approached these tasks differently. Some of those with a record of re-

search-based advocacy, like Amnesty International, believed the VPs were best served by investigating incidents and naming and shaming companies, while at the same time maintaining dialogue with them. Others collaborated with companies to implement the principles. Alert, in line with its policy of engaging with all actors in conflict zones, collaborated and designed the CSBP toolkit based on two years of consultations with dozens of companies and experts. CSBP was meant as a manual for headquarter and field operation managers on how to conduct risk assessments that followed the spirit of the VPs, and it went a step beyond the code by explicitly addressing peace as a desirable goal. It asks companies to "think more creatively about understanding and minimizing conflict risk, and actively contributing to peace."[6]

The CSBP toolkit consists of three parts: a Screening Tool, a Macro Risk and Impact Assessment (M-CRIA) tool, and a Project-Level Risk and Impact Assessment (P-CRIA) tool. The Screening Tool is for headquarter managers of MNCs and aims to help companies determine the types and levels of conflict-related risk in a country. With this knowledge companies can decide quickly whether or not to invest in the country and how to guide more in-depth analysis as the project progresses. The Screening Tool requires approximately two weeks of desk-based research, and final results can be presented in a simple matrix. M-CRIA is the second step. It takes a more detailed look at the country where investments will take place and focuses on the possible impacts of company activity on conflict dynamics. It should allow decision-making staff to identify potential root and trigger causes of conflict by looking at political, economic, cultural, and security variables and at the roles, interests, and capacities of key stakeholders. M-CRIA also seeks to help companies build a transparent relationship with local communities, which is achieved in part by listening and taking into account the communities' views. All this must lead companies to identify opportunities for conflict prevention and peace building. The macro-level analysis should be carried out through desk-based research, consultations with representative stakeholders, and brainstorming in interdepartmental staff meetings. The M-CRIA is meant to be completed in three months but also constantly updated, and its final output can come in the form of a report or a summarized matrix. P-CRIA, the third step, is similar to M-CRIA, but it looks more comprehensively at specific company activities and their impacts on conflict dynamics at the local and regional levels within a country. It should give the company a full picture of the ways in which it may heighten its own risk in a country. According to Alert, stakeholder consultations are the most important element at this stage of the process because they close the information and expectations gaps between local communities and the company and provide the former with a "social license" to operate. Completing P-CRIA takes approximately twelve to twenty-four months.

WORKING ON THE VPS AND INTRODUCING CSBP

In 2003 Cerrejón hired Colombian consultants to provide additional human rights and international humanitarian law training to the local military with whom they had agreements. Cerrejón also began to include some human rights language in its corporate social responsibility discourse. In 2004 new management sought a more comprehensive implementation of the VPs with FIP's collaboration. FIP wrote short, easy-to-read documents that explained the VPs process and the written code; took stock of the company's current practices and identified gaps with respect to expectations in the VPs; designed an overall implementation strategy; adjusted the Protection Division risk matrices in order to evaluate the impact of their security policies; adjusted Cerrejón's management systems to include VPs-related human rights training for employees and security contractors; recommended new categories for the daily compliance sheet to be filled out by workers; and added human rights clauses to the agreements with the military. In the meantime, Cerrejón created a new position for a human rights officer in the Protection Division with the responsibility of developing in-house capacity on the VPs.

OxyCol, the Colombian subsidiary of Occidental Petroleum, began working on the VPs in 2003. That year the company developed its own Security and Human Rights Policy, which was inspired by the VPs. Soon after, the policy flowed up to the corporate headquarters, prompting the leadership in Los Angeles to confirm its adherence to the VPs and to issue a policy for its operations worldwide.[7] Subsequently, the 2004 corporate-level Human Rights Policy reinforced the local process. To put into practice its new Security and Human Rights Policy, throughout 2003 and 2004 OxyCol designed a reporting mechanism to detect possible human rights violations connected to its operations; developed its own human rights and international humanitarian law training program and materials for employees and contractors by adapting standard manuals used by the Red Cross and the International Committee of the Red Cross; and began creating tools to conduct political and security risk and impact analyses. For this last task, staff in the Legal and Government Affairs Departments borrowed methodologies from the Health, Environment, and Safety (HES) Department, but they reached a dead end when they tried to convert their knowledge about the political, social, and security situations into variables that could fit the matrices and to quantify the effects of events like a massacre by corrupt armed forces or harms caused to the company's reputation. FIP was then asked in 2005 to solve the puzzle of adapting HES methodologies for political and security themes, to incorporate VPs elements into the design of the matrices, to "translate" and teach the new methodology to the nontechnical staff assigned to social, legal, and government affairs, and to run an assessment for the Caño-Limón field in Arauca, which OxyCol had discovered in 1983.

A year later, in 2006, FIP and Alert worked with Cerrejón and OxyCol and its new local partner, the Colombian state-owned oil company Ecopetrol, to introduce and test CSBP. FIP arranged meetings in London between the companies and Alert, and a couple of months later the parties involved signed a Memorandum of Understanding containing basic rules of engagement: NGOs would respect confidentiality when dealing with sensitive company information, while the companies would respect FIP's and Alert's independence and refrain from using their names for public relations purposes. The OxyCol-Ecopetrol CSBP pilot was applied to a new, enhanced recovery project in the Cira Infantas field in the Magdalena Medio region, Oxy's first project in Colombia since its 1983 discovery of oil in Arauca. The pilot was divided into two phases. The first phase consisted of introductory workshops on CSBP and a gap study to assess the companies' weaknesses and strengths in risk and impact analyses. One key objective was to provide time and space for all parties to get to know each other first before delving into activities that required more commitment and the sharing of more information. During the second phase additional workshops on the conceptual dimensions and technicalities of CSBP were held, Alert conducted control research interviews with various stakeholders to learn more about the local political context, and FIP and Alert guided a project-scale risk and impact assessment by company staff. The key leading persons on the side of the companies were the corporate-level Corporate Social Responsibility (CSR) manager, OxyCol's general legal counsel, and Ecopetrol's integrated responsibility manager. The local managers constantly reported back to their CEOs, who monitored the exercise closely. Others involved in the workshops included the joint OxyCol-Ecopetrol team in charge of the social issues, which was staffed with eight people, mostly engineers. The Cerrejón pilot was slightly different. It focused mainly on the Protection Division in charge of the company's security policies. FIP and Alert trained staff on conflict analysis and stakeholder consultation. Apart from the corporate affairs manager, the exercise on the ground was led by the Protection Division manager, a local former military officer, and the new human rights officer.

FIP and Alert planned and carried out all the activities together, although each organization had different abilities, which delineated an implicit division of labor. FIP was stronger in methodology and pedagogy and knew better the inner workings of the companies as well as the local conflict and political dynamics in the Colombian provinces. Therefore, it had concrete ideas on how to pilot Alert's CSBP tool. Due to its international work in peace building and its role in the VPs, Alert acted as a moral benchmark, and its international experience allowed it to transfer teachings from other cases.

FINDINGS

How It All Happened: Actors' Incentives

Not all multinational and national extractive businesses operating in weak governance zones have embraced emerging standards, especially the codes and tools concerning human rights and peace building. Nor is it common to find companies willing to work so closely with NGOs on issues of great sensitivity, such as the assessment of their impacts and risks, which are usually topics of high confidentiality. Trust is an issue. Companies think that NGOs are biased and will distort information in order to target them publicly. Likewise, many NGOs eschew collaboration with companies, as they fear being manipulated and losing independence.[8] What drove OxyCol and Cerrejón to work on the VPs and then join with FIP and Alert for the CSBP pilot?

In 2004 Cerrejón hired a new public affairs manager, Andrés Soto, who had just stepped down as Vice Minister of Defense and had worked in the past for OxyCol. At OxyCol, he became aware of the VPs, the lawsuits against oil and mining MNCs in U.S. courts under the Alien Torts Claims Act (ATCA), and increasing NGO attention to the conduct of extractive businesses. At the ministry he had witnessed complex security situations on the ground and faced the challenge of boosting capacity and confidence within the Colombian armed forces while holding them accountable for corruption and human rights crimes. With this background, Soto set out to implement the VPs at Cerrejón. "My view was that one had to work with the institutions, but have safeguards to guide Cerrejón through the complexities of reality. The VPs seemed like a good option; they were practical and had the international political acceptance by those who count in today's global politics," he explains. Soto also saw this as an opportunity to position Cerrejón before its owners as a corporate responsibility leader and make the site attractive to further investment. "The VPs were good for business, society and the country," asserts Soto. Cerrejón's shareholders welcomed the company's decision on the VPs. Two of the owners, BHP Billiton and Anglo American, were VP signatories.

The local political context of the moment made this decision all the more pertinent. As had many other extractive firms, Cerrejón had been attacked by left-wing guerrillas, at least twenty-six times from 1990 to 2006. Extortion of employees and contractors by both guerrillas and paramilitaries was also a problem. For its protection the company hired local private security and relied on a cooperation agreement with the Ministry of Defense and other justice and law enforcement agencies, which entailed company donations of nonlethal equipment to the local brigade and frequent joint meetings to assess the security situation in the region. External observers, therefore, could misconstrue the nature of the company's interaction with public security. Moreover, recent conflict dynamics had begun affecting Cerrejón's reputation. Some NGOs claimed Cerrejón had benefited from the Bahía Portete massacre, which triggered the displacement of at least 250 members of the Wayuú indigenous community from the town located a few kilometers from Cerrejón's port facilities that ship coal abroad. NGOs attributed the massacre to paramilitary groups who, along with corrupt military and law enforcement, wanted to gain control over local drug-trafficking routes and had thus cleared the way by assassinating local Wayuús. They argued that Cerrejón was indirectly responsible given its agreements with the local military. For instance, one report stated that "it is obvious to the Wayúu community from Bahía Portete that the massacre was meant to shatter their resistance to the exploitation by multinationals" in the area and explained how some radical leaders in the community blamed Cerrejón for "supporting the army even when the company knew that the army worked directly with the paramilitary."[9] In addition, locals were disappointed because they believed Cerrejón had not done enough to ensure the appropriate investment of coal revenues—paramilitary forces had penetrated local government and stolen or misallocated public moneys, including coal royalties. Furthermore, the paramilitary demobilization was becoming a dilemma. While cooperation with demobilization and reintegration programs would bring criticism from NGOs and the international community, inaction would elicit discontent from the government and risk driving former combatants back into crime. Within this context Cerrejón's more routine challenges related to resettlements and relations with local communities and with the Wayuú indigenous group became more complex. Mistakes in past resettlements, such as the relocation of Tabaco, a small village, were being revived constantly by a few local leaders who had found support from campaigning international NGOs that had gained an interest in Colombia and could affect the MNCs in their home countries.[10]

Soto approached FIP in 2005 for help. Compared to other codes, the VPs successfully translate general principles on good behavior in weak governance zones into simple and practical actions companies can undertake. Still, implementation requires interpreting what recommendations mean within local contexts and figuring out how to proceed with the day-to-day operations. "We didn't know how to go about the VPs. Our shareholders had, at first, provided little guidance on how to do things and lacked a nuanced understanding of the particularities of La Guajira and Colombia's conflict."[11] FIP had recently created a Business and Conflict Program to promote corporate participation in peace building in Colombia and was familiar with the international VPs process. Not being an NGO but rather a private sector–funded think tank, and having staff with business experience and firsthand knowledge of the discussions in New York, Washington, DC, and London that were shaping the new codes for businesses operating in conflict zones, made FIP an attractive collaborator. FIP saw this as an opportunity to learn more about corporate behavior and conflict challenges by having access to information from the "inside" and to advance its agenda through practical work, not just research and dissemination.

OxyCol's path to the VPs was somewhat similar. Among the reasons that led local management to implement the VPs was a growing awareness of the risks posed by Colombia's situation given the shifts in international corporate standards. In 2001 competition between the FARC and the ELN guerrilla groups in the rural province of Arauca, where Oxy operates, led to a sharp rise in attacks on the Caño Limón-Coveñas oil pipeline, which carries 25 percent of the country's oil. At the same time, it had become evident that local royalties were being stolen by the guerrillas and by corrupt public authorities. The losses and fears that the guerrillas would use the cross-border region with Venezuela to smuggle drugs and weapons prompted an increase of military operations in Arauca, which were later backed by U.S. special forces under the Pipeline Protection Program. More military activity meant more interaction between the company and the Colombian and U.S. armed forces, which in turn exposed the company to greater NGO scrutiny and legal risks.[12] OxyCol already had been the subject of bad press due to the 1998 Santo Domingo incident, during which Colombian armed forces in pursuit of guerrillas opened fire on some guerrilla members dressed as civilians. The public security forces had been funded indirectly by Oxy through its payments to the state oil company Ecopetrol, who had signed an agreement with the armed forces to guard the pipeline and the Caño Limón oil facilities.[13] OxyCol's problems in the late 1990s and early 2000 with the U'wa indigenous community, who lived north of Arauca where Oxy was exploring for new oil, also heightened the company's awareness of the implications of operating in difficult contexts. The U'wa community vehemently opposed these projects for religious and cultural reasons. The U'wa threatened to commit mass suicide if exploration took place, blamed the companies for militarizing the zone and stigmatizing them as guerrilla sympathizers as a strategy to eliminate them, and even filed legal actions in Colombia against OxyCol and Ecopetrol for allegedly being given environmental license by the state to carry out works without fully realizing the indigenous group's right to previous consultation. These incidents attracted the attention of local and international NGOs.[14]

The year-long collaboration between FIP and Oxy and Cerrejón in 2005 paved the way conceptually and politically for the CSBP pilot. The companies learned enough about the emerging standards to understand the basic elements and technical value of the CSBP. For Oxy's executives the CSBP was a way to put into practice the new Human Rights Policy. "By then, we had already adjusted our CSR policies but had no practical instruments to translate aspirational statements into action. My interest as corporate CSR Manager went even beyond Colombia. My mandate was to implement new policies on all our operations around the world and I needed material for internal training and learning," recounts a senior Occidental official. Also, as the business case for the VPs became clearer, nontechnical staff working on these issues gained greater visibility and legitimacy within their organizations. This helped managers like Soto at Cerrejón and OxyCol's legal counsel to garner their CEOs' consent for the CSBP pilots.

Moreover, constructive interaction with FIP, seen as a "special kind of NGO," exposed companies to the idea of engaging NGOs, at least the less radical ones like Alert. Current political affairs in Colombia added a premium to such engagements because they became an opportunity for companies to "tell their story to NGOs who were not only influential among key audiences abroad, but also unbiased and willing to listen." Armed conflict in Colombia had acquired an unprecedented international political dimension: a struggle among all sides to gain the sympathy of foreign states, NGOs, and international organizations for their cause as a way of increasing their legitimacy. Therefore, discriminating between facts and fiction about local dynamics had become a difficult task. In addition, the government's stiff security policies had overexposed it to radical, left-wing, transnational advocacy networks critical of President Uribe's policies, who also claimed businesses were benefiting from state-promoted human rights violations. Therefore, showing Alert firsthand the realities on the ground became important for the companies. Alert's participation in the pilot was also attractive because the companies could validate their human rights policies through the engagement with the NGO.

OxyCol had an additional key interest: making sure that its new investment in La Cira Infantas, which they expected would pose far more difficult challenges than the Caño Limón field in Arauca, complied with company policies. La Cira Infantas had a complex history and was the birthplace of Ecopetrol's USO (Unión Sindical Obrera) union, one of the largest and most powerful worker associations in Colombia. Like other unions in Colombia, it had been infiltrated occasionally by left-wing guerrillas in the past. Moreover, the field was located in the Magdalena Medio region, an area far more convoluted politically than Arauca. It had been afflicted by a brutal power struggle between the ELN and the paramilitary and was home to very active left-leaning civil society groups and, more recently, to hundreds of demobilized paramilitary combatants seeking jobs. In that context, some of the expected impacts of the project, such as relocating an uncertain number of persons living in the field and cutting illegal gas and water services historically provided by Ecopetrol to dozens of families in the area, would inevitably complicate relations with local communities. Given the structure of the new joint venture, whereby Ecopetrol would be operating the field and would have to deal with the issues, it was key for OxyCol to bring Ecopetrol into the CSBP pilot. Ecopetrol had incentives to do so; it was in the middle of a reform that was intended to make the company competitive on the domestic and international markets. However, the idea of developing risk assessment skills in collaboration with NGOs was an issue of concern, especially since Ecopetrol belonged to the state and Uribe's government had tense relations with international NGOs. This is why Ecopetrol's president Isaac Yanovic decided to travel to London himself, in order to undertake a proper due diligence on FIP and Alert.

Finally, the presence of FIP as an interface between Alert and the companies helped to build trust. Intermediation was more than just facilitating preliminary meetings; it was about bridging two worlds: one more technical, dominated by engineers, result-oriented, and used to dealing with hard facts and quantitative indicators, and the another more centered on discourse, used to the fuzziness of social themes, and process-oriented. There also was bridging to do between local understandings about Colombia's reality and foreign perceptions as well as local and international interpretations of human rights. "Had the NGOs involved been others than FIP and Alert, this whole experiment wouldn't have taken place. FIP played a key role in diffusing tension and potential prejudices," claimed an Oxy senior executive.

Changing the Way Companies Think

The implementation of the VPs on the ground, especially of the risk assessment recommendations using CSBP, revealed the code's potential to change both how companies think and what they think, which can ultimately have permanent effects on corporate behavior with respect to conflict and peace issues. Changing the way companies act and think, however, was challenging.

Understanding Human Rights
The companies found that the implementation of the VPs and the introduction of CSBP had to begin with basic human rights and international humanitarian law training for company employees. Due to their technical professions, most had simply never been exposed to formal education on the theme, and the politics of armed conflict in Colombia had distorted their thoughts on the issue. Human rights was for many, in particular those with a military background, linked to radical left-wing ideology; thus, being in favor of human rights meant supporting guerrilla violence. As a result, pedagogic work by FIP and Alert heavily relied on the business case for the VPs in order to combat initial reticence and address misperceptions. In order to do that, accurate knowledge about both local politics and Western ideas of human rights was needed. Top management also had to develop a relatively sophisticated discourse on human rights and send strong signals to employees to gain their commitment. As workshops progressed, discussions about human rights helped staff to grasp that it was possible for businesses to be directly or indirectly involved in human rights violations and to exacerbate conflict.

Understanding Conflict: Security as a Political Phenomenon
We found that since armed conflict was associated with violence, analyzing conflict was left primarily to security departments, which often missed the full picture of the conflict. They tended to focus on hard-core, immediate manifestations like bomb attacks, sabotage, homicides, theft, and kidnappings and spent more time keeping statistics than reflecting on the reasons behind security incidents. The fact that security departments were staffed mostly by former military contributed to this analytical weakness since they tended to lack skills in social and political analysis.

Moreover, the aura of confidentiality attached to security themes discouraged interdepartmental and, therefore, an interdisciplinary analysis of conflict, which could have led companies to grasp conflict as dynamic power and economic struggles involving not only armed groups but also other parts of the populations rather than understanding conflict merely as security incidents.

The VPs and CSBP helped to overcome some of these problems by introducing armed conflict as an analytical category that should be assessed by departments other than security. The tools also helped staff identify the political, economic, and social dimensions of conflict and encouraged interdepartmental analysis. In fact, in the case of Oxy they were the catalyst for an important organizational change. Social and security issues now reside under a common roof. OxyCol's Legal Counsel was promoted to External Affairs Vice President in charge of Community Affairs, Security, and Government Affairs and Communications.

In all, the exercise helped companies assess more comprehensively their impacts on conflict dynamics and peace building, the risks emerging from conflict situations, and their root causes. OxyCol and Ecopetrol, for instance, were able to identify the demobilization of former combatants as an issue and understand that demobilization was not something good or bad in itself but rather a complex post-conflict process. "We know now that not hiring former combatants may pose risk, but helping them out is problematic as well. The conclusion is that we need to analyze demobilization further and have a clear policy," explains an Oxy manager. "The VPs and CSBP also helped us understand that security went beyond the company's physical integrity. It referred to the security of local communities also," added another Oxy manager. Finally, a positive side effect of the interdepartmental analyses of conflict was the greater accountability of the security departments since the content and quality of their assessments was opened to others.

Understanding the Two-Way Interaction between Companies and Context

Following common practice in the industry, the companies regularly conducted social and environmental impact assessments and political and security risk assessments. Each assessment was carried out by different departments, the first by the HES Department along with Community Affairs, and the second by the Security Department. This distorted the companies' understanding of their interaction with conflict dynamics since they usually considered politics and security only when assessing the direct negative effects of these issues on them as opposed to their effects on political and conflict dynamics. So, for instance, the companies would typically identify illegal armed group presence or radical NGO activism as a "risk" but would not be able to analyze the effects of company activities, including security policies, on the interests and actions of these and other actors, which, of course, could then have an impact on local communities as well as company operations. The fact that in common parlance both impacts and risks were called simply "risks" also seemed to impede a clearer understanding of who was doing what to whom and the chain of causation between events. "The realization that we, and not just the various armed groups, could impact the security environment or the security of the local communities, really struck our staff. Now they are aware," says Soto. He continues:

> For instance, one of our security policies was to prevent people from transiting the area next to the river because it was a way in for thieves stealing our copper cables. The black market for copper, by the way, flourished with armed conflict, as copper became a source of extra cash for illegal armed groups. CSBP allowed us to realize that the restrictions were affecting artisan fishermen, and that such grievances could then affect us. Resentful locals could easily be bought off by FARC.

The VPs and CSBP were able to bring analytical clarity simply by unpacking the questions companies had to ask and providing a slot in the matrices where staff could explain how and why impacts and risks occurred. In this way, they sharpened companies' understandings of their interaction with society and made them aware of the effects their operations had on political and security issues. By doing so, they helped companies identify a role in peace building by either "doing no harm" or actively engaging in peace-related activities while also reducing legal risks stemming from the complicity in human rights violations. OxyCol and Ecopetrol, for instance, concluded that if contractors engaged in illicit relations with guerrillas, paramilitaries, or criminal networks—for example, through extortion payments—this could exacerbate conflict and at the same time harm the company's reputation and bring legal and financial risks.

Companies' Analytical Skills

Organizations think through their people and the systems and procedures they have in place. We found important obstacles to producing good collective analysis of company-society interaction and conflict and peace issues: the lack of staff trained on social sciences; a cultural bias in favor of "technical" and "practical" knowledge; time constraints that prevented staff from reading expert reports or developing more sophisticated ideas by writing reports to share with others; competition among various departments; and tight hierarchical structures that prevented information and analysis to flow to all relevant employees. Introduced through various training workshops, the tools managed to address, at least while the exercise lasted, some of these hurdles. The CSBP pilot, for instance, provided staff with basic skills in conflict analysis and a forum for collective analysis.

NGO Strategies and Communication Skills

Whether NGO collaboration with companies or a "stick" approach through boycotts, bad press, and lawsuits is more effective in getting companies to think and act constructively on conflict and peace issues is yet to be established. In the absence of a global regulatory framework, a combination of both is probably needed. As for engagement, the cases presented here illustrated how an NGO and a think tank were able to influence companies in a positive way. The process, however, was not easy or automatic. The parties had to work constantly to build trust and adjust to each others' worlds.

For the companies, one component of trust was FIP's and Alert's interpretation of local realities. The companies were not seeking either organization to echo their own views but rather to demonstrate the ability to understand local culture and be objective. This would prove that the NGOs did not have a hidden adversarial agenda. In this regard, Alert's decision to partner with FIP signaled to the companies that the international NGO was honest about its intentions and would approach local analysis with rigor. Effective communication also proved an important ingredient of trust and indispensable for introduction of the tools. FIP and Alert had to adjust social science jargon to simple terms that nonspecialists could grasp easily. Method also played a role. Because of the characteristics of the audience, the CSBP tool could not be a manual intended to be read and immediately applied. Using the tool required a more intense accompaniment by FIP and International Alert in the form of training workshops tailored specifically for engineers and technically minded staff. Internal politics within companies was another factor to consider. As with any organization, each company had internal divisions and power struggles. This meant that FIP and Alert's agreements with one section of the company did not necessarily have the endorsement of another section; overall company approval of the exercises required time and diplomacy.

CONCLUSIONS

Many private businesses, especially MNCs, are understandably reticent to engage in the politics of conflict resolution, peace making, and peace building. It is simply not their natural role in society, and it exposes them to unnecessary criticism if things go wrong. Taking sides in complex conflict scenarios is risky, as companies may end up supporting former combatants rejected by the liberal international community or backing the opponents of the incoming government, thereby putting their current or future investments in danger. There are, however, other options for contributing to sustainable peace. The adoption of human rights and "do-no-harm" codes of conduct is one. Strategic social investment that addresses the root causes and manifestations of conflict is, of course, another. The VPs and CSBP are examples of such codes, and if thoroughly applied they may also help companies refine their social investment policies. The actual impact of these instruments on armed conflict is yet to be evaluated, but as far as changing private sector attitudes toward conflict prevention and peace, they have proved to have great potential. Surely, it is a mix of factors that drives companies to incorporate human rights and peace into their CSR agendas. However, wanting to act differently and effectively doing so are two different things. Companies need procedures, methods, and time to internalize ideas. Time is needed for the organization to debate, to reorganize its formal structures and hire new personnel, to carry out the necessary internal political transactions, and to learn and to adopt a new identity as its own. Here is where the VPs and CSBP have proven useful: they provide a platform for these adjustments to take place. In that sense they are as important as other incentives, such as laws and social pressure, in bringing about change.

NGOs are useful partners for companies that want to adjust their CSR policies. Consultants may be efficient and have sophisticated technical expertise, but they lack "principled direction"—a moral agenda—and are not the actors leading normative change. Thus, they tend to be one step behind emerging standards. NGO-corporate collaboration, however, is not easy. "Norm entrepreneurs" within companies—those pushing for change within their organizations—NGOs, and international organizations eager to see change in companies need to keep in mind what it takes to introduce such codes and tools into private businesses. International NGOs with a peace agenda and general ideas on how businesses can be a source of positive influence can collaborate with multinational and national companies, but they need to build trust and adjust their organizational capacity. What is trust about? There are features that are common to all NGO-corporate relations, but local context shapes its meaning. In the Colombian setting the private companies considered an international NGO trustworthy if it conducted rigorous research, was able to understand local realities with all its nuances, used confidential information discretely, did not get entangled in the local political fights between the radical left and the radical right, and did not support guerrilla violence and crime. Being open to private business as a legitimate activity helps as well. There are radical antimarket NGOs that argue that private businesses should simply disappear; collaboration with this type of organizations is simply impossible. What is the other side of the coin? What do NGOs expect from businesses and what do companies need to do in order to gain NGO trust? They need to be willing to share accurate information about their operations and challenges and demonstrate that they are prepared to learn and change. Companies also need to be careful not to use alliances with NGOs as a public relations exercise. Practical issues also play a crucial role in NGO-company collaboration. NGOs seeking to collaborate with companies need to speak the corporate language, be acquainted with corporate management systems, be methodic, and offer tangible "deliverables." Adding partners to a collaborative engagement can be seen as complicating interaction. When collaboration is between international human rights or peace-building NGOs and a private sector company, third parties can be helpful. Their profile is key, however. The third party must be able to manage local and global conditions and speak the corporate and NGO languages. For this, "hybrid" staff is required—people who are locals but have lived abroad (or vice versa) and people who are trained in social sciences and can manage the type of methods companies use to guide their policies and measure performance.

This is how NGOs and companies can collaborate in order to galvanize business' potential for conflict prevention and peace building, but what exactly does it mean to work on peace issues? An important finding from the implementation of the VPs and CSBP is that there is much work to do inside the companies. Companies can work on peace issues by transforming their risk and impact assessment methodologies and their management systems—that is, the way they think. Thinking differently about human rights and learning how operations and policies affect political, social, and economic dynamics connected to social and armed conflict and creating operational procedures that can identify concrete actions for company staff to carry out within their daily activities can contribute to a more profound and long-lasting change in corporate conduct.

NOTES

1. The analysis presented here is the author's, who was directly involved in all the activities described below. The text is based on FIP's own research and on the preliminary findings of the CSBP pilot project, and quotes from company and NGO employees were gathered during this research. The CSBP pilot was still underway when this chapter was written, but the parties agreed that initial findings could be presented at the Peace Through Commerce conference held in November 2006 at the University of Notre Dame. A final and more comprehensive report that contains the views of all parties is in the making. The author would like to thank the companies, Alert's team, and FIP analyst Giovanni Mantilla, who directly participated in the projects and gathered additional information for this article.

2. The United States and United Kingdom were the original convening governments in 2000. The Netherlands and Norway joined in 2001 and 2003, respectively. Original companies included Chevron and Texaco—before they merged—British Petroleum, Shell, Rio Tinto, Freeport McMoRan, and Conoco. By 2005, Anglo American Oil, Occidental Petroleum, Newmont Mining, ExxonMobil, Statoil, NorskHydro, Amerada Hess, BHP Billiton, Marathon Oil, and the BG group had signed on as well. The first NGOs to join were Human Rights Watch, Amnesty International, International Alert, the International Business Leaders Forum, Business for Social Responsibility, and the Fund for Peace. Pax Christi, Human Rights First, Oxfam International, the International Council on Mining and Metals (observer), the International Committee of the Red Cross

(observer), and the International Petroleum Industry Environmental Conservation Association (observer) joined the process later.

3. The Alien Torts Claims Act (ATCA) grants jurisdiction to U.S. Federal Courts over "any civil action by an alien for a tort only, committed in violation of the law of nations or a treaty of the United States." According to the most recent report of the United Nations' Secretary-General Special Representative on Business and Human Rights, John Ruggie, so far more than forty cases have been filed against private enterprises under ATCA.

4. "BP Hands 'Tarred in Pipeline Dirty War,'" *Guardian,* October 17, 1998; "Lawsuit Filed Against Occidental Petroleum for Involvement in Infamous Colombian Massacre," *Los Angeles Times,* April 24, 2003; "Oil For Nothing: Multinational Corporations, Environmental Destruction, Death and Impunity in the Niger Delta," *Essential Action,* January 25, 2000; "Mobil Oil and Human Rights Abuse in Aceh," *Down to Earth,* no. 39 (November 1998); International Labour Rights Forum, "ExxonMobil: How the Company Is Linked with Indonesian Military Killings, Torture and other Severe Abuse in Aceh, Indonesia," http://www.laborrights.org/projects/corporate/exxon/index.html; Bennett Freeman and Genoveva Hernández Uriz, "Managing Risk and Building Trust," in *Business and Human Rights: Dilemmas and Solutions,* ed. Rory Sullivan (Sheffield, UK: Greenleaf, 2003).

5. The full text of the VPs is available at in http://www.voluntaryprinciples.org.

6. International Alert, *Conflict-Sensitive Business Practice: Guidance for Extractive Industries* (London: International Alert, 2005).

7. Senior Oxy staff had participated in the making of the VPs but postponed formal adherence until 2002 because they wanted to analyze further the specific implications of the code.

8. Collaborative for Development Action, "Corporate-NGO Relationships," Issue Paper, Corporate Engagement Project (Cambridge: CDA, 2003).

9. Stephan Suhner, "Das Massaker von Bahía Portete und die Interessen eines Schweizer Multis" [Bahía Portete's Massacre and the Interests of a Swiss Multinational], *Arbeitsgruppe-Schweiz-Kolumbien* (February 2006): 1–2. The translation is the author's. See also "Colombian Makes BHP Plea for Justice," *The Age,* May 14, 2005; Tribunal Permanente de los Pueblos, "Resolución del jurado" [The Jury's Verdict] (paper presented at session on Transnational Enterprises and the Rights of the People of Colombia, second hearing, November, 10–11, 2006).

10. The Mineral Policy Institute, Friends of the Earth Australia, and Pressure Point US, "NGOs Condemn BHP Billiton's Human Rights Abuses in Colombia" (June 4, 2004, http://www.mpi.org.au/campaigns/rights/cerrejon/).

11. Later on both MNCs developed their own tools. BHP Billiton designed a Human Rights Self Assessment tool, which it tested in various sites, including Cerrejón, in January 2006. In 2005 Anglo American issued the user friendly

Anglo American Implementation Guidelines for the Voluntary Principles on Security and Human Rights, which contained simple explanations of the code and check-lists to help its staff comply with the VPs. Cerrejón received the guidelines in 2006 and they were translated into Spanish in 2007.

12. By then, the ATCA was already being used to sue U.S.-based MNCs for alleged complicity in human rights violations abroad, and at least one case had occurred in Colombia. Drummond, a mining company, had been sued under the ATCA and the Torture Victims Protection Act for the murder of the three Colombian union leaders in 2001. The complaint explicitly cited the actions of individual company executives, including Augusto Jiménez, president of the La Loma Mine. See *Estate of Rodriguez, et. al. v. Drummond Company, Inc., et. al.,* CV-02-0665-W (N.D. Ala. 2002).

13. In 2003 Occidental Petroleum was sued under the ATCA in Los Angeles court because of the Santo Domingo incident.

14. Project Underground, "Occidental Threatens U'wa of Colombia: Tribe Contemplates Mass Suicide" (May 1998), http://www.hartford-hwp.com/archives/41/157.html; "Colombia Indians to Fight on Against Oil Firm," *Reuters* (August 26, 1999); World Rainforest Movement, "Action for the U'wa People in Colombia," *WRM Action Alerts* (January 2000), http://www.wrm.org.uy/alerts/january00.html; Colombia Labor Monitor, "Oxy Invades Uwa Territory; The Army of Colombia with 5000 Men at the Service of the Oxy" (January 2000); "U'wa vs. Occidental Petroleum," *National Catholic Reporter* (September 2000).

CHAPTER 19

Bristol-Myers Squibb Company

Secure the Future

Thomas Costa

Bristol-Myers Squibb's "Secure the Future: Care and Support for Women and Children with HIV/AIDS" program was announced on May 6, 1999. With a $100 million commitment, it was designed initially for implementation in five countries in southern Africa: Botswana, Namibia, Lesotho, South Africa, and Swaziland. The company moved forward in November 2001 with an additional $15 million for use in four countries in West or Francophone Africa: Burkina Faso, Cote d'Ivoire, Mali, and Senegal. By 2007 the commitment of Bristol-Myers Squibb through Secure the Future (STF) had grown to $150 million, providing for more than two hundred grants for innovative and cost-effective model programs. These programs support people living with HIV in clinics and at home; build medical capacity and infrastructure; and encourage development of sustainable programs that can be replicated elsewhere in Africa and in other parts of the world. It was determined that additional costs for staff, administration, and infrastructure would be paid separately and outside of the $150 million STF commitment.

By 1999 approximately 14.8 million people in sub-Saharan Africa had died of HIV/AIDS. More than 20 percent of those deaths were children. Even though sub-Saharan Africa accounted for only one-tenth of the world's population, by then it accounted for almost 80 percent of all AIDS deaths worldwide and about 70 percent of all those living with HIV/AIDS. Also by 1999 Bristol-Myers Squibb—a leader in the global pharmaceutical industry with a large HIV/

AIDS antiretroviral franchise and a significant business presence in Africa—was searching for an appropriate role to play in fighting the pandemic. There were issues around pricing of HIV/AIDS pharmaceuticals and concerning intellectual property protection. Nevertheless, even with such challenges, it was evident that doing nothing was unacceptable. Bristol-Myers Squibb's stated mission as a company is to "extend and enhance human life."[1] The HIV/AIDS issue clearly needed attention.

Since its establishment STF has focused on two areas: community outreach and education, and medical research and care. Its aim, from the outset, has been to develop public-private partnerships to help women and children. After all, more than half of all infected adults in the region are women aged fifteen to forty-nine. In some countries more than 25 percent of pregnant women are infected, and over 90 percent of all AIDS orphans have been African. As a result, two program components were formally established: Medical Research, and Community Outreach and Education. Research was to receive the bulk of the funding ($85 million), and the activities of the Community Outreach and Education component would focus on priority areas, including home-based care, destigmatization, and care and support for infected and affected children. Capacity building, which was an essential element of both programs, was explored in many ways, including through newly created fellowship programs at the Medical University of Southern Africa's National School of Public Health and exchange programs with the Baylor College of Medicine in Texas.

Also from the beginning, it was decided that STF, as it reviewed and approved grant proposals, would emphasize those that were funded locally and supported African organizations, rather than through U.S. organizations. If proposals from U.S. organizations were to be funded because their ideas were appropriate for the program, STF would insist that there be a strong skills transfer component to those grants. The emphasis was on building capacity on the ground in Africa, so it was critical that local organizations be supported and local skills enhanced.

Why were the specific countries selected? Southern Africa is the region hardest hit by the epidemic. If an impact was to be made by STF, work had to be directed to where the need was greatest. Working in the most difficult environment created an opportunity to test the cost-effective models of intervention in the worst possible circumstances. If achievements were possible here, they could likely be repeated; the company already had established facilities in South Africa, where it had been operating a business since 1936. In addition, a relatively sophisticated medical infrastructure already existed in the urban areas of South Africa, including potential partners like the Medical Research Council (MRC) and its tertiary-level hospitals. HIV/AIDS was high on the region's political agenda and was an issue of deep and growing concern. It seemed likely that any help offered would be welcomed.

At its core, STF seeks to prevent HIV/AIDS and STD transmission; reduce the impact of HIV/AIDS on individuals by empowering infected and affected women and children; and expand access to treatment by informing public health policy leaders. To achieve these goals the program has focused on sustainability and capacity building in order to ensure that a positive legacy from the program would remain after its completion. Most critically, an agreement was reached on key principles for making future decisions relating to funding and other issues. These principles would make the program's activities transparent and easily understood, and they set a level playing field for all the actors involved. They declared that STF would be a public-private partnership as embodied in government policies against HIV/AIDS; compatible with and complementary to health care priorities; governed cooperatively; sensitive to the local context; ethically unassailable; a catalyst for expanded participation; promoting equity; and characterized by grants that were innovative, sustainable, and replicable.

These principles translated into several key actions and decisions. First, STF would not be simply a free or low-cost drug distribution program. While the pressure on pharmaceutical companies for free or low-cost drugs mounted, the gap in the infrastructure in countries to deliver drugs and treat patients had widened. Second, it would not be directed and controlled centrally, with ideas for projects coming from a distant corporate headquarters. Instead, local independent advisory boards were formed and local staffs were hired in Johannesburg and Mali. Third, the active participation of ministries of health, local medical and educational institutions, and local NGOs would be integral elements of project creation and funding. Fourth, independent auditors (Pricewaterhouse-Coopers) would ensure financial and other controls in funded agencies, and Yale University's Center for Interdisciplinary Research on AIDS at the Yale School of Public Health would direct and train evaluators on the ground to assess program efforts. All these things would help make the effort ethically unassailable.

All grant candidates presented their proposed programs as innovative, replicable, and sustainable. They have sought to address such questions as the following:

> What models could be developed that could endure long after this program ended?
>
> How could sustainable institutions be created and fostered that would allow the people in the region to learn to cope with the tragedies of HIV/AIDS?
>
> How could small organizations grow into larger organizations and attract additional funders?
>
> How could programs be developed and then appropriately evaluated by independent professionals?
>
> How could financial and other controls be ensured?
>
> How does STF fit into the other efforts of the Bristol-Myers Squibb Foundation?

Clearly, STF is consistent with the mission of the foundation, which took the lead in developing and overseeing the program for the company. Throughout its history, the foundation has sought to become involved in innovative projects that could be a meaningful catalyst for change in specific areas of interest, including health, women's issues, science, and education.

At the same time, by its very nature STF has differed from earlier foundation-supported and developed projects. It has involved funding well beyond the normal annual operating budget of the foundation, and it has focused on a large geography and on the opportunity to affect the lives of millions. Furthermore, program objectives were shaped with local stakeholder input and were continually revised and revitalized as the epidemic evolved and as the science as well as the social and political context in the region changed. Projects were reviewed by independent technical advisory committees and ratified by ministries of health in accordance with national priorities.

How has the program progressed? Since its inception, about 190 grants have been authorized in southern Africa and another 25 in West Africa. They run the gamut from theatrical troupes that tour villages to promote HIV awareness and sex education, to programs that offer economic opportunities and training for the grandmothers who have now become the caregivers for many of the millions of AIDS orphans in the region. New lower-cost tests to monitor HIV blood levels have been developed. Programs that help orphans deal with the loss of their parents have been generated. Public health fellowships have been funded, lay health workers have been trained, parish nurses have been given new tools to counsel and care for the sick and dying—and for those they leave behind. New approaches to prevent mother-to-child HIV transmission have been explored. Home-based care solutions have been developed, counseling programs funded, orphans cared for, capacity built, and various forms of community outreach encouraged.

As the program has progressed, it has shifted emphasis and resources as appropriate. On the community side, capacity-building and workshop-based efforts increased. In addition, the focus on children was expanded. Innovative projects such as civic education to increase access to social and health services, capacity building for caregivers, and counseling services directed specifically at children were funded. The Medical Research Program identified three "Big Idea" programs: Tuberculosis (TB), Prevention of Mother-to-Child Transmission (PMTCT), and Post-Exposure Prophylaxis for survivors of sexual violence. In the fields of TB and PMTCT, gaps were identified and requests for proposals issued. For tuberculosis funding was provided for research to diagnose smear negative TB, to determine the best use of prophylactic therapy in HIV-infected children, and to determine how long curative TB therapy was needed in children with HIV. For PMTCT funding was provided to studies evaluating comparative PMTCT regimens and for determining the development of resistance. Researchers investigating the psychosocial aspects of PMTCT were also supported.

Indeed, STF is now working on its legacy programs. What will it leave behind? It is already establishing the roots of a new NGO Training Institute, where the best practices of leading and established NGOs in the five southern African countries will be assessed and developed into training modules for existing and emerging community-based organizations. It is also seeking to develop a number of community-based treatment sites in the region that will serve as models for integrated treatment, care, and disease management at the community level and in resource-limited settings.

It should be noted that STF could not work in a vacuum. Around it, even as the pandemic raged, a variety of issues concerning pricing and access continued to arise. In seeking to address those issues, Bristol-Myers Squibb entered into a new UN/Industry Accelerating Access Initiative, a partnership program with five other pharmaceutical companies as well as UNAIDS, other UN agencies, and governments to facilitate the availability of antiretroviral medicines. In March of 2001 the company announced that it would make its two AIDS medicines, VIDEX and ZERIT, available in sub-Saharan African countries below cost, amounting to a combined price of just one dollar a day. And at the same time, it announced that it would ensure that its patents did not prevent inexpensive HIV/AIDS therapies in Africa. The patent for ZERIT would be made available at no cost to treat AIDS in South Africa. The company had no other patent rights in Africa that prevent AIDS therapy there and the fight against AIDS in that region of the world. STF funded the construction and equipping of clinical centers in Botswana, Lesotho, and Swaziland that would be operated by the Baylor International Pediatric AIDS Initiative with the assistance of host government funding. Centers in Burkina Faso and Uganda opened in 2007. The centers provide multidisciplinary care for children and their families, state-of-the-art infrastructure, and education and training for medical professionals. STF and Baylor College of Medicine have created a program to send up to 250 pediatricians and family practitioners to Africa over five years—50 doctors per year—to treat approximately 80,000 children and train local health care professionals. Seven pediatricians are already serving in Africa, and additional members of the first wave of 50 doctors began work in August 2006. The doctors are to be assigned to the countries that have children's clinical centers.

Today STF has come to be identified as a successful model of a public-private partnership, even by earlier critics (among them the minister of health of South Africa). It is a program that has been enriched by collaboration and consultation, and by an unstinting willingness to provide skills and practical support to a wide range of both established and relatively young organizations and individual researchers—both large and small. STF fostered a number of important lessons around gaining government participation, communication, the value and cost of active management, the need for early consultation, and building public-private partnerships. While a discernible impact on people's lives will be made by the program, it is expected that the real impact of STF will be the capacity and sustainability of each program created as a result of STF funding. The ultimate test is whether the people affected and touched by STF are better off today than they might have been otherwise. The success of STF also will be measured by the criteria for success set at the initiation of each of the grants—and by then evaluating how far the grantees have come in achieving their goals. It will be measured by the good that these organizations and groups do in contributing to their communities and to the people they help. It will be measured by their ability to sustain their efforts and expand them—and, eventually, by the additional public-private partnerships that will be created to begin to reverse and eventually help defeat the HIV/AIDS pandemic over time. STF raised the bar on corporate responses to HIV/AIDS. And nearly seven years later, it remains the largest philanthropic corporate commitment to HIV/AIDS.

NOTES

I am grateful to the members of the Secure the Future Team, who contributed to the writing of this chapter.

1. See http://www.bms.com/aboutbms/content/data/ourple.html.

PART VI

Some Conclusions and a Vision for the Future

CHAPTER 20

Multinational Enterprises

Interacting with Nongovernmental Organizations

Lee Tavis

As has been demonstrated in this volume, it is to the advantage of both corporations and nongovernmental organizations to collaborate if each is to achieve its objectives in today's information-rich, integrated world. Corporate management is increasingly aware of the need to position their firms to serve social preferences well beyond the basic market model. This awareness is reflected in the burgeoning corporate social responsibility (CSR) efforts. For their part, managers of NGOs see increased opportunities to leverage the extensive human and material resources of the business enterprise in order to achieve the social impact desired by the NGO.

These partnering opportunities will be analyzed in this chapter, first from the point of view of the business enterprise and then from that of the NGO. Both will be demonstrated through cases discussed elsewhere in this volume. The relevance of the literature on conflict resolution as reflected in this volume and the possible roles of NGOs with regard to issues in multinational management are extensive, including reassessing the unanticipated development of global policies; enhancing the possibility of dialogue and coalition building; and understanding the nuances of local issues.

POSITIONING THE ENTERPRISE

The driving force for corporate involvement with NGOs can be analyzed in terms of operations, outreach beyond the firm's operating environment, and donation programs. The business units of a multinational enterprise are located in diverse economic, political, social, and cultural environments. Each of these settings provides a unique situation that can challenge the uniform standards and policies a firm attempts to apply across its enterprise network. The most difficult component of this managerial tension has to do with the interpretation of local cultures and communities.

Policy Effectiveness

Management must position each firm to compete in its core business operations. Beyond the overall economic/political/social positioning, when operating in different cultures the enterprise must reassess assumptions about the impact of its standard policies. Mary Anderson posits caution in this regard. Her comments, although directed toward "destructive, often violent, intergroup conflict," apply to all situations of multinational corporate presence, particularly in developing countries (chap. 6).[1] Anderson begins with a distinction between context and conflict, where context is a comprehensive review of issues while conflict focuses on key driving factors in a specific situation. Contextual analysis can be related to corporate policy formulation while conflict analysis would be the implementation of these policies.

A central premise of global management is to identify a set of standards and translate these standards into policies that apply across the firm's enterprise network. The role of the local business unit is then to apply these policies to local situations.[2] The Anderson challenge is to emphasize how destructive the blind application of network-wide policies can be. This does not mean that the universal policies are not appropriate to an enterprise, but it does mean that some policies may be totally inappropriate for local circumstances. As an example, standard corporate-wide policies to hire on merit, invest in infrastructure, or pay premium wages in developing communities as a means of contributing to development may create local tensions and conflict.[3] Again, this does not mean that the enterprise policies are not valid. Nevertheless, it indicates that these policies must be modified or set aside in specific local situations.

How does the manager know when to depart from a corporate policy? This involves an understanding of local nuances. The larger the firm as a presence in a community, the more critical this understanding becomes (see chap. 8). The nuances of local communities are always complex. This is abundantly clear in situations such as the informal sectors across Latin America, in slums everywhere, or when local people are under oppression, as was the case in South Africa during apartheid. This caveat applies to a manager from the local community as well as one promoted into that position from another assignment in the enterprise network. The local person is a member of a specific relational group and influenced by its viewpoint, while the outsider may simply miss the point.

Interpreting local uniqueness as a basis for policy application is a role that could be fulfilled by the local NGO in the NGO-business partnership. Beyond understanding, there is the issue of who will represent the local community. The responsibility of the business unit manager is to represent the interests of the firm. From that viewpoint, contributing to the local geographic community is an opportunistic part of the basic business plan. Local contributions build the local economy and contribute to trust, both of which will lead to stability and positive returns for the business in the long run. The NGO can directly represent these interests in the partnership.

In this volume Anderson (chap. 6) reports on the findings of her Corporate Engagement Project. These are right on target and recognizable to the manager of any local business unit because they challenge many accepted managerial perspectives. The experience of the Freeport-McMoRan mine in Irian Jaya (West Papua) Indonesia demonstrates Anderson's concerns. Lowry (chap. 7) poignantly analyzes the inscrutability of the local communities, the interweaving of issues, the unanticipated and unintended consequences of local economic and social actions, short-term disruption while awaiting long-term benefits, differences between perception and fact, and the same action being viewed as beneficial or disastrous depending on the viewpoint of the community involved. An additional example of a challenging local situation is the case of promoting sustainable development in Darfur and Southern Sudan (chap. 12). Given the fluidity and uncertainty in the area, the coalition has chosen the anthropological approach of participative action research, where the field staff are involved in developmental conflict research as well as reacting to specific local needs. The focus is on entrepreneurial capacity, particularly for women. As it turns out, "Women often emerge as entrepreneurs in turmoil. . . . They may play an initial trigger role in stimulating positive cycles of change" (chap. 12). Details of the struggle of internally displaced persons in Southern Sudan are unnerving. Still, researchers found resilient enterprise models even in the confusion and conflict of this area. It reminds us of the determination of bottom-up, grassroots development even in areas of conflict. The multiple-party partnership network consists of Sudanese and Canadian universities, Sudanese governmental agencies and NGOs, and bilateral and multilateral institutions.

Involvement in the Local Community

Local operations are more productive in an environment of favorable local interactions. Employees as well as many contractors and suppliers are members of the surrounding communities. Employees want to be proud of their employer, and the firm needs dependable local contractors and suppliers. When organized properly, these kinds of employee community programs can have an important positive influence on corporate culture. Most of the programs designed to involve employees in local volunteer work are motivated by the desire to enhance this local appreciation and employee pride.

As discussed by Litow in chapter 15, IBM has formed On-Demand Communities to use on-demand computing. Employees and retirees have access to a Website containing technology tools, lectures, online tutorials, and best practices for supporting contributions to local communities. Across the world, often in conjunction with NGOs, IBM has formed learning centers with donated computers. The goal is to support 1,500 such centers. IBM recognizes the contribution these kinds of programs make to reputational capital. Likewise, the Nestlé case presents an extension of the firm's dairy operations in ways that contribute directly to the firm's economic performance while also addressing local needs (chap. 14). Operating in two countries prone to violence—Colombia and Pakistan— Nestlé focuses on milk production. Supporting the transition of demobilized militias to dairy farming in Colombia assures Nestlé access to a reliable source of quality inputs while keeping the militia members demobilized. In Pakistan Nestlé establishes farmers in business and supports their milk production efforts. To reach the scattered farmers in the Punjab, Nestlé trained female agricultural extension workers. In these cases, the firm deals with what it knows well—the production of milk. In Nigeria Nestlé again focuses on sustainable farming methods, here to support food distribution. Confronted with the impact of HIV/AIDS on worker productivity, Nestlé created an education program in partnership with the International Red Cross; the firm also partnered with the NGO Search for a Common Ground to produce films aimed at promoting peace in this divided society.

Outreach Programs

Beyond the interactions between business and NGOs involving an extension of operations into local communities, there is a good deal of collaboration in which the enterprise reaches beyond its neoclassical economic function. Some of these collaborations are normatively based on pure humanitarian concerns, and many come from management's understanding of the changing social preferences and judgments in our increasingly integrated, information-rich world.[4] Partnering with NGOs, particularly international NGOs, is a key dimension in conceptualizing and implementing outreach programs. The engagement of NGOs, and other institutions such as agencies of the United Nations, provides knowledge and insight based on worldviews that can be substantially different from those of business management. Beyond that, these trusted institutions bring legitimacy to the activity, which then translates into reputational capital for the enterprise.

GE has made a major commitment to outreach in Ghana in terms of technology, products, and experience, although this company is explicit about not donating cash (see chap. 16). The initial phase of GE's program in Ghana involved hospital upgrades. During this phase GE modified the technical products donated and the nature of their planning process. In the second phase the lessons from hospital upgrades were incorporated into a broader participation with Ghanian Millennium Village Projects. Here GE is involved with planning synergies (regional hospitals, district hospitals, village cluster clinics) as well as equipment donation and training. There are a number of partnerships involved, from hospital interaction in the first phase of the project to the numerous governmental agencies, businesses, and civil society institutions participating in the Millennium Village Projects.

Donations

In other cases the enterprise provides funds or products to other institutions, usually NGOs or governments, for them to manage in community or humanitarian development with little or no control over allocation of the moneys. Here the corporation is depending on the other institution to make a positive contribution to society. A second donation dimension is that the firm is not contributing managerial skills, as is the case for operations or outreach programs where management is involved in the long-term development of the specific project. In some situations, however, when the social need is so far removed from corporate expertise, the risk of direct involvement too high, or available corporate management limited, donations are the best option. In these cases the Anderson (chap. 6) and O'Neill (chap. 8) caveats outlined earlier apply—local communities can be inscrutable and introducing resources into a resource-scarce economy can easily increase tensions. In this sense, corporate management is well advised to choose the donor recipient with great care.

For example, the Angola Enterprise Program (AEP) focuses on economic development through the support of micro, small, and medium sized enterprises. Under the guidance of the United Nations Development Program (UNDP), AEP implements the overall UNDP mission of "Poverty reduction for sustainable human development" (see chap. 10). Angola is a difficult entrepreneurial environment. In addition to the economic marginalization and health issues present in all of Africa, Angola is rated by the World Bank as one of the most difficult countries in which to establish a business, and the nation is emerging from three decades of civil war. Beyond that, as in all developing countries, micro and small business development is contained within its own distinct culture.[5] AEP focuses on enhancing microfinance structures, starting Business Development Services Centers, studying the micro, small, medium business environment, and working toward appropriate governmental policy and legislative reforms. The program creates and participates in a broad range of partnership networks. Given the complexities of these circumstances, ChevronTexaco's partnership with AEP has been in the form of funding ($3 million) as part of the company's broader $25 million program, the Angola Partnership Initiative.

THE BUSINESS MODEL

There is a distinction in business strategy between operations sensitivity, outreach programs, and donations. In our current environment, strategies are selected by management within an informed global society that is re-evaluating its preferences relative to corporate behavior. Social preferences are reflected in the actions of external stakeholders and in evolving international legal structures.[6] There is a direct payoff of increased productivity for the firm's operations through commitment to local communities. Enhancing productivity is the key to success in the basic market model of finance and economics where optimizing productivity within regulatory constraints is the necessary condition for survival in competitive markets. Indigenous NGOs, in their role of interpreting local communities, aid the firm in meeting competition in this basic market model by effectively channeling corporate human, technical, and material resources to social objectives as counseled by the NGO.

For outreach programs and donations, partnerships can be motivated by (1) the long-term benefits that accrue to the firm through external stakeholders, or (2) the existence of a humanitarian need that the company is in a position of mitigating. Leisinger makes this distinction as it applies to a pharmaceutical company's responsibility in terms of "ought" versus "can" (chap. 9). When a social outreach strategy will lead to benefits for the firm in terms of reputational capital or employee pride, these activities ought to be undertaken. He notes that outreach of this sort is leveraging not only the resources of the firm but also those of the NGO. Beyond this enlightened self-interest, some firms commit resources to outreach efforts with no benefits other than the satisfaction of a humanitarian contribution. The cases in this volume demonstrate both "ought" and "can" projects. The distinction is important for planning purposes even though it is difficult to judge, even for management, what sort of a venture a program will be at its inception.

Law, in the form of setting minimum standards or encouraging a proactive business stance, is a central component of the business model. Cassel and O'Brien assess the role of law in guiding the human rights efforts of the firm (chap. 3). Addressing the question, "By what means and through which laws should TNCs be regulated?" they note the beneficial impacts of the law in terms of being a stimulant to enhance corporate behavior, to standardize good practice, to create an environment conducive to good conduct, and to catch corporate laggards. Legal constraints and guidance begin with the nation-state, a point strongly made by Leisinger (chap. 9) as well as Cassel and O'Brien (chap. 3). Beyond national law, Cassel and O'Brien note five categories of international law that apply to the multinational corporation (MNC): (1) individuals, including corporations, have definable duties under international law; (2) corporate activity that aids and abets, or is otherwise complicit in, state violations of human rights can lead to corporate liability; (3) corporations that undertake privatized governmental functions may be liable in some jurisdictions as state actors; (4) some international law obligations are nominally directed at states but in reality seek mainly to govern private conduct; and (5) international law imposes the duty to respect human rights on corporations and their executives.

Within this context, Cassel and O'Brien evaluate the Norms of the Responsibilities of Transnational Corporations and Other Business Enterprises with Respect to Human Rights, as promulgated by the United Nations Sub-Commission on the Promotion and Protection of Human Rights. While the Norms of this document cover essentially the same ground as the ten principles of the United Nations Global Compact (UNGC), unlike the voluntary compliance of the UNGC, the sub-commission includes legal obligations on the part of the multinational enterprise. In these ways Cassel and O'Brien are helpful in explaining the context within which the business/NGO partnership takes place, and they raise the issue of voluntary compliance versus legal requirements.

BUSINESS-NGO JOINT VENTURE PARTNERING

Just as the operating purpose of the firm is to meet the demands of the basic market model and, beyond that, to ensure long-term sustainability, so is the goal of the NGO to efficiently and effectively meet the needs of its clients and, beyond that, to mature into a sustainable organization capable of revising and expanding its client services. NGOs have become the formal, although varied, voice of civil society.[7]

NGOs—more precisely defined as nonprofit, nongovernmental entities—have flourished in the industrialized world for a long time. They have become a force in developing countries since the 1960s, paralleling the process of globalization. Organizationally, NGOs cover a broad spectrum, including development nongovernmental organizations, professional associations, producers' organizations, social movements, labor unions, religious groups—for example, congregations, orders, or base communities—and even the mass media.[8] The diversity of NGOs is captured by the Commission on Global Governance: "Some are issue-oriented or task-oriented; others are driven by ideology. Some have a broad public interest perspective; others have a more private, narrow focus. They range from small, poorly funded, grassroots entities to large, well-supported, professionally staffed bodies. Some operate individually; others have formed networks to share information and tasks and to enhance their impact."[9]

There is a distinction between indigenous and international NGOs. Most indigenous groups are grassroots organizations. Firmly rooted in the local communities, they are formed to serve the specific interests of their members or for general community support. Fisher estimates that there are over 200,000 indigenous NGOs in the developing world alone.[10] Indigenous NGOs are a remarkably diverse group. Other NGOs operate on an international level. These groups generally seek legitimization through association with indigenous NGOs and are often the source of financial, informational, and strategic support for their grassroots associates. International NGOs provide more aid than the entire UN system.[11] The Commission on Global Governance counts 28,900 international NGOs with operations in three or more countries.[12]

Governance

The rules of the game are not as well established for NGOs as they are for either governments or the private business sector. For government, there are the rights and responsibilities of the sovereign. For the private business sector, there is the acceptance of competition as the driving force within legitimate regulatory constraints, with legally required transparency and accountability. NGOs are largely self-appointed within loose legal structures. As nonprofit institutions NGOs must be licensed and defend their nonprofit status to tax authorities. Direct accountability is to their funders, as that of the corporation is to its shareholders. Accountability is not as distinct as in the case of the corporation, however, since reporting and accountability standards vary. Access to, and uniformity of, information are not required. Beyond that, since NGOs do not have traded shares, they lack the benefit of in-depth critique from a sophisticated financial analysis profession.

Early efforts toward transparency and accountability are being undertaken by groups such as the International NGO Accountability Charter, which was initiated by a serious group of influential NGOs. The theme of the charter is responsible advocacy. NGOs that subscribe to the charter commit to maintaining their financial independence and not practicing discrimination. The charter assures that NGOs will practice advocacy that is consistent with their mission, will assume generally accepted standards of technical accuracy and honesty, will be responsible in their public criticism of individuals and organizations, and will encourage inputs by people whose interests may be directly affected.[13] Other NGOs in search of a code of conduct have joined the United Nations Global Compact. Like corporations, NGOs have a broader social responsibility beyond self-interest. Indeed, in the overwhelming number of cases, this is the reason for their creation and the responsibility they continue to take seriously, with a genuine concern and determination for the specific issues they represent.

Strategy

Business-NGO partnerships cover a wide spectrum, as reflected in the case studies discussed in this volume. From the NGO point of view, the strategy for forming these partnerships revolves around what issues they will embrace and the balance between collaboration and confrontation. NGO decisions as to the most effective approach depend not only on the nature of the issue but also on the culture of the corporation. Fort and Westermann-Behaylo, in chapter 2, identify three corporate cultures in terms of trust. For firms pursuing the neoclassical economic model with little attention to social issues, they propose a "Hard Trust" activist, confrontational approach. For firms pursuing a long-term strategy of social involvement as a means of enhancing brand image and reputational capital, they suggest a partnering, "Real Trust" collaboration. For corporations committed to social enhancement as a worthwhile end in itself, they recommend "Good Trust" partnerships—"built on inspiration and common commitments." Long-term successful partnerships can evolve from Real Trust to Good Trust. Overall, there seems to be an increasing willingness to collaborate as reflected in the numerous partnerships discussed in this volume.

> While a number of NGOs continue to exert direct pressure on the business community to accelerate change, a majority of NGOs have

shifted from the pre-Seattle anti-globalization movement (polarizers) to a more constructive alter-globalization movement (integrators), which seeks change through alliances and partnerships built upon the complementary competencies, objectives, and resources of NGOs and business. The WTO Summit in Seattle in 1999 was a major shifting point in the NGO movement, which was urged to make constructive alternative proposals to those issues which they denounce.[14]

Two case examples from Ford demonstrate NGO confrontational and collaborative approaches. First, after Ford pledged to increase the fuel economy of its pick-up trucks and SUVs by 25 percent by 2005, a group of environmental NGOs placed a full-page ad in the *New York Times* charging that "Ford's fleet continues to produce more global warming pollution than any other major automaker" (qtd. in chap. 13). Alternatively, NGOs were part of the "summit" group convened by Ford in 2000 that "identified human rights as a key issue for multinational corporations," a conclusion that came as a surprise to Ford management. NGOs then participated in the preparation of Ford's Code of Basic Working Conditions, which upon completion, was then reviewed by human rights experts from other NGOs (see chap. 13).

A recently reported example shows how confrontation can turn to collaboration. NGOs (Environmental Defense and the National Resource Defense Council) challenged a utility company's (TXU Energy) plans to construct eleven coal-fired generating plants. Broadcasting through a Website, these NGOs built a national coalition to oppose the construction. During the period of confrontation, a leveraged buyout group proposed to purchase TXU. At this point, through negotiations with the takeover company, the NGOs gained a number of environmental concessions in return for supporting the buyout.[15]

The Promise of Collaboration

Based on his experience in situations of conflict, Lederach outlines the great promise of interrelationships and the potential contribution of business to conflict resolution (chap. 4). He identifies the challenge of peace building: "Peace building represents the intentional confluence— the flowing together—of improbable processes and people to sustain constructive change that reduces violence and increases the potential and practice of justice in human relationships." The phrase "improbable people and processes" suggests that people and activities that would not likely come together on their own volition and connection are encouraged to do so with intentionality. This means that people who are not like minded and not like situated within the conflict find themselves in relationship—flowing together—with a purpose of finding greater understanding and constructive engagement. In a word, this kind of confluence points toward the idea of creating space for meaningful though very unusual interaction. Constructive change provides a goal and a direction for this flowing. In more specific terms it suggests that transformation is needed that reduces violence and increases justice in human relationships.

As a strategic approach, Lederach identified three conflict-creating gaps—vertical, justice, and interdependence—pointing to the potential contribution of business in bridging all three of these gaps. He places the contribution in terms of pursuing what has been outlined above as the "basic market model"—the need for business to build relationships among a wide group of constituencies—as well as the extension of that model into longer-term sustainability strategies in what Leisinger (chap. 9) calls "ought" and "can." In dealing with Lederach's vertical gap, we are again reminded of Anderson's (chap. 6) caution about the inscrutability of local situations and the need for local managers to find "people who are not like minded and not like situated."

The Business Humanitarian Forum promotes partnerships among the public sector, business, and NGOs with the conviction that "comprehensive and widespread cross-sector collaboration is essential to ensure sustainable development initiatives that are imaginative, coherent, and integrated enough to tackle the most intractable problems" (chap. 11). The forum's nine phases of the partnering process—from identifying opportunities and partners, to building sustainability or agreeing on appropriate conclusions—provide solid guidance. The process has been demonstrated with a project to produce generic medicine in the challenging environment of Afghanistan. The hurdles were substantial, including the difficulty of overcoming the Afghan "brain drain" of technical people and the hesitancy of Western technicians to travel to Afghanistan. A key lesson learned is to approach the project as a business case, not a humanitarian effort, and to select partners based on what they can deliver.

Demonstrating that AIDS is the worst health crisis of all human history, the Global Business Coalition (GBS) on HIV/AIDS works with business to take action. Although not discussed in this volume, the Business Coalition is an important voice in encouraging businesses to get involved in the HIV/AIDS crisis. Economically, HIV/AIDS is a "potential threat to the creation of value" in terms of damage to economies, threats to security, diminishing workforces, and cuts in productivity and profits. Beyond these effects, consumers are changing their attitudes toward business with new expectations and shifting balances of trust, which enable cause-related marketing. Among the many companies participating with GBS, two demonstrate this approach—Unilever and M.A.C. On its Kenyan tea plantations, Unilever partners with a number of local groups from the Kenya HIV/AIDS Business Council to support local schools. The fashion cosmetic producer M.A.C. works with retailers in its cause-related marketing, contributing portions of its earnings and raising external funds for its M.A.C. AIDS Fund.[16]

An area of collaborative promise is in the formal NGO assessment of corporate performance—particularly challenging in that assessments of this sort often involve the reporting of unwelcome news. A pioneer in this approach is the Fair Labor Association (FLA). From its foundation as a business-dominated group, roundly criticized by NGOs upon its founding, the FLA is now the leader in transparent monitoring and remediation efforts of developing country apparel production. Other groups such as the International Center for Corporate Accountability conduct more in-depth analysis on a contractual basis.[17]

Sustainable Long-Term Partnerships

The goal of both the business enterprise and the engaged NGO is to ensure the sustainability of the joint venture—a true challenge given that business-NGO partnerships are unions across diverse cultural lines. For NGOs consisting of unusually bright, committed, and determined people, the institutional organization can be more like a university than a business enterprise. Compounding this cultural difference, many work in the nonprofit sector due to a disdain for business and fear being compromised and used for public relations purposes. For business, interacting with NGOs is generally well beyond management's comfort zone. Partnerships involve relinquishing control to others whom they believe may turn from collaboration to confrontation when things go wrong and are in a position to use shared information against the firm. Still, bridging these differences is the key to achieving the great partnership potential. The cases in this volume present ample evidence of this tension and how it can be overcome. Lessons learned are a central component in the reporting of each experience. These lessons reflect a surprising consistency across a range of situations.

Trust is the key for long-term sustainability. Given the cultural differences, members of the partnership need mentoring regarding the establishment and maintenance of trust. O'Neill (chap. 8) provides an insightful set of guidelines for enhancing long-term relationships, including the following recommendations: the relationship needs to be formalized, input should be roughly equal, trust should be built on shared achievement, and third parties, including government, should be involved if necessary.[18] An example of building partnership trust across extreme ideological barriers is the Middelburg Forum (chap. 17). South African apartheid put all businesses in the untenable position of trying to operate according to unjust laws. In the late 1980s Middelburg Steel and Alloys (MSA), a subsidiary of Barloworld, found itself in the middle of a major local political issue as well. The town of Middelburg had turned off the lights and water for the local black township for nonpayment of bills. Malan outlines the situation:

> The white council was in financial trouble as a result of nonpayment for services, the black councillors from the township did not have any legitimacy in their own community, the comrades (a term for activists within the Mass Democratic Movement) were facing intimidation and threats from the security forces, and the trade union leaders were branded as sellouts by many comrades as a result of their participation in the Forum.

Assuming the role of political activist, MSA assembled the parties as the Middelburg Forum, which, over time, transformed the town.

The interaction among two multinational extractive companies (Occidental Petroleum and Cerrejón, the largest open-pit coal mine in Latin America), a London-based NGO (International Alert), and a Colombian think tank (Fundación Ideas para la Paz, or FIP) provides a clear example of building trust among the partners as a way of avoiding inadvertent contributions to the Colombian conflict and a way of moving ahead positively. Against a history of confrontation between NGOs and business over the conflict in Colombia, Guáqueta (chap. 18) outlines how FIP worked with the partners:

> The presence of FIP as an interface between Alert and the companies helped to build trust. Intermediation was more than just facilitating preliminary meetings; it was about bridging two worlds, one more technical, dominated by engineers, result-oriented, and used to dealing with hard facts and quantitative indicators, and the other more centered on discourse, used to the fuzziness of social themes, and process-oriented. There was also bridging to do between local understandings about Colombia's reality and foreign perceptions as well as local and international interpretations of human rights.

There were many lessons learned from this partnership:

> The companies were not seeking either organization [Alert or FIP] to echo their own views but to demonstrate the ability to understand local culture and be objective. As with any organization, each company had internal divisions and power struggles. FIP and Alert had to adjust social science jargon to simple terms that nonspecialists could easily grasp. The parties had to work constantly to build trust and to adjust to each others' worlds.

A key partnership that has not been discussed in detail in this volume is the business and NGO partnership with government. Esterhuyse outlines the leadership role of the South African government in the transition from authoritarian rule to democracy in South Africa (chap. 5). He describes the transition in terms of "structural transformations—managed transformations over time, not adaptations." In this process "The old apartheid state has been transformed into a market-friendly developmental state—a social democracy, and not into a typical liberal democracy." He emphasizes, however, that, "The transition to democracy gave additional leverage to the private sector to play a more decisive social role than the role it was allowed to play under authoritarian conditions." The South African process is evolving in four steps: (1) stable democracy, (2) rising incomes, (3) reasonable distribution of incomes, and (4) stable social fabric.

Esterhuyse points out that South Africa has done well with the first two steps but has been less successful with the third, while the fourth is "still in a very problematic condition." Business can play a major role here because "The state, and its institutions, is not able to create a stable social fabric—in any case not if the state is of a democratic nature."

PURPOSE OF THE BUSINESS ENTERPRISE

This volume is rich in examples of the potential for partnerships between business and NGOs to contribute to development through promoting peace and dampening conflict, as well as the lessons to be learned from these partnerships. Evaluating the contribution of these partnerships involves a judgment as to the appropriate role of the business enterprise and its responsibility to society. Smurthwaite opens the volume (chap. 1) with an analysis of the many crosscurrents in this debate: analyzing whether the corporation is a legal entity or a community, whether it is or can be a moral agent, and the conflicting views of its appropriate role. She concludes that the corporate purpose is built upon the neoclassic theory but its responsibility goes beyond the dictates of that model. For her that "more" is based on Catholic Social Thought:

> For our purposes, we argue that the corporation is a part of the society and that, while its profit-making role is clearly important, this role may not eclipse its relationship or role with regard to human beings, be they employees or those affected by the policies and practices of the corporation. Responsibilities to the common good include responsibilities for the environment in which the corporation operates and for environmental damage these operations may have caused. The corporation, for our purposes, bears both legal responsibilities and moral responsibilities and cannot merely have recourse to carrying only legal responsibilities and obligations.[19]

Assessing the appropriate purpose of the firm is a different undertaking than it was a quarter century ago. A more informed global society is changing its mind about what it expects from the individual business enterprise, and from the global system. This is, indeed, a "New Role for the Firm in the Global Community."

NOTES

1. Parenthetical references in the text refer to chapters in this volume.

2. See Lee A. Tavis, "Determining Standards for the Implementation of CSR/CST" (paper presented at the Sixth International Symposium on Catholic Social Thought and Management Education, October 5–7, 2006, Rome, Italy).

3. For a concrete example of these policies and their local impact, see Lee A. Tavis, "Case 1, The Dolefil Operation in the Philippine Islands," in *Power and Responsibility: Multinational Managers and Developing Country Concerns* (Notre Dame, IN: University of Notre Dame Press, 1997), 169–204.

4. For a discussion of the changing global economic/political/social system, see Lee A. Tavis, "Corporate Governance, Stakeholder Accountability, and Sustainable Peace," *Vanderbilt Journal of Transnational Law* 35, no. 2 (March 2002): 487–547.

5. See Lee A. Tavis, "Microentrepreneurial Development at the Grassroots," in *Power and Responsibility: Multinational Managers and Developing Country Concerns* (Notre Dame, IN: University of Notre Dame Press, 1997), 60–93.

6. Underlying each strategy are managerial assumptions and decisions about the appropriate role of the business enterprise. For an analysis in terms of (1) the basic market, (2) an extension to include long-term enterprise sustainability, and (3) normative departures from the basic market model, see Tavis, "Determining Standards for the Implementation of CSR/CST," 2–6.

7. Technically, civil society is composed of all nongovernmental formal and informal organizations. Business is generally separated as a distinct category from this milieu. NGOs are often identified as the spokespersons for civil society.

8. Charles A. Reilly, "Balancing State, Market and Civil Society: NGOs for a New Development Consensus," in *Poverty and Inequality in Latin America: Issues and New Challenges,* ed. Guillermo O'Donnell and Victor Tokman (Notre Dame, IN: University of Notre Dame Press, 1998).

9. Commission on Global Governance, *Our Global Neighborhood: The Report of the Commission on Global Governance* (Oxford: Oxford University Press, 1995), 254.

10. Julie Fisher, *Non-Governments: NGOs and the Political Development of the Third World* (Bloomfield, CT: Kumarian Press, 1998), 6.

11. Robert O. Keohane and Joseph S. Nye Jr., introduction to *Governance in a Globalizing World,* ed. Joseph S. Nye and John D. Donahue (Washington, DC: Brookings Institution Press, 2000), 1, 15.

12. Commission on Global Governance, *Our Global Neighborhood,* 32.

13. See http://www.mallenbaker.net/csr/nl/97.html#anchor1659.

14. For a definition of these strategies, see Brak Chabuca and Pierre Echard, "Business and NGO Partnerships—For Maximum Impact," *CRS and Accountability,* http://www.sustdev.org/getfile.php?id=283.

15. Thomas Friedman, "Going Green with Greenbacks Internet," *Palm Beach Post,* March 17, 2007, 15A.

16. Mark Holloway, "Harnessing the Power of Business to Fight AIDS: Unilever and MAC Cosmetics" (paper presented at the conference Peace Through Commerce: Partnerships as the New Paradigm, November 13, 2006, University of Notre Dame).

17. Tavis, "Corporate Governance," 508.

18. Although these guidelines are based on the experience of the extractive industry, they apply to all business-NGO partnerships.

19. For an analysis of the appropriate role of the enterprise in a social contract framework leading to support of the United Nations Global Compact as the universal social standard, see Tavis, "Determining Standards for the Implementation of CSR/CST."

CHAPTER 21

Responsible Corporate Citizenship and the Ideals of the United Nations Global Compact

Oliver F. Williams, C.S.C.

INTRODUCTION

This final chapter will offer some overarching reflections that may apply to many of the essays in this volume. The premise of the chapter is that while corporate social responsibility (CSR), or corporate citizenship, is not a new idea, what is emerging in some of these company accounts is a new role for the firm within society. Some companies have a view of corporate citizenship that envisions a state-like role for the corporation, which becomes a quasi-public institution that goes far beyond the traditional division of labor between corporations and governments. In this view CSR is not necessarily undertaken because in some way or another, at some future time, it will enhance profits but rather because the firm is understood to be a socially responsible political actor in global society. The chapter further shows how the work of Adam Smith, the eighteenth-century moral philosopher and author of the "bible of capitalism," could easily accommodate this new responsible corporate citizenship in light of the globalization of the economy. The final section of the chapter highlights how good corporate governance can offer guidance on how this new political role of the firm can be implemented while preserving the democratic nature of society. In all of this, a crucial role for the United Nations Global Compact is underscored.

CAPITALISM: THE MOVING TARGET

> The proper guardians of the public interest are governments, which
> are accountable to all citizens. It is the job of elected politicians to
> set goals for regulators, to deal with externalities, to mediate among
> different interests, to attend to the demands of social justice, to pro-
> vide public goods and collect taxes to pay for them, to establish col-
> lective priorities where that is necessary and appropriate, and to
> organize resources accordingly. The proper business of business is
> business. No apology required.[1]

With this reassertion from neoclassical economics concerning the strict
division of labor between the private and public sectors, the *Economist* offered an uncharacteristically muddled critique of corporate social responsibility, or corporate citizenship, in a recent twenty-two-page survey.[2]
The gist of the argument in the *Economist* is that proponents of CSR have
"a mistaken analysis of how capitalism serves society." In the *Economist*'s
view, those promoting CSR do not believe that free enterprise, *as such,* advances the public good, but rather business must take on projects in the
wider society as their way of contributing to social welfare. These projects then "redeem" business and give it legitimacy for its quest in seeking
profits—which is a purely private good.

Who are these authors who advance the notion of CSR with the mistaken idea that business, as such, does not advance the public good? I
must say, I do not know and the *Economist* never tells us. As a would-be
scholar in this area, I follow the literature closely, and almost everyone
writing in the CSR field acknowledges that business is responsible for
tremendous gains in not only the quantity of goods and services available
but in the quality of life. Advances in life expectancy, infant mortality,
medicines that bring cures and comfort, technology that enables enjoyment of music, and so on are all attributable to the work of business, as
such. Why, then, do many argue for corporate citizenship or CSR?

The Changing Context: A Globalized World

In the 1980s Leon Sullivan, the well-known civil rights leader and pastor,
asked me to serve on the board of directors of the Sullivan Principles for

South Africa. These principles were formulated in a series of meetings involving numerous NGOs (civil society members) and many companies that had operations in South Africa.[3] The principles were designed to promote the human rights of blacks in South Africa. If a company wanted to remain in South Africa, the Sullivan Principles required that company to actively oppose all apartheid legislation and to promote and protect the civil and political rights of blacks in the workplace as well as the community. At its height, the Sullivan Principles had over three hundred U.S. companies as signatories. While the Sullivan Principles were not without controversy, for our purposes the significant point here is that the Sullivan Principles were the first instance of a shift from state-centric regulation to a new form of regulation created and implemented by the private sector and civil society. Opposing apartheid in South Africa was also the first instance where political ends were pursued by *directly* pressuring businesses without going through the government. NGOs, through their research and advocacy work, helped shape public opinion on the evils of apartheid. Up to this time, it was assumed that promoting and protecting civil, political, and social rights were the exclusive domains of the nation-state. What we observe here is the beginning of the demise of the strict division of labor between the private and public sectors. In large measure, this new role of business in society—advancing citizenship rights—was advocated by civil society because the government of South Africa was either unable or unwilling to do it on its own.

Leon Sullivan, the charismatic leader of the Sullivan Principles, advanced another, and perhaps more compelling, argument for companies assuming this new role in society. Sullivan was fond of telling the companies, "Where there is power, there is also responsibility."[4] Sullivan's point was not that companies had caused apartheid, or that they could buy legitimacy by dismantling it. Simply put, apartheid was wrong, and because the companies had the economic power to dismantle it, they should do so. It was the right thing to do. If a company would not work to dismantle apartheid, Sullivan would publicly shame it and force it to leave South Africa. This notion that organizations that have power have to be accountable to society or else they lose their legitimacy is not new. In the business context, Keith Davis, in 1966, coined the phrase "the iron law of business responsibility."[5] In contemporary business literature, including the essays in this volume, the term *license to operate* is often used to convey the idea that society has certain expectations of business. If business does not meet those expectations, business loses its legitimacy, and there is a price to pay as a result. In the South African apartheid struggle, there are many examples of U.S. society influencing the *license to operate* of companies perceived to be sustaining apartheid. For example, in the 1980s, 168 state, city, county, and regional authorities had some form of policy restricting their business dealings with U.S. companies thought to be irresponsible in using their corporate power in South Africa.[6] Thus, the City of Chicago was precluded by one of these "selective purchasing ordinances" from buying buses from General Motors. GM understood the power of the people.

Jeffrey Sachs, arguing with a logic not unlike that of Leon Sullivan, makes the point that with some moderate assistance from the developed world, the dire poverty characterizing the lives of millions of people could be overcome. His position, summarized by Marshall Greenhut in chapter 16 of this volume, has caught the attention of many large companies. Greenhut details how General Electric is advancing the war on poverty in Africa. General Electric is clearly meeting society's expectations by participating in this venture. Laws like the selective purchasing ordinance in the City of Chicago prepared large companies to be proactive in meeting society's expectations and to see the wisdom of collaborating with NGOs in designing and implementing ethical rules for the global community. The UN Global Compact, for example, entails self-regulation, rule making, and rule implementation without the assistance of governments. "Soft" transnational law complements "hard" national law, and the impetus for this law comes not from national political discussion but from transnational civil society. At least in practice, there is clearly a change underway in the way the responsibilities of the private and public sectors are apportioned. More reflection on the conceptual foundations of this recalibration may be helpful.

While the *Economist* article cited above attributes these new consumer expectations that business take on projects in the wider society to "a mistaken analysis of how capitalism serves society," most of the companies profiled in this volume have a different perspective. Most business leaders are thinking and feeling human beings who realize that their companies might have the managerial talent and resources to help overcome poverty, especially where governments are unable or unwilling to do so. These leaders respond to the sort of consumer expectations, outlined in chapter 16, from the Environics Institute Millennium Poll on Corporate Responsibility.[7] That survey, mirroring others, reported that two-thirds of consumers want companies to go beyond the traditional division of labor between the private and public sectors and to take on projects that might build a better society. Are these consumers and business leaders ill-informed concerning the nature and purpose of capitalism?

I am reminded of a book by a *New York Times* business editor, Leonard Silk, entitled *Capitalism: The Moving Target.*[8] Silk's point in this book was that the free enterprise system survived and even thrived because leaders understood that it was an evolving system that needed to respond to the times. The biggest change in business in our time is its overwhelming success in producing goods and services that consumers want—hence the business world's vast economic power. Large businesses, because of their success, dominate our economies and our world. For example, General Electric has sales of over $100 billion a year and has over 300,000 employees; IBM has sales of over $80 billion and some 300,000 employees. There are some 190 nations in the world, and very few have government revenues that come near these figures and those of other large companies.[9] This is a remarkable change from the world of Adam Smith, the eighteenth-century moral philosopher who first helped us understand the dynamics of wealth creation in his famous "bible of capitalism," *The Wealth of Nations.* Smith championed the strict division of labor between the private and public sectors, and this division clearly made sense in his time. With the enormous growth in the power and capacity of business, would Smith still champion such a strict division today? I think not.

As indicated in the introduction to this volume, I advocate the United Nations Global Compact as a forum and an instrument to bring the best minds together from business and civil society. There is a growing consensus that with the large aggregates of money and power, multinational corporations (MNCs) have a moral obligation as corporate citizens to assist the poor in the global community, but the extent of these obligations is unclear. The Global Compact offers a forum under the umbrella of the United Nations—with its visibility, global reach, and convening power—where some of the best members of civil society—nongovernmental organizations, academic and public policy institutions, individual companies, business associations, and labor representatives—can come together to discuss the changing role of business and its *moral* purpose.

Retrieving the Moral Purpose of Business in a Global Economy

Perhaps the moral philosopher who has developed the intellectual under-
pinnings for the most demanding vision of the moral purpose of business
is Alasdair MacIntyre.[10] Will the higher standards of living, if they ever
come to poor countries, in fact lead to a better quality of life? MacIntyre,
in the face of a globalized economy he characterizes as marked by individualism and acquisitiveness, opts for an economic community where
the virtues of character essential for the good life can flourish. He uses the
example of two fishing communities, one characterized by a single-minded
quest for profits and the other by a wider range of objectives including
sustainability, community preservation, and promoting excellence in the
task of fishing.[11] It is helpful to focus on the convergence in the views of
MacIntyre and the Global Compact in that both are trying to retrieve the
notion of the moral purpose of business.

One way to view the Compact is as an attempt to revive the moral un-
derpinnings of the economy that were assumed by Adam Smith. While
many would characterize the worldview of MacIntyre's first fishing village as that of Adam Smith, I join those who have another interpretation.[12]
In *The Wealth of Nations,* Smith sought to understand why some nations
were wealthier than others.[13] Part of his answer was that nations that encouraged free competitive markets were wealthier. In a curious kind of
way, in the context of the economy, *when each person pursues his or her self-
interest the common good is enhanced* and all are wealthier. Given competition, the baker bakes the very best bread possible and sells it at the lowest
price feasible so that he will have the resources to buy what he wants. Although motivated by self-interest, the result is that the community has
good bread at a reasonable cost. Thus, Smith showed how economic self-
interest is beneficial for the community.

In my view, however, the crucial point in Smith's analysis is his assumption in *The Wealth of Nations* that becomes quite explicit in his *The
Theory of Moral Sentiments.*[14] The "self-interest" of business people could
be shaped by moral forces in the community so that self-interest did not
always degenerate into greed and selfishness. Wealth creation enabled
and sustained a humane community when it was practiced by virtuous
people.

The Compact is not going to shape global business into something like MacIntyre's ideal fishing community any time soon. My argument is that Smith assumed that an acquisitive economy existed in the context of a moral community, which would ensure that a single-minded focus on making money would not perdure. Yet it is precisely this challenge of fostering the growth of humane values in the *global* society, a challenge heretofore managed by nation-states for their own domestic situation, that marks the unique mission of the Global Compact.[15] The argument made by Global Compact officials is that unless the moral purpose of business is retrieved, economic globalization is doomed to failure:

> It is precisely because a backlash to globalization would represent a historically unmatched threat to economic prosperity and peace that the Global Compact urges international business leaders to take reasonable steps to secure the emerging values of global civil society in exchange for a commitment on the part of the United Nations to market openness.[16]

Globalization critics see little value in the Compact unless "the emerging values of global civil society" are somehow mandated by a worldwide legal framework. The creators of the Compact, seeing little prospect for worldwide legal statutes, advance a vision of the moral purpose of business that relies on transparency and the interest companies have in maintaining their good reputation as the ultimate sanction.

There is a growing awareness by multinational companies that global business is only possible in a world where basic ethical principles are assumed. Some evidence for this moral sensitivity of MNCs is seen in the formation of the Caux Principles, a set of moral ideals not too unlike the Compact and subscribed to by a number of prominent global companies. Founded in 1985, the Caux Principles do not have the visibility, global reach, and convening power with many stakeholders that accrue under the umbrella of the United Nations, but they do represent a significant attempt by companies to accent the moral purpose of business.[17] Largely because of the UN sponsorship, however, I argue that the Compact has the potential to be a more effective vehicle than Caux.

The moral context assumed by Adam Smith in his *Wealth of Nations* and made more explicit in *The Theory of Moral Sentiments* is retrieved with the notion of the Global Compact. Without the values embedded in the Compact—for example, trust, fairness, integrity, and respect for people— global capitalism would neither be effective nor considered legitimate for long. In my view, Smith offers two sorts of justification for doing the right thing. In the *Wealth of Nations* a utilitarian moral logic is the primary justification, whereas in *Moral Sentiments* one does the right thing because it is the right thing to do. Both of these types of justifications are assumed by the Compact. Principles concerning the environment and safety in the workplace, for example, are justified by the first sort, while the Principles concerning human rights are largely matters justified by the second type. The Compact brings to the fore that business has a moral purpose, and this is highlighted by a quote from Ban Ki-moon, the current Secretary-General of the United Nations: "Business practices rooted in universal values can bring social and economic gains."[18] To be sure, the Global Compact of today is a far cry from a force that might shape significant changes in the moral values of the global community. Yet one has to start somewhere, and the authors of the Compact envision it as an incremental process of learning and improvement rooted in local networks sharing the same universal values—but it is now only at the starting gate.

Of course, one premise of the Compact is that there will always be NGOs, activists, social investors, and others who will be on the scene to pressure firms and the Global Compact to be better corporate citizens.[19] There is a growing realization that NGOs or organizations of civil society play an important role in such a dialogue because their focus is properly the common good—the culture of civility, health, environmental protection, and so on. This is certainly not to say that NGOs are always above reproach, for they too need accountability structures. In economic terms NGOs focus on overcoming the negative externalities of business. Already major NGOs, including Amnesty International, Oxfam, Human Rights Watch, World Conservation Union, World Wildlife Fund, and Transparency International have joined and are participating in the deliberations of the Compact. The International Confederation of Free Trade Unions, business associations, and academic and public policy institutions have joined as well. The business schools endorsing the Principles for Responsible Management Education are the most recent new category of partners with the Compact.

GOOD CORPORATE GOVERNANCE IN A GLOBAL ECONOMY: THE LICENSE TO OPERATE AS A QUESTION OF TRUST

Several of the essays in this volume have referred to the crucial role of trust for the fruitful interaction of business and society. It may be that this focus on trust can shed light on the movement toward an expanded role of business in society. When the cities and states passed the selective purchasing ordinances in the 1980s, thereby changing the terms of the license to operate, the root cause was a lack of trust in business and a growing divide between the values of business and those of society. This divide most often results in public pressure for additional regulation and legislation to control business, what economists call "transaction costs." Francis Fukuyama, in his important book on trust, shows how a low-trust society has higher transaction costs than a high-trust society, and he likens these costs to a kind of tax.[20] Perhaps the most dramatic, recent example of a change in the social contract and of new transaction costs for business is the 2002 U.S. Sarbanes-Oxley law enacted after the accounting scandals, which has increased auditing expenses 200 to 300 percent. The movement for good corporate governance is, in large measure, a response to a decline in trust.

Compared to ten years ago, most surveys on trust levels in countries throughout the world show that public trust in business institutions and leadership is at a low level. Perhaps the most respected survey is that done under the leadership of the World Economic Forum (WEF), an NGO funded by over one thousand of the world's most influential corporations. A 2004 WEF report indicated that in a survey of some eighteen countries, the percentage of persons saying that they had "A Lot" or "Some Trust" in the executives of multinational companies averaged 33 percent.[21] That same survey indicated that the leaders themselves enjoy less trust than the institutions they lead and that the attributes of leadership considered most important in garnering trust are honesty and vision. A 2007 survey conducted by Harris Interactive and the *Wall Street Journal* ranking the corporate reputations of the most visible companies in the United States concluded that "the majority of people (69%) continues to characterize corporate America's reputation as either 'not good' or 'terrible.'"[22] What is the best way for corporations to restore and build new public trust in business? To answer this, it will be necessary to explore just what trust is and why it is given and withheld.

The immediate causes of lack of trust in business are not difficult to catalogue: financial frauds such as those at Enron, WorldCom, and Parmalat; corporate governance that approves exorbitant executive pay unrelated to performance; the volatility in world stock markets; and corporate deception, such as false dating of stock options. My concern, however, is to probe the underlying causes and nature of the trust deficit and thus be in a position to offer strategies to renew trust that are likely to be successful. A more comprehensive understanding of trust may also help us understand the move toward corporate citizenship and the changing role of business in society.

I have found the work of Onora O'Neill, principal of Newnham College, Cambridge, most helpful in probing the underlying nature of trust.[23] O'Neill suggests that placing and refusing trust is an age-old problem, and she refers us to the method of Socrates to clarify the issues. Active inquiry—asking questions and assessing answers, listening and checking information, or what is sometimes called the Socratic method—is the way we most often place or refuse trust. In O'Neill's view the calls for complete openness and global transparency, while possibly important values for a number of reasons, are not the best remedy for restoring trust. We need to follow the Socratic model and give people the opportunity to ask specific persons in business about specific information and specific actions that have been implemented. Through this process of active inquiry, a firm foundation for building and restoring trust is realized. Delving further into the nature of trust, the work of Mayer, Davis, and Schoorman in developing a model of trust in organizations helps to us understand why the method of Socratic active inquiry builds trust.[24] They define trust as "the willingness of a party to be vulnerable to the actions of another partly based on the expectations that the other will perform a particular action important to the trustor, irrespective of the ability to monitor or control that other party."[25] Thus, active inquiry serves to provide a rational basis for taking a risk, for making oneself vulnerable. The goal of their work is to highlight the reasons why one person would trust another—that is, what facilitates a trustor (trusting party) to trust a trustee (the party to be trusted)?

After an extensive review of the literature, Mayer, Davis, and Schoorman conclude that although numerous characteristics of the trustee enhance the development of trust in the trustor, these may all be related to three core characteristics: ability, benevolence, and integrity. Ability is defined as "that group of skills, competencies, and characteristics which enable a party to have influence within some specific domain." Benevolence is "the extent to which a trustee is believed to want to do good to the trustor." Integrity includes a strong sense of justice and fairness and is a part of character; it entails a trustee adhering "to a set of principles that the trustor finds acceptable."[26] Trustworthiness is conditioned on the perceptions that one has ability, benevolence, and integrity. If these core characteristics are perceived as high in a trustee, then a trustor will allow the personal vulnerability we commonly know as trust.

To be sure, trustworthiness is a continuum. When reports of polls speak of a decline in trust in corporations and their leaders, there is no implication here that people have lost all trust. Most are still purchasing products from these companies and many continue to invest in them.

What is being said, however, is that the perceptions of the characteristics and actions of business leaders by many people lead them to trust business less and to perceive that there is more risk involved in trusting behavior. This perception of greater risk leads many citizens to lobby for stronger organizational control systems, for example, the U.S. Sarbanes-Oxley law. The irony here, however, is that such control systems may actually inhibit the development of trust since the good behavior of the business leader may now be perceived to be the result of the law rather than because of integrity or benevolence—that is, trustworthiness. People will begin to move to a more robust trust from a modest trust when trust (not control systems) actually yields good outcomes. When business leaders show by their actions that they actually have ability, benevolence, and integrity, then people will trust them more. Responsible corporate citizenship activities have the potential to enhance trust.

Many of the discussions of companies involved with corporate citizenship activities in this book demonstrate that at least some companies understand that they are a crucial part of contemporary society. As Sir Mark Moody-Stuart put it in the foreword, "All of us, including everyone in business, have a strong stake in the sound working of society." These companies have a mission statement embodying societal expectations, including an acceptance of corporate citizenship, a widened purpose, and ethical values. Corporate citizenship activities, then, are a factor in building and maintaining trust because they enhance the perception that the firms have integrity and benevolence. Another method for building trust, however, is to have ongoing, open, and honest communication available for all interested stakeholders. Supporters and critics alike must know that they are able to engage in a dialogue with business officials and that they will be treated honestly and fairly. Such communication also ensures that this new political role of the firm is congruent with the democratic nature of society.

Many believe that simply including moral values in corporate mission statements and issuing a code of conduct will enhance and build public trust in business, but just the opposite is true. Prakash Sethi argues that a code without independent external monitoring, verification, and public disclosure will often be dismissed as impotent and irrelevant.[27] Similar to O'Neill's insight, Sethi makes the point that in order to avoid adding to public cynicism, there must be some provision for objective measurement, independent verification, and transparency regarding a code of conduct for a business. The Global Reporting Initiative (GRI) is making some progress in meeting these concerns.[28] This move toward more transparency, monitoring, and reporting is crucial as the corporation becomes more of a political actor in the global economy. The *King Report* addresses these issues.

Contrary to the position of the survey in the *Economist,* which argues that CSR is based on "a mistaken analysis of how capitalism serves society," contemporary corporate governance guidelines take full cognizance of the changing role of business in society and advocate CSR and responsible corporate citizenship. Perhaps the resource that summarizes the best international practices in corporate governance most effectively and comprehensively, especially for a developing country, is the 2002 *King Report on Corporate Governance for South Africa,* published by the Institute of Directors in Southern Africa.[29] This study draws on that report. The *King Report* opens with a quote from Sir Adrian Cadbury, a highly regarded business leader in the United Kingdom: "Corporate Governance is concerned with holding the balance between economic and social goals and between individual and communal goals . . . the aim is to align as nearly as possible the interests of individuals, corporations and society."[30] It is clear from this understanding of corporate governance that every attempt will be made by business "to adhere to a set of principles that the trustor finds acceptable." Thus, the overall objective is to be a corporation of integrity and to be perceived in that way.

From the start the *King Report* raises the question as to whether the corporate governance model should be *inclusive* or *exclusive*—that is, should it be addressed to all relevant stakeholders or simply to shareholders. This is a crucial question for, in terms of this study, the issue is to whom is a company responsible—the shareholders alone or all relevant stakeholders? The *King Report* argues that in the world we live in today, there is no choice. The inclusive model that considers key stakeholders such as employees, customers, suppliers, and communities is the only relevant one. The report argues that, while in the past to obtain a "license to operate" boards only needed to influence the appropriate government regulator, today a board has to consider a whole host of stakeholders, including consumers, ethical pressure groups, investigative media, investors, communities, etc. With this approach, the political role of the firm can be in harmony with the democratic nature of society. Thus, in terms of this study, good corporate governance will have to be such that the perceptions of all these stakeholders about the ability, benevolence, and integrity of the company and its leaders are positive.

It may be helpful to review what the *King Report* suggests with regard to ability, benevolence, and integrity for a well-run firm. The point here is that the best-run companies are not simply putting their fingers to the wind, determining what consumer expectations are, and then designing appropriate CSR activities. This "flavor-of-the-month" approach is rightfully criticized by the *Economist* and others. Companies discussed in this volume and others demonstrating good corporate governance have a corporate culture in place that permeates the whole organization and reflects an understanding of the role of business in today's society as well as its limitations. I now consider how the report addresses the issues of integrity, benevolence, and ability.

Integrity

The *King Report* offers a number of recommendations for enhancing the major stakeholders' perception of the integrity of a business and its leaders. Included among these are the following.

Right to Information. In numerous places the report stresses the need for honest communication with a business's shareholders and relevant stakeholders and highlights that this communication should be done "openly and promptly and with substance prevailing over form."[31]

Character. Board members as well as management in the firm must be men and women who "will behave honestly and with integrity in regard to their shareholders and others."[32]

Integrated Sustainability Reporting. In addition to financial reports, companies should report on social and environmental issues (the triple bottom line). For example, black economic empowerment, advancement of women, workplace safely issues, and HIV/AIDS issues are just a few of the crucial ethical issues currently facing South Africa, and they should be discussed with stakeholders.[33]

Organizational Integrity. This section of the *King Report* outlines a significant program for enhancing the perceptions of integrity by stakeholders and merits being quoted in full:

> Every company should engage its stakeholders in determining the company's standards of ethical behavior. It should demonstrate its commitment to organizational integrity by codifying its standards in a code of ethics.
>
> Each company should demonstrate its commitment to its code of ethics by:
>
> - Creating systems and procedures to introduce, monitor and enforce its ethical code
> - Assigning high level individuals to oversee compliance to the ethical code
> - Assessing the integrity of new appointees in the selection and promotion procedures
> - Exercising due care in delegating discretionary authority
> - Communicating with, and training, all employees regarding enterprise values, standards and compliance procedures
> - Providing, monitoring and auditing safe systems for reporting of unethical or risky behavior
> - Enforcing appropriate discipline with consistency
>
> Disclosure should be made of adherence to the company's code of ethics against the above criteria. The disclosure should include a statement as to the extent the directors believe the ethical standards and the above criteria are being met. If this is considered inadequate there should be further disclosure of how the desired end-state will be achieved.

Companies should strongly consider their dealings with individuals or entities not demonstrating its same level of commitment to organizational integrity.[34]

In summarizing the *King Report*'s recommendations on integrity, it is clear that the authors believe that there is no substitute for men and women of character in leadership roles in business. Integrity is not just an *instrumental* value—although good ethics may be good business—but rather integrity is an *intrinsic* value. Integrity is not simply a value when rational, self-interested calculations demonstrate that it will yield more profit but rather honesty and fairness are a constitutive dimension of what it means to be human. Business leaders are first of all human beings and only secondarily managers of wealth creation. To check our human values at the office door is to invite chaos and spread distrust in business.

Ability

After Enron many came to have serious doubts about the ability of board members and the top management of leading companies. Good corporate governance is designed to ensure that only the most able performers are promoted and retained in major leadership positions. Stakeholder perceptions of the ability of corporate leadership would be enhanced by a number of *King Report* recommendations, including the following.

Qualities of a Board Member. The *King Report* specifies that nonexecutive directors (directors not involved in the day-to-day management of the company) "should be individuals of caliber and credibility, and have the necessary skills and experience to bring judgment to bear independent of management."[35] Skills to deal with issues such as equity, standards of conduct, evaluation of performance, and strategy are considered essential. It is recommended that background checks be carried out on potential directors to ensure they are "fit and proper."[36] The report recommends a majority of nonexecutive directors and a consideration of the demographics of South Africa "in relation to the composition of the board."[37]

Evaluation of Board Members. The report recommends a self-evaluation of the board as a whole as well as its committees and each individual member. Skills, experience, demographics, diversity, and performance should be evaluated.[38] Risk management processes in the company are a key oversight responsibility of a board and should be evaluated.

Benevolence

As indicated above, benevolence is understood as "the extent to which a trustee is believed to want to do good to the trustor." The *King Report* opens its section on sustainability reporting with a quote from the work of the World Business Council on Sustainable Development that highlights the role of business in shaping a better life for all: "Corporate citizenship is the commitment of business to contribute to sustainable economic development, working with employees, their families, the local community and society at large to improve their quality of life."[39] The report touches on the area of the perceived benevolence of business in numerous ways, including the following.

Reputation. If doing the right thing because it is the right thing is not enough to direct corporate behavior, the report reminds companies that "reputation is a function of stakeholder perception of a company's integrity and efficiency" based on observation of a company's environmental practices, community relations, customer service, etc. The investment community increasingly factors reputation into an "ethical premium" in valuing companies. Thus "'non-financial issues' have financial consequences for business."[40]

Corporate Citizenship. Corporate social responsibility or corporate citizenship is defined, borrowing from Business for Social Responsibility, as "business decision-making linked to ethical values, compliance with legal requirements, and respect for people, communities and the environment."[41] The report notes that sustainability and corporate citizenship are concepts closely related to the idea of *Ubuntu,* African humanism. "Ubuntu means humanness and includes supportiveness, co-operation and solidarity." It highlights the "inter-dependent relationships between an enterprise and the community in which it exists."[42] In the context of South Africa, the *King Report* recommends that specific issues be addressed in sustainability reporting:

> Every company should report at least annually, on the nature and the extent of its social, transformation, ethical, safety, health and environmental management policies and practices. The board of directors should, in determining what is relevant for disclosure, take

into account the environment in which the company operates. For South Africa, the board should disclose:

i.   Whether it has adopted an appropriate HIV/AIDS strategy plan and policies to address and manage the potential impact of HIV/AIDS on the company;

ii. Whether it has developed format procurement policies that take into account black economic empowerment;

iii. Whether it has developed and implemented a definitive set of standards and practices in the company based on a clearly articulated code of ethics.[43]

The *King Report,* not unlike many other reports offering guidance on good corporate governance, especially in developing countries, assumes that business has a wider role in society. It focuses on the "inter-dependent relationships between an enterprise and the community in which it exists." CSR or responsible corporate citizenship is taken to be one manifestation, among many, that a firm realizes that where there is power, there is also responsibility.

The hypothesis in this section on trust is that if members of society perceive ability, benevolence, and integrity in a business leader, then there will be trust. Further, the point is made that following good corporate governance entails demonstrating ability, benevolence, and integrity. It is these qualities in a corporate culture, especially benevolence and integrity, that engender responsible corporate citizenship.

Thus, the business case for responsible corporate citizenship is made on the basis that it engenders trust, a key factor in the free enterprise system. Without "a comprehending and supportive climate of opinion,"[44] as the *Economist* put it, transaction costs go up and wealth creation goes down. To be sure, this theoretical model only sets the stage for empirical studies that may add further insight in understanding how to improve the trust levels in business and its leaders. One survey adds some credibility to the hypothesis that following good corporate governance enhances trust levels. The 2004 World Economic Forum survey on trust levels shows that 63 percent of South African citizens trust global MNCs operating in the country.[45] This is more than 20 percent higher than the reported global average trust levels. The research, conducted in South Africa by

GlobeScan, indicates that, in part, this higher trust of companies in South Africa results from large companies following the *King Report* and listening and responding to the plea of citizens for antiretroviral drugs for those suffering from HIV/AIDS.[46] Companies such as Coca-Cola, Anglo American, Old Mutual, Anglo Gold, De Beers, Heineken, Ford, and Daimler-Chrysler have a continuous dialogue with key stakeholders and have provided medicines. Global companies have also become leaders in black economic empowerment as a part of their role as corporate citizens. The 2007 report on the annual poll by Harris Interactive and the *Wall Street Journal* also confirmed that social responsibility can play a big roll in positive survey results.[47] Microsoft and Johnson & Johnson ranked numbers one and two, respectively, in corporate reputation in that poll.

CONCLUSION

Some of our authors have suggested that a business case has to be made to sustain responsible corporate citizenship, as, for example, Klaus Leisinger has argued with his suggestion of enhancing reputational capital. Tim Fort, on the other hand, suggests his "good trust model," where a firm acts for other reasons than those entailed in its economically productive role. Many companies discussed in this book have not clearly articulated whether they expect a commercial gain from their CSR activity. It may be helpful to draw an analogy between an individual and a firm. Just as an individual citizen has two sets of responsibilities, a role responsibility (husband, lawyer, father, for example) and a citizenship responsibility (taxpayer, volunteer for projects for the common good—playgrounds, eldercare, neighborhood watch, for example), so too does a firm. A business has a *role* responsibility—to produce goods and services while returning on investment—and a *citizenship* responsibility. This citizenship responsibility can take many forms, as shown in the discussions in the volume, and it may or may not enhance the firm's economically productive role. In my view, to try to determine whether being a good citizen, as an individual or as a firm, has a cash value in monetary terms is beside the point. Corporate citizenship activities that enhance life both for the firms and for people in the wider society have value. Again, we return to the purpose of business and its relation to the common good. Echoing much of the secular literature, Catholic Social Thought says it well: "In fact, the purpose of a business firm is not simply to make a profit, but is to be found in its very existence as a *community of persons,* who in various ways, are endeavoring to satisfy their basic needs, and who form a particular group at the service of the whole society."[48]

A lingering issue identified by several of our authors is the question of when a firm has done enough to meet its corporate citizenship responsibilities. Mainstream neoclassical economics has noted correctly that business firms and their managers are not democratically controlled. When multinational companies assume state-like roles, there must be dialogue and open communication with relevant stakeholders in accord with good corporate governance. Thus, the firm as a political actor has more democratic processes and internal structures. Yet sometimes stakeholders can demand more than a firm can possibly deliver; for example, some have asked pharmaceutical firms to give free antiretroviral medicines to all 25 million people in sub-Saharan Africa who have the HIV virus. Where do you draw the line on what constitutes responsible corporate citizenship? This requires an informed public and much discussion. The forum provided by the UN Global Compact holds much promise in addressing this issue. Time will tell if it is successful.

NOTES

1. Clive Crook, "The Good Company: A Survey of Corporate Social Responsibility," *Economist,* January 22, 2005, 22.

2. Ibid., 1–22.

3. S. Prakash Sethi and Oliver F. Williams, *Economic Imperative and Ethical Value in Global Business: The South African Experience and International Codes Today* (Notre Dame, IN: University of Notre Dame Press, 2001).

4. Ibid., xii.

5. Keith Davis and Robert Blomstrom, *Business and Its Environment* (New York: McGraw-Hill, 1966).

6. Sethi and Williams, *Economic Imperatives and Global Business,* 295–97.

7. See http://www.iblf.org/docs/MillenniumPoll.pdf.

8. B. Leonard Silk, *Capitalism: The Moving Target* (New York: Praeger, 1974).

9. For the most recent figures, see http://www.money.cnn.com/magazines/fortune/global500/2007.

10. See Alasdair MacIntyre, "A Partial Response to My Critics," in *After MacIntyre,* ed. John Horton and Susan Mendus (Notre Dame, IN: University of

Notre Dame Press, 1994), 283–304. This section was previously published in Oliver Williams, "The U.N. Global Impact: The Challenge and the Promise," *Business Ethics Quarterly* 14, no. 4 (2004): 755–74.

11. While I find MacIntyre insightful and provocative, in the final analysis, I side with Andrew Wicks: "I find enough coherence, hope, and possibility in both capitalism and 'modernity' to cast my lot with those who see the Enlightenment (and what followed) as something other than a disaster." See Andrew C. Wicks, "On MacIntyre, Modernity and the Virtues: A Response to Dobson," *Business Ethics Quarterly* 7, no. 4 (1997): 133–35.

12. See Patricia H. Werhane, "Business Ethics and the Origins of Contemporary Capitalism: Economics and Ethics in the Work of Adam Smith and Herbert Spencer," *Journal of Business Ethics* 24 (2000): 185–98; see also Oliver F. Williams, "Catholic Social Teacher: A Communitarian Democratic Capitalism for the New World Order," *Journal of Business Ethics* 12 (1993): 919–23. The 1991 encyclical letter of Pope John Paul II, *Centesimus Annus,* makes this central point: "If economic life is absolutized, if the production and consumption of goods become the center of social life and society's only value, not subject to any other value, the reason is to be found not so much in the economic system itself as in the fact that the entire socio-cultural system, by ignoring the ethical and religious dimension, has been weakened, and ends by limiting itself to the production of goods and services alone" (John Paul II, *Centesimus Annus* [Washington, DC: U.S. Catholic Conference, 1991], para. 39).

13. Adam Smith, *The Wealth of Nations,* 5th ed., ed. Edwin Cannan (1776; London: Methuen, 1904).

14. Adam Smith, *The Theory of Moral Sentiments,* 6th ed. (1759; London: A. Millar, 1790).

15. A good overview of the issues addressed by the Global Compact was presented in the keynote address to the Society of Business Ethics and the Social Issues in Management Division of the Academy of Management meeting in Chicago, August 7, 1999. See Douglass Cassel, "Human Rights and Business Responsibilities in the Global Marketplace," *Business Ethics Quarterly* 11, no. 2 (2001): 261–74.

16. Sandrine Tesner and Georg Kell, *The United Nations and Business* (New York: St. Martin's Press, 2000), 51.

17. Participants in the Caux Principles have been from twenty-seven countries and include such U.S. companies as 3M International, Chevron, Time Inc., the Prudential Insurance Company of America, Procter and Gamble, Chase Manhattan Bank, Medtronic Inc., Monsanto Company, Honeywell Inc., Cargill Inc., and the Bank of America. See the Website at http:// www.cauxroundtable.org. Accountability as discussed here is even less a requirement in the Caux Principles, and this endeavor has much less visibility. For the text of the Caux Principles, see Oliver F. Williams, ed., *Global Codes of Conduct* (Notre Dame, IN:

University of Notre Dame Press, 2000), 384–88. See in particular in this volume Gerald Cavanagh, "Executives' Code of Business Conduct: Prospects for the Caux Principles," 169–82; and Kenneth E. Goodpaster, "The Caux Round Table Principles: Corporate Moral Reflection in a Global Business Environment," 183–95.

18. See http://www.globalcompactfoundation.org.

19. For an example of this countervailing power of NGOs, see the letter by Louise Frecheete, Deputy Secretary-General of the United Nations, of June 3, 2003, responding to the officers of Oxfam, Amnesty International, Lawyers Committee for Human Rights, and Human Rights Watch, who are pressuring for more accountability in the Compact (http://www.globalpolicy.org/ngos/business/2003/0626secret.htm. For a recent, similar criticism, see "Global Compact Leaders Summit: NGO Participants Raise Concerns," June 24, 2004, http://web.amnesty.org/pages/ec-letter-240604-eng.

20. Francis Fukuyama, *Trust: The Social Virtues and the Creation of Prosperity* (New York: Free Press, 1995).

21. See http://www.teresearch.com/local/World_Economic_Forum.pdf.

22. See http://www.harrisinteractive.com/services/reputation.asp.

23. Onora O'Neill, *A Question of Trust: The BBC Reith Lectures* (Cambridge: Cambridge University Press, 2002).

24. R. C. Mayer, J. H. Davis, and F. D. Schoorman, "An Interactive Model of Organizational Trust," *Academy of Management Review* 20, no. 3 (1995): 709–34.

25. Ibid., 712.

26. Ibid., 714.

27. S. Prakash Sethi, *Setting Global Standards: Guidelines for Creating Codes of Conduct in Multinational Companies* (Hoboken, NJ: John Wiley and Sons, 2003). See also Andreas Georg Scherer, Guido Palazzom, and Dorothée Bauman, "Global Rules and Private Actors: Toward a New Role of the Transnational Corporation in Global Governance," *Business Ethics Quarterly* 16, no. 4 (2006): 505–32.

28. See http://www.globalreporting.org.

29. Institute of Directors in Southern Africa, *King Report on Corporate Governance for South Africa–2002* (Parklands, South Africa: Institute of Directors in Southern Africa, 2002).

30. Ibid., 5.

31. Ibid., 21.

32. Ibid., 18.

33. Ibid., 37.

34. Ibid., 37–38.

35. Ibid., 24.

36. Ibid., 25.

37. Ibid., 23.

38. Ibid., 29.

39. Ibid., 96.

40. Ibid., 104.

41. Ibid., 96.

42. Ibid., 99.

43. Ibid., 39.

44. Crook, "The Good Company," 10.

45. See http://www.weforum.org.

46. Rob Rose, "SA Trust in Global Companies High, WEF Survey Finds," *Business Day,* April 2, 2004.

47. See http://www.harrisinteractive.com.

48. Pope John Paul II, *Centesimus Annus,* 35.

Appendix 1

The Principles for Responsible Management Education

INTRODUCTION

The Principles for Responsible Management Education (PRME), launched at the 2007 Global Compact Leaders Summit on July 5 in Geneva, provide a framework for academic institutions to advance corporate social responsibility through the incorporation of universal values into curricula and research. The PRME have been developed by an international task force consisting of sixty deans, university presidents, and official representatives of leading business schools and follow from a recommendation of all academic stakeholders of the Global Compact. For further information, see the Website of the UN Global Compact http://www.unglobalcompact.org.

THE PRINCIPLES FOR RESPONSIBLE MANAGEMENT EDUCATION

As institutions of higher learning involved in the education of current and future managers we are voluntarily committed to engaging in a continuous process of improvement of the following Principles and their application, reporting on progress to all our stakeholders and exchanging effective practices with other academic institutions:

Principle 1. Purpose: We will develop the capabilities of students to be future generators of sustainable value for business and society at large and to work for an inclusive and sustainable global economy.

Principle 2. Values: We will incorporate into our academic activities and curricula the values of global social responsibility as portrayed in international initiatives such as the United Nations Global Compact.

Principle 3. Method: We will create educational frameworks, materials, processes and environments that enable effective learning experiences for responsible leadership.

Principle 4. Research: We will engage in conceptual and empirical research that advances our understanding about the role, dynamics, and impact of corporations in the creation of sustainable social, environmental and economic value.

Principle 5. Partnership: We will interact with managers of business corporations to extend our knowledge of their challenges in meeting social and environmental responsibilities and to explore jointly effective approaches to meeting these challenges.

Principle 6. Dialogue: We will facilitate and support dialog and debate among educators, business, government, consumers, media, civil society organizations and other interested groups and stakeholders on critical issues related to global social responsibility and sustainability.

We understand that our own organizational practices should serve as examples of the values and attitudes we convey to our students.

Appendix 2

Developing the Principles for Responsible Investment

In early 2005 the UN Secretary-General invited a group of the world's largest institutional investors to join a process to develop the Principles for Responsible Investment (PRI). Individuals representing 20 institutional investors from 12 countries agreed to participate in the Investor Group. The Group accepted ownership of the Principles, and had the freedom to develop them as they saw fit.

The Group was supported by a 70-person multi-stakeholder group of experts from the investment industry, intergovernmental and governmental organizations, civil society and academia. The process, conducted between April 2005 and January 2006 involved a total of five days of face-to-face deliberations by the investors and four days by the experts, with hundreds of hours of follow-up activity. The Principles for Responsible Investment emerged as a result of these meetings.

The process was coordinated by the United Nations Environment Programme Finance Initiative (UNEP FI) and the UN Global Compact. The PRI reflects the core values of the group of large investors whose investment horizon is generally long, and whose portfolios are often highly diversified. However, the Principles are open to all institutional investors, investment managers and professional service partners to support.

Following the launch of the Principles, Phase 2 of the process will promote adoption of the Principles by additional investors, provide comprehensive resources to assist investors in implementing the Principles and actions, and facilitate collaboration among signatories.

THE PRINCIPLES FOR RESPONSIBLE INVESTMENT

As institutional investors, we have a duty to act in the best long-term interests of our beneficiaries. In this fiduciary role, we believe that environmental, social, and corporate governance (ESG) issues can affect the performance of investment portfolios (to varying degrees across companies, sectors, regions, asset classes and through time). We also recognise that applying these Principles may better align investors with broader objectives of society. Therefore, where consistent with our fiduciary responsibilities, we commit to the following:

1. We will incorporate ESG issues into investment analysis and decision-making processes.

Possible actions:
- Address ESG issues in investment policy statements
- Support development of ESG-related tools, metrics, and analyses
- Assess the capabilities of internal investment managers to incorporate ESG issues
- Assess the capabilities of external investment managers to incorporate ESG issues
- Ask investment service providers (such as financial analysts, consultants, brokers, research firms, or rating companies) to integrate ESG factors into evolving research and analysis
- Encourage academic and other research on this theme
- Advocate ESG training for investment professionals

2. We will be active owners and incorporate ESG issues into our ownership policies and practices.

Possible actions:
- Develop and disclose an active ownership policy consistent with the Principles
- Exercise voting rights or monitor compliance with voting policy (if outsourced)
- Develop an engagement capability (either directly or through outsourcing)

- Participate in the development of policy, regulation, and standard setting (such as promoting and protecting shareholder rights)
- File shareholder resolutions consistent with long-term ESG considerations
- Engage with companies on ESG issues
- Participate in collaborative engagement initiatives
- Ask investment managers to undertake and report on ESG-related engagement

3. We will seek appropriate disclosure on ESG issues by the entities in which we invest.

Possible actions:
- Ask for standardised reporting on ESG issues (using tools such as the Global Reporting Initiative)
- Ask for ESG issues to be integrated within annual financial reports
- Ask for information from companies regarding adoption of/adherence to relevant norms, standards, codes of conduct or international initiatives (such as the UN Global Compact)
- Support shareholder initiatives and resolutions promoting ESG disclosure

4. We will promote acceptance and implementation of the Principles within the investment industry.

Possible actions:
- Include Principles-related requirements in requests for proposals (RFPs)
- Align investment mandates, monitoring procedures, performance indicators and incentive structures accordingly (for example, ensure investment management processes reflect long-term time horizons when appropriate)
- Communicate ESG expectations to investment service providers
- Revisit relationships with service providers that fail to meet ESG expectations
- Support the development of tools for benchmarking ESG integration

- Support regulatory or policy developments that enable implementation of the Principles

5. We will work together to enhance our effectiveness in implementing the Principles.

Possible actions:
- Support/participate in networks and information platforms to share tools, pool resources, and make use of investor reporting as a source of learning
- Collectively address relevant emerging issues
- Develop or support appropriate collaborative initiatives

6. We will each report on our activities and progress towards implementing the Principles.

Possible actions:
- Disclose how ESG issues are integrated within investment practices
- Disclose active ownership activities (voting, engagement, and/or policy dialogue)
- Disclose what is required from service providers in relation to the Principles
- Communicate with beneficiaries about ESG issues and the Principles
- Report on progress and/or achievements relating to the Principles using a "Comply or Explain"[1] approach
- Seek to determine the impact of the Principles
- Make use of reporting to raise awareness among a broader group of stakeholders

The Principles for Responsible Investment were developed by an international group of institutional investors reflecting the increasing relevance of environmental, social and corporate governance issues to investment practices. The process was convened by the United Nations Secretary-General.

In signing the Principles, we as investors publicly commit to adopt and implement them, where consistent with our fiduciary responsibilities. We also commit to evaluate the effectiveness and improve the content of the Principles over time. We believe this will improve our ability to meet commitments to beneficiaries as well as better align our investment activities with the broader interests of society.

We encourage other investors to adopt the Principles.

NOTE

1. The "Comply or Explain" approach requires signatories to report on how they implement the Principles, or provide an explanation where they do not comply with them.

Appendix 3

Report on the AACSB Task Force on

Peace through Commerce

Carolyn Y. Woo

AACSB International (Association to Advance Collegiate Schools of Business) is the association of business schools committed to the advancement of business education through accreditation, transfer of best practices, and thought leadership on key issues pertaining to business education. In April 2005 the AACSB International Board of Directors established the Peace through Commerce Task Force. The charge to the Task Force is to "consider, plan, and execute strategies that will enable and encourage business schools to help faculty, students and others to understand and engage in activities that harness the connection between business; social, political, and economic stability; and peace."

The power of business as a global agent for positive change is recognized by many prominent players, including the United Nations, the U.S. Department of Commerce, and nongovernmental organizations across the world. Business not only has the potential to contribute to the financial stability and economic development of a country but also transcends governments and religion to foster cooperation. In seeking the benefits that can come from trade, countries have learned to go beyond or work with language, culture, political, and other challenges. AACSB's influence is broad and deep as it comprises over a thousand member schools, with a sizeable percentage located outside of the United States. AACSB has the "power to convene" through its conferences, workshops, seminars, survey capability, and web resources. That business and thus business schools can contribute to peace making aligns strongly with AACSB's mission to provide thought leadership on key issues.

The Task Force was made up of Richard Cosier (Purdue University), Manuel Escudero (United Nations Global Compact), John Fernandes (AACSB), Timothy Fort (George Washington University), Andrea Gasparri (SDA Bocconi), Anne Graham (AACSB), Fenwick Hess (Georgia State University), Rita Jordan (U.S. Air Force Academy), Robert Karam (Holy Spirit University Foundation), Georg Kell (United Nations Global Compact), Joseph E. McCann, III (University of Tampa), Mark David Milliron (SAS Institute), Sung Joo Park (Advanced Institute of Science and Technology, KAIST), Niranjan Pati (Indiana University–Kokomo), and myself serving as chair. A report, *A World of Good: Business, Business Schools, and Peace* (2006),[1] further articulated the reasons for the impact of business on world stability, provided illustrations of how different business schools engaged their students on this topic, and provided a set of recommendations. The rest of this essay will summarize the nature of the efforts of business schools and the future steps forward.

The Task Force conducted a survey of member schools concerning their activities related specifically to the relationship between business and peace. Over fifty schools responded with detailed descriptions. The respondents included schools from New Zealand, Ecuador, Italy, Switzerland, France, India, China, Taiwan, and the United States. The group included both large and small schools. The types of initiatives undertaken include the following: in-depth country studies by students that may culminate in international site visits; collaboration between business school students and counterparts in the host countries; business plan development for micro ventures and entrepreneurial training for international partners; outreach to schools in emerging countries through faculty exchange and joint degree programs; volunteer work to assist youths in other countries; a model U.N. program; and fund-raising projects. These initiatives are characterized by an impressive scope of outreach, which extended to Northern Ireland, Israel, Palestine, Darfur, Bosnia, Brazil, Guatemala, Sarajevo, Cuba, Vietnam, Mongolia, Namibia, Ghana, Azerbaijan, Cairo, Nigeria, Kenya, Moscow, and Jordan.

These initiatives have emerged from well-established foundations within business schools developed over the last few decades for international exchange, start-up of international programs, and collaborative ventures. The most popular form of activity centers around the development of micro ventures. These are of a scale that aligns with the students' ability to "put their arms" around the issue, formulate recommendations, and actually contribute to the implementation. The Internet clearly contributes to the design, implementation, and success of these programs: communication challenges relating to collaboration across distances diminish; much work is completed before teams actually make site visits; and often times relationships are already in place before student teams and their country hosts meet in person to work on their projects. Students were also comfortable with travel and have not held back working in countries operating under various tensions or conflicts.

Despite these inspiring and effective learning experiences, the survey responses indicate some important gaps. Students are not likely to engage corporations in their contribution to the Peace through Commerce activities. The focus on micro ventures has shifted attention almost exclusively to very small local enterprises rather than established local and multinational companies. The entry and exit points into the conversation tend to be regional economic studies and business plan development. We did not see curriculum devoted to a systemic, longitudinal and multidimensional exploration of the role of business in stabilizing or destabilizing an economy, nor the interaction of business with other political and cultural factors. Responses to the survey did not mention initiatives related to the issue of human rights, labor rights, or environmental sustainability. The extent of faculty research in both conceptual and empirical work is limited. Usually a single faculty member is the driving force behind the program and is also the individual with research interests in the topic. These gaps represent areas for future investment and attention if the positive impact of business as a change agent is to be recognized.

As we move forward, there are some encouraging developments that will likely bring further attention and scrutiny to the impact of business on society. There is extensive growth in the number and size of socially responsible funds. Social investing now has broad public appeal. Watchdog groups such as Transparency International and Shareholder Services Incorporated (SSI) will increasingly call companies to accountability through various metrics in highly visible and vocal ways. Surveys of consumers indicate trends of their willingness to use their purchases to support social causes of importance to them. The UN Global Compact has developed a voluntary program that engages companies across the world to abide by human rights principles, protect labor rights, refrain from corruption, and operate in ways that have positive effects on the environment. It is also in the process of convening business schools to develop principles for responsible education.

From AACSB International, the Peace through Commerce Task Force concludes with the following recommendations for its next steps.[2]

1. *Scholarship:* Encouraging scholarship and research that examines the link between commerce and peace and the roles, contributions, and potential impact of business schools in this area.
2. *Collaborative Efforts:* Building relationships with other organizations that are already engaged in strengthening the Peace concept.
3. *Utilization of AACSB Structures:* Leveraging educational programs, communications channels, and other resources to bring together those with a shared interest in this topic.
4. *Curriculum:* Encouraging business schools to integrate peace concepts into the curriculum by providing platforms that facilitate exchanges of ideas and demonstrate best practices.
5. *Private Sector:* Creating specific strategies for ensuring connections and communication between the business community and business schools around the Peace concept.

NOTES

1. AACSB International, *A World of Good: Business, Business Schools, and Peace* (Tampa, FL: AACSB International, 2006), http://www.aacsb.edu/Resource_Centers/Peace/Final-Peace-Report.pdf.

2. Ibid., 13.

Contributors

SAMER ABDELNOUR is a research associate with the Centre for Refugee Studies, York University, Toronto, and a founding member of the Foundation for Sustainable Enterprise and Development. After a brief corporate marketing career with leading automotive and retail companies, he left the corporate environment to work with refugees in the Middle East, and is now actively engaged as both a field researcher and coordinator of a project promoting sustainable enterprise development and postwar reconstruction in Sudan. In the summer of 2006 he conducted field research with internally displaced persons (IDPs) in Darfur and Southern Sudan as part of a joint research project between York University and Ahfad University for Women (Sudan). The research formed the foundation for a Forum for Sustainable Enterprise Development in Sudan held in Sudan on April 1–3, 2007, in conjunction with Ahfad University for Women and the World Bank, in which Abdelnour took a lead coordinating role. He holds an undergraduate degree in Management and Economics from the University of Toronto and is currently pursuing a Master in Environmental Studies at York University.

MARY B. ANDERSON, executive director of CDA Collaborative Learning Projects and president of CDA, Inc., has worked in international development assistance for over forty years. Named "the most influential theorist in the world of humanitarianism" (*New York Times Magazine,* February 11, 2001), she is more typically known for CDA's pragmatism and grounded approach to solving problems faced by the staff of international agencies. Dr. Anderson was program officer at the Harvard Institute for International Development, director of the Bunting Institute at Radcliffe College, and director of the International Relief/Development Project at the Harvard Graduate School of Education. She received her Ph.D. in economics from the University of Colorado, Boulder, and held a postdoctoral fellowship at the Massachusetts Institute of Technology. CDA Collaborative Learning Projects, a nonprofit entity established by Dr. Anderson in 2003, broadens the scope of collaborative training, learning, and new project development with many international governments and NGOs.

BABIKER AHMED BADRI received a Ph.D. in Human Geography from the University of Liverpool and is associate professor in the School of Rural Extension Education and Development of the Ahfad University for Women (Sudan) and general director of the Rural Extension Program at the university. Areas of research include livelihoods and culture and development interactions.

JOHN BEE is communication manager for public affairs at Nestlé S.A., based in Vevey, Switzerland. He specializes in corporate social responsibility communications and was responsible for coordinating the writing, production, and communications programs around "The Nestlé Commitment to Africa"; "The Nestlé Concept of Corporate Social Responsibility as Implemented in Latin America"; "Nestlé, the Community and the UN Millennium Development Goals"; and "The Nestlé Water Management Report." Prior to coming to Nestlé, Bee held a range of positions with UK communications agencies, specializing in the food, telecommunications, energy, and personal finance industries before joining the consumer health division of Swiss pharmaceutical multinational Novartis in 2000 as worldwide internal communications manager. A move to Zurich-based global human resources solutions leader Adecco as Internet and knowledge management director followed, before his appointment to his current role in February 2004. Bee is a graduate in German from the University of London and is fluent in French and German. He is also a member of the Chartered Institute of Public Relations.

DAVID BERDISH is the manager of social responsibility for the Ford Motor Company.

OANA BRANZEI is assistant professor and deputy director of the Erivan K. Haub Program in Business and Sustainability at the Schulich School of Business and Executive Faculty with York University's Institute for Research and Innovation in Sustainability. As an academic, teacher, and consultant in the field of sustainable value creation, she enables managers, executives, and students to successfully transform the challenges of local and global pressures for social and environmental sustainability into sources of advantage. Dr. Branzei's current research initiatives, in collaboration with academics and executives in North America, Africa, and Asia, explore the contribution of grassroots microenterprise to poverty alleviation and post-conflict stabilization, the creation and appropriation of economic, social, and environmental value, and the diffusion of pro-poor, for-profit institutions. Her ongoing projects in Sudan, Rwanda, Tanzania, and Uganda are in collaboration with the International Labour Organization, the United Nations Development Program, the World Bank, and Care Enterprise Partners. Her research is supported by grants from Canada's Social Sciences and Humanities Research Council, the International Development Research Centre, and the Investment Climate and Business Environment Research Fund.

DOUGLASS CASSEL is a scholar, attorney, and journalist specializing in international human rights and international criminal and humanitarian law. Current or former president of two international organizations assisting justice reform in the Americas, he has been human rights consultant to numerous nongovernmental organizations as well as the United Nations, the Organization of American States, the U.S. Department of State and Department of Justice, and the Ford Foundation. He lectures worldwide, and his articles are published internationally in English and Spanish. Cassel's commentaries on human rights are published in the *Chicago Tribune* and broadcast weekly on Chicago Public Radio. He is currently professor of law and director of the Center for Civil and Human Rights at the University of Notre Dame Law School.

GERALD F. CAVANAGH, S.J., holds the Charles T. Fisher III Chair of Business Ethics and is professor of management at the University of Detroit Mercy. He is the author of more than forty research articles and five books, the latest being *American Business Values: A Global Perspective,*

5th ed. (Prentice Hall, 2005). Cavanagh previously was academic vice president and provost at the University of Detroit Mercy and held the Gasson Chair at Boston College and the Dirksen Chair of Business Ethics at Santa Clara University. He has received honorary doctorates from Loyola of Baltimore and Siena Heights University. He chaired the Social Issues Division of the Academy of Management and the All-Academy of Management Task Force on Ethics. He referees papers for several journals and for national professional conferences. Cavanagh has served on the board of trustees of Fordham, Santa Clara, Xavier, Holy Cross, Loyola University of New Orleans, and the University of Detroit. Cavanagh holds a B.S. in engineering, graduate degrees in philosophy, theology, education, and a doctorate in management. In his free time, he enjoys the national parks and backpacking.

BOB CORCORAN is vice president of corporate citizenship and president of the General Electric Foundation, where he is responsible for GE's global citizenship activities and reporting; philanthropic activities, including public education, community building, and disaster relief; and volunteerism initiatives throughout the company. Corcoran's twenty-eight-year GE career has included key human resources leadership roles in GE's medical, aircraft, lighting, and aerospace businesses. Prior to his current position, Corcoran spent five years as chief learning officer responsible for GE's Management Development Institute at Crotonville and prior to that was vice president of human resources for GE Medical Systems. He was elected a corporate officer by the GE board of directors in 2000.

THOMAS E. COSTA is vice president of international policy and government affairs and deputy general counsel for Bristol-Myers Squibb. Tom joined Bristol-Myers Squibb in 1987 as worldwide regulatory counsel. For eighteen years he had legal responsibility for mergers and acquisitions, licensing, global marketing, the Pharmaceutical Research Institute, patents, technical operations, and U.S. pharmaceuticals. In addition, Costa spent two years in London leading the Bristol-Myers Squibb International Legal Team. He received his B.A. degree from Mount Saint Mary's College and his law degree from the University of Notre Dame in 1980. Before joining Bristol-Myers Squibb, he worked with the law firm of Hunton and Williams and the A. H. Robins pharmaceutical company. Costa is a member of the Philadelphia Museum of Art Board of Corporate Directors.

WILLIE ESTERHUYSE is a visiting professor of business ethics and corporate governance at the University of Stellenbosch Graduate School of Business. A professor of philosophy at Stellenbosch University from 1974 to 1998, his career includes nonexecutive director of the boards of Murray and Roberts, Metropolitan Life, Medi-Clinic Plexus, and Stellenbosch Vineyards; member of the South African Academy for Science and Art and the Philosophical Society of Southern Africa; board member of the Foundation for Global Dialogue and the Centre for Development Enterprise; and trustee of the Sanlam Demutualisation Trust and Nations Trust. He is also a recipient of the Stals Prize for Philosophy from the South African Academy of Arts and Science; the *Sunday Times* Prestige Prize for political literature; the Leon/Fox Community Relations Award; the NP van Wyk Louw Medal from the South African Academy of Arts and Science (October 1999); and the IPM Presidential Award (November 1999). Esterhuyse is a writer of a regular column in *F & T Weekly,* a financial journal, and a weekly column in *Die Burger, Beeld,* and *Die Volksblad* on ethical issues.

OFELIA C. EUGENIO is the program coordinator of the Angola Enterprise Programme, a public-private partnership between the Government of Angola, the United Nations Development Program, and Chevron to promote the development of a robust and dynamic micro, small, and medium enterprise sector in Angola.

TIMOTHY L. FORT is the executive director of the Institute for Corporate Responsibility and holds the Lindner-Gambal Professorship of Business Ethics at George Washington University Business School. He is also an academic advisor for the Business Roundtable Institute for Corporate Ethics and a fellow of the William Davidson Institute. He is the director of the Program on Peace through Commerce at George Washington University's Business School and is also an adjunct faculty at the George Washington University School of Law. He holds B.A. and M.A. degrees from the University of Notre Dame and received his J.D. and Ph.D. from Northwestern University. Fort is co-author of *The Role of Business in Fostering Peaceful Societies* (Cambridge University Press, 2004). He has authored two other books: *Business, Integrity, and Peace: Beyond Geopolitical and Disciplinary Boundaries* (Cambridge University Press, 2007) and *Prophets, Profits, and Passion: How Corporations Can Be Instruments of Peace and Enhance Religious Harmony* (Yale University Press, 2007).

MARSHALL GREENHUT is a recent graduate of the M.B.A. program of the University of Notre Dame's Mendoza College of Business. He holds a B.A. in philosophy from the University of Maryland at College Park and a B.S. in biology from Sonoma State University.

ALEXANDRA GUÁQUETA is academic director at the Fundación Ideas para la Paz (FIP), a Bogota-based independent think tank supported by the business community that examines issues relating to peace and conflict in Colombia. At FIP she has conducted research and practical work on the theme of business, conflict, and peace building. Before joining FIP in 2004, Guáqueta worked at the Foreign Affairs, Defense and Trade Division of the Congressional Research Service in Washington, DC, and served as senior program officer for the Economic Agenda and Civil Wars Program at the International Peace Academy in New York. In Colombia Guáqueta has taught international relations at several universities and worked as government affairs analyst for Occidental Petroleum. Her publications focus on doing business amidst conflict. She holds a D.Phil. in international relations from Oxford University.

MARY ANN HAZEN is professor of management in the College of Business Administration at the University of Detroit Mercy, where she teaches in the undergraduate and M.B.A. programs. She studies and continues to write about dialogue in organizations, polyphonic organizations, grief in the workplace, business and social responsibility, and management education. She has published articles in *Human Relations,* the *Journal of Organizational Change Management,* the *Journal of Business Ethics,* and the *Journal of Management Education.* Hazen has served on the editorial board of *JOCM* and is currently an associate editor of *JME.* She earned an M.S.W. at the University of Michigan and a Ph.D. in organizational behavior at Case Western Reserve University. Her eight grandchildren— and everyone else's grandchildren—are her primary motives for working toward a more just, sustainable, and peaceful world.

JOHN PAUL LEDERACH is the author of *The Moral Imagination: The Art and Soul of Building Peace* (Oxford University Press, 2005), *The Journey Toward Reconciliation* (Herald Press, 1999), *Building Peace: Sustainable Reconciliation in Divided Societies* (USIP, 1997), and *Preparing for Peace: Conflict Transformation Across Cultures* (Syracuse University Press, 1995). Widely known for his pioneering work on conflict transformation, Lederach is involved in conciliation work in Colombia, the Philippines, Nepal, and Tajikistan, as well as countries in East and West Africa. He has helped design and conduct training programs in twenty-five countries across five continents. Lederach holds a Ph.D. in sociology from the University of Colorado (1988). He is a member of the faculty of the Joan B. Kroc Institute for International Peace Studies of the University of Notre Dame.

KLAUS M. LEISINGER is president and CEO of the Novartis Foundation for Sustainable Development in Basel (Switzerland); since July 2002 he has served as president of the board of trustees of the foundation. He studied economics and social sciences at the University of Basel, Switzerland, earned his doctorate in economics, and did postdoctoral work in sociology, focusing on health policy for least developed countries. The foundation has consultative status with the Social and Economic Council of the United States. In addition to his position at Novartis, Leisinger is professor of sociology at the University of Basel. He has contributed to the academic debate widely through articles in peer-reviewed journals and books in several languages. He is a member of the European Academy of Sciences and Arts and was awarded an honorary doctorate in theology by the University of Fribourg (Switzerland) in November 2004. Leisinger has held advisory positions in a number of national and international organizations, such as the United Nations Global Compact, the United Nations Development Program (UNDP), the World Bank (CGIAR), the Asian Development Bank, and the Economic Commission for Latin America (ECLA). In September 2005, Kofi Annan appointed Leisinger special advisor to the United Nations Secretary-General for the UN Global Compact.

STANLEY LITOW is the president of the IBM Foundation and IBM's vice president for corporate community relations and corporate affairs. He heads global corporate citizenship efforts at IBM, which contributes nearly $150 million across 170 countries. Under his leadership, IBM has developed new innovative technologies to help nonliterate children and adults learn to read, helped people with disabilities access the Internet, created a humanitarian grid to power research on cancer and AIDS, and developed technology to increase economic growth and small business development. Litow's articles and essays have appeared in numerous books and publications including the *Yale Law Review,* the *Annual Survey of American Law, Brookings Papers,* the *American Academy of Sciences,* the *Journal for the Center for National Policy,* the *New York Times,* and *Newsday.* He has served as an adjunct professor at New School University, the City University of New York, and Long Island University. He helped create and chairs the Global Leadership Network and serves on the board of Harvard Business School's Initiative on Social Enterprise, Independent Sector, Citizen's Budget Commission, and the After School Corporation.

DAVID B. LOWRY served for fourteen years as a vice president at Freeport-McMoRan Copper and Gold, Inc., where he had responsibility for community relations and human rights. He retired from Freeport in 2004. He currently is managing director of the International Center for Corporate Accountability, an Episcopal priest serving as rector at Christ Church in Manhasset, New York, and adjunct professor of religion at the United States Merchant Marine Academy (King's Point). He has written for a number of journals on ethics and globalization and has lectured at universities in the United States, Europe, and Asia.

DANIEL MALAN is a senior lecturer in ethics and governance at the University of Stellenbosch Business School (USB) in South Africa and also associate director in the Sustainability Services Unit of KPMG South Africa. He is the regional coordinator for Ethics and Integrity Services of KPMG Forensic in the Europe, Middle East, and Africa regions. His focus areas include the development and implementation of ethical codes, ethical climate measurements and risk assessments, ethics training, corporate governance, and sustainability reporting. Malan is a member of the International Society of Business, Economics, and Ethics (ISBEE), as well as a member of the Southern African Institute of Directors' portfolio committee on sustainability. He also serves on the editorial board of the *African Journal of Business Ethics.* He holds an M.A. in philosophy as well as an M.B.A. from the University of Stellenbosch.

SUSAN MCGRATH is director of the Centre for Refugee Studies and associate professor in social work at York University, Toronto. Her research interests include social development, community organizing, settlement of refugees, and collective responses to trauma. She has extensive experience in organizational management in the not-for-profit sector. Publications for 2007 included an article in *Social Development Issues* on social justice and a co-authored book on community organizing with Wilfrid Laurier University Press. Dr. McGrath is currently working on a capacity-building project in the Black Creek West area of Toronto, a mental health project in Rwanda, and a local enterprise development project in Sudan. She is a member of the editorial board of the journal *Refuge* and vice-president of the International Association for the Study of Forced Migration.

SIR MARK MOODY-STUART is chairman of the board of the United Nations Global Compact Foundation and chairman of Anglo American, a global mining and natural resources company. From 1998 to 2001 Sir Moody-Stuart was chairman of the Royal Dutch/Shell Group of Companies and also chairman of the Shell Transport and Trading Company from 1997 to 2001, after having served six years as both managing director of Shell Transport and managing director of the Royal Dutch/Shell Group of Companies. He remains on the board. He is also a director of HSBC Holdings and Accenture. Sir Moody-Stuart is a governor of Nuffield Hospitals and a vice president of the Liverpool School of Tropical Medicine. He was co-chair of the G8 Task Force on Renewable Energy in 2000 and 2001 and is the chairman of the Global Business Coalition on HIV/AIDS. Sir Moody-Stuart was a member of the UN Secretary-General's advisory council for the Global Compact from 2001 to 2004. He holds a doctorate in geology from Cambridge University and is a fellow of the Geological Society, the Royal Geographical Society, and the Institute of Petroleum, which awarded him the Cadman Medal in 2001. He is an honorary fellow of St. John's College Cambridge, an honorary fellow of the Society of Chemical Engineers, and was awarded an honorary doctorate in business administration from Robert Gordon University, Aberdeen. Sir Mark Moody-Stuart became a knight commander of the Order of St. Michael and St. George in June 2000.

LISA H. NEWTON is professor of philosophy and director of the Program in Applied Ethics at Fairfield University in Fairfield, Connecticut. She has authored or co-authored several textbooks in the fields of ethics and environmental studies, including *Wake Up Calls: Classic Cases in Business Ethics* (Wadsworth, 1996), *Watersheds: Cases in Environmental Ethics,* 2nd ed. (Wadsworth, 1997), and *Taking Sides: Controversial Issues in Business Ethics and Society,* 6th ed. (McGraw-Hill, 1998). She has authored over seventy articles on ethics in politics, law, medicine, and business, and was the writer and ethics consultant for Media and Society's 1990 series *Ethics in America,* which is still occasionally aired on public television. She has been president of the Society for Business Ethics and the American Society for Value Inquiry and has made numerous presentations on current issues in business ethics, including the International Conference on Business Ethics in Milan in 1992. Newton consults with several regional health care providers, corporations, and professional associations.

SEAN O'BRIEN is the assistant director of the Center for Civil and Human Rights and a concurrent assistant professor of law at the University of Notre Dame Law School. He holds three degrees from the University of Notre Dame, most recently graduating *summa cum laude* from the LL.M. program in international human rights law in 2002. His international legal experience includes work on the Bloody Sunday Inquiry in Derry, Northern Ireland, and extensive litigation in the Inter-American System for the Protection of Human Rights. Immediately prior to joining the center in 2005, he served as chief counsel for Immigration and Human Rights at the Center for Multicultural Human Services (CMHS) in Falls Church, Virginia, where he directed a legal services program for survivors of torture and war trauma.

DONAL A. O'NEILL graduated from the National University of Ireland in 1968 with degrees in mechanical engineering and is now a partner in Lansdowne Consultants, which provides advice in the area of the impact of industry on host societies, with emphasis on socioeconomic factors and long-term effects. Prior to founding Lansdowne with Australian associates, O'Neill spent some thirty-six years with Shell, almost a third of them in sub-Saharan Africa. O'Neill held many senior positions, including running Shell's Exploration and Production companies in Turkey and Venezuela.

His last role in Shell, from 2000 to 2004, was vice president of external affairs and social performance, a position specifically requested by him so that he could institutionalize the experience he had gained in managing oil and gas ventures in challenging environments and implement his belief that management of the energy industry's impact on its host societies is as important as its technical and economic management of its oil and gas assets. He came to this topic through his fascination with how societies as diverse as those in the Netherlands, Norway, Great Britain, Nigeria, and Venezuela had reacted socially, culturally, and economically to the presence of extractive industries and with how incapable—or unwilling—private business often was of appreciating or managing the impact that its presence had on host societies. O'Neill's philosophy is that business is in business to make money, but to do so decently and ethically. He knows from experience that it can be done but that it does not happen automatically, and it demands intellectual rigor in analysis, imagination in planning, open-mindedness in alliance building, and endless vigor and sensitivity in execution.

BRIGITTE HÉLÈNE SCHERRER holds an M.A. in international relations from the Graduate Institute for International Studies in Geneva, Switzerland, and worked with the Business Humanitarian Forum (BHF) in Switzerland as a project manager from July 2003 to November 2006. She is currently working as a senior advisor for Global Development Alliances on a USAID project called Afghanistan Small and Medium Enterprise Development (ASMED) and is based in Kabul, Afghanistan.

BRAD SIMMONS is the director of the Office of Executive Chairman, President, and CEO of the Ford Motor Company.

MARILISE SMURTHWAITE is the coordinator and head of the Department of Applied Ethics at St. Augustine College, South Africa, where she teaches business ethics. She has had many years of experience in education and has also had experience as a director of a company. Her area of research is economic justice, with a focus on economic injustice in South Africa. She completed her Ph.D. at St. Augustine College with a dissertation entitled "Corporations and Economic Justice in South Africa 1994–2003: An Ethical Analysis."

LEE R. TAVIS is the C. R. Smith Professor of Business Administration, founding director of the Program on Multinational Managers and Developing Country Concerns, and faculty fellow of the Helen Kellogg Institute for International Studies and the Joan B. Kroc Institute for International Peace Studies at the University of Notre Dame. His work focuses on the trade-off between corporate economic optimization and the contribution to development in the poor countries of Africa, Asia, Latin America, and Central Europe. He is the editor of four volumes, the latest being *Power and Responsibility* (University of Notre Dame Press, 1997), and co-editor of another. He received his B.S. from the University of Notre Dame, his M.B.A. from Stanford University, and his D.B.A. from Indiana University.

MICHELLE WESTERMANN-BEHAYLO holds a J.D. from Vanderbilt University. She is currently a doctoral candidate at George Washington University in the Department of Strategic Management and Public Policy, with research interests in business ethics and leadership. She has presented her research at various academic conferences including annual meetings of the Academy of Management, the Society for Business Ethics, and the International Association for Business and Society. In 2005 and 2006 she received the Society for Business Ethics Founder's Award for promising scholars.

DAVID WHEELER is the dean of the faculty of management of Dalhousie University, Halifax, Nova Scotia. His research interests include international development, with a special focus on the role of the private sector in enhancing self-reliant development in Africa. Recent research has been published in the corporate strategy, sustainability, organizational change, finance, and corporate governance literatures. He is a member of the National Round Table on the Environment and the Economy Capital Markets Task Force, co-chair of the UNDP task force on cases in private sector development, chairman of the Foundation for Sustainable Enterprise and Development, an advisor to the International Finance Corporation (World Bank Group), and a board director of Zero Footprint.

OLIVER F. WILLIAMS, C.S.C., is a member of the faculty of the Mendoza School of Business at the University of Notre Dame and is director of the Center for Ethics and Religious Values in Business. He is an ordained Catholic priest in the Congregation of Holy Cross. Williams is the editor or author of fourteen books as well as numerous articles on business ethics in journals such as *Harvard Business Review, California Management Review, Business Ethics Quarterly,* the *Journal of Business Ethics, Business Horizons,* and *Theology Today.* A recent book, co-authored with S. Prakash Sethi, is *Economic Imperatives and Ethical Values in Global Business* (Kluwer, 2000; University of Notre Dame Press, 2002). He served as associate provost of the University of Notre Dame from 1987 to 1994 and is a past chair of the Social Issues Division of the Academy of Management. In 2006 he was appointed a member of the four-person board of directors at the United Nations Global Compact Foundation. Williams is serving as a visiting professor with a joint appointment in the Graduate Schools of Business of the University of Cape Town and Stellenbosch University. He is also a Donald Gordon International Scholar at the University of Cape Town.

CAROLYN YAUYAN WOO is the Martin J. Gillen Dean and Ray and Milann Siegfried Chair in Entrepreneurial Studies at the Mendoza College of Business at the University of Notre Dame. She assumed the deanship of the Mendoza College of Business in 1997. Before then she served as associate executive vice president for academic affairs at Purdue University. Her research focuses on strategy, entrepreneurship, and organizational systems. In 1998 *Change* magazine, a publication of the American Association for Higher Education, named Dr. Woo one of forty Young Leaders of the Academy. She currently serves on the boards of AON Corporation, Circuit City, and NiSource Incorporated. In 2003 she was elected chair of AACSB International, the accrediting association for business schools, and she was also elected to the board of Catholic Relief Services. She is a member of the Committee of 100, an organization of Chinese American leaders devoted to enhancing U.S.-China relations and the full participation of Chinese Americans in American life. She has published widely, including in the *Academy of Management Journal, Administrative Science Quarterly, Harvard Business Review, Management Science,* and the *Strategic Management Journal.*

Index